873.01
V497P
K71v

D1094233

873.01   Knight
V497P   Vergil
K71v

VERGIL: EPIC AND ANTHROPOLOGY

VERGIL

EPIC AND ANTHROPOLOGY

Comprising
VERGIL'S TROY, CUMAEAN GATES
and
THE HOLY CITY OF THE EAST

BY

W. F. JACKSON KNIGHT, *1895 — 1964*

EDITED BY
JOHN D. CHRISTIE

BARNES & NOBLE INC
New York

EDITORIAL PREFACE

Over the past two years I have had occasion to read, or to re-read, all the classical writings of the late W. F. Jackson Knight* and I have been greatly impressed, among so much else, by the striking unity of thought and imagination that binds together his several works on seemingly disparate topics. It is now planned that as much of his work as possible should be made more easily available. Already *Roman Vergil* has been republished in a revised and augmented edition: and next year, to complement this, there will appear some of his writings, including unpublished work, on Homer. Other volumes are planned. Meanwhile, the present volume brings together three works which have an obvious unity of theme and approach, within the larger unity.

Part One, *Vergil's Troy*, was first published in 1932, and Part Two, *Cumaean Gates*, in 1936, both by Basil Blackwell. And here I should like to express thanks to Sir Basil Blackwell himself for his kindly interest and ready co-operation over this volume. Part Three appeared originally as 'The Holy City of the East in Vergil' in *Vergilius*, Volume 2, 1939; and I thank the Editor, Professor J. A. S. Evans, for permission to reprint the article here. I have inserted a few interesting additions found in manuscript on an offprint among the author's papers. (The substance of this article appeared earlier as 'The Sumerian Provenience of Greek Defensive Sanctity' in *The Proceedings of the American Philological Association*, Volume 68, 1937.)

When I was invited by the author's brother, G. Wilson Knight, to edit these three texts, I accepted readily, knowing I could rely on his expert advice and shrewd judgment at all stages. I should like here to declare my indebtedness to him for his constant and devoted interest in the progress of the work. He on his part wishes me to record his gratitude to Mr John R. T. Pollard for advice and encouragement in his plans for publication.

* Bibliographies have appeared in *The Proceedings of the Virgil Society*, No. 4, 1964-5, and in *Pegasus* (University of Exeter Classical Society) Nos. 4 (Oct. 1965) and 6 (June 1966).

In editing the texts I have made corrections and adjustments where these were obviously called for. Egyptian dating, especially in Chapter IV of *Cumaean Gates*, has been adjusted to conform with more recently established chronology. Rather more substantial adjustments were called for on pages 168, 211, 235, 239 and 253 either to remove inaccuracies or to make for greater clarity. In making these changes I have acted only with Wilson Knight's approval, often relying on his gift for creating the appropriate phrasing that would at once remedy the defects and yet be consonant with his brother's personal style. I never cease to marvel at the swift brilliance with which he not only grasped the essence of problems referred to him but often devised their solutions, in what is, as they say, 'not his field'.

I have been able to check all but a very few of the references cited in the notes, making corrections wherever necessary and adjustments where it seemed desirable; for instance, I have sometimes cited editions that experience tells me are now more easily accessible, and occasionally I have redrafted a note to present the same data but with more clarity. In the long labour of verifying several thousands of references, I have been greatly helped by the rich resources of the University Libraries of Glasgow and Edinburgh, and by the efficient and courteous staffs of both. Naturally I was helped most by having direct access to Jackson Knight's own library and papers in his house in Exeter, put readily at my disposal at all times by his brother. (In editing a volume like this, there is a special delight in working in the very work-room and among the books and documents of such a remarkable scholar.)

As it proved in any case necessary to standardize the references in the three parts, I have taken the opportunity to simplify the format of the references and to renumber the notes in separate series for each chapter: this has helped to cut down the repetitions of complicated titles and at the same time makes cross-reference between notes much simpler. Notes added by myself are set within square brackets.

I have deliberately made no attempt to bring the bibliographical references up to date, with a few exceptions some of which relate to the author's own later publications. I refer in notes 32 and 34 on page 161 to more recent work by Dr John

Layard, and I am especially grateful to him for going over all the Malekulan material in *Cumaean Gates*.

The Indexes have been entirely recomposed and cover the notes as well as the text, giving access to an exceptionally rich mine of references to the basic literature on the themes of this volume.

I should like now to make acknowledgments, with gratitude for their indispensable co-operation, to Mr L. J. Lloyd for again providing illustrations; to the Librarian of the Society of Antiquaries of London for making available a fresh photograph of Maiden Castle; to the Librarian of the Warburg Institute for efficient help in tracing a suitable illustration of the Wooden Horse and for supplying a print; to the Editor of *Folklore* for permission to quote extensively from an article by the late Robert W. Cruttwell; to Miss Olivia Mordue for valuable help in locating documents; to Mr Raymond Clark for the courtesy of a helpful correction; to Dr Tristan D. M. Roberts for practical advice at every stage of the work and for expert help with proof-reading; and to Mr Rayner Unwin for his generous collaboration.

It is a pleasure to point to Mr Michael Ayrton's forthcoming essay 'The Path to Daedalus' in the Virgil volume of *Studies in Latin Literature and its Influence* (edited by D. R. Dudley and T. A. Dorey) in which he discusses the relation of *Cumaean Gates* to certain aspects of his own creative work; and also to record our gratitude for his great kindness in designing our dust-jacket, a service freely offered as a personal tribute to Jackson Knight.

Lastly, *illuc unde abii, redeo*: without Wilson Knight's fraternal piety this volume might never have been conceived; without his enthusiasm and expert care, its execution would have been a much more anxious task for its editor.

JOHN D. CHRISTIE

University of Glasgow
October 1966

CONTENTS

ILLUSTRATIONS

PLATES

FIGURES

ABBREVIATIONS

AJA	*American Journal of Archaeology*
ARW	*Archiv für Religionswissenschaft*
BSA	*Annual of the British School at Athens*
CAH	*Cambridge Ancient History*
CIL	*Corpus Inscriptionum Latinarum*
CJ	*Classical Journal*
CP	*Classical Philology*
CQ	*Classical Quarterly*
CR	*Classical Review*
CW	*Classical Weekly* (now *Classical World*)
G & R	*Greece and Rome*
IGSI	*Inscriptiones Graecae Siciliae et Italiae*
JDAI	*Jahrbuch des deutschen Archäologischen Instituts*
JEA	*Journal of Egyptian Archaeology*
JHS	*Journal of Hellenic Studies*
JRAI	*Journal of the Royal Anthropological Institute*
JRS	*Journal of Roman Studies*
MKAW	*Mededeelingen der Koninklijke Akademie van Wetenschappen, Afdeeling Letterkunde*
OLZ	*Orientalistische Literaturzeitung*
RE	Pauly-Wissowa, *Real-Encyclopädie der Klassischen Altertumswissenschaft*
RM	*Rheinisches Museum für Philologie*
SHAW	*Sitzungsberichte der Heidelberger Akademie der Wissenschaften*
SIFC	*Studi Italiani di Filologia Classica*
SMSR	*Studi e Materiali di Storia delle Religioni*
TAPA	*Transactions* (and *Proceedings*) *of the American Philological Association*

I. The Wooden Horse at Troy and the Breaking of the Wall

(Engraving, Fontainebleau School, Bartsch xvi, 394, 45: XVIth cent.)

PART ONE

VERGIL'S TROY

Essays on the Second Book of the Aeneid

(1932)

MATRI
MONSTRANTI
VIAM

AUTHOR'S PREFACE

The interest of the Second *Aeneid* is rarely denied, but it does not now attract as much investigation as it deserves. The reason for this may be that the Second *Aeneid* still presents several large problems of unusually discouraging aspect. Yet these problems belong to questions which there is at present a strong tendency to ask. Of this tendency there are many signs: a certain Vergilian quality, apparent in the English poetry of today, is probably one of them. Accordingly, I have tried to find new orientations, and I offer in the course of these essays conclusions to which I have thus been directed.

Some of the results of my enquiries, treated again here, have been published during the last three years in *The Classical Review*, *Latin Teaching*, *Classical Philology*, *The Classical Quarterly*, *The Classical Journal*, and *The Journal of Hellenic Studies*. I sincerely thank the editors of these journals for the encouragement which they have thus given to me. For the kindest of advice and criticism during my investigations I am deeply grateful to Professor J. L. Myres, who has freely and repeatedly afforded me the advantage of conversations with him, to Professor H. J. Rose, and to Mr J. D. Denniston; and for generous encouragement, and in one place for an important expansion of a theory of my own, to Professor R. S. Conway. To these scholars I owe much more than this small book can clearly show. Lastly, I am greatly indebted to my brother, G. Wilson Knight, whose thought has continually influenced my views, and whose suggestions have helped my work.

References in the text of the essays to the *Aeneid* of Vergil are made with numbers only, of books and lines. I have used the Oxford Edition of Vergil (*P. Vergili Maronis Opera* rec. F. A. Hirtzel [Oxford, 1900]).

W.F.J.K.

Bloxham School
19 *September* 1932

I

INTRODUCTION

Of all the work of Vergil, the Second *Aeneid* is the easiest part to love, but it is hard to investigate, because, equally in itself and in its context, it is a pure work of art.[1] Deceptive criteria cannot, however, be applied to the Second *Aeneid* so easily as to other books, in which parts of the artistic pattern are more readily exposed to isolation for thought and judgment. In the Fourth *Aeneid*, for example, the story of Aeneas and Dido[2] is pure poetic tragedy. But it may be discussed ethically, as a conflict of right and wrong, or politically, as an allegory in which Vergil deprecates the influence of Oriental attractions upon the rulers of Rome. These aspects belong to Vergil's story legitimately, but they can easily be emphasized in abstraction from Vergil's primary and immediate poetic vision; so that it is sometimes made to seem that such a play of thought, invested with grand and subtle verse externally overlaid, is the poetry itself. But however long and deep may have been the thinking with which the poetic act has been prepared or reinforced, great poetry is not made by mechanical combination only, and even when elements, which seem to have been contributed by prosaic faculties of invention and design, have been examined in abstraction from the poetic whole, the very difficulties and discussions which arise show that some of the self-dependent and self-evident truth of great art has gone.

The tragic and epic unity of the Second *Aeneid* offers little to this critique by abstraction, and invokes, instead, the judgment of receptivity and contemplation. There is less temptation to discuss parts or single members of the poetic organism as if the material taken for criticism were not poetry at all. This does not mean that there are not questions in this book to be asked and diffidently answered by careful investigation. There are many: concerning the right place which a detail should hold in the main poetic unity; the forms of old myths and old beliefs which Vergil has inherited and transmuted; and the method by which the intellect of Vergil worked, in the service

of his sovereign vision. But the vision itself must remain sovereign
and unforgotten, for it alone gives full reality to everything that
it has comprised.

Great poetry enriches human experience and justifies it. The
poetry of the greatest poets has sometimes, perhaps, enriched
and justified all human experience, actual and possible, as long
as men are human. The *Aeneid* in particular is near to this kind
of completeness: probably there is no human situation and no
kind of emotion which is not poetically consecrated in it. It is
important to know what is to be expected from poetry, because
a mistake at the start may mean a pitiful waste of learning,
thought, and even love of beauty. A typical mistake is made
by those who think that a poet is a moral teacher. It is quite
often made about Vergil; and it has naturally led to the de-
plorable complaint that Vergil has failed, because we feel equal
sympathy for his bad characters and his good. The mistake
comes from illegitimate abstraction. A character is abstracted
from a situation and from the poetic unity in which alone it
exists at all. A new hypothetical character is accordingly
fancied, and supposed to be acting in some modern situation
in a fashion inferred as likely from the speech and action of the
original character of the poem. This result is many degrees
removed from reality. Pathetically, all the grace of poetry has
flowed away. It is unfortunate that such misunderstandings
often beset the keenest intellects, whose very vitality and
critical power involve them in premature questions before they
have given poetry time to possess them; so that in this way
scholars sometimes incur the blame of insensibility.

There is also an argument that great susceptibility to an
ancient work of poetry must be insincere or unreal because such
a work cannot now be read as it was intended originally by the
poet, and differences communicated by a modern reader trans-
form the original work of art. This seems unphilosophical, and
untrue to common experience and the whole basis of knowledge.
A work of art is something which can contain a certain great
spiritual quality which seems to be in some relation to a certain
kind of truth and beauty. To receive the influence of the work
of art, the percipient must bring himself into a right relation to
it by habituation and knowledge. He must acquire opinions and
beliefs as near as possible to the truth: the truth for him, now.

If this seems subjective or arbitrary, it cannot be helped. The Greeks found that a good work of art is a work of art approved by the best critics and that the best critics are those who approve the best works of art. We are in the same vicious circle still. It does not matter. ἐν τῇ αἰσθήσει ἡ κρίσις. But we can watch the master work and sometimes catch the tricks of the true play of his skill. This can only be done by thinking hard about the impressions gained from years of passive contemplation, supported by honest attempts to master the language of the work of art and the circumstances of its composition. Presently analysis furnishes a set of critical instruments, theories which help and enrich the perceptions. The theories are provisional answers to questions which we do and must ask here and now, generally questions why, or at least in what circumstances, we are conscious of certain reactions before the work of art under our view. These theories are in no way more abstract or more disreputable than the theories of physical science. Both are reached in a similar way, and both are necessary to guide our behaviour towards the material before us, whether it is the physical universe or the *Aeneid*. Because a piece of iron meant one thing to Thales and means something else to a modern investigator of the base of matter, the iron is not the less iron to both, though all things are, of course, varied by the mental context in which they are experienced. The *Aeneid*, like everything else, has never been quite the same to any two people—not even to Varius and Tucca. It is not the same to us as to Vergil himself. But it must be judged objectively; and 'the most concrete thing in the world' is a thought of the right kind. It is the adversaries of poetic interpretation who fall into the fallacy of subjectivism. When they postulate an *Aeneid* as it seemed to Vergil himself, they do what Locke did in postulating 'matter' as a base of qualities—'something, he knew not what'. Protons and electrons are provisional answers to present questions about matter. But they are not usually blamed for being assumptions. Yet that is what they are; and they are none the less provisionally true and useful because of it. So it is also in attempting to answer questions about poetry. Poetry is *given*, like 'matter'; but there is less doubt about poetry. We must investigate what we find. What the poet may have intended to commit to his poetry has little relevance, beside what, with due care and education, we find

in it. We must try to ask sensible questions and to answer them
provisionally as well as we can; but above all, we must submit
to the influence of the poetry, or we shall be discussing something that is entirely unreal and fanciful.

It is high praise of Vergil to say that his 'bad' characters earn
as much sympathy as his 'good'. He takes us to a world in which
'it would be strange not to forgive', even the unforgiving, like
Dido. Poetry is imitation and creation too.[3] It cannot be
defined, but the great poets and others, too, especially since
Aristotle, have often understood its power. Poetry justifies
God's ways to man; even if Milton himself thought that theology
would do that part, in the midst of a great poem. Poetry imposes a mysterious reconciliation, because it is poetry. Beyond
the tragic climax, and nowhere else on earth, the riddle of the
universe is answered. Samson hath quit himself like Samson:
and the good prevails. This is the work of poetry. It intensifies
in beauty and truthfulness both good and evil, and the greatest
kinds of poetry prove, by the tragic synthesis, the goodness of
the universal whole.

In the Second *Aeneid* the passions are fierce and swiftly
changing. The suffering is made as keen as genius can make it:
it is hardly less than the agony in *King Lear*. It is necessary to
read those books of the *Aeneid* which carry even numbers as
both epic and tragic also.[4] In each there is the form and force
of tragedy, but they are not, therefore, any the less part of the
epic scheme. The second book is very high tragedy, and it is
perfected perhaps chiefly by an amazing control of poetic
emotion always in exact balance, and generally near an intense degree of exerted power. If Vergil is read receptively and
for a long time, there is an impression of titanic resources very
seldom applied in full pressure, but always ready for release at
his touch. In the Second *Aeneid* Vergil seems to be near his full
power more often than in any other book; so that when, at the
climax of Priam's death, he has still more hurricane force to give,
it is a miracle, and when at the end, peace, in the classical
manner, comes, the very peace is a shock.

This controlled power in the poetry is one with the whole
poetic unity. But it is legitimate to analyse the impression, or
rather to describe it, if the provisional isolation of phenomena
by which alone thought can work is used with humility to help

in the apprehension of the whole. New truth is always waiting in great poetry, and the hope of finding a little of it is worth the quest. As usual, Shelley[5] is right:

All high poetry is infinite; it is as the first acorn, which contained all oaks potentially. Veil after veil may be undrawn, and the inmost naked beauty of the meaning never exposed. A great poem is a fountain for ever overflowing with the waters of wisdom and delight; and after one person and one age has exhausted all its divine effluence which their peculiar relations enable them to share, another and yet another succeeds, and new relations are ever developed, the source of an unforeseen and an unconceived delight.

The *Aeneid* is not out of date, though the Rome of Augustus is gone. For, like the Troy which the Grecians overcast, the Rome of Vergil lives still, a spiritual city.

Notes

1. The view of the nature of poetry and especially of tragedy adopted here owes much to G. Wilson Knight, *The Wheel of Fire* (London, 1930); id. *The Imperial Theme* (London, 1931).
2. For a recent commentary on the Vergilian Dido, where the practical thought is not greatly stressed, *cf.* Corso Buscaroli, *Virgilio, Il libro di Didone* (Milan, 1932).
3. *Cf.* Gilbert Murray, *The Classical Tradition in Poetry* (London, 1927) 44 ff., and *passim* esp. 248.
4. R. S. Conway, *Vergil's Creative Art* (London, 1931) 11 ff.
5. P. B. Shelley, *A Defence of Poetry.*

II

THE POETRY

The words which Vergil uses and the verse in which he sets them are true to his supreme vision. It is worth while to watch how they dominate perception, though the subtlety of them must often be elusive. The Vergilian hexameter has many different ranges of conditions, and all are varied in harmony. The permutations are countless. Vergil himself seems to have understood partly, though not of course entirely, how his effects were determined.

The metre alone, if purely metrical occurrences could be extracted from the whole of the verse technique, provides great emotional flexibility.[1] The effects of dactyls and spondees individually and in changing proportions, and of the variety of divisions in the sense and between words, within or at the end of a verse, are widely recognized. Sinon is caught by the Trojans, and pretends fear:

> medio turbatus, inermis,
> constitit atque oculis Phrygia agmina circumspexit: . . .
> (II, 67 ff.)

The unusual spondaic ending—Vergil, in his wealth of resources, only uses it once in this book—quickly renders a beating heart and nervous eyes. In the night-fighting a tower on a house is nearly dislodged. The Trojans push the tower over onto the attackers:

> . . . conuellimus altis
> sedibus impulimusque; ea lapsa repente ruinam
> cum sonitu trahit et Danaum super agmina late . . .
> (II, 464 ff.)

impulimusque undeniably reproduces by its metrical form the last impulse, the moment's hang before the crash; and the rest of the line with its quick dactyls—helped by other conditions—gives the violent successive collisions of the fall. Nowhere else in the book is there the same combination of dactyls, word-pauses, and caesura. Vergil contrasts the old wealth and glories of Tenedos with its derelict present:

Est in conspectu Tenedos, notissima fama
insula, diues opum Priami dum regna manebant,
nunc tantum sinus et statio male fida carinis: . . .

(II, 21 ff.)

There is here another metrical usage which is worth examining. It is very characteristic of Vergil, and is found elsewhere in variations. It is the employment of a dactyl followed by a pause to give a sense of sadness and futility.[2] Here the pause after *sinus* leaves a suggestion of disappointment and contrast. The verse itself seems to wait for a return of prosperity. The falling rhythm falls away to nothing. So it does, in a different metrical form, in another line, where the sense of ineffectual sadness is present also. Aeneas, saved from the smoking wreck, searches for lost Creusa without success. But presently her ghost appears:

infelix simulacrum atque ipsius umbra Creusae . . .

(II, 772.)

The sadness is all the greater because Creusa is not only lost, but forgotten, too. Her part is over; and her memory does not count in Aeneas' later loves. This is one of the places where Vergil spares no suffering, so that the tragedy may be perfect. Besides, humanity does forget. The falling rhythm renders this sadness. The last syllable of *simulacrum* trails off into silence, and is lost in the elision.

But it becomes increasingly difficult to investigate the technique in a classification of purely metrical effects. It is not enough to consider whether syllables are short or long and whether the break between words coincides with the break between metrical feet. Other qualities of the syllables are too important for that. The falling rhythm of *infelix simulacrum* gains most of its force from the richness of the vowel sounds of *infelix*, standing at the beginning of a line in its usual place, and contrasted with the lightness of very short syllables. There is a like contrast with the short syllables of *sinus*. Elsewhere Vergil has the closely comparable

infelix puer atque impar congressus Achilli, . . .

(I, 475.)

to describe Troilus at his death. It is the imposition and quick withdrawal of weight which expresses suspense, disappointment, and sadness. The words which follow *simulacrum* continue the same effect. *ipsius* is light and insubstantial, with its short *i* sounds and coincidence of the end of the foot and of the word. The assonance[3] at the last two feet is darker, and seems to enforce the aspect of an ill-defined, shadowy ghost.

Vowel-weight and vowel-tonality seem metaphorical conceptions; but they cannot be neglected if we are trying to find why, or at least how, we experience certain feelings in reading certain passages of Vergil. The importance of these qualities is shown in the beginning of the book.

> conticuere omnes intentique ora tenebant.
> inde toro pater Aeneas sic orsus ab alto:
> 'infandum, regina, iubes renouare dolorem,
> Troianas ut opes et lamentabile regnum
> eruerint Danai, quaeque ipse miserrima uidi
> et quorum pars magna fui. . . .'
>
> (II, 1 ff.)

There is weight in the first line, and some solemnity, as the banqueters at Dido's court prepare to listen to the story. The scene must be imagined visually, like many—but not all—in Vergil, who is a poet to both the eye and the ear. There are rich hangings in the tall palace, and many signs of eastern comfort. The Carthaginians, following their queen, are intent on the stranger prince. Dramatically and with slow dignity the prince begins—and he must be imagined heroic, as we ought to imagine a Homeric hero. Aeneas is already famous over the Mediterranean world, and the suspense for his own story of great events is breathless. The second line has a neutral tonality. There is no preponderance of any strong vowel sound. The line is light, and strengthens by contrast the next. The beginning of the speech breaks on the hearers with very great force indeed. The vowel sounds are long and rich, more grand than expectation. It seems impossible that Vergil can match the rest of the tale with the splendour of the beginning. The audience is not disappointed: it begins to realize the greatness of the sorrow now to be awakened and how deeply it had been felt by the man before it. The fourth line is different. Depth and strength of sadness change to a kind of far-away bitterness rendered in this line by long, open sounds of *a* in great predominance. This use of this

sound is almost a general principle. Catullus presents the same
kind of sadness with it:

> namque mei nuper Lethaeo gurgite fratris
> pallidulum manans adluit unda pedem, . . .
>
> (LXV, 5 ff.)

The open *e* is also compatible with sadness, of a softer kind,
as Vergil often shows; especially at the sorrow of Orpheus for
Eurydice:

> te ueniente die, te decedente canebat.
>
> (*Georg*. IV, 466.)

The next line in the story of Aeneas continues the theme. There
are seven *i* sounds and five *e* sounds. Of the other syllables one
has a short *u* and the other four *a* or *ae*. The whole pitch is
higher and tenuous. The weak, thin sounds seem to say that
the past is irrevocable and the disaster irretrievable. The significance of the change of pitch is proved by the reversion to
deeper sounds in *et quorum pars magna fui*. Here Aeneas clearly
remembers that he himself and his men are still unconquered
except by gods and fates, that his own honour stands, and his
own valour has come through justified. His reasoned pride
returns: the pride with which he can afterwards say:

> sed mea me uirtus et sancta oracula diuom . . .
>
> (VIII, 131.)

The deeper steadiness and dignity, the concrete nearness of
et quorum pars magna fui, seem to be given first by means of a
long *o* in contrast with the light vowels, secondly by the two
m's—the Romans recognized that *o* and *m* expressed solemnity
—and thirdly by the occurrences of consonants together, with
a vowel following another vowel only once, at *fui*. Here a
rhyme is provided, with *uidi*, in the same verbal inflexion, and
with *Danai*. There is some interest in this, because it is one of
the usages so typically Vergilian that it may be treated as a
principle. Dido, telling the story of her life at its end in a manner
which recalls Roman epitaphs, says:

> uixi et quem dederat cursum fortuna peregi,
> et nunc magna mei sub terras ibit imago.
> urbem praeclaram statui, mea moenia uidi,
> ulta uirum poenas inimico a fratre recepi, . . .
>
> (IV, 653 ff.)

The balance and unity in diversity given by the rhyme are exquisite. The interplay of rhymes and assonances reaches its greatest perfection in a passage of which there will be more to say later, a passage which high authorities have thought not written by Vergil. Aeneas suddenly sees Helen, hiding alone:

> Iamque adeo super unus eram, cum limina Vestae
> seruantem et tacitam secreta in sede latentem
> Tyndarida aspicio; dant clara incendia lucem
> erranti passimque oculos per cuncta ferenti.
>
> (II, 567 ff.)

But of this there is too much to say and the discussion of it must be postponed. Rhyme and assonance are old in Latin poetry; they are common already in Latin comedy. Vergil is careful not to use them mechanically, except perhaps to suggest archaic ruggedness as in:

> haec genus acre uirum, Marsos pubemque Sabellam
> adsuetumque malo Ligurem Volscosque uerutos
> extulit, haec Decios Marios magnosque Camillos, . . .
>
> (Georg. II, 167.)

The end of this habit is as interesting as the beginning. From the occasional and irregular use of rhymes, practised most perfectly by Vergil, in part developed the regular use of rhyme as a metrical principle in the poetry of the Middle Ages and of modern Europe.[4] The whole process can be traced, through pagan Latin lyrics and mediaeval Latin hymns; and now devolution has begun, for English poets at present are practising internal rhymes, like the rhymes of Vergil.

But it is time to return to the beginning of the Second *Aeneid*, which must be carefully examined, so that we may be sensitive to the subtle influences of Vergil from the start. After the full stop at *fui* there seems to be a pause, and then a quickening of pace:

>   quis talia fando
> Myrmidonum Dolopumue aut duri miles Vlixi
> temperet a lacrimis? et iam nox umida caelo
> praecipitat suadentque cadentia sidera somnos.
> sed si tantus amor casus cognoscere nostros
> et breuiter Troiae supremum audire laborem,

quamquam animus meminisse horret luctuque refugit,
incipiam.
            Fracti bello fatisque repulsi
ductores Danaum . . .

(II, 6 ff.)

The hot passions return to Aeneas, and hate and pity combine.
The dramatic question is a brilliant device. It would never
have been expected. It is part of the technique by which
Vergil maintains suspense by cunning delay, which is itself part
of the broader technique, mastered supremely in the Second
Aeneid, by which he generates mystery and infinite recession of
hope and horror. The memory of the hated Achaeans is
expressed in a rough collocation of sounds, with many short
o's and *u*'s. It is followed by another change. Aeneas recovers
from his sudden memory, and thinks of the lateness of the time,
for after the long banqueting the night has come. *Suadentque
cadentia sidera somnos* is famous: the peculiar technique which
gives it its quality of expressive sleepiness must be left for a
treatment later. The next line is neutral: but in the rich
sounds of *supremum audire laborem* the tragic dignity of the first
line of the tale returns, and with it, partly in the characteristic
elision, a kind of sunset softness: and all is ready for a new
contrast. For the mood changes again to harshness and hatred,
in the *s*'s of *animus meminisse*, and the graceless but strong elision;
and then the introduction ends with a finish to a paragraph,
not at the last, but after the first few syllables of a line; a new
and rare device, which Vergil used again at the beginning of
the Seventh *Aeneid*.[5] When the next paragraph starts, the verse
is hard and practical, and dreams are over for the time.

It is clear that if we want to examine the Vergilian technique at all deeply and to carry further the understanding of
his effects, very many different kinds of artifice have to be
regarded. A certain amount of rational analysis is necessary,
but, since the art is single and unitary, it is best to avoid isolation as much as it can be avoided. In the beginning of the
Second *Aeneid* there is already much to be apprehended besides
metrical form; but that must not be forgotten, especially in the
significant variety of the caesura and changes in the metrical
position of breaks in the sense. These questions are generally
understood, but the contribution of vowel and consonant values,

besides other conditions, is sometimes forgotten. Yet a purely metrical analysis is partly misleading.

The consonant values are not so easy to understand as the vowel values, except in a few of their appearances. Of course, they are often neutral: it is already clear that neutral effects are important in contrasts. To the more specific uses belong the solemn *m* and the hissing *ss*. The meaning of this *ss* is splendidly displayed in the 'Helen scene', perhaps a passage where Vergil is not very far from the full exertion of his tremendous powers of poetry. Aeneas longs to kill Helen:

> exstinxisse nefas tamen et sumpsisse merentis
> laudabor poenas, animumque explesse iuuabit
> ultricis flammae et cineres satiasse meorum.

> (II, 585 ff.)

In these three lines are sixty-three consonant sounds. As a single consonant of the alphabet—to assume, not quite accurately, of course, that each single consonant sound is to be expected equally often—*s* should be entitled here to either four or five occurrences. But the *s* sound occurs fourteen times, and, if *exst-* of *exstinxisse* is counted, double *s* four times. If there is anyone whom Aeneas is tempted to hate, above all it must be Helen, whose ways were not his ways, and who, more than any single being, seemed to have devastated his home. Besides, if contrast and alternation are significant at all in Vergil—and they are very significant indeed—the following lines, in which the creative holy love of his divine mother intervenes to deflect Aeneas from the anger which the unholy loves of Helen have made him feel, require this hatred of Helen for their contrasting force. Vergil's alliterations have often been noticed. The alliteration of *u* is favourite, and seems to give softness, as it is used, for example, at the appearance of the doves of Venus:

> uix ea fatus erat geminae cum forte columbae
> ipsa sub ora uiri caelo uenere uolantes,
> et uiridi sedere solo.

> (VI, 190 ff.)

In general it is perhaps best to count alliterations with other kinds of assonance as part of the technique by which elements of the verse are knit together across it, by many different kinds of answering and alternating balance.

One of the conditions which control the movement and quality of Vergilian hexameters is particularly important, but has nearly always been neglected. It may be described by the term *texture*.[6] This texture is determined, not by metre only, but also by the position of the stress accent which belongs naturally to most Latin words. A Latin word consists of one or more syllables, either short or long. On one of those syllables, independently of its quantity, and sometimes apparently on more than one, there is a stress accentuation. This stress accentuation seems to have been like the accentuation on English words with which the metres of English poetry operate. The position of a stress accent on a Latin word is generally the position at which it would be if the word were English and were pronounced naturally. The accents on both *Julius* and *Caesar* fall on the first syllables, whether the names are pronounced as English or as Latin. On the whole, though there is some uncertainty, the position of the stress accent on most Latin words can be fixed with confidence. It is usually believed—but not universally—that the earliest Latin poetry was scanned by stress, not by quantity; and that the principle of scansion by quantity was adopted from Greek poetry. There is evidence that the use of stress was never altogether abandoned. In designing the *clausulae* at the end of his sentences, Cicero seems to have regarded quantity in his more literary compositions, but stress accent in informal letters. At any rate, not very long after the classical periods of Latin literature stress accent began to predominate again. Certainly stress accent has retained importance, in conversation at least, throughout the life of the Latin languages.

It is not accordingly strange that accentuation by stress should have some relevance in the Vergilian hexameter. There is a suggestion that typically Vergilian incidences of stress were noticed and copied by a late writer, Commodianus, who shows no sign that he understood the prosody of the hexameter.[7] At any rate, Latin hexameters certainly differ according to the place, within the metrical form, at which the stress accentuation of the words falls. In the metrical scheme the first syllable of every foot takes a certain emphasis which is called metrical *ictus*. Syllables carrying the metrical ictus must, of course, be long; but they may or may not also carry a stress accent. Both metrical ictus

and accent fall on the first and fourth syllables of *cónticuére*.
But in *infándum regína* the first, third and fifth syllables carry
the metrical ictus, while the second and fifth carry an accent.
Thus in the hexameter there are two series of impulses which
may or may not coincide. The coincidence I have called
'homodyne', and the opposite condition, when there is not
coincidence, 'heterodyne'.

Homodyned verses and feet are quite different from those
which are heterodyned. The two kinds of impulse either reinforce each other, if they coincide, or oppose each other, if
they do not. Thus homodyne has the quality of freedom, but
heterodyne of resistance, effort, and conflict: these conditions,
therefore, control the *texture* of the verse, whereas the proportion
of quick dactyls and slow spondees controls its natural *rapidity*.

Texture seems to be more important for Vergil than for any
other Latin poet. Apparently, he alone uses texture both frequently and artistically. The texture of his verse must always
be considered if a full account of his versification is to be given.
Now at last a comment can be made on:

suadéntque cadéntia sídera sómnos.

(II, 9.)

In all four feet, at the syllables indicated by ', stress and ictus
coincide. The four feet are, therefore, fully homodyned, and
they flow freely and unresistingly. They accordingly seem to
suggest the irresistible appeal of sleep. The alliterations and
assonance help the effect by their sense of monotony. There is
an obvious difference between this rhythm and the rhythm of:

Fracti bello fatísque repúlsi
ductores Danaum . . .

(II, 13 f.)

Here the heterodyne clearly renders conflict and difficulty
exactly appropriate to the frustrated effort which is described.
There is homodyne only in two places, in the fifth and sixth
feet. In these positions it is almost universal, because convention required that a hexameter should normally end with a
word of two syllables or of three, with no break after the first
syllable of the fifth foot. In accordance with the usual place of
the stress accent on Latin words, this means that the last two

feet are nearly always homodyned. The texture may, in fact, have been the main consideration determining the typology.

Homodyne and heterodyne may be examined in any part of the verse, but they seem to be most important in the fourth foot, where the main weight of the hexameter appears to fall. At this point there are some exceptionally interesting artifices of technique to be noticed. Vergil forms patterns of fourth-foot texture in succeeding lines. He allows homodyne and heterodyne to alternate in the fourth foot; and the effect is a steady, sometimes rapid, controlled momentum. Frequently he constructs a period or 'movement' of three or more lines, all heterodyned in the fourth foot, until the last, which is homodyned before some strong punctuation. If such a movement is a unit of thought as well as of rhythm, and begins at the beginning of a line, I call it a 'released movement', because a pressure of energy seems to be generated by the heterodyne and released by the homodyne at the end. Homodyne thus giving release at the end of a period or movement, or of a paragraph, is important generally, and not only in formally correct 'released movements'. It may be applied at any time, after a succession of fourth-foot heterodyne; and sometimes the effect is strengthened by the employment of the finishing homodyne in a pair of lines, not one.

Vergil's apparent preference for those two patterns of fourth-foot homodyne seems to be connected with some psychological predisposition which has been independently observed in its more general effects on his poetry. Vergil's thought fits naturally into the forms of alternation and reconciliation.[8] The alternation is perpetually evident in contrasts large and small; for example, in the tragic form and quality of alternate books of the *Aeneid*;[9] in the whole construction of the *Georgics*,[10] and probably the *Eclogues*;[11] and in balances of emotion and of poetic weight and colour, examples of which have occurred here already. Some of this Vergil may have derived from the elaborate balances of moral and emotional qualities which he may have found in Sophocles, perhaps the greatest master of the most subtle and perfect kind of poetry in the times before Vergil. But however that may be, the importance of many kinds of alternation to Vergil himself is certain: as he says, *amant alterna camenae*. The principle of reconciliation is if anything more general still. It dominates all Vergil's belief[12]—reconciliation in religion, in politics, in moral life, in nationalities, and, above all, the reconciliation by the tragic synthesis of the ideal and the real in human things. Vergil's thought is comprehensive. It has lately been compared to Holism.[13] Vergil cannot help seeing things in their relation to their whole context, which makes them, of course, what they are. That is one reason why he is a supremely great poet; for he discloses deep truth which narrower minds miss, because they do not see existence steadily and whole, like Sophocles and Vergil. This tendency to reconciliation, then, no less than the delight in balance and alternation, really seems to appear in patterns of rhythmic texture.

This possibly needs some more proof. But first a very interesting application of the general principle of reconciliation must be indicated, although the discussion of it belongs to another place. Vergil even tries to include versions of legends which flatly contradict the version which he has adopted.[14] Apparently to exclude them altogether would be partial—perhaps almost 'un-holistic'—and so untrue to intellectual and poetic reality. Vergil's way is ingenious. He finds an occasion when the contradicting version may with dramatic fitness be specifically denied by a character; or he makes that version into the utterance of some enemy of Aeneas and the Rome that is to be as a taunt or accusation, which the whole poem proves to be untrue, or at least true only as the inferior truth of two. If Vergil had been living now he would probably have agreed with a thinker who asserts—in the tradition of Leibniz and Spinoza—that 'there is room for error' in a perfect universe, as there is for other kinds of 'evil'.

But it is in the tragic scheme that the principle of reconciliation, and its application to patterns of rhythmic texture, are most clearly seen. In Greek tragedy there is first δέσις or 'tying up', then λύσις, 'release', dénouement.[15] The problem is created, and the solution comes at the end. The Greeks, of course, did not fully understand the nature of the solution or λύσις. It is usual for poets not to understand what they are doing. Milton himself, involved with this same question of tragic synthesis, in *Samson Agonistes* expressed what happens almost perfectly, but in *Paradise Lost* expected the solution to come by theology, not by the inherent power of tragic poetry. This is exactly why Milton, against his will, has made Satan the hero of his poem, as Shelley saw.[16] Socrates, after questioning the poets, decided that they themselves did not know what they meant by their poetry:[17] a fact profoundly true, but unhappy, since both Socrates and the poets were in quest of the same thing, which each, unintelligibly to the other, had really found. It is even likely that Euripides, at the end of his tragedies, comes particularly near to the truth of poetry and human existence in the very device which is generally thought most unreal and unsatisfactory—the *deus ex machina*, the theophany which seems to give no right λύσις, but to cut the tragic knot instead.[18] This, however, is probably the best way of all in Greek tragedy; for by it Euripides, without abandoning old forms, represents the ultimate and ideal truth that somehow, amid an unearthly peace, all is well in spite of the unfairness and the pain. How Vergil uses this very theophany will be seen presently.

It is time now to notice more clearly how the rhythmic pattern corresponds with Vergil's tendency to think by reconciliations, especially by the special kind of reconciliation in the tragic λύσις, following the tragic δέσις. The first seven lines of the whole *Aeneid* show how thought and rhythm are harmonized:

> arma uirumque cano, Troiae qui primus ab oris
> Italiam fato profugus Lauinaque uenit
> litora—multum ille et terris iactatus et alto
> ui superum, saeuae memorem Iunonis ob iram,
> multa quoque et bello passus, dum conderet urbem
> inferretque deos Latio—genus unde Latinum
> Albanique patres atque altae moenia Romae.
>
> (I, 1 ff.)

This astonishing period is a 'released movement': it is a unit of thought, and all the lines have heterodyne in their fourth feet except the last, which has homodyne; not only in the last three feet, but in the first two also. There are other interesting things about the passage. For example, it is modelled on the beginnings of both the *Iliad* and the *Odyssey*, by a peculiar power of Vergil, which will be met again presently, to copy and blend two originals at once.[19] But the main importance

here is the correspondence of the rhythm with the thought. The
whole scheme of the *Aeneid* is very brilliantly foreshadowed. The
elements, with which the story begins, are given. It is localized.
Then the many kinds of opposition which Aeneas had to face
are indicated, and there is a reference to the gods whom he
always obeyed. In these six lines the heterodyned rhythm,
helped by the lack of breaks in the sense at the ends of verses,
renders the persistent undaunted effort, in conflict with increasing opposition, that the words describe. Then, in the last
line, victory comes. The Roman nation is founded, and the
race of men and their walled cities are triumphantly secure.
There is peace after the conflict; and the freedom of the rhythmic texture declares it as clearly as the words themselves.

There is one more Vergilian artifice to examine before the
set of critical instruments is roughly and sufficiently complete.
It is the Vergilian echo. Vergil often uses similar words to refer
to similar things, but seldom the very same words in the same
setting.[20] It has been shown that he does not use 'Epic repetition': he avoided 'τὸν δ' ἀπαμειβόμενος'.[21] In fact, when exact
repetitions are found, they are sometimes actually a sufficient
reason to emend the text.[22] When Vergil echoes his own words
used elsewhere, there are three most probable reasons. There
is little doubt that Vergil had a great love of beautiful sound-
complexes; that they stayed somewhere in his memory and
came to the surface of his consciousness, offering themselves to
be used again and again. These sound-complexes, so remembered, might equally belong to Vergil's own earlier work or to
the work of others. He echoes Lucretius alone, according to
one computation, once every four or five lines, on the average,[23]
besides countless other poets, some probably not very much
less often. Frequently he cannot have remembered the original
context of the words, and sometimes he recalls his own verses
without knowing it. That has been practically proved,[24] and it
is anyway likely. Imagination works to create something new
out of old-remembered elements which it reassembles. Vergil's
imagination works greatly by ear as well as by the eye; he has
'*l'imagination auditive*'.[25] But sometimes the repetitions are
consciously adopted. Some of course are simple dramatic
necessities; for example, when the same words are used in a
question and in the answer to it. At other times a principle of

ancient poetry, known in Vergil's day, and before and after, is in operation: the principle of the ἀγών and *retractatio*.[26] Poets, according to their classical fashion 'in search of the matchless word or phrase',[27] were in competition (ἀγών) with each other and with themselves to perfect their expression, frequently of a simple and ordinary thought, by a rehandling (*retractatio*) of old words and combinations of words. It is surprising how many ways Vergil finds to describe nightfall and sunrise, no two quite alike.[28] The last reason for echo seems as clear as the others; but it has generally been excluded by them from consideration. Vergil significantly uses the same words to give cross-references to corresponding places in the epic, places sometimes thousands of lines apart. Dido is *pallida morte futura* (IV, 644). Long afterwards the very different Cleopatra, who yet, in the poetic vision and perhaps also in the practical thought of Vergil, is her counterpart, is *pallentem morte futura* (VIII, 709).[29] When the fleet of Aeneas reaches Italy the anchoring is described thus:

> obuertunt pelago proras; tum dente tenaci
> ancora fundabat nauis et litora curuae
> praetexunt puppes.   (VI, 3 ff.)

After the passage to the world below and a vision of heaven and hell, time and eternity, after which Aeneas is never the same again, the fleet is anchored farther up the coast, and the words at the beginning and end are alike:

> tum se ad Caietae recto fert litore portum.
> ancora de prora iacitur; stant litore puppes.
>   (VI, 900 f.)

The poetic impact of such a repetition, sharply representing sameness and diversity in one, is strong enough to be part of Vergil's magic. But we have not yet finished with the opening passage of the Second *Aeneid*. All are silent to listen to Aeneas:

> conticuere omnes intentique ora tenebant.
>   (II, 1.)

At the end of the Third, Aeneas, having come to the conclusion of his story, is silent in his turn, and the same words recur:

> Sic pater Aeneas intentis omnibus unus
> fata renarrabat diuom cursusque docebat.
> conticuit tandem factoque hic fine quieuit.
>   (III, 716 ff.)

This reference, at the end of a tremendous poetic experience, to the beginning of it, seems to set on that experience a seal, and to confirm it in compact unity for ever. The intense validity of the repetition is there, however hard it is to describe. The best example of all is not far from the second book. When Aeneas starts his years of wandering, in little knowledge of the future and in sore dependence on his faith, he says

>   feror exsul in altum
> cum sociis natoque penatibus et magnis dis.
>   (III, 11 f.)

The little gods of his home and the great gods of his race go with him. The metrical rhythm is strange, and will not be forgotten. Five books later another line ends with the same words.[30] The last fight for Aeneas is approaching. His hope is nearer: the future is declared to him on the new shield which Vulcanus has made for him; and on it Augustus Caesar is pictured, winning his final victory, with the might of Italy behind him:

> hinc Augustus agens Italos in proelia Caesar
> cum patribus populoque, penatibus et magnis dis, . . .
>   (VIII, 678 f.)

The faith has been kept.

These are a few of the rough categories within which the poetry of Vergil ought to be experienced. They must all be ready to be used at once; I have tried at some risk not to isolate them too much from each other even in discussion. Their usefulness is mainly poetic. They help us not to miss the intensest experience of Vergil, by passing by some exquisite soft voices of poetry, or by hearing only the storm, when the tumult of mighty harmonies is filling the skies.

The direct power of the poetry is worth investigating specifically here and there in the book. Aeneas begins his narrative; and it continues without great passion until the appearance of Laocoon before the Trojans, who are debating what to do with the wooden horse; the Achaeans, having departed, have left it on the shore. There are two passages in which Laocoon is met, and both are detachable, without dislocating the rest of the story. Of this there will be more to say. Laocoon denounces the horse, in lines in which excitement is rendered by great variation in the place of the caesura, and coherence gained, in spite of that, by answering rhymes and assonances. Vergil's single verses are not self-dependent, but exist as parts of long organic periods. Laocoon's speech falls into a group of three lines and another of four, with an eighth epigrammatic line alone after them. The three- and four-line groups are almost stanzas. Lines often cohere in groups of four, sometimes clasped together by rhythm and sometimes by rhymes and assonances, as here. Laocoon hurries from the citadel:

> et procul 'o miseri, quae tanta insania, ciues?
> creditis auectos hostis? aut ulla putatis
> dona carere dolis Danaum? sic notus Vlixes?
> aut hoc inclusi ligno occultantur Achiui,
> aut haec in nostros fabricata est machina muros,
> inspectura domos uenturaque desuper urbi,
> aut aliquis latet error; equo ne credite, Teucri.
> quidquid id est, timeo Danaos et dona ferentis.'
>
> (II, 42 ff.)

The rhymes *ciues Vlixes*, *hostis dolis* in their places are important. They make the first three lines hold together. The next four have still more elaborate organization. The two halves of the first are steadied by the rhyme of *i*, which recurs at the end of the next two lines but one; that line ends with *os* rhyming with the *os* of *nostros* in the same line and of *domos* in the next, where it separates *inspectura* from *uentura(que)*, which also rhyme. The three *aut*'s also contribute a unity, and the whole stanza is interlaced. If the lines are read aloud several times, the power and beauty of them is quickly apprehended; and soon afterwards, the importance of the assonance in creating the effect is apparent too. The unusual pause at *error* seems to render a sort of shudder: there are fears darker than can be explained. The last line is a fitting finish, and points on to the increasing doubt and horror to come. Laocoon throws his spear at the horse:

> insonuere cauae gemitumque dedere cauernae.
>
> (II, 53.)

This is probably one of the cleverest onomatopoeic lines in all literature. If the spear had only broken into the horse,

Troiaque nunc staret, Priamique arx alta maneres.

(II, 56.)

There is great pathos in the change of person (sufficiently justified by the authority of MSS.). Vergil allows something to remain unsaid; he goes on, leaving a long story to be guessed, and hints at the end of it when it has yet hardly begun. To this technique much of the dark questioning and mystery of the first part of the Second *Aeneid* is owed.

Sinon is suddenly brought in by some Trojans, and he begins his deceptive story with a question. Sinon speaks very rich and stately poetry, a part of the dramatic plan:

> fando aliquod si forte tuas peruenit ad auris
> Belidae nomen Palamedis et incluta fama
> gloria, quem falsa sub proditione Pelasgi
> insontem infando indicio, quia bella uetabat,
> demisere neci, nunc cassum lumine lugent: . . .

(II, 81 ff.)

The long word groups, the fourth-foot homodyne in the second two verses and in the last, the deep open vowels, the unspared alliteration, and the many different places in the verse where the pauses come, give these lines the strength and richness which their use requires. This grandeur in thought and word occurs again when Sinon has explained that Ulixes had plotted his death as a sacrifice for the return of the Achaeans:

> quod te per superos et conscia numina ueri,
> per si qua est quae restet adhuc mortalibus usquam
> intemerata fides, oro, miserere laborum
> tantorum, miserere animi non digna ferentis.

(II, 141 ff.)

It occurs again in another perjurious profession, when Priam has asked him the meaning of the wooden horse:

> 'uos aeterni ignes, et non uiolabile uestrum
> testor numen,' ait, 'uos arae ensesque nefandi,
> quos fugi, uittaeque deum, quas hostia gessi:
> fas mihi Graiorum sacrata resoluere iura, . . .'

(II, 154 ff.)

Sinon explains the anger of Pallas at the theft of the palladion from Troy by Ulixes and Diomedes:

ex illo fluere ac retro sublapsa referri
spes Danaum, fractae uires, auersa deae mens.

(II, 169 f.)

Vergil has his own manifold strength and subtlety sternly under
his control. At the beginning of the first of these lines comes the
falling rhythm which has expressed failure and futility before.
Vergil has each artifice ready for its place. Of the fifteen vowels
only four are long by nature, and the neutrality of tone
renders helplessness. In the next line the tonality is enriched
again, and the decisiveness of the anger of the goddess seems
to be expressed. The line has three distinct parts. This is not
unusual at the end of a period or movement. A few lines later
Sinon recounts the signs of anger which the statue of the goddess
was supposed to have shown:

. . . terque ipsa solo (mirabile dictu)
emicuit parmamque ferens hastamque trementem.

(II, 174 f.)

There is again a division into three parts on a different principle, with more assonance; but again the division seems to
present a decisive energy. Sinon explains how the horse is to
expiate the crime and to placate the goddess. But if the Trojans
take it into their city, the Achaeans will be frustrated, and the
victory will be with Troy. He is believed:

Talibus insidiis periurique arte Sinonis
credita res, captique dolis lacrimisque coactis
quos neque Tydides nec Larisaeus Achilles,
non anni domuere decem, non mille carinae.

(II, 195 ff.)

This is another carefully knit unit of four lines. The pauses are
greatly varied; but the caesurae are alike in alternate verses.
The three successive sounds of -is following two others seem to
express hate. In the third line the open vowels and fourth-foot
homodyne give solemnity to the thought. The rhymes of
periurique and *captique*, and of *Tydides* and *Achilles*, and the
double pair of negatives, interlace the parts of the movement
together.

At this point occurs the second passage in which Laocoon
appears. He, mysteriously enough—of this there will be more

to say—was sacrificing a bull to Neptunus on the shore. Suddenly two snakes approach swimming over the sea, and kill Laocoon and his two sons. The terrible description is worth a discussion, for the great perfection of its fourth-foot texture if for nothing else:

Hic aliud maius miseris multoque tremendum
obicitur magis atque improuida pectora turbat.
Laocoon, ductus Neptuno sorte sacerdos,
sollemnis taurum ingentem mactabat ad aras.
ecce autem gemini a Tenedo tranquilla per alta
(horresco referens) immensis orbibus angues
incumbunt pelago pariterque ad litora tendunt;
pectora quorum inter fluctus arrecta iubaeque
sanguineae superant undas; pars cetera pontum
pone legit sinuatque immensa uolumine terga.
fit sonitus spumante salo; iamque arua tenebant
ardentisque oculos suffecti sanguine et igni
sibila lambebant linguis uibrantibus ora.
diffugimus uisu exsangues. illi agmine certo
Laocoonta petunt; et primum parua duorum
corpora natorum serpens amplexus uterque
implicat et miseros morsu depascitur artus;
post ipsum auxilio subeuntem ac tela ferentem
corripiunt spirisque ligant ingentibus; et iam
bis medium amplexi, bis collo squamea circum
terga dati superant capite et ceruicibus altis.
ille simul manibus tendit diuellere nodos
perfusus sanie uittas atroque ueneno,
clamores simul horrendos ad sidera tollit:
qualis mugitus, fugit cum saucius aram
taurus et incertam excussit ceruice securim.
at gemini lapsu delubra ad summa dracones
effugiunt saeuaeque petunt Tritonidis arcem,
sub pedibusque deae clipeique sub orbe teguntur.
tum uero tremefacta nouus per pectora cunctis
insinuat pauor, et scelus expendisse merentem
Laocoonta ferunt, sacrum qui cuspide robur
laeserit et tergo sceleratam intorserit hastam.
ducendum ad sedes simulacrum orandaque diuae
numina conclamant.

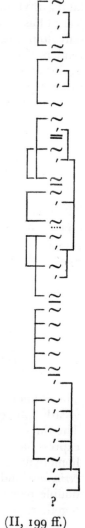

(II, 199 ff.)

This is one of many passages in Vergil where the scheme of

the fourth-foot homodyne can be worked out usefully according to its elaborate but regular pattern. The usefulness of the attempt is declared at once, if the lines are carefully read aloud with a slight emphasis on the homodyned syllables in the fourth feet. Homodyne is indicated by ′ and heterodyne by ∽ in the margin; where bracketing lines show what the scheme seems to be. The beginning has two panels of ∽″∽, like the beginning of several other elaborate rhythmic structures in Vergil. Also characteristically, the second panel is fused with a released movement, ∽∽′, ending at a full stop. In the *Aeneid*, about one line in every seven on the average forms part of a released movement, so that they are frequent enough to be thought typical. The effect of the pattern so far seems to be this. The poetry is carefully articulated. The two four-line panels have a steady balance, with a pause for breath between them. The released movement confers a stronger finality, and the whole system has become a firm, even base on which the greater fierceness and rapidity of the following rhythms can be founded, so that they gain something from the contrast. Meanwhile the released movement has itself turned to an alternation of five lines, which develops pace, but still preparatively. It ends with heterodyne at *linguis uibrantibus ora*. The last three lines ∽′∽ are copied by the next two groups of three, each also ∽ ′ ∽, in an expanded kind of alternation. This retains the momentum and symmetry, but allows heterodyne to help the solemn pathos of . . . *et miseros morsu depascitur artus*. Laocoon's attempt to help the children is made vigorous by homodyne, as well as by the assonance of *subeuntem* and *ferentem*, and the energy is retained in the next line in spite of heterodyne by the unusual pause after *ingentibus*. The last panel of ∽ ′ ∽ forms also the first three lines of a normal alternation, in which dramatic rapidity seems to be developed still more. It ends at *altis*, and after it there are five lines of fourth-foot heterodyne, lines of helpless misery, heaviness, and ill-omen. Then, starting with *at gemini lapsu delubra ad summa dracones . . .*, there is another alternation, more strong and irresistible than ever, consisting of seven lines ending firmly with homodyne. It has a tremendous swing and majesty, as if the agony of mortal men is a slight thing for the divine emissaries of the terrible goddess. The effect owes something to the preceding sequence of fourth-foot heterodyne, often a base on which an alternation is constructed. Possibly the best example of this is at the end of the First *Aeneid*, where a potent and impressive alternation, nine lines long, which finishes the book and leaves everything without finality and ready for the start of Book Two, is based on a sequence of fourth-foot heterodyne of sixteen lines. The snakes glide on their way; and the spring and momentum of the texture are helped by richer vowel sounds, massed in some variety, though the sound of *u* predominates; notably in the answering assonances *effugiunt petunt teguntur*, which possibly contribute to the dark mystery of the deed. At any rate, the nervous terror of the Trojans seems well rendered by weaker vowels, and a jump of fear by the unusual pause after *insinuat pauor*. The whole passage ends with an unfinished line; possibly because Vergil could not, at the time, find a satisfying solution of the problem how to finish his structure of rhythmic texture. The incomplete lines of the *Aeneid*—most numerous in the second book—have been much discussed: it is now nearly certain that they are unfinished, for however beautiful they may seem, it cannot be decided that they would have been less beautiful if Vergil had completed them.

This, then, is part of the poetic mechanism of the Death of Laocoon. The modulation of rhythmic texture is one of Vergil's many devices, like others that have been met. He does not always make it clearly significant, content with other means. But when he applies this technique at all, it gives to his art a perfection that nothing else could have given.

The horse is taken into Troy with festivity, and night falls. Then the Achaeans sail back from Tenedos:

> et iam Argiua phalanx instructis nauibus ibat
> a Tenedo tacitae per amica silentia lunae
> litora nota petens, . . .

> (II, 254 ff.)

The word music, with the alliteration of *i*, *t*, and *l*, and the rhyme of *ae*, perfectly renders a soft moonlit sail. Sinon, receiving a fire signal from the fleet, opens the hatch of the horse, and the heroes emerge and assault the Trojans.

The spirit of Hector appears to Aeneas in a dream, at the time when first sleep comes to suffering men:

tempus erat quo prima quies mortalibus aegris
incipit et dono diuum gratissima serpit.

(II, 268 f.)

The sound of *s* is usual for sleep, and the alliteration of *d* and
the open *o*'s give softness. There is a quick transition to a more
tumultuous verse: Hector is as he was on the day of his death

. . . atérque cruénto
púluere pérque pedes traiéctus lóra tuméntis.

(II, 272 f.)

Of the eight feet seven are homodyned, and the texture, helped
by many short syllables and the alliteration of *p*, suggests force
appropriate to the dragging of Hector behind the chariot of
Achilles. Hector tells the terrible news, and commits to Aeneas
the Trojan sanctities which he is to guard for a new home in a
far land. All is still a dream.

But the noise of battle gathers and dawns on Aeneas:

Diuerso interea miscentur moenia luctu,
et magis atque magis, quamquam secreta parentis
Anchisae domus arboribusque obtecta recessit,
clarescunt sonitus armorumque ingruit horror.

(II, 298 ff.)

A low roar seems to grow into crashes and distinguished sounds,
chaotically; but chaos is not rendered by chaotic art. The fourth-
foot homodyne is alternate in this four-line group. The sharp-
ness of *et magis atque magis* and the broken heterodyne of *armorumque* seem to give hurry and confusion. Aeneas wakes to it.
By a stroke of genius, the noises are made to force their way into
his sleep; he wakes after the sounds of battle are described. He
finds the destruction in full progress, and watches it, like a
shepherd watching a forest fire. The simile begins with three
lines of fourth-foot homodyne, a use of this technique which
may be called regular. The texture defines the simile from the
narrative. This simile is used in the Homeric fashion, to inter-
pose relief—or suspense—at a moment of great passion or
activity.[31] Burning houses collapse, and even the channel at
Sigeum is lighted by the fires.

exoritur clamorque uirum clangorque tubarum.

(II, 313.)

—another brilliantly onomatopoeic line. Aeneas can form no

plan; but he arms himself, hoping only for a glorious death. All this is told in sharp, short sentences, in contrast with Vergil's usual narrative, but of great effect in this rapid succession of impressions and ideas.

Aeneas meets the old Panthus, Apollo's priest, who says:

> uenit summa dies et ineluctabile tempus
> Dardaniae. fuimus Troes, fuit Ilium et ingens
> gloria Teucrorum; . . .
>
> (II, 324 ff.)

It is possible to see how the overpowering sadness of the first line is achieved. The three open sounds of *e* are regular for sadness. Here they are, perhaps also regularly, helped by the homodyne of the fourth, and, still more, of the first foot, where *uenit* is a spondee, commensurate with the foot, and homodyned, so that there seems to be a catch and a pause after its self-dependent rhythm. Panthus explains that the Achaeans are in occupation:

> obsedere alii telis angusta uiarum
> oppositis: stat ferri acies mucrone corusco
> stricta, parata neci; . . .
>
> (II, 332 ff.)

There is a change to fierce, active energy. The sharp visual image has been compared with the images of angels with their flaming swords, in the Old Testament;[32] and the comparison can perhaps be added to many others, which seem to show that Vergil was somehow influenced by Hebrew literature. This passage deserves another comment also. Vergil has a habit of using words, not only in their commonly accepted meanings, but also in meanings closer to their etymology. *acies* is one of the words which he uses in this way, with a clear recollection of its probable etymological sense. *acies* should be anything with a sharp edge. Elsewhere Vergil employs it for the sharp glance of keen eyes, an ordinary use. Elsewhere, again, he adopts it to mean the sharp, clear-cut edge of mountains seen against the sky,[33] apparently deducing from the root meaning of the word that this use is good and legitimate, though there seems to have been no precedent. In *ferri acies* the same intention is evident; and the phrase is exactly right for a jagged but regular line of bare steel.

There is soon another sharp and real visual image. Aeneas is joined by other Trojans:

> addunt se socios Rhipeus et maximus armis
> Epytus, oblati per lunam, . . .

(II, 339 f.)

Epytus, a large man, seems larger than life in his battle-order, looming up in the moonlight. Everything is concrete: another of Vergil's excellences. Names are given, and some quality makes them into individuals, who can be known. Coroebus meets them, too, the lover of Cassandra: his history is shortly told, partly for the sake of concreteness, and partly because his future appearance will be important.

Together these Trojans go forth to certain death. Aeneas tells them:

> una salus uictis nullam sperare salutem.

(II, 354.)

The line is of some interest, because it seems to have been written three generations too soon. It is probably the only line in Vergil which looks more like a line of Lucan. Presently the Trojans take Androgeos and his large party of Achaeans by surprise. They annihilate them, and disguise themselves with the captured Achaean arms. After that they have some more success, and some of the enemy are positively routed. Next they see Cassandra being dragged from the temple of Athena; Coroebus cannot bear it, and hopelessly attempts to rescue her. Meanwhile, the Trojans are falling, hit by their own friends, who are also deceived by the disguise. The Achaeans recognize them, and counter-attack: most of Aeneas' small party seems to be killed:

> ilicet obruimur numero; primusque Coroebus
> Penelei dextra diuae armipotentis ad aram
> procumbit; cadit et Rhipeus, iustissimus unus
> qui fuit in Teucris et seruantissimus aequi
> (dis aliter uisum); pereunt Hypanisque Dymasque
> confixi a sociis; nec te tua plurima, Panthu,
> labentem pietas nec Apollinis infula texit.
> Iliaci cineres et flamma extrema meorum,
> testor, in occasu uestro nec tela nec ullas
> uitauisse uices, Danaum et, si fata fuissent
> ut caderem, meruisse manu.

(II. 424 ff.)

The first six lines are in alternation of fourth-foot homodyne, which seems to maintain steadiness of momentum in the succession of short sentences and to make all the events seem nearly simultaneous. The alternation is followed by two lines of fourth-foot homodyne; but after the passion of *flamma extrema meorum* there is calmer sadness in heterodyne. Most of the heroes who were named when they joined Aeneas are mentioned at their death: Coroebus, in his character of a forlorn lover, and as the first to charge, in the attempt to rescue Cassandra, first; then Rhipeus, Hypanis and Dymas, whose names occur in the same order, and occupying the same places in the lines as before, with an effective echo. Rhipeus and Panthus are further characterized by their goodness, which does not save them: Vergil has here taken some earlier motive, duplicated it, transferred it, and presented it infinitely enriched.[34] The technique has energy; but it culminates in *nec te tua plurima, Panthu, labentem pietas*, where the long deep vowels and alliterations of *t* and *p* seem to shed a sunset glow of high tragedy, bathing away the injustice and pain. The apostrophe in the next line is brilliantly unexpected. As often, Vergil misses a step. Aeneas appeals to nothing that is, but to 'ashes of Ilion and the last glow of the burning' of lives that he held dear: a tremendous assertion of destruction, as if truly nothing were left but dry cinder and the flicker of a flame. The use of *tuorum* at the end echoes other uses, where sadness is joined to dignity; Aeneas said to Hector's ghost:

> ut te post multa tuorum
> funera, post uarios hominumque urbisque labores
> defessi aspicimus!

> (II, 283 ff.)

Once the sound *-orum* is doubled at the strongest places in a single line, and it is impressive to notice where this power is applied. At the last long climax of the whole *Aeneid*, Turnus, bewitched and soon to die, says, in the broken sob of an unhappy dream, to the spirits of death:

> sancta ad uos anima atque istius nescia culpae
> descendam magnorum haud umquam indignus auorum.

> (XII, 648 f.)

There is a more definite echo of the invocation 'Ashes of Ilion . . .'

later in the Second *Aeneid*, when Aeneas wishes, by killing Helen, to avenge his people and his house:

> animumque explesse iuuabit
> ultricis flammae et cineres satiasse meorum.
>
> (II, 586 f.)

The echo almost amounts to a *retractatio*. However, there is a further interest in the appeal which Aeneas makes. He avows that he shirked no danger. This is a good instance of Vergil's habit of including unfavourable alternatives to the versions which he adopts.[35] It was sometimes said in antiquity that Aeneas should not so readily have forsaken his home: there were even strong traditions that he betrayed it. In the earliest story he seems to have left Troy immediately after the death of Laocoon. Vergil—strangely perhaps, but with supreme poetic power—explicitly faces and denies the imputation, at a moment of high tragedy.

Aeneas, with Iphitus and Pelias, hearing shouts at Priam's palace, starts in that direction:

> diuellimur inde,
>
> Iphitus et Pelias mecum . . .
>
> (II, 434 f.)

Questions have been asked about *diuellimur*: whether it means that Aeneas was parted from his comrades, or torn away from the place of the engagement.[36] Reasons can be found against either view. The truth seems to be that Vergil likes to mix thoughts, for the sake of a poetic impression. Here the thoughts are mixed in a single word, which contains both the suggested meanings at once, but not fully explicit. Vergil writes by word-complexes rather than single words, and rational contents are not sharply divided. But nothing could serve better than the strong, violent *diuellimur*: it renders at once the separation of man from man in the press and confusion of battle, and the hurried dangerous disengagement, under stress of fear for Priam.

They find the palace closely besieged and the attackers on the point of forcing an entry. They join the defence from the roof, but it is in vain. All is fiercely and violently told. Then Priam, with the enemy almost upon him, arms himself. Hecuba

reproves him, and tells him that he is far too old to fight; it is
much wiser to take sanctuary at the altar. This reproof has
been thought comic.[37] There is humour in Vergil: there must
be, because epic should be complete, and should, if possible,
traverse the whole range of human emotion. But Vergil's pure
comedy seems to occur only in the alternate books which carry
odd numbers. Hecuba's reproof is tragic; all the more tragic, not
less, because Vergil knew that sometimes the deepest tragedy
grows from the seeds of laughter.

The death of Priam, next related, is the climax of all that
has come before. Its force and horror are over-powering:
partly because it somehow achieves a violent rapidity, and
successive acts and speeches seem almost simultaneous. How
this is done is not at first obvious. There is no great dependence
on rich vowels or homodyne, though there is some. Nor is the
verse peculiarly dactylic. On the whole, the effect is contrived
intellectually and visually, though word manipulation is
significant also. The beginning is important:

> Ecce autem elapsus Pyrrhi de caede Polites,
> unus natorum Priami, per tela per hostis
> porticibus longis fugit et uacua atria lustrat
> saucius. illum ardens infesto uolnere Pyrrhus
> insequitur, iam iamque manu tenet et premit hasta.
>
> (II, 526 ff.)

How intensely this is individualized will be shown best later
by a comparison with the kind of material Vergil seems to
have used here. The images are visually realized, especially
perhaps by the scene that is set—long colonnades and empty
galleries—and by the brilliant picture of Pyrrhus in pursuit
with his presented spear. The verse itself owes some power to
alliteration and to variation of pauses, but more still to the haste
and confusion rendered by many short but stressed syllables,
one of the less usual effects of heterodyne, especially in the third
and fifth alternate lines: *portícibus fúgit uácua: inséquitur mánu
ténet prémit.*[38] Polites is killed at Priam's feet. The first five lines
of Priam's speech gain dignity because they form a released
movement and because they return to long open vowels, in
an appeal to Heaven that recalls the blasphemous appeal of
Sinon, which Priam himself believed:

di, si qua est caelo pietas quae talia curet,
persoluant grates dignas et praemia reddant
debita, qui nati coram me cernere letum
fecisti et patrios foedasti funere uoltus.

(II, 536 ff.)

Priam is selfless in defiant hate: he even hopelessly throws a
spear. The cruelty of Pyrrhus is idealized equally: he drags
Priam right up to the altar and kills him there:

hoc dicens altaria ad ipsa trementem
traxit et in multo lapsantem sanguine nati,
implicuitque comam laeua, dextraque coruscum
extulit ac lateri capulo tenus abdidit ensem.

(II, 550 ff.)

Rich assonances, in the first two lines, are contrasted with
short stressed syllables in the next two.

The death of Priam is related in a sequence of simple pre-
dications, acts and thoughts following each other naturally.
This quick and simple succession may account for some of the
rapidity. There are also balances of quality in the verse.
Every four or five lines there is a change of tone or pace. There
is some interest in what Vergil has not done in this passage.
He has avoided the 'interlocking and embracing word groups',[39]
which he developed in his earlier work, from the model furnished by his predecessors, especially Catullus. Of this technique the 'golden line' is most typical of all—a line 'with two
adjectives and two substantives and a verb in between',[40] like:

mollia luteola pingit uaccinia calta.

(*Ec.* II, 50.)

There are many variations of this schematism, and some have
been shown in lines that have been met here. But, graceful
though this technique is, Vergil gradually abandoned it,
perhaps because it turns the line into the primary unit, and
Vergil preferred his unit to be a long structure of many lines.
In the scene of the death of Priam there is very little indeed
of this technique. The whole passage of thirty-three lines is the
unit, and the elements are complexes of lines, sharply broken
into distinct clauses, with little convolution of order. The order
is, in fact, sometimes not unlike the order of English.

After the death of Priam, which apparently—though there is disagreement—he saw, Aeneas for the first time was afraid: afraid for his father, his wife, and his son left behind at his own home. He realized that he was now alone.

Suddenly, he noticed Helen herself, hiding in terror:

> Iamque adeo super unus eram, cum limina Vestae ∼
> seruantem et tacitam secreta in sede latentem ʹ
> Tyndarida aspicio; dant clara incendia lucem ʹ
> erranti passimque oculos per cuncta ferenti. ≃/‖/
> illa sibi infestos euersa ob Pergama Teucros ‖/
> et poenas Danaum et deserti coniugis iras ʹ
> praemetuens, Troiae et patriae communis Erinys, ∼
> abdiderat sese atque aris inuisa sedebat. ≃/‖/
> exarsere ignes animo; subit ira cadentem ≃/∼
> ulcisci patriam et sceleratas sumere poenas. ʹ/‖/
> 'scilicet haec Spartam incolumis patriasque Mycenas ∼/‖/
> aspiciet, partoque ibit regina triumpho, ∼
> coniugiumque domumque patris natosque uidebit ∼
> Iliadum turba et Phrygiis comitata ministris? ≃/⋯
> occiderit ferro Priamus? Troia arserit igni? ≃/⋯
> Dardanium totiens sudarit sanguine litus? ʹ
> non ita. namque etsi nullum memorabile nomen ≡/‖
> feminea in poena est nec habet uictoria laudem, ∼
> exstinxisse nefas tamen et sumpsisse merentis ∼
> laudabor poenas, animumque explesse iuuabit ʹ
> ultricis flammae et cineres satiasse meorum.' ∼
> talia iactabam et furiata mente ferebar, . . . ʹ

> (II, 567 ff.)

There has only been a short break and the full passion is awakened again. The texture is worth attention. The beginning is a four-line group ∼ ʹ ʹ ∼ followed by another ʹ ʹ ∼ ∼. The homodyne in the first group, and the rich assonances, seem to render the fiery horror of the scene, in strong contrast with the succeeding picture of human weakness in the fourth line. The next two homodyned lines forcibly express the reason of Helen's fear, and the return to heterodyne again helps to present a lonely helplessness. In the rest of the passage single occurrences of fourth-foot homodyne give rhythmic punctuation after fourth-foot heterodyne. Partially there is the effect of released movements, though the rhythmic units do not quite satisfy the definition. The balance of thought is more exact than usual,[41] and the order almost as direct as in the death of Priam. Again, the visual presentation is brilliant, perhaps especially in:

> dant clara incendia lucem
> erranti passimque oculos per cuncta ferenti.
>
> (II, 569 f.)

and in:

> partoque ibit regina triumpho, . . .
>
> (II, 578.)

The sharp questions, themselves balanced, in the second half of the passage, are contrasted exquisitely with the richer tones of the answer; and there is yet another balance in the second part of the answer itself, where the sound of the verse renders an ideal hate, strengthened by the violent personification in the last line.

This passage has often been bracketed by editors on both external and internal evidence. All such evidence is insufficient. The internal evidence includes objections to some of the verbal usages, which have been supposed un-Vergilian. Of course, Vergil, especially in such a passage as this, delights in strange ways of expression. The word *sceleratas* has been thought un-Vergilian as an epithet of *poenas*. But, even if the use is surprising, Vergil habitually offers something new. This time, however, there seems to be a particular point in the strange usage. Vergil—and not here only—is using a word in two senses at once. By *sceleratas poenas* he means both 'punishment for a crime' and 'punishment even at the cost of a crime'. It would have been a crime if Aeneas had killed Helen, who was a woman, and in a sense a guest. In fact Vergil himself seems to have agreed to the excision of this whole passage,[42] partly, perhaps, because the intention of Aeneas seemed wicked, and partly because the account of Helen conflicts with a reference to her in the Sixth *Aeneid*, where she actively helps the Achaeans.[43] In consequence, Varius and Tucca deleted the whole scene, and it is not preserved, except by Servius and a few inferior MSS. This is, of course, no reason why the passage should now be bracketed. It is certainly Vergilian, and necessary in its context. To suppose that Vergil's supreme poetic judgment could have been influenced by two objections artistically quite irrelevant may at first seem strange. But on the other hand it is found that a poet, when he turns to criticism, may be hardly the same man. There is a very good parallel in English literature to Vergil's supposed decision. Wordsworth, overruled by Coleridge, deleted some great and important lines from the *Ode on Intimations of Immortality*. Yet Coleridge, though he was himself a great poet and a thinker, notoriously misunderstood Wordsworth; and the lines are necessary.[44] As a critic Wordsworth apparently misunderstood what he had meant as a poet. Like the poets questioned by Socrates, he did not know his own meaning; and accordingly he deferred to what he supposed to be the superior critical judgment of Coleridge. If the Helen scene is deleted from the Second *Aeneid*, there is a dislocation. The passage is not detachable or inorganic. For the tenses of the line before it . . . *misere* . . . *dedere* . . .(566) are perfect, and the indicative after *cum* in the line after it (589) requires the imperfect in the main clause. But imperfects are found in the last line of the Helen scene.[45]

However, the poetic contrast between the vision of Helen, symbol of an impure love, and the quickly succeeding vision of Venus, symbol of a divine love that moves the world and guides Aeneas, is so perfect that it must be Vergilian:

> talia iactabam et furiata mente ferebar,
> cum mihi se, non ante oculis tam clara, uidendam
> obtulit et pura per noctem in luce refulsit
> alma parens, confessa deam qualisque uideri
> caelicolis et quanta solet, dextraque prehensum
> continuit roseoque haec insuper addidit ore: . . .
>
> (II, 588 ff.)

All the softness of Heaven and of home is interposed amid the blood and battle wrack and ugly murk of the burning city. This is the second great climax of the book. Vergil, surely remembering his own mother, has fixed an emotion for ever, and made it absolute. The Divine Mother of Aeneas is quite different from the frivolous character of Aphrodite which Venus sometimes assumes even in the *Aeneid*: she is, on the other hand, a type of mothers, and her care of Aeneas is a perfect expression of universal human truth—as alive in memories of the European War as in Vergil's Troy. At her touch in this very moment hope comes to Aeneas, and a seed of faith is sown. The poetry is perfect and self-sufficient. But the impact of it and the intensely real picture of a true, happy dream gains by an echo. When his mother declares herself to Aeneas in the First *Aeneid*, the same words and thoughts are used, in the same softness:

> Dixit et auertens rosea cervice refulsit,
> ambrosiaeque comae diuinum uertice odorem
> spirauere; pedes uestis defluxit ad imos;
> et uera incessu patuit dea.
>
> (I, 402 ff.)

'To Vergil the greatest thing in life was the relation between parent and child.'[46]

Venus warns Aeneas to go to guard his home, and tells him not to blame Helen or Paris:

> non tibi Tyndaridis facies inuisa Lacaenae
> culpatusue Paris, diuom inclementia, diuom,
> has euertit opes sternitque a culmine Troiam.
>
> (II, 601 ff.)

The stately words show Aeneas what mind his destiny requires in him: not passionate impulse, but humility and restraint in the presence of truth. Venus withdraws the dark cloud of mortal vision:

> aspice (namque omnem, quae nunc obducta tuenti
> mortalis hebetat uisus tibi et umida circum
> caligat, nubem eripiam; tu ne qua parentis
> iussa time neu praeceptis parere recusa): . . .
>
> (II, 604 ff.)

There is overpowering softness and gentle pity for the blindness of mortality; but Aeneas must give his faith. Then all the terror and grandeur of the truth are revealed, for the Olympian gods themselves are visible, wrecking Troy:

> apparent dirae facies inimicaque Troiae
> numina magna deum.
>
> (II, 622 f.)

It is unlikely that any words contain more solemnity and stateliness than these. Some of the greatness comes from the vague mystery of the terrible forms and mighty powers of gods, and some from the sparing *meiosis* of *inimica*. The half-line *numina magna deum* is one of the hardest to believe capable of improvement, if it had been completed. This sudden revelation of divine agency has been compared, like a former image in the Second *Aeneid*, to the prophetic visions of the Old Testament.[47]

All Troy is now seen settling into the fires, tottering to its fall like a felled mountain ash. The simile is given in six lines, of which the first five are homodyned in their fourth feet, perhaps, as elsewhere, to emphasize the distinctness of the simile from the narrative. Aeneas, guarded and guided by Venus, makes his way home to take his family to safety in the mountains. But Anchises declines to leave Troy: he says that it is the will of the gods that he should perish with his home. Even loss of burial is a light thing:

> facilis iactura sepulcri.
>
> (II, 646.)

This is a divided line, beginning again after a strong stop at the caesura. It is heterodyned in the fourth foot. This is unusual, because, though the absolute percentage of fourth-foot homodyne in the *Aeneid* is about 35 per cent—a lower figure than most Latin poets show, and a reason for Vergil's greater flexibility of texture—yet in divided lines the figure of fourth-foot homodyne is over 70 per cent. This is one of the proofs that changes of texture are important and significant; for statistics show that there is here one place where homodyne is preferred. Often in divided lines homodyne is not inevitable without a change of words, but can be avoided by a simple change of order:

> stat dúctis sortibus urna.
>
> (VI, 22.)

It would have been just as easy to write

> ductis stat sortibus urna;

which would have given heterodyne. When a divided line has heterodyne there is often an expressional reason why the strong impulse of homodyne should be avoided. In

> facilis iactura sepulcri. . . .
>
> (II, 646.)

the reason seems to be the dull resigned hopelessness of the
thought.

Aeneas is in despair, for their plight is worse than ever. But
for a brave man the worst can turn suddenly to the best. Three
omens convert the opinion of Anchises: a flame playing about the
head of Ascanius, thunder on the left, and a shooting star.
Anchises says:

> 'iam iam nulla mora est; sequor et qua ducitis adsum,
> di patrii; seruate domum, seruate nepotem.
> uestrum hoc augurium uestroque in numine Troia est.
> cedo equidem nec, nate, tibi comes ire recuso.'
> dixerat ille, et iam per moenia clarior ignis
> auditur, propiusque aestus incendia uoluunt.
>
> (II, 701 ff.)

Most of the verse in this last part of the book has a certain
distant lightness, almost unreality sometimes, of dawning peace
after pain. But the theme of battle is occasionally interposed; for
the battle is still near. At these times the verse is strengthened
and enriched, as in the last two of these six lines, often, as here,
with verbal echoes from moments in the fighting.

They begin their escape: Ascanius finds it hard to keep up:

> dextrae se paruus Iulus
> implicuit sequiturque patrem non passibus aequis.
>
> (II, 723 f.)

This is a picture of great brilliance, and the 'unequal paces' are
a perfection of isolated relevance, a rule of art which Vergil
especially obeys. Ascanius knows neither the full terror of the
night and of his loss nor the splendour of his star. But he is not
afraid, as he is in another version.[48]

There is an alarm: the enemy are seen approaching. In the
hurry, Creusa is separated from the rest. Aeneas never misses
her till they reach their rendezvous, a derelict shrine of Ceres:

> nec prius amissam respexi animumue reflexi
> quam tumulum antiquae Cereris sedemque sacratam
> uenimus: . . .
>
> (II, 741 ff.)

In spite of the lavish enrichment of all the book so far, Vergil
has not traversed his whole range. He still has a new rhyme,

a strange note of tearfulness for this new sudden disappointment, just when safety seemed near. Aeneas goes back to Troy, to the walls and then to his home:

> inde domum, si forte pedem, si forte tulisset
> me refero: inruerant Danai et tectum omne tenebant.
> ilicet ignis edax summa ad fastigia uento
> uoluitur; exsuperant flammae, furit aestus ad auras.
>
> (II, 756 ff.)

The swift fright and dying hope in *si forte pedem, si forte tulisset*, made final in the breathless words, are succeeded by more echoes of the battle theme. *ilicet* comes again, with the force that was in *ilicet obruimur numero*. The fierceness of the last two lines masters the tiny hope in the first with its contrasts. Aeneas risks shouting:

> impleui clamore uias, maestusque Creusam
> nequiquam ingeminans iterumque iterumque uocaui.
>
> (II, 769 f.)

Endless effort, given in the quick repetition, only brings him back, as the assonance *impleui . . . uocaui* confirms, to his first hopelessness. Then the wraith of Creusa appears:

> quaerenti et tectis urbis sine fine ruenti
> infelix simulacrum atque ipsius umbra Creusae
> uisa mihi ante oculos et nota maior imago.
>
> (II, 771 ff.)

Again there is great power in the rhyme, and the very greatest delicacy in the rhythm of the second line. The third, with *uisa mihi ante oculos*, recalls the vision of Hector. The comfort offered by Creusa is almost the saddest part of all. It is the will of God, she says, and:

> . . . lacrimas dilectae pelle Creusae.
>
> (II, 784.)

How can he, at the sweetness of the words? But, she goes on, she will at least not be in slavery to Achaeans, she who is

> Dardanis et diuae Veneris nurus; . . .
>
> (II, 787.)

There is a pride of the high beauty of times for ever gone in the lightness of short *i*'s and *e*'s, a pride that can gladly resign even joy.

> haec ubi dicta dedit, lacrimantem et multa uolentem
> dicere deseruit, tenuisque recessit in auras.
> ter conatus ibi collo dare bracchia circum;
> ter frustra comprensa manus effugit imago,
> par leuibus uentis uolucrique simillima somno.
>
> (II. 790 ff.)

Again and again, unique perfection is disclosed and the infinite power is not all spent. It is easy to show where a rhyme or an assonance or an unexpected impulse or pause helps the greatness to be revealed. But here, if anywhere, it is better to listen, and remember.

Aeneas finds his company meanwhile increased. Dawn after the night of horror comes up bright and new; with solemn thoughts Aeneas carries his father to the mountains:

> cessi et sublato montis genitore petiui.
>
> (II, 804.)

But the rhythms of the last four-line group have hope and life in them, and the way of revelation has begun.

This is the end of one of the grandest adventures of the human spirit. Vergil has not failed to sustain his gigantic design. His music and thought are oracular and yet directly clear, in many forms. His vision is absolute, and coextensive with humanity. He is not out of date, if time after time he fits perfect artistic form to the very hopes and fears and intense living of our own generation; and he does. The Emperor Napoleon I found the tactics of Vergil's Sack of Troy unsound. But the human truth of it goes on in its living harmony, faultless for even the slightest moods of men who can still be in danger and agony, and hope again.

Notes

1. For a thorough analysis of these conditions *cf.* S. E. Winbolt, *Latin Hexameter Verse* (London, 1903) *passim*.
2. This effect of a dactyl is explained at *Aen.* VI, 886 by R. S. Conway, *New Studies of a Great Inheritance* (London, 1921) 138–9. *Cf.* J. D. Meerwaldt, *Mnemosyne* 59 (1931–2) 184 ff., esp. 190 ff., 198 ff., for an independent consideration of sound-values in the Second *Aeneid*, on principles similar to the principles used in the present chapter.

3. On Vergilian assonance, *cf.* R. G. Austin, *CQ* 23 (1929) 46 ff. *Cf.* also on Homeric assonance, A. Shewan, *CP* 20 (1925) 193 ff.

4. Austin (above, note 3) 55; R. B. Sedgwick, *G&R* 1 (1931–2) 103–4; *cf.* Stephen Gaselee, *The Transition from the Late Latin Lyric to the Medieval Love Poem* (Cambridge 1931) esp. 22 ff., and a review of the book by F. J. E. Raby, *CR* 46 (1932) 142–3, for the question whether Celtic practice contributed to the development of rhyme: apparently the contribution is unlikely.

5. J. W. Mackail, *The Aeneid of Virgil* (Oxford, 1930) 48.

6. [The present argument (pp. 31–4) was subsequently expanded in *Accentual Symmetry in Vergil* (Oxford, 1930). J.D.C.] For a partly different critique of rhythm, *cf.* G. Funaioli, *L'Oltretomba nell'Eneide di Virgilio* (Palermo-Rome, 1924) 38, 42 ff.

7. Sir Henry Newbolt, *A New Study of English Poetry* (London, 1917) 34 ff.

8. R. S. Conway, *Vergil's Creative Art* (London, 1931) 7 ff., 13 ff., esp. 18–19.

9. Ibid. 5 ff., 10 ff.

10. Ibid. 7 ff.

11. Ibid. 6.

12. Ibid. 17 ff. and *passim.*

13. T. J. Haarhoff, *Vergil in the Experience of South Africa* (Oxford, 1931) 111 ff.

14. A.-M. Guillemin, *L'originalité de Virgile* (Paris, 1931) 59 ff.

15. Conway (above, note 8) 11 ff.

16. P. B. Shelley, *Preface to Prometheus Unbound.*

17. Plato, *Apol.* 22 B-C.

18. *Cf.* Gilbert Murray, *Euripides and his Age* (London, 1913) 222 ff., esp. 225 ff.

19. H. R. Fairclough, *CP* 25 (1930) 45–6, after Nettleship in J. Conington and H. Nettleship, *P. Vergili Maronis Opera*[3] (London, 1883) III, 519.

20. John Sparrow, *Half-Lines and Repetitions in Virgil* (Oxford, 1931) 71 ff.

21. Ibid. 87 ff. (citing Heinsius *ad* Verg. *Ecl.* V, 37; the ref. in Heinsius I have not been able to see).

22. Sparrow (above, note 20) 111 ff.

23. According to the material collected by W. A. Merrill, *Parallels and Coincidences in Lucretius and Virgil* (Berkeley, California, 1918) 135 ff.; true reminiscences are estimated by Cyril Bailey, *Proc. Class. Ass.* 28 (1931) 21–4, at about one in every twelve lines.

24. Sparrow (above, note 20) 57–8.

25. The principle was established by F.-X. M. J. Roiron, S.J., *Étude sur l'imagina-tion auditive de Virgile* (Paris, 1908); *cf.* esp. i ff., 13 ff., 24–5.

26. Guillemin (above, note 14) 125 ff.

27. R. B. Steele, *CP* 25 (1930) 329; *cf.* 328 ff. *passim.*

28. Collected by Sparrow (above, note 20) 85 ff.

29. For this instance *cf.* Guillemin (above, note 14) 91.

30. For this instance *cf.* W. Warde Fowler, *CR* 27 (1913) 85.

31. *Cf.* C. M. Bowra, *Tradition and Design in the Iliad* (Oxford, 1930) 123 ff.

32. R. W. Raper, *CR* 27 (1913) 21.

33. W. Warde Fowler, *Virgil's 'Gathering of the Clans'* (Oxford, 1916) 64 ff., on *Aen.* VII, 695.

34. *Cf.* Quint. Smyrn. XIII, 178 ff., where a source of Vergil is probably followed; *cf.* Ch. IV below.

35. Guillemin (above, note 14) 42 ff., esp. 44–5.

36. Mackail (above, note 5) *ad loc.*

37. Guillemin (above, note 14) 81–2.

38. On the words of this list the accents indicate stress only, not coincidence of stress and ictus as elsewhere.

39. Arthur M. Young, *CJ* 27 (1931–2) 518.

40. Ibid. 515; *cf.* ff. for a discussion of the development.

41. H. R. Fairclough, *CP* 1 (1906) 221 ff., where the passage is discussed and the Vergilian authorship of it defended.

42. Serv. *Vit. Verg.* 39; for the reff. to authorities *cf.* C. G. Heyne, *P. Virgilius Maro . . .*⁴ rev. G. E. P. Wagner (London, 1830–41) II, 346–7.

43. Mackail (above, note 5) *ad loc.*

44. G. Wilson Knight, *The University of Toronto Quarterly* 1 (1932) 228 ff., esp. 233. [Id. *The Starlit Dome* (London, 1959) 44 ff. J.D.C.]

45. See also the views of J. Conington, *P. Vergili Maronis Opera*² (London, 1872) II, *ad loc.*

46. R. S. Conway, *CR* 45 (1931) 33.

47. Raper (above, note 32) 21.

48. Quint. Smyrn. XIII, 320–1.

THE EPIC TRAGEDY

In the dramatic structure[1] of the Second *Aeneid* three scenes of nearly equal length stand out from the narrative: one on the shore outside Troy, another in the city during the night-fighting, and a third, less coherently localized, which begins after Aeneas has reached his home.[2] Vergil has contrived to unite the epic and dramatic technique in one poem: or it may be truer to say that the greatest works of art are not capable of inclusion in a rigid classification.[3] But it is at least certain that something important in Vergil's art will be missed if those qualities in it, which are elsewhere most characteristic in dramatic poetry, are neglected.

Besides the structure, another dramatic characteristic is significant in Vergil. In epic poetry, each moment is almost complete in itself. The plot, however elaborate, is unfolded gradually and steadily. In a tragedy there is a sharper kind of unity. The whole drama must be apprehended almost in a single view, dominated by the same poetic quality: a kind of unity of theme in the full poetic sense. Everything must have a significance for this unity. In epic the unity is looser, and much may be admitted which is interesting for itself alone.[4] The *Iliad* has a very elaborate design indeed, as elaborate as the system of answering panels on the Shield of Achilles, and almost pedimental in its symmetry.[5] But Homer has much to tell which is not inherently necessary to the design. Although in the formal scheme everything has its right place, yet the matter is often chosen for its own sake, simply because it is too good to be left out. Vergil's plan is different; perhaps chiefly because he admits influence not only from epic models but from tragic models also.

In fact, the main theme of the *Aeneid* is much more easily handled tragically than epically. Vergil asks questions about God, Man, and Immortality, justice and destiny; and satisfies them poetically. For this the tragic method is appropriate. Pure epic is concerned more objectively with what is given in experience. That is not necessarily a less exalted kind of art. But it is possible that, with the publication of the *Aeneid*, the time for composing pure epic of the less reflective Homeric sort was gone for ever.[6]

Not only is it legitimate to call Vergil's epic technique a tragic technique also, but it is practically safe to call much of his tragic method Sophoclean. Some balances of spiritual and poetic qualities in the minor technique of the Second *Aeneid* have already seemed like the balances of Sophocles. The sisters Dido and Anna partly recall the sisters Antigone and Ismene in their mutual differences;[7] and it is not necessary to think that the likeness came by chance. How Sophoclean[8]—but not exclusively Sophoclean—is the Second *Aeneid* itself will soon be clear. Nor is it surprising that the book should be in some sense Sophoclean. In certainly three, and probably more than three, tragedies now lost, Sophocles handled events which Vergil afterwards handled in the Second *Aeneid*. It is incredible that Vergil should have been unfamiliar with those tragedies or that, if he knew them, he either could or would have excluded their influence, however many other influences he may have admitted besides. Sometimes a typically Sophoclean thought can even be extricated from the Latin hexameters.

Almost from the beginning in the Second *Aeneid*, as in the *Oedipus Tyrannus*, the shadow of the future is cast over the present. The revelation of the truth is gradual. The brightness of the freedom after the siege does not remain unclouded. Thymoetes first advises that the wooden horse should be taken into Troy—either in treachery or because the fates had already begun to have their way.[9] It is the first suggestion and threat of Sinon. There was a story that Thymoetes was destined by a prophecy to be the cause of the ruin of Troy. The dark questioning has now begun; and with little delay Laocoon is introduced. He denounces the folly of the Trojans, for he fears the Danai, even with gifts in their hands—almost a translation of a thought in the *Ajax* of Sophocles,[10] which may equally have occurred in another play. But when he throws his spear at the horse the mystery only deepens: there is a hollow echo, but the chieftains inside give no sign. Aeneas, telling the story, reflects that under destiny all the life of Troy hung on that cast of a spear.

Sinon was a well-known character in drama. The Vergilian

Sinon is usually traced to Greek plays.[11] He enters dramatically
enough, a captive, his hands tied behind his back, and pretends
to be terrified. The whole scene is governed by a perfect
dramatic sense. Sinon even seems unwilling to talk, until
Priam kindly tells him not to fear: *'noster eris'* (II, 149). This is a
cryptic remark. In another version[12] it appears as 'you will be
our friend'. Both seem to render some former Greek original
which had a more cryptic meaning still: probably an ironically
ambiguous phrase which might equally mean 'you will be
within our lines'. Sinon laments that now both Achaeans and
Trojans hate him: the same thought is known in Sophocles.[13]
He offers the Trojans a 'great' reward for their kindness: it is
hard not to think of the Greek, or even the Sophoclean, usage of
'great' to mean 'terrible'. It has already been supposed[14] that
when Sinon says that he will 'lift to the open air' all the secrets
of the Achaeans, he ironically means that he will open the hatch
of the horse for the Achaeans to come out. He also says that he
'is held by no laws of his own land': another ambiguity, for in
Latin that may equally mean either that he no longer owes those
laws obedience, or that he is guiltless before them.

Throughout the Sinon scene, apart from the tragic irony of
individual thoughts, there is a gradual development greatly
helped by suspense and mystery.[15] The magnificent storm of
harmonies in which Sinon recites his connection with Palamedes, and the origin of the enmity of Ulixes against him,
seems all the time to say more than the hearers can apprehend
in the rapidity of the narration, while they are still under the
influence of their first surprise. But gradually the grim personality
of Ulixes grows in the background, and is alone definite and
self-dependent. To Vergil he is always—except once[16]—malig-
nant, cold, and of devilish cunning. In the first few lines of this
book he is a symbol of cruelty. In Sinon's speech his malignity
is all the more real for the dark uncertainties of its action—*inuidia
postquam pellacis Vlixi (haud ignota loquor)* . . .(II, 90 f.)—*uerbis
odia aspera moui* (II, 96)—*criminibus terrere nouis, hinc spargere
uoces in uolgum ambiguas et quaerere conscius arma* (II, 98 f.). There
is always some omission, and room for another word—to say
whose fierce hate was stirred, what was the 'complicity', and
what is meant by 'arms'. The poetry is spoilt if too much care
is taken to interpret its rational content. At the climax of this

speech, just when a clearer explanation is expected, Sinon breaks off, maddeningly, as though the topic were hateful to him, and of no interest to the Trojans. But he remembers to say last of all that his death would please the Achaeans.

No drama intended for the stage can have excelled this scene in dramatic technique. But at this point a question arises. Vergil needs a chorus, and of course he has none. True to his principle of contrast, he interposes three lines of description: the Trojans are all the more anxious for the full story, not suspecting how wicked Pelasgian cunning can be; and Sinon, trembling and deceitful, goes on.

His continued tale is in more detail and again maddeningly deliberate. Slowly it becomes clear how Ulixes intended to destroy him. But there is still a depth of mystery—in the storm, which grew more intense when, and even possibly because,[17] the wooden horse was made, the oracle demanding a human life, the doubt who the victim should be, the silence of Calchas for 'twice five days', and the unexplained escape of Sinon from his chains.

Vergil shows perfect judgment in limiting these speeches. At the right moment Sinon thinks it worth while, now, to appeal for pity, and he stops. Again he is questioned—this time by Priam himself—about the wooden horse: the main question, of course, which has not been mentioned for nearly a hundred lines, except once, in a dark hint about the storm. But even now Sinon maintains the suspense, and adds weight to it, by a horrifying and blasphemous appeal to Heaven, entirely opposite in quality for the reader and for the hearing Trojans. With almost incredible cunning Sinon reinterprets the mysteries of forgotten cult and manipulation.[18] All kinds of old hopes and fears are built into Sinon's tale, and again strength comes out of the darkness. The horse was an expiation. Pallas was angry with the Achaeans for the theft of her image from Troy by Diomedes, and—never long forgotten, in the background—Ulixes. The image itself had given terrible signs of anger. Then the plan of Calchas is outlined, unintelligibly enough to the Trojans. The Achaeans must return home for new omens and a divinity 'that they had carried away by sea'. They had done so; but they would soon return. If the Trojans damaged the 'gift to Minerva' they would be destroyed; but if with their own hands they should take it into their citadel, they in their turn would bring war to the walls of cities in Greece. The horse, in fact, had been made too big to be taken into the gates—ostensibly so that it must remain outside, but really—as will become clear below—for a very different reason, which makes the cunning seem more diabolical still.

Again the speech ends, and is succeeded, like the first part of it, by four lines, a kind of substitute for a comment from a tragic chorus. These four lines are, however, more reflective and almost lyrical: they recall that Sinon's treachery and false tears succeeded where the heroes and resources of Achaea had failed.

But only those four lines intervene, before the action becomes more intense than ever, gradually working up to the final catastrophes. As if the Trojans were not sufficiently convinced by Sinon, Athena herself sends snakes to destroy Laocoon. The technique is still tragic: it recalls the ῥῆσις or messenger's speech of many Greek tragedies. The passage has been quoted already, and its rhythms have been discussed. Its magic effect is shattering and ironic; for the men of the city, whose doom it foreshadows—in the oldest known version[19] the incident was so interpreted by Aeneas himself, who, warned by the prodigy, immediately departed to Ida—actually think that Laocoon has sinned against their own safety. Greek ideas of destiny are suggested, in which it is almost impious to forestall, even by goodness, an evil fate that is already decreed.

This is the end of the first tragic division, the drama of Sinon, with which has been blended the drama of Laocoon; perhaps not quite finally. The mechanics of the construction will be discussed later. Between this dramatic part and the next there is a kind of panel, where epic narrative is used. The Trojans in great delight pull the horse into Troy. They do this as if they were engaged in a religious festivity. The shadow of destiny is darker, because of the references to old folklore in the story here, and the contrasts of brightness and gloom. It is already mysterious why the horse should help the Trojans if it entered their city 'by their own hands' and should then empower Asia to make war in Greece, and equally mysterious why, if they harmed it, they would bring destruction on themselves. Then in festal joyfulness the young Trojans take it in, singing, and delighting to touch the rope, which, of course, puts them into magical connection with something that they believe holy.[20] Immediately Vergil recalls that the horse threatened them all: Aeneas appeals in emotion to the holiness of his home. For the Trojans have violated the city by 'severing the walls and opening the battlements'. Yet—though they have broken their walls for it—it is at the threshold of the gate that the horse halts four times: a necessity, as it will appear, which has become an omen. The arms clash inside: but the Trojans have no thoughts for the truth. They are supernaturally bewitched. They set the thing of horror in their holy citadel—*monstrum infelix sacrata sistimus arce* (II, 245), the contrasting words together. Cassandra warns them, in vain: on their last day they decorate their temples with flowers, and amid rejoicings go to rest.

The epic style continues. The Achaeans sail back to Troy, and Sinon lets the heroes out of the horse, fulfilling the truth of his former ironic proposal. Together they assault the guards and occupy the defences.

The vision of Hector in a dream has parallels both epic and dramatic. But it is dramatic in the connection of it with the main action. Hector brings the first news of the capture of the city, and very fitly gives Aeneas the first injunction to preserve the life of Troy in a far land. The first revelation comes from an informant who is near to humanity. The deep beauty of the passage owes something to a rational inaccuracy. Aeneas says that Hector looked as he looked at the day of his death; but in the dream he speaks to him as if he could not understand his dishevelment and wounds.[21] The poetry is perfect; and it does not matter whether this inconsistency is the inconsistency of dreams or of great poetry. They are, anyway, nearly the same. Again, Aeneas carried with him on his journey the visible sanctities of Troy. But they were given to him by Hector in the dream. It has been asked when he actually took them, and whether Panthus afterwards gave them to him; for he was met carrying 'conquered gods'.[22] This again does not matter. It is best that Aeneas should receive his gods from Hector, the very spirit of the manhood of Troy. There is no firm boundary between poetry and dream here: as little as in Shakespeare's *Cymbeline*,[23] where Posthumus possesses, awake, a tablet which he has received from Jupiter in a dream.

The waking of Aeneas and the beginning of the sack are given in epic narrative, with a simile. In the fighting, until the death of Priam, the epic treatment is continued in high rapidity, with dramatic treatment of individual characters and incidents perfectly blended with it. This combined treatment is carried just far enough. It is important to notice how Vergil maintains intensity by quick changes of matter and method whenever they are wanted. The death of Coroebus is of some interest. For Vergil he is very sympathetic, a young lover who died for his love. Elsewhere[24] he is represented as a rough and clumsy fool. But Vergil creates his own characters: here his only concession to tradition is to allow Coroebus to use hasty, perhaps reckless words. Elsewhere again, Coroebus is killed, not by Peneleos, as in Vergil, but either by Neoptolemus[25] or by Diomedes.[26] Neither fits Vergil's plan. Diomedes will, at the end of the *Aeneid*, become the friend of Aeneas, and he must not, therefore, kill so sympathetic a character as Coroebus. This is a kind of consistency for which Vergil cares. Nor can Neoptolemus kill Coroebus; for Neoptolemus must be reserved for the climax of Priam's death, where his tremendous entry on the heels of Polites may only be forestalled by the mere threat of his presence at the gate. Neoptolemus is the type and symbol of the impiety and inhumanity of the Achaeans, as Ulixes is the symbol of their cunning. Coroebus is necessary for the poem. He is one of the instances of bitter injustice which great poetry must face. Other instances are furnished by Cassandra, loved by Apollo, Rhipeus, with his righteousness, Panthus with his holiness, and Priam himself with the sanctity of his kingship. The poem would be incomplete without them: *heu nihil inuitis fas quemquam fidere diuis!* (II, 402).

Neoptolemus appears at the threshold of the Palace in a metallic glitter, and baleful as a snake. Other Achaeans are with him. He breaks in the door.

This localizes visually the scene of Priam's death, which may be called fully dramatic, even to the altar which is characteristic of the Greek theatre. The scene is strangely prefaced by *forsitan et Priami fuerint quae fata requiras* (II, 506), a line which seems to reorientate the larger dramatic situation and to give warning of the intensity to come. Everything is done to increase that intensity. The pathos of Hecuba, above all in her appeal to

Priam, so helpless and solicitous that it has been thought comic, and then the helplessness of Priam himself and his pitiful intention to fight, are a preparation for the helplessness of Polites, who is a young warrior, but, no more than Priam and Hecuba, able to resist Neoptolemus. Vergil's Priam denounces Neoptolemus with royal courage,[27] concerned more for the horror of the deed to be done than for his own imminent suffering. Priam dies; and Vergil admits a lament in retrospect for the bitter reversal of his fortune, which has the quality of a tragic ode.

The death of Priam, like most of the book, is sharply organic. It is necessary in its place for the gradual realization of the utter horror of the destruction. Aeneas thinks of his own family and is for the first time afraid. He looks round to see what men he still has with him. But he is alone, except that there, below him, is Helen. He is so hopeless that he forgets his family: at least he may have revenge, as that seems to be the only hope left. Artistically there could be no better moment to reveal one single human cause, on which may be concentrated all the hatred for what has happened. Yet there is some pity for Helen—she, too, is afraid, of retribution from either side. Aeneas is still very human and fallible, and has not yet achieved the calm selflessness which his divine mission gradually imposes on him.[28] He is a soldier, and his spirit is still young. And he deeply feels his loss. Therefore, his natural impulse is to kill Helen,[29] and probably he would have killed her if his divine mother had not intervened.

This intervention is the greatest contrast in the book, a contrast between the impurity of earth and the purity of Heaven. It is also of intense epic and dramatic importance. Epically, the advice of Venus directs Aeneas on his mission more than any other influence, and turns him towards the settled faith which he will need. Dramatically, her appearance corresponds with the theophany of a tragedy, and assures Aeneas that, after all the suffering, somehow it is well with him. This moment is the turn from despair to hope. Vergil has carried the method of Euripides nearer still to the truth; and it is interesting that he has clearly remembered the end of the *Hippolytus*. His passage in the Second *Aeneid* has been shown to be very like another in the First, where Venus also appears, and that passage is paralleled by phrases used in the *Hippolytus*[30] at the appearance of Artemis. But the Artemis of Euripides is cold and careless of mankind, whereas Vergil has made his goddess of divine love almost Christian. How great is this prophetic act will be seen better later, in the comparison between the sources which Vergil used and the result which he achieved.[31] The vision of her here brings Heaven close, even in all the horror of blood and fire. A question which Venus asks is typical: *quonam nostri tibi cura recessit?* (II, 595). It is generally, but not always, supposed that *nostri* means the whole family of Aeneas—his father, mother, wife and son.[32] But Venus is not closely associated with her human family in daily life. Nor is it clear why Aeneas should specially be remembering Venus herself at this time. It is better, as so often, to let the uncertainty remain. *nostri* probably means all the people whom it might mean, regardless of logical exclusions; but above all, poetically it means all who are of another world than the battle, all who are different from Helen, all, whether powers above or those whom Aeneas loves on earth, who would not endorse a dark act of passion. Vergil, without knowing it, has very nearly given a poetic form to the command 'Love your enemies'. Venus tells Aeneas that neither Helen nor Paris is to blame— an astonishing change of some old poem, which seems to have said in this place that *not* Helen *but* Paris should be blamed[33]— for the gods themselves are overthrowing Troy. She shows him the truth, and with his own eyes he sees the giant forms at the destruction. He knows, therefore, that this is not the time to take the sword, greatly though he would prefer it. He cannot fight against gods. Venus promises her protection; the light goes and she vanishes into thick darkness. The giant forms remain.

This is the end of the second tragic motive, but epically it is a beginning.[34] There has been the δέσις, and a λύσις, by the most profound theophany of classical literature. The rest of the book has a new theme, which is really the start for the new home prophesied by Hector.

For the story—and Vergil, as a mere story-teller, deserves at least the praise generally given to Herodotus—the difficulties are not over. The strain is prolonged, and in the manner of Sophocles sometimes, there is another climax to come at no great interval. Anchises refuses to leave his home. The emphasis is now mainly on religious duty[35] and obedience to Heaven—a right sequel to the battle scenes, in which the revelation to Aeneas began. The gods are nearer now: they seemed far away at the death of Coroebus and at the death of Priam. At the home of Aeneas events come in quick succession; and it is not long before three divine signs have justified the start. Anchises carries the Trojan sanctities. This he did on the pictorial representations. Vergil characteristically finds a reason for it: Aeneas may not touch them till he is ceremonially clean from the blood of battle. Again obedience before Heaven is made to govern the action.[36]

At the last, the strain is prolonged to heart-break, in the loss of Creusa. As often, Vergil serves two purposes at once, this time a mechanical and a directly poetic purpose. Creusa cannot survive, because her presence would be in conflict with the later parts of the story. But the poetic reason is much more valid to any reader. The book must end as its whole splendour requires. It would be spoilt if all lived happily ever after: it would lack the full tragic force and consolation. The last scenes of all are the stronger for the suddenness of the new loss and for the quick succession of passionate emotions in the discovery that Creusa is not there, the breathless and dangerous search, and the apparition of Creusa herself, who, like Hector and Venus, prophetically reveals to Aeneas his divine mission. The stately ghost of the delicate, proud lady fills the cold dawn with longing; and, chastened and purified in spirit by the pity and the terror, the Trojans prepare for the long task that destiny has set before them.

Vergil has himself created with a strong hand the characters which he needed to serve his grand poetic unity. Some of them have emerged already. All are subordinate and necessary to the design. It is not always noticed how carefully Vergil has created these characters. They are not the characters whom he inherited from Greek poetry, in spite of their names, and they are not directly borrowed from the earlier Latin poets, whose work Vergil also used; for those poets seem to have followed their Greek sources much more closely. The diabolical Ulixes has scarcely anything in common with the long-enduring prince of the *Odyssey*, the steady, sound warrior of the *Iliad*, or the good

and humane man of experience in the *Ajax* of Sophocles. Even
the Odysseus of Euripides, stupid, mean, and cunning as he is,
could never have been mistaken for the Ulixes of the *Aeneid*.
Lost poetry may have helped in the creation of the character,
but it seems certain that it owes almost everything to Vergil.
Neoptolemus, too, is greatly, but perhaps not mainly, Vergil's
work. These two symbolize the evil qualities of the Achaeans.
It is, of course, important to remember that Vergil must be on
the Trojan side, whereas his most important authorities were
Greeks, and necessarily on the side of the Achaeans; though
Greek writers are marked by their sympathy for enemies.

Accordingly, Sinon also must be in large part a creation of
Vergil. To Greek writers he is a brave patriot, sometimes a very
gallant hero, whom the Trojans most cruelly maltreat.[37] There
are vestiges of this in Vergil. Sinon is *fidens animi atque in utrum-
que paratus* (II, 61), and the Trojans *certant inludere capto* (II, 64).
But this is nothing in comparison with the terrible denun-
ciations of Sinon's treachery—Vergil seems to find in him a
kind of *Punica fides*, though his ruse would not seem very dis-
honourable to us, in warfare—or with the royal magnanimity
of Priam—which we might call incautious credulity.

Priam himself has gained a princely heroism which is not
incompatible with his character in the *Iliad*, but which seems
to have been very greatly magnified by Vergil from the given
Greek treatments of his death.[38] His bold defiance, and the
utter, unnecessary brutality of Neoptolemus are Vergil's
additions. Helen to Vergil is both vile and pathetic. Her love-
liness is nothing for the Roman. Homer pitied and admired
her. Stesichorus[39] maligned her, and perhaps Vergil owes
something to him. Lost Greek poetry[40] seems to have represented her doubtful fears at the sack, but, even in a few lines,
Vergil must have greatly enriched the composite Helen whom
he formed from these elements.

Of the other characters, some have been treated already; and
more must be said anyhow in a later place. Only Aeneas
himself need have some comment now. He is generally *pius
Aeneas*, and for that he and Vergil have been endlessly blamed.
This is to misunderstand the poetry, and to be unfair. Aeneas
is intensely real in the Second *Aeneid*, a man of strong passions
and individuality, as his emotional exclamations prove, and a

soldier prince of great gallantry, as his courageous and commanding part in the battle declares. This is the Aeneas of the beginning of the *Aeneid*. He is different afterwards. It has been said that a tragic hero cannot be a strong and silent man, because to be a tragic hero at all he must give way articulately to his emotions. Aeneas does, at the beginning. In the First *Aeneid*[41] he almost shows cowardice during the storm at sea which drove him onto the Carthaginian shores. But none of this is good enough for the founder of the race of Rome. Some of his old self is left behind in the ashes where Troy once stood, and some on Dido's pyre. Aeneas must be more sublime than any tragic hero. He must reach a perfection of selflessness, and for that the selves, which he loves and which others can admire, must die. At the end of the *Aeneid* he seems to us sometimes less than human: the truth is that he is more, for he is a symbol of enduring, toiling, and relenting Rome.

NOTES

1. R. S. Conway, *Vergil's Creative Art* (London, 1931) 7 ff., 13 ff., esp. 18–19; C. G. Heyne, *P. Virgilius Maro ...*[4] rev. G. E. P. Wagner (London, 1830–41) II, Exc. I, 387–8.
2. R. Heinze, *Virgils epische Technik*[3] (Leipzig, 1915) 6; *cf.* 13, 17, 37, 44, etc., 445, 468; Norman W. de Witt, *CJ* 26 (1930–1) 19 ff.
3. E. Cesareo, *SIFC* 6 (1928) 251 ff. on the Second *Aeneid*.
4. J. T. Sheppard, *The Pattern of the Iliad* (London, 1922) 1 ff., 204 ff., and *passim*; A. R. Burn, *Minoans, Philistines, and Greeks* (London, 1930) 9.
5. J. L. Myres, *The Twenty-fourth Book of the Iliad: its Place in the Structure of the Poem* (a paper read to the Hellenic Society on 3rd May, 1932); id. *Who were the Greeks?* (Berkeley, California, 1930) 511 ff.
6. Conway (above, note 1) 11.
7. Thelma B. DeGraff, *CW* 25 (1931–2) 148 ff.
8. *Cf.* Heinze (above, note 2) 7, 37, 133 ff., etc.; Heyne (above, note 1) II, Exc. IV, 404–5. Euripides also was probably much used by Vergil: see Heyne, *passim*.
9. Cesareo (above, note 3) 236–7 (on Sinon and Thymoetes). *Cf.* Quint. Smyrn. II, 9 ff. (for the probable traditional qualities of Thymoetes, adopted here by Vergil).
10. Soph. *Ajax*, 665.
11. Heyne (above, note 1) II, Exc. IV, 404–5; Carl Robert, *Die griechische Heldensage* (Berlin, 1923) II, iii, ii, 1243.
12. Tryph. 286.
13. Soph. *Ajax*, 457 ff.
14. J. W. Mackail, *The Aeneid of Virgil* (Oxford, 1930) *ad loc.*
15. Cesareo (above, note 3) 288 note 1, and, for a general appreciation of poetic qualities in the Second *Aeneid*, 251 ff.
16. *Aen.* III, 613 ff.

17. W. F. J. Knight, *CP* 25 (1930) 360 and note 9; *cf.* Ch. V below.

18. *Cf.* Ch. V below, where an explanation of the wooden horse is offered.

19. Proclus, *epit. Iliu persis*.

20. Eugene S. McCartney, *CJ* 21 (1925–6) 112 ff.

21. Heyne (above, note 1) II, 309.

22. Ibid. Exc. IX, 418 ff.; Heinze (above, note 2) 34 ff.; *Aen.* II, 318 ff.

23. Shakespeare, *Cymbeline*, V, iv, 1 ff., esp. 28 ff., 109–10, 133 ff.

24. Heyne (above, note 1) II, Exc. X, 426. *Cf.*, for the character of Coroebus in *Margites*, T. W. Allen, *Homeri Opera* (Oxford, 1908, etc.) V, 157–8; Euphorion gave him a like character according to Servius *ad Aen.* II, 341, who thinks his speech at *Aen.* II, 390, an instance of his folly.

25. Paus. X, 27, 1.

26. Ibid.; Quint. Smyrn. XIII, 168 ff.

27. *Cf.* Heinze (above, note 2) 43.

28. *Cf.* William Warburton, *The Divine Legation of Moses* (London, 1738–41) I, Book II, 189, etc.; Henry W. Prescott, *The Development of Virgil's Art* (Chicago, 1927) 477 ff., esp. 479–80.

29. *Cf.* W. P. Clark, *CJ* 27 (1931–2) 39 ff., esp. 41–2. It should be remembered that the Horatius who survived the battle with the Curiatii of Alba and who killed his sister for mourning one of them was acquitted by the populus (Liv. I, 26).

30. Eur. *Hipp.* 1282 ff.; *cf.* 1391–2 with *Aen.* I, 403–4. (See Ch. II above). *Cf.* de Witt (above, note 2) 23: 'Upon the final scene the rescuing goddess makes her appearance, and the unwilling agent of heaven is saved to a distant, retreating destiny. The epic emerges from the tragedy.'

31. See Ch. IV below.

32. Serv. *ad Aen.* II, 595.

33. See Ch. IV below.

34. De Witt, as quoted at note 30 above.

35. *Cf.* Serv. *ad Aen.* II, 681 ff.

36. *Cf.* also here Prescott (above, note 28) 335.

37. Quint. Smyrn. XII, 360 ff., esp. 370 ff.; *cf.* Tryph. 219 ff., 291 ff.

38. Quint. Smyrn. XIII, 220 ff. and Tryph. 634 ff. clearly suggest what the quality of earlier Greek treatments may probably have been.

39. *Cf.* W. Schmid and O. Stählin, *Griechische Literaturgeschichte* (München, 1929) I, i, 475 (with note 8), 476.

40. *Cf.* Ch. IV below, and *cf.* Quint. Smyrn. XIII, 356–7, 386–7, Tryph. 630 ff., with *Aen.* II, 567 ff.

41. *Aen.* I, 92 ff.

IV

THE LEGENDS

Octavius Avitus compiled eight books of 'Vergilian Correspondences'. They are lost; but the very large number of parallels between Vergil and extant poetry that are usually cited show that the size of the collection which Octavius made should not be surprising. How frequently Lucretius alone is remembered by Vergil has already been remarked. He is only one of the small proportion of poets whose work has survived for comparison. The number of the poems which Vergil might have used, but which are now lost, is very great indeed. Of Greek hexameter poetry alone—composed in the earlier periods—the names of over eighty poems, by more than fifty poets, are known; but only a small part has survived, under the names of Homer, Hesiod and Apollonius of Rhodes.

The utility and aesthetic justification of this dependence on predecessors and contemporaries has been continually discussed, and there has been some progress towards a right perspective. Vergil was blamed for his borrowing in his lifetime. His reply is famous: 'It is easier to rob Hercules of his club than Homer of a single line.' This dependence was a strong convention in Latin poetry. Seneca[1] only gives the first principle of the matter when he explains that Vergil imitated others with the clear intention that his imitations should be recognized. They were even sometimes meant as compliments to other poets. The convention does not contradict the originality of Latin writers: it provides the confining boundary, within which most of them are very original indeed. Their method is not, after all, different from the method of great poets of other times, Homer and Shakespeare included: and it is recognized today, especially by T. S. Eliot, both in theory and practice. But the special care of Latin poets for their models is part of their classical quality, which is shown in the desire for an ultimate and absolute beauty and fitness, in an art where the mean was golden and there was no competition for gain in tuning the strings. Besides, words are not self-identical and sharply delimited in content through time. They are, like most other things, symbols of all their history, and they are the poorer without the recognition and use of their past associations. But anyhow, no justification is needed for Vergil beyond the sovereignty of his own great verse, the power of Hercules' club in his hand, which can yet touch like a rapier or a magic wand.

In minor technique, therefore, Vergil perpetually availed himself of the work of others. But the result is often and, of course, in some senses always quite different from the original. There are some strange instances, which have suggested the belief that Vergil could make terrible mistakes in translating Greek. *Omnia uel medium fiant mare* (*Ec*. VIII, 58) clearly recalls the πάντα δ'ἔναλλα γένοιντο of Theocritus.[2] If so, the obvious criticism has been to accuse Vergil of confusing ἔναλλα, which means something like 'reversed' in the sense of 'upside down', with εἰς ἅλα 'into the salt sea'.[3] Even then he has said 'become the sea' instead of 'go into the sea'. It is quite likely that Vergil in spite of his wide knowledge of Greek, was capable of this kind of mistake, though hardly, perhaps, of a mistake quite as bad as this. It does not matter if he was. His mind, anyhow, had not the tendency to accuracy in mechanical processes of thought. It worked in the appropriately poetic way, by associations of ideas, the method which Locke believed to be the sign of a madman, and which Berkeley announced to be the basis of all thinking. Whichever is right, association of ideas, or thinking in symbols, is a main poetic process—poetic and lunatic, too, as Shakespeare would say. This shows what Vergil does. A phrase suggests to him an idea, a visual image, or a sound complex. In his memory is registered a poetic impression which may be quite incoherent with the logical content of the words which suggested it. He probably knew that ἔναλλα had nothing logically to do with sea; but his poetic consciousness immediately created, in response to the stimulation, a new image which appealed to him, an image suggested by the likeness of ἔναλλα to εἰς ἅλα (or perhaps to ἐν ἁλί, 'in the sea'). That is to say that Vergil, when he imitates, may imitate any of many different things that in his mind belong to the original. A thought, an image, or the mere colour or tone of a feeling reappears in quite a different context from the well of his deeper consciousness, probably long after the original experience.[4] This is implied in the very interesting anecdote recorded by Donatus, which is altogether credible in its main outline.[5] Vergil had left unfinished a line of the Sixth *Aeneid*: *Misenum Aeoliden . . .* (VI, 164). Eros, his secretary, was reading it aloud when in a flash the completion came to Vergil: *quo non praestantior alter aere ciere uiros . . .* (VI, 164 f.). If the story is rightly told, the same thing must have happened again, and the completion of this line also must have been given on the same or another occasion in the same way: *Martemque accendere cantu* (VI, 165). A great part, in fact, of Vergil's creative process happened in some unconscious part of his mind. This is characteristic of great poets: the composition of Coleridge's *Kubla Khan* is only an unusually clear instance of a general law.

But it is not in minor technique only that this habit of the detachment of particulars is typical of Vergil. It is even more remarkable in the major technique of epic and dramatic construction. Vergil quite ruthlessly, but yet with a sharp economy of material, transfers[6] and transmutes references of every kind, and constructs quite new combinations of them in the service of his grand poetic vision. This method has been called the Vergilian integration.[7] Vergil seems to have carried it much farther than any other poet, though Homer himself may have given him some important examples to follow. It is, perhaps, just because he has carried it so far, that the method, though it is both characteristic and important, has hardly been sufficiently recognized.

There is some mystery about the sources of the Second *Aeneid*. Parallels to its thoughts and phrases are continually cited, from Homer, Greek dramatists, Ennius and Pacuvius, and from others. But no extant poetry written before Vergil's time gives a continuous version of the occurrences related in the book; and there is strong reason to think that Vergil must have used some, at least, of the many previous poems now lost which might have furnished him with a continuous source. On this Macrobius,[8] in the person of one of his characters, made a very important, but mysterious, statement: that 'as every schoolboy knows' Vergil copied most of the Second *Aeneid* almost verbally from Peisander. Unfortunately, this statement fits none of the Peisanders of whom anything is known.[9] One, for example, lived after Vergil's time, and another, of the seventh century B.C., who might otherwise have provided a very useful source, is only recorded to have composed poetry about Heracles, though one of the notices gives a warning that much other work attributed to him is spurious.[10] It is best to conclude that Macrobius has made a mistake about the name, and to accept what he says as very strong evidence that Vergil did make great use of some unknown Greek narrative poem when he was composing the Second *Aeneid*. Macrobius was a keen Vergilian scholar, and would hardly have thought of introducing so emphatic a statement on an important question if there had been no ground for it at all. It will appear later how echoes of this unknown poem can sometimes be detected.

Of the lost poetry which Vergil might have used, the probability that he used plays of Sophocles has already been noticed. Of the rest, the old 'cyclic' epic has a special interest. This poetry seems to have been composed to complete Homer's work, some of it soon after the age when Homer lived. The events which followed the time covered by the *Iliad* were described in the *Aethiopis* by Arctinus of Miletus, in the *Ilias parva*, attributed less securely to Lesches of Mitylene, and in the *Iliu persis*, by Arctinus also. The contents of these poems are known from the epitomae of Proclus, which are themselves preserved at second hand by Photius, and from a few scattered notices. But even this knowledge of these poems is not quite satisfactory. It has been supposed that Proclus himself had not access to them, but depended on mythological handbooks. That is unnecessary, especially as there is scarcely any doubt that the early epic survived at least to the time of Proclus.[11] Most losses of ancient literature belong to later centuries. But there are still difficulties.[12] The notices disagree about the points at which the poems begin and end. Aristotle,[13] for example, seems to have thought that the *Ilias parva* went on to the finish of the sack of Troy, and to have included the *Iliu persis* in it. Tzetzes[14] even carried it to the death of Neoptolemus after the war, and to the settlement of Aeneas and Andromache in North Greece. Proclus himself makes the *Ilias parva* end after, and the *Iliu persis* begin before, the introduction of the wooden horse into Troy: even though he seems to have been partly concerned to give a coherent story of the legendary events, and not merely to epitomize the poems accurately.[15] It used to be thought that the *Aethiopis*, *Ilias parva*, and *Iliu*

persis together formed a single continuation of the *Iliad* up to
the fall of Troy. Welcker[16] proved that this is not so. It is
probable that, as Robert[17] says, the middle of the *Aethiopis*
(in which he includes the *Iliu persis*) and the beginning and end
of the *Ilias parva* are missing from the epitomae. If so, the *Ilias
parva* and the poetry of Arctinus give parallel and different
continuations of the *Iliad*. It has been suggested that the poems
of the epic cycle were ill-defined at the joins, and overlapped
considerably, but it is doubtful whether this accounts for the
conditions. It is even possible that several different texts of these
poems existed; they were edited, but perhaps not so carefully
or so soon as the Homeric poems themselves.

It is almost certain that Vergil used early Greek hexameter
poetry now lost, because the few fragments of it that survive
furnish parallels, and because scholiasts sometimes cite it to
explain Vergil.[18] There is hardly any doubt that if this poetry
was in the hands of scholiasts it was in the hands of Vergil too:
especially as their information is sometimes inherited from the
generation or even the friends of Vergil himself.[19] The notices
refer to lost Hesiodic poetry, and to an unknown 'Homer',
which may easily mean the cyclic epic, often attributed to
Homer himself. This argument makes it, on the whole, likely
that Vergil used some cyclic version of the events of the fall of
Troy; and the uncertainties about the early poems make it
hard to prove that he did not. The cyclic epic is said to have
been well known: that is, the greater popularity of Homer and
the dramatists did not drive it out of circulation, as might have
been expected. Propertius and other writers not far from
Vergil's time seem to derive material from Arctinus.[20] Sophocles,
who was very fond of the epic cycle, used its material for many
tragedies;[21] and Vergil is likely to have agreed with him.
Occasionally Vergil seems to preserve an incident which agrees
remarkably with something recorded to have been in this lost
poetry.[22] Heyne,[23] though he wrote more than a hundred years
ago, was probably right to think that of the lost material
Vergil used especially Greek tragedies and the cyclic epic as
sources for the Second *Aeneid*.

They, of course, do not nearly exhaust the possibilities.[24] Of
the remaining poems, in so far as they are known, the *Iliu
persis* of Stesichorus is one of the most important in this con-

nection. Stesichorus was compared to Homer, and he was well known at Rome. His importance to Romans partly consisted in his share in the creation of the legend of Aeneas.[25] He was probably the first to say that Aeneas left Troy guided by Venus, when the fighting was nearly over, and sailed to Italy. Sophocles[26] also seems to have adopted a version of the departure of Aeneas not entirely unlike this. That Stesichorus was a famous authority until late times is shown by Tzetzes[27] who refers his readers to Stesichorus for the return of heroes from Troy. Tzetzes could do worse things than give impossible advice, and there is no reason to think that the poetry of Stesichorus was still surviving then; but the reference suggests that Stesichorus was widely known well into the Christian era.

Tzetzes is one of three Greek poets who told the story of the sack of Troy long after Vergil. The other two are very important indeed for the Vergilian question. They are Quintus Smyrnaeus, who wrote the *Posthomerica* in fourteen books probably during the fourth century, and Tryphiodorus, thought to have been an Egyptian, who wrote an *Excidium Ilii*, probably soon after the time of Quintus. The importance of Tzetzes, who wrote three books of *Antehomerica*, *Homerica*, and *Posthomerica*, is less; this is a pity, for he is exceedingly comical. He is often lost in his attempts to write hexameters which will scan, and sometimes it is hard to think that he had heard of the caesura. He seriously reproves Tryphiodorus for saying that the Trojans put flowers on the wooden horse,[28] since Troy was taken in the winter, when there would be no flowers. It is wrong, he says,[29] to tell a lie; and he carefully explains that he is indebted for that valuable rule of life to Orpheus, who learnt it from someone else: he does not identify this unknown benefactor of humanity. But it would be irrelevant to say more, either about the private domestic difficulties of his own life, without which he thinks his poem would be incomplete, or about his elaborate description of the physical qualities of the Achaean heroes, except to record the hope that he did not forget the rule of Orpheus in these passages. For, unfortunately, it is not likely that the lost poems, which were the common sources of Quintus, Tryphiodorus, and Vergil himself, survived until the time when Tzetzes lived.

Whether the two late poets used the sources of Vergil himself has been debated intermittently but with some vigour for more than a hundred years. It has been thought, sometimes almost generally, that they copied him; but the view that they are not directly dependent on Vergil, a view adopted principally by Koechly in 1850 and Heinze in 1901, is now almost certainly right. The conditions are interesting. The late poets describe in full the events which fall within the Second *Aeneid*. Their spirit is entirely different from Vergil's, and they do not present their legends quite in the Vergilian form. As Heinze[30] said of Tryphiodorus, if they knew Vergil, they certainly did not love him. On the other hand, both the late poets persistently show great similarity to Vergil in their phrases and thoughts. Sometimes similar words occur in the same places in the lines; and sometimes the sequence of events, including quite small details, is the same for long passages. These similarities have been supposed to be a strong argument in favour of the dependence of the late poets on Vergil. But a closer examination shows some strange facts. The comparable thoughts and phrases often occur at different places in the Latin and Greek versions; and it is quite clear, in very many instances, that the Greek versions have them in their original context, where they must have belonged in the earlier tradition, and that their occurrences in the Latin poem are governed by redistribution, according to a new artistic plan. Again, though Tryphiodorus sometimes follows Quintus, he often diverges from him; and when this happens, Vergil agrees sometimes with the one and sometimes with the other. The best proof, however, is this: the late poets are on the whole consistent and accurate, but Vergil most certainly is not. Yet sometimes, when a detail is found with verbally similar expression, in both Vergil and one of the late poets, but in different contexts, a restoration of the detail, in the poetry of Vergil, to the place where it belongs in the Greek poem, will remove the inconsistency or correct the inaccuracy. Occasionally Vergil actually suppresses some mention which the rest of his narrative assumes: a mention which the late poetry, however, supplies, so that the original meaning of Vergil is declared.

There seems to be only one solution of the problem: that there were two important poetic sources, one used by Vergil and Quintus, and the other by Vergil and Tryphiodorus.

They must have been poetic sources: no mythological hand-books, which are sometimes thought to have been used by later poets to the exclusion of original poems, could account for the verbal similarities. In fact, if the dates at which the three poems were composed had been unknown, it would long ago have been agreed that the Second *Aeneid* partly represents a combination of elements of the other two.

What these mysterious lost poems were is hard to discover, and it is not very safe to try to identify them, at least without a long argument. Critics have often thought that the cyclic epic was not used by the late poets or by Vergil either. That is not finally proved; Quintus, for example, diverges quite as much from Homer as he does from the cyclic epic, but it is certain that he used Homer; it has been said that he saturated himself in Homeric poetry.[31] But at least one thing is clear, that of the unknown sources of Vergil and the late epic, one must be the very poem which Macrobius said that Vergil almost transcribed.

The utility of this discovery chiefly lies in the opportunity that it gives of watching Vergil at work. Something has been said of his general method of imitation and transferred integration. The comparison with the late epic offers some remarkable instances.

The Achaeans sailed away to Tenedos, having burnt their camp, and left Sinon and the wooden horse behind. This belongs equally to nearly all the versions. But with Sinon the divergences begin. In the *Iliu persis* he seems to have found his way into Troy disguised, and to have had no previous role. The Sinon of Quintus[32] allows himself to be captured near the horse. The Trojans question him, and presently treat him very cruelly, even cutting off his ears and nose. First he bears it all heroically: and then, very inconsequently, begins telling his lies. This inconsequence may show that Quintus himself is using a combined version here, as elsewhere. Sinon's tale is like part of his tale in Vergil. The Achaeans, tired of the long war, had gone home. At the suggestion of Calchas the horse had been made as a dedication to Athena, who was angry with them. Then, at the advice of Odysseus, they had decided to sacrifice Sinon to the gods of the sea for their return. He had escaped and taken sanctuary at the feet of the horse, where the Achaeans dared not touch him. Afterwards, he signals to the Achaeans at Tenedos with a beacon, and warns the Achaeans in the horse that it is time to act.

The Sinon of Tryphiodorus[33] is seen by the Trojans, who are standing round the horse, moving over the plain towards them, already showing the marks of ill-treatment, for he had allowed the Achaeans to mutilate him as a confirmation of his story. He supplicates Priam to save him, for he can preserve Troy: the Achaeans had outraged him, as they had also injured Achilles, Philoctetes and Palamedes, because he would not go home with them. They had stripped and flogged him. Priam ought to save him, for it would please the Achaeans if the Trojans killed him. Besides, he can prevent the Trojans from having to fear a return of the Achaeans. Priam replies kindly, saying that Sinon shall be the friend of the Trojans, and asking him questions. Sinon then tells who he is, and explains that if the Trojans leave the horse on the shore, the Achaeans will take Troy, but if they bring it to their citadel, the enemy will retreat home. Afterwards, as in Quintus and the *Iliu persis*, Sinon signals to the Achaeans, this time with a torch.

A comparison with Vergil shows what has happened. Vergil has included almost as many as he could of the details of treatment used by the other two poets, though he has added particulars and made some changes. For example, the plan to sacrifice Sinon is taken from the tradition of Quintus, and the alternatives for dealing with the horse—preserved only by Vergil and Tryphiodorus—from a version used by Tryphiodorus. Vergil clearly realized the dramatic value of Sinon, and employed all means to make that value effective. He even seems to have used material, derived from earlier treatments of Sinon, for his scene in the Third *Aeneid*[34] in which Achaemenides is found in Sicily by the Trojans. However, he carefully does not allow the Trojans to treat Sinon with any cruelty, except a little mockery.

Sinon has now a part to play very different from his part in the cyclic epic. There he may not have been needed to persuade the Trojans to take in the horse: for there seems to have been an inscription on it which would influence them. In the *Iliu persis* Sinon seems to have been disguised: a motive which has turned into his mutilation, either by Achaeans or

Trojans, perhaps under the influence of the mutilation of Odysseus when he secretly entered Troy, or of stories like the story of Zopyrus, who thus entered Babylon according to Herodotus.[35] But it is hard to be certain which elements of the story are older than others.

It is a remarkable thing that in this part of the book Vergil follows exactly the same sequence of events as Tryphiodorus,[36] but interposes the two passages about Laocoon, of which Tryphiodorus has nothing to say. But the form of Laocoon's story, which is nearest of all that are known to the form of it in Vergil, is given by Quintus.[37] Clearly Vergil began by following the tradition of Tryphiodorus; but finding that the story of Laocoon—as it was told in some source of Quintus— had very great possibilities, imposed it, in two pieces, on his narrative. The result is inconsistent,[38] because Laocoon has to come down from Troy after all the Trojans are supposed to be on the shore. This seems to be because Vergil has created the picture of Laocoon's arrival from a picture of Priam's arrival, given in the tradition of Tryphiodorus[39] quite appropriately. It is equally hard at first to see why Laocoon should be sacrificing a bull to Neptunus at an altar near the shore, particularly at this exciting moment. If he came down from the citadel to sacrifice, he ought not to be represented as hurrying down to stop the Trojans from madly trusting the wooden horse. Besides, there ought hardly to be an altar still, as Vergil seems to say, in regular use, out in the open where a long war has been fought. The truth is that Vergil has imperfectly combined traditions. Laocoon ought to be sacrificing inside Troy: he has nothing to do with the scene on the shore. Nor should he have thrown his spear at the horse. There is imperfect combination even in the older version as Quintus seems to reproduce it; but in Quintus, when the snakes devour Laocoon's sons—not, however, Laocoon himself also, as in Vergil—the Trojans think he is punished because they have maltreated Sinon, whereas in Vergil they think that he is punished for damaging the horse.[40] This is again clearly a piece of Vergilian integration: Vergil must have thought a sin against the horse more darkly tragical than a sin against Sinon, and besides, his Trojans cannot treat Sinon very badly. Vergil has only to be read to be justified, but it is due to him to understand how much had to be done before such a result was possible. As G. K. Chesterton has said, a great deal of science is needed to produce even a little art. Another mark of imperfect adjustment is shown by the words with which Vergil introduces the scene of Laocoon's death. He says that 'another still more terrible thing' was going to happen. But nothing else terrible has occurred; for the mere discovery of the wooden horse could not be meant by Vergil's very strong expressions. However, almost the same thought, in very similar words, is used by Quintus;[41] but for him the comparative expressions are justified, since Laocoon has just been punished by a painful blindness and threatened by an earthquake,[42] and he is about to be punished again, since he has persisted in his warnings, by the death of his children. This shows clearly that Vergil has imperfectly adapted material from a source of Quintus. Now, in Quintus, Laocoon only warns the Trojans about the horse; but Cassandra, who in Tryphiodorus[43] warns the Trojans to break into it, in Quintus[44] actually tries to damage it. Cassandra's activities happen in Troy, after the horse has been taken through the gates, at the moment at which Vergil just mentions that she vainly prophesied. It is easy to see why he says little about her. When he decided to develop Laocoon to the greatest intensity, he transferred to him the attributes of Cassandra, her warning as given by both Quintus and Tryphiodorus, and her threat of violence to the horse—reproved as impious by Priam—which Quintus alone records.

The story of Laocoon had a long history, and underwent many variations, before Vergil used it. This history—analysed and determined by Carl Robert[45]—begins in literature with the *Iliu persis* of Arctinus. There two snakes appear, after the wooden horse had been taken into Troy, and kill Laocoon and one of his sons. At this portent Aeneas and his following depart to Mount Ida. Robert explains that the death of Laocoon and one son meant the destruction of Troy and the senior branch of the lineage of Tros. Aeneas and the younger branch, represented by the other son, might survive. The next writer known to have dealt with the story is Bacchylides, who mentioned Laocoon and his wife, and serpents who came from the Calydnae islands and were changed into men. An account of this is given by Hyginus, who says that Apollo's priest, Laocoon the son of Capys and the brother of Anchises, had, against the will of

Apollo, married a wife and begotten children. As punishment
Apollo, 'taking his opportunity' when Laocoon, chosen by lot
to offer sacrifice to Poseidon-Neptunus on the shore, was engaged in this rite, sent two serpents over the sea from Tenedos
to kill his sons, Antiphates and Thymbraeus. Laocoon tried to
help them, and the serpents coiled round him and killed him
also. The Trojans thought he was killed because he had thrown
his spear at the wooden horse. Robert argues that much of this
is interpolation from the Second *Aeneid* itself, either introduced
by Hyginus himself or by some later interpolator, to reconcile
Vergil with the Greek story. The original notice of Hyginus,
derived possibly from the lost *Laocoon* of Sophocles but much
more probably from the version of Bacchylides, only mentioned
the identity of Laocoon, his sin, and the expiation of it in his
two sons; though Laocoon may have died himself in an early
version. (It is, of course, equally possible that Hyginus took his
language from Vergil, but his facts from another authority.)
The most important new detail is the guilt of Laocoon. In this
tradition he suffers for his sin, and not only so that Aeneas may
be warned. This may correspond with the form of the story used
by Sophocles, which, however, is more securely reported by
Dionysius, who records that Aeneas prepared to leave Troy,
instructed by Anchises, on a warning from Aphrodite, but
also inferring the city's fall from the fate of Laocoon's sons.
Sophocles differs from Arctinus in saying that both sons were
killed, but agrees with him in supposing that the disaster was
a sign to Aeneas. Scholiasts add the information that the snakes
had names, Porces and Chariboea—one male, one female—,
that they 'sailed' from the Calydnae Islands, and that they
destroyed the sons of Laocoon (given as son of Antenor) in the
temple of the Thymbraean Apollo. Lysimachus, an important
writer of prose *Nostoi* much used by scholiasts, is reported to
have given names to the snakes, besides Sophocles; and Robert
concludes that the notices of Bacchylides and of Sophocles go
back to Lysimachus, and that he must have given both the
traditions. He also thinks that, since the snakes have names and
'sail' instead of swimming, they were in Sophocles human
beings, who were changed into snakes for the purpose of their
deed. Sophocles disagrees with Arctinus and may have followed
Bacchylides (but we are told that, according to Bacchylides,

the change was from serpents to men). Besides, the action now takes place in the temple of Apollo, not on the seashore. According to Servius, the sin of Laocoon was union with his wife in the presence of the god's (Apollo's) statue. If so, in the tragedy, the sin and expiation may have happened both in the same place. That is appropriate to tragic custom. Hyginus seems to have given Capys (the word is an almost certain emendation of the text), not Antenor, as the name of Laocoon's father; and from this Robert suggests that the whole story did not originally belong to the fall of Troy, but that the events of it happened long before.

Robert estimates Vergil's innovations, and his reasons for them. Aeneas must, of course, stay in Troy to the last, and so he cannot use the fate of Laocoon for a warning. Laocoon's old sin and guilt are irrelevant also, and, in fact, Vergil might have left him out altogether. But actually he only left out the causes and setting of the calamity, and retained the incident itself. The sign is now not the sign of the fall of Troy, but, by a mistake of the Trojans, of the sanctity of the horse. Again, Laocoon cannot now be punished by Apollo, as elsewhere, because he has not injured him; accordingly Athena, whom he has injured, sends the snakes. The disaster must happen outside the walls, to fit the connection with the wooden horse; and, therefore, Vergil makes Laocoon priest of Poseidon-Neptunus and engages him in a sacrifice to Neptunus on the shore. Vergil, again, relates that all three, Laocoon and both his sons, were killed. No other writer is known to have related that; though, of course, it seems to be intended in the Vatican group representing Laocoon's death. Robert, without fully discussing the question, believes that the Vatican group is later than Vergil; a more recent critic,[46] however, dates it at about 50 B.C. Robert himself does not believe that Vergil made all the innovations that are found in his version. He would not, he thinks (without very strong ground for the opinion), have allowed the sons to be killed, as well as Laocoon himself, if he had not taken this part over from a predecessor. Besides, Euphorion may have already told the story with some of the Vergilian changes. Euphorion explained that the Trojans had at the beginning of the war stoned their priest of Poseidon for not preventing the arrival of the Greeks. That was why an

acting priest had to be chosen by lot for the sacrifice to Neptunus after the war. The note continues—but probably as the
contribution of Servius, who cites this notice of Euphorion, not
of Euphorion himself—that the Trojans were deceived about
the cause of Laocoon's fate, because they did not know of his
sin, and that others instead maintained that there had been
no priest of Neptunus since Laomedon's quarrel with the god,
who now showed, in the fate of Laocoon, what all the Trojans
had deserved. The inference is that Euphorion's version must
have been like Sophocles', with differences: that in it the father
and both sons seem to have been killed and there was a sacrifice to Neptunus; but that the previous sin of Laocoon in the
temple of Apollo was retained and brought into relation with
the new ending. Vergil, therefore, may depend on Euphorion:
neither Vergil himself, nor Petronius, who follows him, imply
that Laocoon was really Neptunus' priest. Vergil, accordingly,
did not invent these changes. Robert cannot suggest what the
precedent for the story of Laomedon's sin and the stoning of the
priest of Poseidon in this context may have been. Vergil omits
Laocoon's previous sin against Apollo (who, of course, is now
irrelevant). However, Servius thought that Vergil understood
that Laocoon really died for this sin, but that the Trojans mis-
took the reason for his death. He explains that the serpents
went to the *arx*, that is to the temple of Athena-Minerva,
either because she was also the enemy of the Trojans or because
this was a sign of the fall of Troy. But in Vergil it is Athena,
not Apollo, who sends the serpents; and that contradicts the
possibility that Vergil intended Laocoon's past sin to be understood or assumed. On the other hand, there is no proof that
Euphorion ever handled the incident of Laocoon at all. He may
have explained why the Trojans had no priest of Poseidon in
quite a different context. Robert notices that Quintus has a
version connected with the Vergilian; but adds that since,
according to him, Laocoon's sons only are killed, he must have
followed an old saga version, which he could have got either
from an hypothesis of Sophocles' play or from a handbook; and
that after all Lessing was, in fact, right to say that Vergil is
the first and only writer known to have recounted that Laocoon himself and both his sons were killed.

Robert's analysis is open to some criticism, but by it several

facts are established. There was an early version of the story of
Laocoon in which Laocoon, priest of Apollo, was punished by
Apollo for a sin against him. With this has become conta-
minated quite a different story, in which Laocoon's death was
a sign of the fall of Troy. These versions begin for us respectively
with Bacchylides and Arctinus; and, of course, Arctinus is
the earlier poet, though it does not follow that his was in all
senses the earlier version. The Vergilian story is an intricate
combination, in which the variant of Arctinus may perhaps
predominate. But, unless Vergil made more innovations even
than Robert supposed, there must be some missing links in the
chain of tradition.

It appears that Vergil combined, with a composite Laocoon-
story which preserved elements from both the early variants, a
new composite motive which he found ready for him in sources
of the late epic, and derived from it all but one of the additions
which distinguish the Vergilian account. These additions were
shown by Robert's analysis to be the warning of Laocoon
against the wooden horse; the subjection of the whole incident
to the will, not of any other god or goddess, but of Athena; the
attempt to damage or test the wooden horse; the time and place
of the events; and perhaps, also, but by no means certainly,
the connection of Laocoon with Poseidon-Neptunus. All but
the last of these additions can be derived from the unknown
sources of Quintus and Tryphiodorus, either directly or by
transference. The last may possibly be the one invention left
to Vergil. The version of Quintus is itself a combination, partly
because the snakes, though they are sent by Athena, disappear
at the temple of Apollo. Heinze[47] thought that Quintus himself
duplicated the punishment of Laocoon; but the comparison of
his with Vergil's introduction to the narrative of Laocoon's
death practically proves that both he and Vergil used a version
in which two successive punishments were inflicted.

Having partly disintegrated Cassandra for the creation of
Laocoon, Vergil used some of her other attributes for Helen, as
she appears in the Sixth Aeneid,[48] and Amata, the Latin queen,[49]
still farther away in the Seventh. The account of Helen given
in the Second Aeneid is so different from the account in the
Sixth, that the difference may have helped to determine Vergil
himself to reject the reference to her at the sack of Troy,[50] where

she is merely found hiding in terror at the thought of the vengeance in store for her at the hands of either Trojans or Greeks. This is part of the Helen of the late epic.[51] In the Sixth *Aeneid*[52] Deiphobus in the world below after his death tells Aeneas that Helen, whom he had married after Paris was killed, summoned the Achaeans by displaying a torch. This also belongs to the version of Tryphiodorus.[53] According to him, Helen visited the wooden horse in the night and called to the heroes, an incident recorded by Homer[54] in one of his two short references to the events of the fall of Troy. But Aphrodite warned her not to do this, but to go to her house and wait for the Achaeans with a torch. Accordingly, Helen all night long showed the fire signal. So far all is simple, for Vergil has taken one part of the character of Helen, as the late epic pictures her, for his second, and another part for his sixth book. Interesting suggestions have been made about the torch. Helen, holding her torch above the ramparts, seems to appear on a gem.[55] She used to be identified with the moon: and ΕΛΕΝΕ and ΣΕΛΕΝΕ certainly might be confused. Accordingly, it has been proposed that Helen with her torch only means that the Achaeans sailed back from Troy by moonlight,[56] as Arctinus and Vergil say that they did. In one part of the night-fighting Vergil refers to the moonlight again; though elsewhere characteristically he implies that there was black darkness that night. There is little doubt that Helen was a human princess, and not the moon. But it is just possible that she became confused with quite another Helen, who, according to a skilful but hardly certain train of argument,[57] has been inferred as a requisite figure in the mythology of the sun and of the trees which the Greeks may have acquired from North Europe. If so, according to Frisian etymology, Helen ought perhaps to be the real name of Calypso. 'Helen' may also contain an element equivalent to the Anglo-Saxon root which means 'light', and Hesychius explains ἑλάνη as 'torch'; there certainly was a tree spirit in Rhodes worshipped under the name of Ἑλένη δενδρῖτις.[58]

All this is too interesting to be left out altogether, but it does not explain another difficulty about Helen. In the Sixth *Aeneid*, but apparently nowhere else, she leads the Trojan women in a pretended bacchic dance as an excuse for showing her torch. The late epic explains why. Vergil has added to

Helen actions of Cassandra, who, according to Tryphiodorus,[59] strayed like a bacchanal, shaking a laurel bough, and, according to Quintus,[60] took a torch of blazing pine, not to make signals, but to set fire to the wooden horse. The verbal expressions of both are reproduced by Vergil, some of them for Helen and others for Amata, who engages in bacchic revelry later in the *Aeneid*;[61] a kind of *retractatio*. It is possible that Vergil had another detail in mind: the fire signal shown in other versions by Sinon, which he has transferred to the flagship of the Achaean fleet.[62] However, Vergil's success is again apparent, for he has intensified the action of Helen, to make her seem more heartless still, in revelling on that terrible night.

In the Sixth *Aeneid* Helen secretly takes away the arms of Deiphobus while he is asleep. This seems to be imitated from the *Odyssey*,[63] where Odysseus and Telemachus take the arms secretly out of the hall, in preparation for killing the suitors. As they did so Athena showed an unearthly light to help them; and this may also have contributed to Vergil's picture of Helen. In the same context there is another reference from the *Odyssey* and another difficulty. Aeneas tells Deiphobus that he had heard that he died fighting heroically.[64] This is the Homeric[65] story. Deiphobus replies that, weighted with cares, he fell into a deep sleep, like death, in his home, and that meanwhile Helen took the arms away. Apparently Deiphobus was killed asleep or half-awake. This is very like the account of Quintus,[66] who says that Menelaus found Deiphobus, 'weighted' (almost certainly) with wine by the bed of Helen; that is, of course, in his house—though in the Second *Aeneid* the house of Deiphobus collapsed early in the fighting. What has happened is interesting. Vergil, characteristically giving both sides of a question, has followed both Homer and the unknown source of Quintus. Either there is a contradiction, or it can be supposed that the Homeric rumour about the death of Deiphobus which Aeneas had heard was wrong. Vergil as usual leaves some doubt, and Deiphobus is not robbed of his heroic stand. But in Quintus Deiphobus must have been very drunk to sleep through so much fighting. This Vergil has carefully mitigated; he keeps the expression 'weighted', but insists that it was with cares, not wine; as elsewhere he suppresses the recollection that the Trojans were drunk on their last night.

The Vergilian death of Priam is one of the most brilliant examples of the method of transference and combination. Vergil has combined[67] the version of the *Iliu persis*, in which Neoptolemus killed Priam at the altar, and the variant of the *Ilias parva*, in which he dragged him from the altar to the door. Vergil intensifies the horror of the deed very greatly by relating that Priam was dragged, not from, but to, the altar, and there killed. This combination is quite a simple device, but, used as frequently and ingeniously as Vergil uses it, it has surprising power in it. The late epic here follows the usual version, the version of the *Iliu persis*, content neither to defend Neoptolemus nor to exalt the courage of Priam. But Vergil has another of his apparent contradictions. He says that Priam was stabbed, and Tryphiodorus seems to say the same.[68] But soon afterwards he writes as if Priam had been beheaded. This variant, usually traced to Pacuvius, was chosen by Quintus:[69] according to whom Priam's head rolled far along the ground, away from his other members, in the blood of other men. The reference to the blood of other men reappears in Vergil typically transmuted: in the *Aeneid* it is the blood of Priam's own son, slain before his eyes, and Priam slides in it before, not after, his death.

Some reasons why Vergil may have wanted to say that Priam was beheaded, even though that was not quite in harmony with the account which otherwise he preferred, are interesting. At almost any moment, apparently, Vergil's poetry may become 'allegorical'. He certainly began to use allegory early; it is important in the *Eclogues*.[70] The whole scheme of the *Aeneid* may be called in some sense allegorical.[71] Vergil, planning his great epic in advance, calls it a marble temple—using almost the same expression which he used later for a real temple—with Caesar in the middle.[72] Caesar Augustus, in fact, often corresponds in some sense with Aeneas. This is why Aeneas has shocked nearly every reader by descending on one occasion[73] to human sacrifice; for Augustus himself had been guilty of that crime, and Vergil, with great subtlety, thus suggests that in certain circumstances such rigour could be justified.[74] Another instance of the ingenious use of figurative meaning is at the beginning of the Sixth *Aeneid*. On the gates of the temple at Cumae there is in Vergil's description[75] a picture of a maze or labyrinth with the minotaur in the middle.

It seems that the book partly conveys the doctrines of the Eleusinian Mysteries,[76] and that a symbolic maze-treading was part of the introduction to these ceremonies.[77] So Vergil, who could not easily represent this literally, makes Aeneas go through a gate on which a maze is pictured.[78] The esoteric meaning seems to have been connected with the common symbolism by which a maze represents the state of doubt and confusion that frequently precedes a revelation of divine truth. Two ways have been suggested in which the Vergilian death of Priam may be allegorical. The description of his headless body on the shore recalls the death of Pompeius Magnus.[79] Again, the dismemberment of Priam may indicate the dismemberment of his empire.[80] If these suggestions are true, the allegory is hardly inconsistent with Vergil's known practice; the double meaning of the picture given intensifies the poetic effect, and there is more reason than ever to wonder both at the complexity of Vergil's design and at the triumphant success with which he achieved it.

The sharply and powerfully individualized Polites of Vergil is no more than his Priam the creation of chance. According to Quintus,[81] and no doubt also to the unknown poem used by both Quintus and Vergil, Polites was killed by the cast of a spear with many other sons of Priam, but apparently out of sight of his father, and attacking, not fleeing. Polites occurs also much earlier in the poem of Quintus, and there he narrowly escapes death from an arrow in a battle.[82] Vergil has clearly worked on material very much like this. He combines the two episodes, and arranges that Polites should be wounded, but escape immediate death. He refers to other sons of Priam, but concentrates attention on Polites. He retains the mention of the spear; but Polites is pursued with it at his back, to die at Priam's feet. Priam's speech to Neoptolemus is full of allusions which occur, not always as part of the speech, in the late poetry near this place. Vergil has shown his power in compressing them all into Priam's heroic and violent words. His Priam is courageous and selfless to the last; but in his sources Vergil probably found a very different Priam, for in Quintus[83] he is resigned, and in Tryphiodorus[84] he querulously appeals for mercy.

But the crowning example and most triumphant vindication of Vergil's method is in the next climax, the encounter with Helen and the intervention of Venus. In some earlier poetry, and probably in the early epic, Menelaus went to the house of Deiphobus and there found Helen. He at first wanted to kill her, but repented at the sight of her beauty. It is clear that this is the material out of which Vergil constructed his great scene. There can hardly be another copy in the world so incomparably finer than its original.

It is worth while to indicate shortly the history of this motive. It has been analysed by Robert,[85] like the story of Laocoon. According to Euripides and Aristophanes, Menelaus at first meant to kill Helen, but seeing her beauty lost his anger and let fall his sword. The scene is the house of Deiphobus and the direct agency of Aphrodite in inspiring Menelaus with forbearance is not asserted. According to Ibycus, however, Helen fled to Aphrodite's temple and there talked to Menelaus; and he for love threw down his sword. But already Stesichorus seems to have said the same, for a *tabula Iliaca*—a Roman earthenware relief, picturing the fall of Troy 'according to Stesichorus' —adds to the scene an inscription, 'The Temple of Aphrodite'; and he may have combined in this incident part of another, in which the Achaeans nearly stoned Helen, but, seeing her beauty, let the stones fall. Robert argues that the story of the temple was not in the *Ilias parva* or the *Iliu persis*: though one of the scholiasts, on whom the argument for the *Ilias parva* rests, connects Ibycus, Lesches and Euripides together as authorities; and the evidence for the *Iliu persis* is negative, since it is drawn from the reticence of Proclus, who merely says that Menelaus found Helen and took her to the ships, having killed Deiphobus.

Robert cites vase paintings of the fifth century for the flight of Helen to a statue of a goddess. At first Cassandra and Helen are both shown at the statue of Athena. The necessity to show the fortunes of both heroines on one vase, and the authority of Arctinus for Cassandra's refuge, could account for the pictorial tradition. Later, Aphrodite's statue is presented, in a posture of encouragement and help to Helen; and, again later, Aphrodite herself appears, to protect her. All this could quite easily have developed without influence from poetry; but in fact Stesichorus, who is thought to have represented the scene in the temple of Aphrodite, is earlier than the vases.

His contribution mainly rests on the authority of the *tabula Iliaca*, and there the identification of the temple of Aphrodite may perhaps be questioned as a late addition to the story. But it is likely enough that Ibycus so handled the incident of Helen's recovery, because the account of the scholiast who asserts this is in some detail and seems carefully written; and it is best to suppose that Stesichorus really placed the recovery of Helen in the temple of Aphrodite. On the other hand, there is little reason to deny that the appearance of Aphrodite, or at least her unseen influence on Menelaus, was described in the early epic. It is at least nearly certain that an account, almost verbally like Vergil's, existed before him; for to this Quintus once more furnishes his testimony.

But whatever older form of the incident is taken for comparison, the ethical and poetic difference between the other accounts and Vergil's is startling. Yet Vergil keeps close to the details of the original or originals which he used, one of which seems, as usual, to have been the source also used by Quintus. He even reproduces, in the words which describe the action of Venus in restraining Aeneas from his anger, exactly the posture of Aphrodite, reassuring Helen, on an Attic vase. It is possible that Vergil may actually have remembered a vase, though this is not necessary. Probably enough, the great wall painting of Polygnotus at Delphi influenced the poets, and among them Vergil himself, who is thought to have followed plastic representations frequently. It has been noticed that the laurel tree by the altar, which Vergil mentions, appears on an *Iliu persis* vase; and there also, apparently, the arms of Priam, which have a reference, at this context, only in the *Aeneid* and here;[86] so that perhaps Vergil did not entirely invent the heroic daring of Priam just before his death.

In the meetings with Helen and Venus, Vergil's transferences are, if anything, more simple than usual. It is Aeneas, not Menelaus, who meets Helen. His cause for anger is, of course, quite different: it is for him an unselfish anger, in vindication of his own race and his own home. But Aeneas, unlike Menelaus, from the first understands that there is no glory in killing a woman. This is another transference; for not long before this part of the story in the version of Quintus[87] Ilioneus, about to be killed, appeals for mercy on the ground that there is no glory in killing an old man. The detail is released, for Vergil to use it in the thought of Aeneas about Helen, because in the *Aeneid* Ilioneus lives on. The intention of Aeneas to kill Helen has far greater tragic significance than the intention of Menelaus; but the difference in poetic value of the change of mind in the two situations is greater still. Menelaus, either by the specific intervention of Aphrodite or by the natural appeal of a sentiment nearer to selfishness than love, is actuated to consult his future pleasure in preference to his present animosity. Aeneas, whose anger is anyhow more righteous, has nothing worldly to gain by sparing Helen. But his divine mother restrains him by a far higher and purer influence, which Vergil as so often has left undefined. She tells him not to blame either Helen or Paris, for Troy is falling by the grim will of gods. Aeneas must resign himself to a higher law. Yet even here Vergil has adopted something from his source and made quite a small change in it. For in the account of Quintus[88] Aphrodite tells Menelaus that not Helen, but Paris is to blame. The words and even the versification are nearly the same; and Vergil betrays by a slight irregularity of syntax[89] the truth that he is following some authority closely: closely, but worlds away.

But Vergil has used not only the meeting of Menelaus and Helen as it was represented in former poetry, but apparently also a meeting between Anchises and Aphrodite. Sophocles seems to have followed a version in which Anchises warned Aeneas to depart from Troy in obedience to the advice of Aphrodite.[90] This advice was given to Anchises, not to Aeneas directly, and quite possibly not at the time of the action, but previously, in prophecy. Vergil apparently developed a change made by Ennius, whose fragments[91] suggest that he constructed a scene in which Venus at the sack of Troy warned Anchises to depart, and that Aeneas also was present at part, at least, of the interview. Vergil, as usual, has accepted all the influences, and by compression and a few dexterous alterations has made the poetic situation infinitely more intense. His biggest change here seems to be a very simple inversion; it is the Aeneas of Vergil who is warned by Venus, his divine mother, and who then persuades Anchises, more appropriately reluctant to leave his home, to start life over again.

The vision which Venus now shows to Aeneas seems to have been suggested partly by two passages in the *Iliad*,[92] and partly by scattered references in the unknown source or sources which Vergil shared with the late epic. It is very likely that Homer himself exercised some transferences. It is even possible that Homer's picture of the gods at war originally belonged to this place in the story, and that such a picture was recorded in this original context by other poetry now lost. But the perfect fitness with which the Vergilian vision follows the stress, despair, and hate of Aeneas is likely to belong to Vergil's technique, though his choice was probably determined by allusions at this point in the lost poetry. There is, however, one very likely indication here of a Homeric transference. Vergil[93] and the late epic[94] describe Poseidon at work, destroying his own Trojan wall. Homer,[95] in grand and majestic poetry, tells how Poseidon destroyed the wall in front of the Achaean camp, after the builders had sailed home. The descriptions are alike, and it seems that Homer invented his situation because, though he did not intend to deal fully with the fall of Troy, he thought the opportunity which the picture of Poseidon gave too good to miss. It must never, of course, be forgotten that Homer had at his command a great volume of earlier poetry which he frequently presupposes, and which was partly reproduced, with less changes than Homer must have made in the passages of it which he rehandled, in other later poems, lost or extant.

But Vergil has other transferences in his vision of the gods. The recognition of one of them removes a difficulty. Aeneas sees Juno fiercely calling the Achaeans from the ships.[96] It is, of course, too late for that.[97] At the beginning of the fighting Androgeos spoke as though he thought all of them should have reached Troy. The reason is that Vergil has compressed into one two appearances of the gods, both of which are given, surely from a common source, by Tryphiodorus: one at the final destruction of Troy,[98] and one earlier, when the wooden horse entered the city.[99] At the first appearance an invitation to the Achaeans would be appropriate, especially if the important thing was that the horse should merely enter the city by a certain way, as even Homer once implies: a view for which reasons will be given later.

The next movements of Aeneas, the events at his home, and

D

the loss of Creusa, Vergil would have found it difficult to derive from any Greek source, since the fortunes of Aeneas are unlikely to have been so fully recounted in the Greek poems. But the actual departure of Aeneas from Troy can be discussed and a difficulty solved by the theory of transference. In the Second *Aeneid*[100] Aeneas goes from the palace of Priam to his own home under the guidance and protection of his divine mother. But elsewhere, in the First *Aeneid*,[101] he speaks as if his mother had guided him from Troy at the start of his wanderings. This has appeared to be an unsolved difficulty,[102] for the earlier guidance of Venus has been missed. Quintus[103] shows the importance of it, for he describes the departure of Aeneas from Troy in almost the same expressions which Vergil uses for the walk of Aeneas from the palace to his home. Vergil has clearly made one of his transferences and forgotten, as usual, to apply the principle that one change ought generally to involve many. Other signs of transference connected with this context help to show that this has happened.

There was a story, which Varro is said to have told,[104] that it was the star of Venus that guided Aeneas, like the star in the New Testament. Vergil has not forgotten this star, but in his account it is hardly recognizable. It appears as the shooting star,[105] which was the final omen which decided Anchises to leave his home. There is still something surprising in this, for the Romans usually thought a shooting star unlucky, not lucky. The omens at the death of Julius Caesar occur obviously for comparison. But the rule is not quite absolute; and a fusion of Greek and Roman ideas helps to account for Vergil's choice.

The version which Quintus gives of the departure of Aeneas seems to be derived from some Greek source that was nearer to Vergil's than any other form of the story. But the Vergilian changes are again to be seen. In Quintus,[106] Calchas warns the Achaeans not to harm Aeneas partly because he is following a high destiny, and partly because, though he might have taken the wealth of Troy with him, he is piously taking his old father instead. This is amusing; and Vergil knew how to suppress things so crude, though he mentions the Trojan treasure not far away.

It would take a long time to analyse fully the elaborate and intricate structure of Vergil's major technique. There are many more instances of his transference and integration which leave little doubt, if any, that the circumstances are as they have been represented here. The comparison of the old with the new has been worth making, for it helps to show how great was the cost of Vergil's creation, and how sublime were the powers of memory, intellect, and artistic intuition which he used in the service of his cardinal vision.

NOTES

1. Seneca, *Suasoriae* III, 7; *cf.* Pliny, *Ep.* VII, 9, 3; Hor. *Ars Poet.* 131 ff. For a discussion *cf.* A.-M. Guillemin, *L'originalité de Virgile* (Paris, 1931) 7 ff.

2. Theocr. *Id.* I, 134.

3. For a discussion of this whole question *cf.* H. R. Fairclough, *CP* 25 (1930) 37 ff.

4. E. K. Rand, *CJ* 26 (1930–1) 38.

5. Donat. *Vit. Verg.* 114 ff. (J. Brummer, *Vitae Vergilianae*, Leipzig, 1912, 7).

6. *Cf.* D. Serv. *ad Aen.* III, 10, who partly understands the conditions, but hardly states them emphatically enough.

7. For arguments in support of the main thesis of this chapter, *cf.* W. F. J. Knight, *CQ* 26 (1932) 178 ff.

8. Macrob. *Sat.* V, 2, 4–5.

9. C. G. Heyne, *P. Virgilius Maro . . .*[4] rev. G. E. P. Wagner (London, 1830–41) II, Exc. I, 394 ff.; W. Schmid and O. Stählin, *Griechische Literaturgeschichte* (München, 1929) I, i, 295 ff., esp. 297, notes 6, 7, 9.

10. Suid. *s.v.* Πείσανδρος; G. Kinkel, *Epicorum Graecorum Fragmenta* (Leipzig, 1877) I, 248 ff.

11. T. W. Allen, *Homer: The Origins and the Transmission* (Oxford, 1924) 56 ff.

12. Schmid-Stählin (above, note 9) I, i, 195 ff., where the reff. are given.

13. Aristot. *Poet.* XXIII.

14. Tzetz. *ad* Lycophr. *Alex.* 1232.

15. Carl Robert, *Bild und Lied* (Berlin, 1881) 222, citing K. O. Müller and Th. Schreiber.

16. F. G. Welcker, *Der epische Cyclus oder die homerischen Dichter* (Bonn, 1835–49) I, 211 ff. (I², 1865, 200 ff.).

17. Robert (above, note 15) 223.

18. Knight (above, note 7) 181 (with note 7)–182.

19. R. S. Conway, *New Studies of a Great Inheritance* (London, 1921) 107.

20. T. W. Allen, *Homeri Opera* (Oxford, 1908, etc.) V, 126–7; *cf.* Hor. *Ars Poet.* 136 ff.

21. Athen. VII, 5, 277 E; *cf.* Aristot. *Poet.* XXIII.

22. *Cf.* E. Fraenkel, *Philologus* 86, 41 (1932) 242 ff., who argues that Vergil seems to show influence from the *Aethiopis*, and is inclined to think, against the accepted view, that he may have used the actual text of it. *Cf.* also Knight (above, note 7) 180 (with note 1)–181 (with note 5).

23. Heyne (above, note 9) II, Exc. I, 387–8.

24. *Cf.* ibid. II, Exc. I, 378 ff. for an account of the material. The important question of Dictys and Dares, whose lost sources Vergil may have used, and who seem now to preserve ancient legends (Allen, above, note 11, 130 ff., esp. 163 ff.), must be omitted here.

25. Schmid-Stählin (above, note 9) I, i, 474–5. For the possible connection between Stesichorus and Vergil in their accounts of the fall of Troy, *cf.* O. Immisch, *RM* 52 (1897) 127 ff.

26. Dion. Hal. *Ant. Rom.* I, 48.

27. Johannes Tzetzes, *Posthomerica* 750 ff.

28. Ibid. 700 ff.

29. Ibid. 705 ff.

30. R. Heinze, *Virgils epische Technik*[3] (Leipzig, 1915) 81. For the arguments and reff. on this controversy, *cf.* Knight (above, note 7) 178 ff.

31. A. S. Way, *Quintus Smyrnaeus* (Loeb ed., London, 1913) Introd. v ff.

32. Quint. Smyrn. XII, 237 ff., 358 ff.

33. Tryph. 258 ff.

34. *Aen.* III, 588 ff.

35. Hdt. III, 154. For the history of the motive of Sinon, as it is mentioned here, *cf.* E. Bethe, *RM* 46 (1891) 516; *cf.* ff. esp. 519, note 3.

36. *Cf. Aen.* II, 39 with Tryph. 250 ff.; *Aen.* II, 57 ff. with Tryph. 258 ff.; *Aen.* II, 189 ff. with Tryph. 296 ff.; *Aen.* II, 232 ff. with Tryph. 304 ff.

37. Quint. Smyrn. XII, 387 ff.

38. For the difficulties, *cf.* Bethe (above, note 35) 511 ff., esp. 512–3.

39. Tryph. 241 ff.

40. Quint. Smyrn. XII, 415 ff.; *cf. Aen.* II, 228 ff.

41. Quint. Smyrn. XII, 447 ff.; *cf. Aen.* II, 199 ff.

42. Quint. Smyrn. XII, 395 ff.

43. Tryph. 358 ff.

44. Quint. Smyrn. XII, 565 ff.

45. Robert (above, note 15) 192 ff.; citing esp. Procl. *epit. Iliu persis*; Serv. *ad Aen.* II, 201, 204, 211; Hygin. *Fab.* 135; *Aen.* II, 201, 203, 216 ff., 229 ff.; Apollodor. *Epit.* V, 17–18; Bacchyl. fr. 32 (Bergk); Dion. Hal. *Ant. Rom.* I, 48; Schol. *ad* Lycophr. *Alex.* 347; Heyne (above, note 9) II, Exc. V, 409–14; Petron. *Troi. hal.* 18 ff. For criticisms *cf.* A. C. Pearson, *The Fragments of Sophocles* (Cambridge, 1917) II, 38 ff. [For a useful recent discussion see R. G. Austin, *Aeneid* II (Oxford, 1964) 94 ff. J.D.C.]

46. W. Rollo, *Rev. des ét. anc.* 31 (1929) 134 ff.; Guillemin (above, note 1) 41.

47. Heinze (above, note 30) 68.

48. *Aen.* VI, 511 ff., esp. 517 ff.

49. *Aen.* VII, 385 ff.

50. *Aen.* II, 567 ff.; Heyne (above, note 9) II, 346–7.

51. Quint. Smyrn. XIII, 356–7, 386–7; Tryph. 630 ff.

52. *Aen.* VI, 518 ff. For the reff. on these passages of the Sixth *Aeneid*, *cf.* E. Norden, *P. Vergilius Maro, Aeneis Buch VI*[3] (Leipzig-Berlin, 1927) 260 ff., where a different and more general theory of sources is adopted.

53. Tryph. 512 ff.

54. Hom. *Od.* IV, 274 ff.

55. Norden (above, note 52) 261, adopting the comparison (suggested by R. Wünsch) of A. Furtwängler, *Die antiken Gemmen* (Leipzig, 1900) I, Pl. XXXVIII 6, described very shortly (without identification of Helen) ibid. II, 181. The view that Helen here is a symbol of the moon is maintained by Norden (260–1), citing for it Schneidewin, *Göttinger Nachrichten*, 1852, 99 ff. (which I have not been able to see).

56. For the strong tradition that there was a bright moon on the night of the fall of Troy, Norden (above, note 52) 261, cites Schneidewin (above, note 55). *Cf. Aen.* II, 255, 340, 621.

57. J. Rendel Harris, *Apollo's Birds* (Manchester, 1925) 45 ff., citing Hesych. *s.v.*

and Athen. XV, 61. In these equations, if they are pursued, the digamma should not be forgotten.

58. Paus. III, 19, 10; the cult may be older than the name.

59. Tryph. 365 ff.

60. Quint. Smyrn. XII, 568 ff.

61. Cf. Aen. VI, 517 ff.; VII, 385 ff., esp. 397–8.

62. Aen. II, 256–7.

63. Hom. Od. XIX, 31 ff.

64. Aen. VI, 502 ff.

65. Hom. Od. VIII, 517 ff.

66. Quint. Smyrn. XIII, 354 ff. The theory that Vergil was following a source of Quintus explains the strangeness of phraseology which Norden notices at Aen. VI, 520 (above, note 52, 267, where he mentions the combination of legends by Vergil).

67. Heinze (above, note 30) 39 ff.

68. Aen. II, 553; Tryph. 634 ff.

69. Quint. Smyrn. XIII, 241 ff.

70. Donat. Vit. Verg. 294 ff. (Brummer, above, note 5, 16–17); L. Hermann, Les Masques et les Visages dans les Bucoliques de Virgile (Brussels, 1930) passim; for reff. cf. esp. 1 ff. and 173 ff.

71. Cf. William Warburton, The Divine Legation of Moses (London, 1738–41) I, 183, etc.; the question is fully examined by D. L. Drew, The Allegory of the Aeneid (Oxford, 1927) passim.

72. Verg. Georg. III, 13–16; Aen. VI, 69–70.

73. Aen. X, 517 ff.

74. Knight (above, note 7) 55 ff.

75. Aen. VI, 14 ff., esp. 24 ff.

76. Warburton (above, note 71) I, 133 ff., esp. 182 ff.; Colin Still, Shakespeare's Mystery Play: A Study of 'The Tempest' (London, 1921) passim, esp. 27–8, 61, 132–3. Still argues that many creations of poetry and religion, including The Tempest and the Sixth Aeneid, give forms of a 'Universal Myth' of the soul's journey to perfection.

77. Still (above, note 76) 133, citing Plato, Phaedo 108 A; Lucian, Catapl. XXII, 644.

78. W. F. J. Knight, CR 43 (1929) 212–3.

79. Guillemin (above, note 1) 60–1; cf. Lucan, VIII, 708 ff.

80. H. Schickinger, Wiener Studien 28 (1906) 165 ff.; J. D. Meerwaldt, Mnemosyne 59 (1931–2) 184 ff. Cf. Heinze (above, note 30) 39: 'Und nun beginnt der letzte Akt des Dramas: der Fall Trojas gipfelt in König Priamos' Tod. Diese Symbolik der poetischen Architektur scheint uns jetzt so selbstverständlich, dass sie bei Virgil, soviel ich sehe, keinem Interpreten als etwas Besonderes aufgefallen ist; . . .'

81. Quint. Smyrn. XIII, 213 ff.

82. Id. VIII, 409 ff.

83. Id. XIII, 222 ff.

84. Tryph. 636 ff.

85. Robert (above, note 15) 76 ff., citing Schol. ad Eur. Andr. 631; Eur. Andr. 629; Aristoph. Lysistr. 155, and Schol.; Stesich. fr. 25 (Bergk); Schol. ad Eur. Orest. 1286; cf. Schol. ad Aristoph. Vesp. 711; cf. Quint. Smyrn. XIII, 385 ff.

86. E. A. Gardner, JHS 14 (1894) 177.

87. Quint. Smyrn. XIII, 193 ff.

88. Quint. Smyrn. XIII, 412 ff.

89. Aen. II, 601 ff.

90. Dion. Hal. Ant. Rom. I, 48.

91. E. M. Steuart, *The Annals of Ennius* (Cambridge, 1925) 3 (frs. 9, 10, 11); *cf.* 103 ff.

92. Hom. *Il.* V, 127; *Il.* XX, 31 ff.

93. *Aen.* II, 610 ff.

94. Tryph. 568–9; *cf.* 680–1.

95. Hom. *Il.* XII, 27 ff.; W. F. J. Knight, *CP* 26 (1931) 417.

96. *Aen.* II, 612 ff.

97. Heinze (above, note 30) 52; *cf. Aen.* II, 370 ff.

98. Tryph. 566 ff.

99. Id. 330 ff.

100. *Aen.* II, 632 ff.

101. *Aen.* I, 381–2.

102. For this difficulty *cf.* Catharine Saunders, *Vergil's Primitive Italy* (New York, 1930) 199 ff.

103. Quint. Smyrn. XIII, 300 ff., esp. 326 ff.

104. Varr. *ap.* Serv. *ad Aen.* I, 382; see Ch. III, note 30, above.

105. *Aen.* II, 692 ff. Servius, *ad Aen.* I, 382, considers that Lucifer at *Aen.* II, 801 represents the star of Venus.

106. Quint. Smyrn. XIII, 333 ff.

V

THE EVENTS

The story of the siege of Troy is the most famous in all literature outside the Bible. It owes the honour to something like an accident. Alexander the Great understood this when he envied Achilles the lucky chance by which Homer himself recorded his deeds. Alexander meant that Achilles would never have won his renown without the genius of the greatest poet to help him, and perhaps, too, that Achilles, after all, was not so very great. There may be truth in this. Homer's poetry is older than any other poetry of Europe; but it is an elaborate, artistic presentation of the events which furnished its material. Homer preserves much history, but often it was necessary, for his artistic purpose, to discard and to alter facts.[1] Among the facts which he altered the achievements and importance of Achilles are to be included. Achilles owes his commanding significance, at least in its familiar literary form, to Homer, who magnified his part by an act of artistic concentration, probably because the character and fate of Achilles were naturally attractive to a great poet. In the original material about the fighting in front of Troy, from which the *Iliad* was composed, Achilles may even have been one of many minor characters; except that it was he who killed Hector.

Homer has probably made other changes. It is likely that the siege of Troy actually lasted about two years, not ten; probably it was hardly a siege at all until after the death of Hector. It is also likely that the Achaeans of the heroic age were not nearly so intellectually broad-minded, so modern, and so free from early or superstitious habits of thought, as Homer has represented them to have been.

The exact historical motive of the Achaeans in their war against the city, perhaps the empire, of Troy, is partly uncertain. Troy commanded the four cross-ways where Europe met Asia and two seas were joined. Its tactical, strategical, and commercial position was exceedingly strong. The Achaeans may have been attempting to liberate commercial enterprise in the Pontus from Trojan control, or they may have been in-

stinctively preparing an access to Asiatic soil which was used
afterwards for the foundation of Greek cities in Anatolia.[2]
New forces had been liberated when the dominion of the
Hittites receded. However, the historical background[3] in world
conditions—among which the revival of Egyptian power under
Rameses III is important—is known; and Helen may actually
have been the immediate cause of the war, for she was a queen
of the older stock, and the Achaeans may have ruled by her
right.[4] Probably some recent suggestions[5] also contain much of
the truth, and most of the Achaeans were seeking nothing but
adventure and loot, in their brilliant and romantic, but un-
productive, way. Even if Homer has exaggerated, they must
have shown considerable resource and tenacity to win a
decisive victory over the Trojans in their almost impregnable
fortress; for that this, at least, happened archaeology makes it
hard to deny.

However, after the war had been long in progress, and when,
in spite of losses, the victory remained in doubt, since the
Trojans, behind their massive walls, might hold out indefinitely,
if they continued to control their supplies, the Achaeans seem
to have fallen into nervousness and some distraction. As usual
in such a case, they turned more and more to superstition.
How natural this is after a strain is shown by parallels: for instance, after the successes of Hannibal at the beginning of the
Second Punic War, and again at the end of it, the Romans
enlisted any supernatural aid they could; and even at the end
of the European War of 1914–18, a superstitious outlook was
clearly spreading among many classes of people. It may be
truer to say that in times of great stress men see things in
spiritual shapes: the regard in which St Joan was held and the
belief in the Angels of Mons can be included among many
examples. At any rate, the legends seem to show that the
Achaeans, having lost Achilles, Ajax, and others of their best
leaders, and no doubt finding it difficult and unpleasant to
maintain themselves on their over-worked camping ground,[6]
began to rely more than before on superstitious devices. The
war seems to become more mythical. The Trojans were helped
first by the queen of the Amazons, who may be the Hittites,
but are well disguised, and then by black Memnon, the son
of the Morning himself. The Achaeans sent for Philoctetes,

whose bow had supernatural power, then for Neoptolemus, the
son of Achilles, who was expected to have some peculiar efficacy,
and lastly for the bones of Pelops, as the Spartans afterwards
acquired the relics of Orestes and the Athenians the remains
of Theseus to help them in times of need. This part of the war
was described by other, 'cyclic', poets, not by Homer. It has
been proposed[7] that Homer refused this theme because it was
not congenial to his humanistic taste and method. That is
possible, for at the end of the war men appear to count for
less and the dark powers for more. The cyclic poets seem to
have had less compunction: they are thought to have been less
anxious than Homer to exclude unpleasant actions or ignorant
thoughts from their poetry.[8]

The Achaeans were now fighting against the divine protection on which the Trojans relied. An obvious method was to
win the Trojan gods to their side; and the most obvious way to
do that was by simple theft. Accordingly, Odysseus and
Diomedes entered Troy secretly and stole the image of the city
goddess[9] on whom the safety of Troy was thought to depend.[10]
This exceedingly interesting manoeuvre is, characteristically
enough, not mentioned by Homer at all. The theft of a divine
statue or talisman was probably not unusual. It has even been
thought that the tale of the abduction of Helen conceals such a
theft; but that is unlikely, for Helen is human enough. Many
instances of talismans, thought necessary to the safety of
ancient cities, are known. A Roman practice corresponds
with the deed of Odysseus and Diomedes—the practice of
'evoking' the deity of a besieged city, and welcoming him
or her to the Roman side; the best known instance is the
evocation of Juno from Veii.[11] Strangely enough, other parallels
between the siege of Troy and the siege of Veii will have to be
noticed later. At present the main question is the theft of the
palladion.

That Athena should have been worshipped at Troy has
seemed surprising. Euripides[12] was shocked at the idea that she
might support Phrygians against her own people. He made a
mistake which has been made often since: the mistake of thinking that Athena was called after Athens, not Athens after
Athena. The goddess is so important in the Second *Aeneid* that
she deserves some investigation here. Besides, if the Poseidon of

Euripides[13] is fair to her, she was somehow entirely to blame for
the fall of Troy.

Athena belongs to the Minoan-Mycenaean element in Greek
religion. She descends from the pre-Hellenic armed goddess of
the home.[14] But gradually she became the goddess not only of
the home, but of the fortress, and when the Greek πόλις evolved,
of the πόλις. This is likely, because she was worshipped as
Athena Larisaia[15] in the Peloponnese, apparently at a place
called τεῖχος, 'the fort'; and Larisa seems to mean the same as
τεῖχος in some pre-Hellenic language.[16] The name of Athena is
also clearly pre-Hellenic:[17] and it probably means something
like 'guardian of the palace'. Another name of Athena, παλλάς,
seems to be etymologically connected with πόλις and in fact to
mean much the same as πολιάς, πολιοῦχος, 'city holding', her
very usual epithets.[18] Athena, therefore, is pre-eminently the
goddess who protects a city. Her other names and epithets endorse this. She is πρόμαχος, ἀλαλκομενηΐς—'defensive', from
ἀλαλκεῖν (Alalcomenae in Boeotia is called after her)—and in
Tegea she is Alea—a name which probably means the same as
ἀλαλκομενηΐς.[19]

Athena and 'Pallas,' however, were not, apparently, identical
originally. In some myths which look old they are quite distinct.
In one of them, Pallas is the daughter of Athena, and in another
she seems to have been a kind of friend, killed by Athena by mistake during a sham fight.[20] Pallas gave a start, at a sudden
movement of the 'aegis' which Zeus interposed to protect
Athena; and a blow from Athena struck her, more effectively
than she herself intended. Again, in another myth, Pallas is a
giant, slain by Athena, who used his skin to protect herself in
battle.[21] Such stories seem to imply that Pallas was also a
defensive and warlike goddess, probably the northern counterpart of Athena; and that the two forms were eventually identified. The kind of defence expected from Athena is shown both
in mythology and history. Sterope, left at Tegea without the
army to defend the city, was afraid of attack. But Heracles
gave her a lock of the gorgon's hair from the aegis of Athena, in
a bronze jar, and told her that if she held it up before the walls
of the city, and at the same time looked behind her, the enemy,
if he attacked, would turn to flight.[22] The gorgon's head is thus
very appropriate to Athena, for it is originally an apotropaic

mask, designed to cast an evil eye, perhaps, on intruders. In fact the gorgon's face certainly existed before the gorgon. The whole creature was probably evolved by the adventurous Greeks who visited south-western Asia Minor before the Trojan war, and told old soldiers' tales, partly inspired by the monsters of Oriental art.[23] The gorgon mask was widely used. It occurs on shields, on the brow-bands of war-horses, and on the doors of ovens, where it was meant to exclude evil influences from the bread. How important it was to Athena, and how characteristic of her method, is shown in the history of the battle of Salamis.[24] The Athenians only consented to leave their city, a movement which sound tactics certainly required, because they supposed that their goddess could protect her own. The god Apollo at Delphi had 'protected his own', apparently relying on the help of the defensive Athena Pronaia.[25] It was because the Athenians had such faith in their goddess that they were so deeply alarmed when Xerxes captured the Acropolis and with it her enclosure.[26] They clearly expected her to use her gorgon for her duty of defence; for when Themistocles wanted a pretext to search the kits of the Athenians to extract money for the provision of the ration allowance that ancient navies required, he could find no better excuse than the announcement that someone had stolen the gorgon from Athena's statue.[27]

This defensive Athena is well known in many cities of Greece, and her cult in them seems to be ancient. Sometimes another goddess is the repository of these protective qualities, but, on the whole, it is quite safe to say that they are peculiarly characteristic of Athena. It is likely enough that she was, in fact, worshipped in the same capacity in Homeric Troy. Homer[28] mentions her at Troy, and in later days her cult there was famous and apparently old. Athena is exceedingly important in the story of the Sack, because it was, perhaps, mainly on her estrangement that the Achaeans thought that their success depended. Tryphiodorus[29] calls her ἐρυσίπτολις before the wooden horse entered; but πτολίπορθος afterwards.

The Achaeans, then, stole the palladion. Sinon says that it showed signs of disapproval. This is possibly one of his lies, and Vergil's account of the behaviour of the statue may have been derived from some later incident, either connected with the large statue which had not been stolen, or belonging to a different story: it seems comparable to the bad omens recorded by Livy at the beginning of the Second Punic War. On the other hand, there may actually have been some ground for the Achaeans to think that they were not quite in the right relation to the goddess after the theft.[30]

The next step was the construction of the wooden horse. The wooden horse has been the greatest mystery of all,[31] mainly perhaps because Homer has set his genius to work on some old soldier's tale. Attempts to explain the artifice sensibly began early, but not very early. In antiquity it was, on the whole, supposed to represent a siege engine of some kind; but the suggestion seems to have taken a long time to appear, which counts against it. Others supposed the horse to have been some kind of ship,[32] and poetical language drawn from the launching of the Argo was applied to it.[33] Sir James Frazer has actually found a parallel incident in Spanish history, in which a town was taken by men introduced surreptitiously by river in a boat.[34] Two large images of animals which could contain men are known in ancient history;[35] one is the famous bull of Phalaris. Such objects may have helped the Homeric explanation of the horse of Troy to evolve.

But none of this seems to suggest any truth about the Trojan War. The story, unless some adjustments can be made in it, is absurd. Among other things, far too many men are recorded to have entered Troy in the horse, even if the number, three thousand, which the *Ilias parva* is recorded to have given, depends on manuscript corruption.[36] Again, if the Achaeans were entering Troy by the horse, the role of Sinon is not convincing. The variations and confusion in the tradition about him seem to admit that adjustments were frequently needed to make more sense of his part in the story. The version of Dares,[37] in which Sinon occurs, but not the horse, and Troy is taken by treachery, is more coherent. Again, Dictys[38] seems to have thought that the horse was solid. It is hard to see how such a version could possibly be invented and repeated if the whole point about the horse was an intention to introduce an armed party by means of it. Furthermore, if that had been the intention, and if it had had the truth on its side, there should have been no need of theories that the horse was a piece of siege-machinery. On the other hand, that it was a piece of machinery is additionally unlikely, because the Achaeans of the time and the earlier Greek writers seem never to have thought of that possibility. Since the construction of the horse is always ascribed to Athena and to Epeus, a Greek eponymous hero, it is hardly credible that it actually was a siege engine, but contrived by Oriental engineers, and accordingly misunderstood by Greek tradition.

It is best to suppose, therefore, that the wooden horse, whatever its purpose, was not intended to introduce an armed party in the rear of the defence. Next, a collection of various references strongly suggests that its importance was religious or superstitious in some sense. An axe was kept at a temple of Athena at Eilenia, which was supposed to be the very axe with which Epeus made the horse.[39] The Trojans proposed to destroy the horse by known methods of horse-sacrifice.[40] The ceremony of the October horse at Rome was traced to the horse of Troy.[41] A rope-dance called the *Cordax* was said to have been derived from the use of a rope to pull the horse into Troy, and to have been introduced into Greece from Phrygia.[42] This rope[43] is emphasized by Vergil, and with it another rope,[44] by which the heroes climbed down to the ground. The attendant circumstances of festivity with which the Trojans introduced the horse into their city have evoked comparison with the Roman religious ceremony at which wagons called *tensae* were ritually drawn up to the Capitol.[45] Tryphiodorus[46] compares the scene with a dance called the 'Crane dance', which seems to have been a kind of maze ritual attributed to Theseus.[47]

Again, the whole context in which the wooden horse is found is more magical than military. The Achaeans were at the time depending chiefly on occult methods; and since Athena is supposed to have directed the construction of the horse,[48] the obvious suggestion is that this was in some way a natural consequence of the theft of her image. Details recorded of the construction enforce the general impression. Servius[49] remarks that the kinds of wood used had symbolical meanings. When the horse was completed, the storm which was raging then seems, according to Vergil,[50] to have become more intense. Vergil does not say definitely that the horse in any way caused the storm, but his words strongly suggest it.[51] Quintus Smyrnaeus,[52] clearly using the same source, supplements him with the direct assertion that when the horse was finished there was a war among the gods about it, some wishing to destroy the horse, but others Ilion. This war, he fully explains, was manifested to mankind as a storm. The recollection immediately occurs that in mythology horses are persistently associated, often genealogically, with the winds.[53] The wooden horse apparently let loose a strong access of new magic, which interfered with the weather.

If so, it was an accident. The wooden horse was meant somehow to damage the Trojan defence by supernatural means. The records are just sufficient to show what these means were. In the account of Dares there is no wooden horse at all, and the besiegers succeed by treachery. But in all other versions the Trojans seem to have demolished part of their wall to admit the horse.[54] In the version of Dictys[55] there is a wholesale destruction, and Odysseus ingeniously contrives that all the Trojan masons should be otherwise engaged when they are wanted to repair it. Usually, however, in spite of the demolition, the horse still enters by way of one of the gates in the wall, probably the Scaean Gate. This is an important indication. For if the horse had been a siege engine, the gate would not have been the right place to apply it; and if it had been intended to introduce armed men secretly, the necessity of the demolition would have counted against the success of the plan. So great is the insistence on the wall that Tryphiodorus,[56] misled by the passage of the horse through the gate, thought fit to describe the demolition of quite a different wall, a wall which had screened the horse during its construction.

It is apparent now that one of the writers[57] who has been thought to support the siege-engine theory writes ambiguously. He says that the horse was generally recognized to have been a device directed against the Trojan wall. He uses the word μηχάνημα, which can equally well mean a piece of machinery or a design in the sense of a plot. Thus he possibly concurs with Dictys, who supposed that the horse was meant to persuade the Trojans to pull down their walls; which, in fact, it did.

The next question is clearly whether anything remarkable is known of the wall of Troy. The answer is obvious. The wall was sacred. It was built by Apollo and Poseidon;[58] but they called in the human hero Aeacus to help,[59] so that the wall might be destructible in at least one place, in case the divine favour to Troy should need to be withdrawn, as, in fact, it was. Homer[60] mentions an oracle that the defence of Troy would be pierced at a certain weak place in the wall; though he, or the oracle, may not be quite accurate here. He also records[61] that it was 'fate' that Troy should fall as soon as the wooden horse should be within the city.

The wall of Troy had a special name: it was called ἱερὸν κρήδεμνον, 'the sacral veil'. κρήδεμνον seems to be derived from κάρα, 'head', and δεῖν, 'to bind':[62] it was used of the veil worn by women and of the seal on a jar of wine. Troy was sealed or veiled by its wall; and it is at once evident that this wall was a magic circle which must be broken if attack was to succeed. Perhaps Euripides,[63] when he interpreted the Greek name for the wooden horse, δούρειος ἵππος, as 'spear horse', a meaning equally possible, implied some of the truth about the piercing of the defence by the horse.

The descriptions of the incident now become more intelligible. Quintus Smyrnaeus[64] says that the Trojans introduced the horse by 'releasing the sacral veil of their great city'. Vergil[65] says that Sinon's purpose was to '*open Troy to the Achaeans*'; and later[66] that the Trojans '*severed their walls and flung wide the ramparts*'. Even Homer,[67] describing the building of the wall by the gods, says that their intention was 'that the πόλις might be unbreakable'; but Poseidon himself is speaking here, and he exaggerates, for the magic circle was broken in the end.

After the time of Homer himself, the 'sacral veil' of a city was still regarded with some awe. In the Homeric Hymn to Demeter[68] good rulers are said to maintain the κρήδεμνα of cities by their righteous judgments—that is, not only by good tactical dispositions. It has been thought that the original meaning of the word was forgotten; but Catullus[69] seems to have understood it quite well, because he writes of 'loosening the Neptunian bonds' of Troy.

The Trojan wall was, therefore, a kind of magic circle, and the wooden horse was meant to neutralize its efficacy. This is not surprising. There are many traces of circle magic in Western Asia and some in Greece. Miltiades met a mysterious fate in 489 B.C., apparently because he jumped over a sacred wall in Paros with the intention of winning military success by this occult act.[70] A version of the story of Romulus and the leap of Remus is known in Boeotia,[71] and seems to be genuine old folk-lore there.[72] Poemander killed his son Leucippus with a mysterious stone, in mistake for his architect, at whom he was aiming, because he had jumped over his wall. In similar circumstances Oeneus killed Toxeus.[73]

From these stories it seems quite evident that there was in each case a magic circle and that an enemy intended to vitiate it by jumping over it. The magic circles of Italy are very well known; and it is now more unsafe than ever to distinguish sharply some of the religious ideas of early Italy and early Greece.[74] In Italy the tracing of a magic circle by ploughing a furrow was an important part of foundation ceremonies. The magic circles were maintained by circular rituals called *amburbia*, or, if the purpose was to maintain the magical protection of farm lands, *ambarualia*. How serious a jump over the line of distinction between the domains of the powers of without and within was thought to be, is fully proved by the infliction of the death penalty on any Roman soldier who entered or left a camp by any way except the gates.[75] There is little doubt that the jump of Remus himself was meant to be an act of effective hostility, not only derision.

Here are two of the very same ideas which belong to the manipulation of the wooden horse. Aeschylus,[76] Ennius,[77] and Vergil[78] all say that the wooden horse jumped over the defences of Troy. If it went through the wall or through the gate or partly through both,[79] there seems no obvious reason why it should be said to jump. It has been suggested that a fact has here been created of a metaphor.[80] But it is more likely that a metaphor has been created out of a fact: the usual history of old magical ideas, which, when they are no longer understood, generally survive in poetic figures.[81] Actually the wooden horse must have jumped the magic circle to vitiate it, like Leucippus, Toxeus, Remus, Miltiades, and presumably some nameless Italians.

The other idea concerns the gate. In Italy only the gates might be used for passage; unauthorized exits and entrances were forbidden. Plutarch explains this excellently.[82] The walls were sacred; but the gates were necessarily profane, since profane or magically dangerous traffic must necessarily pass through them sometimes. That is, of course, why, when a magic circle was first ploughed at a foundation, the plough was always lifted up when it came to the place where a gate was to be.[83] Sinon in Vergil, with even more than his usual cunning, lays down a similar principle for the wooden horse. He says that Calchas had it made specially large so that it should not be able to be taken in through the gates.[84] The Trojans thought that this meant that the Achaeans did not want it to be taken into Troy at all. But the plan was deeper than that. Sinon says what the Achaeans intended the Trojans to think: really, the horse was to be taken in, but not entirely through the gates. If it had gone only through the gates, no harm would have been done to the magic circle, for the gates must have been more or less profane; not entirely, however, as will appear.

The Trojans, then, were to take the horse into Troy and to violate the magical wall in doing so. Why they should have wanted to do this needs explanation. It has been well argued[85] that a recently recovered fragment of Apollodorus means that in an early version of the story, used by Vergil among others, the wooden horse carried an inscription dedicating it to Athena, so that the persuasions of Sinon were in this version unnecessary. The Trojans thought, as Vergil suggests,[86] that the horse would bring them an accession of divine strength. This is more intelligible than it looks for certain reasons: among them, that the instrument chosen by the Achaeans had the form of a horse, and not of any other animal or thing.

One aspect of this is quickly clear. Poseidon, who, with Apollo, built the Trojan wall, was in some sense 'god of horses'. However, the wooden horse was an 'offering to Athena'.[87] Some time ago the right explanation of this was given.[88] The horse was accepted by the Trojans as a fit offering for their horse-god, Poseidon, who was probably enough worshipped on the Trojan citadel, as he was elsewhere, conjointly with Athena in the same temple. Poseidon is often associated with some other divinity like this. At Phigalia he was worshipped as the consort of a horse-headed Demeter;[89] and he is also found in a temple of Athena associated with Medusa the gorgon,[90] who is little more than a symbol of the defensive power of Athena. At Athens the association of Poseidon and Athena is well known, but the myths scarcely explain it satisfactorily by their reference to the gifts of the horse and the olive. It is more likely that, as Athena was the goddess of the defence of the whole citadel, so Poseidon was specially the god of the city wall. Among the indications of this is a passage of Hesiod[91] where Poseidon is said to 'maintain the κρήδεμνον of Thebes and guard the city'. It is clear that he equally guarded the κρήδεμνον of Troy, for he built it. Once in the *Iliad*[92] he seems to claim a general authority over walls, and complains that the Achaeans had built a wall without sacrificing to him.

Here, then, is the reason why the Trojans willingly accepted the horse. They thought that it would be appropriately acceptable to their gods and probably that it would strengthen their magical sufficiency. They seem to have regarded it as they had regarded the splendid white horses of Rhesus, which Odysseus and Diomedes acquired in a night raid just in time. The horses of Rhesus clearly have a magical significance.[93] That is implied by the *Rhesus* of Euripides, who had access to some un-Homeric version of the story,[94] and by the tradition of an oracle[95] that, if the horses of Rhesus once tasted Trojan water and fodder, Rhesus would be invincible, or, according to another version, Troy would not be captured. Vergil also had access to this tradition, for he clearly refers to it.[96] In the *Rhesus* of Euripides, the horses must remain one night at least in Troyland. Obviously, they were to become magically assimilated to Troy. Perhaps the magical process was expected to work more securely by moonlight: the visibility, at least, was good on that occasion.[97] One of the arguments that this is the right interpretation of the play is furnished by the accusation against Hector at the end.[98] The groom of Rhesus accuses him of his master's death and of the theft of the horses. This is unintelligible if Rhesus is only as important as any other ally might be; but if the whole exceptional value of his help lay in his magical horses, Hector might be thought, by one who did not know him, capable of securing them by such quick methods. The warlike association of horses is well known; and there is reason to think that their sanctity must have seemed particularly valuable at Troy. Their warlike quality survives in the omen furnished at Carthage by the horse's head discovered at the foundation, from which it was inferred that the

Carthaginians would prosper and have success in war.[99] Anchises, seeing four horses when the Trojans first sighted Italy, interpreted them to mean that there would be war.[100] It may have been because horses were warlike animals that the Roman *flamen dialis*, who was not allowed to see a *classis procincta*, might not ride a horse.

Such, therefore, seem to have been the associations which helped to induce the Trojans to take in the wooden horse. The associations which appealed to the Achaeans must have been different. They expected the horse-form to be dangerous to the Trojans. Their expectation is fully clear from what is known of early beliefs about horses.

Horses could interfere with sanctity. At Aricia they were excluded from the precinct.[101] Callimachus[102] definitely records that there was a taboo on horses in the unwalled sacred city of Delos. In early thought horses are greatly dreaded. In many parts of Europe and in classical Greece and Italy they are persistently associated with death and disaster.[103] This fear of horses is important in the construction of one of H. G. Wells' novels, *The Undying Fire*: it partly controls the character and development of the hero. In fact, psychologists have sometimes thought the fear and awe of horses a principal factor in the psychology of mankind, and have in particular tried to trace its importance in the psychology of sex and the evolution of myths.[104] The emphasis laid by Tryphiodorus on the wooden horse's mane has been discussed from a psychological point of view.[105] Herman Melville, in *Moby-Dick*, has a fine passage where the emotions with which horses can be regarded are poetically expressed.[106]

It is now no longer unintelligible why both the Trojans and the Achaeans, each with very different motives, should have wished the wooden horse to enter the city of Troy. Other parts of the story become clearer also. It is assumed in the legends that Hector was particularly important to the defence of Troy. In Seneca, Hector and Troy are said to have died on the same day,[107] and Hector is poetically equated with the wall of Troy.[108] The Pyrrhus of Seneca claims that Achilles conquered Troy, and that to have killed Hector was a supreme achievement.[109] Horace[110] faced the difficulty here, but without much success. He explains that the death of Hector made Troy easier for the tired Greeks to capture. Yet, of course, the presence or absence of Hector could make no difference to the success of the artifice of the wooden horse if it was a means to introduce armed men into Troy. It is not credible that Hector alone among the Trojans would have had sufficient sense to piquet the horse and take ordinary precautions. Now in the *Iliad*[111] Achilles chased Hector three times round Troy and then dragged him, tied to his chariot, back to the ships. But there was another version, in which Achilles dragged Hector three times round Troy. Homer has clearly altered the story, much to the improvement of the poetic situation. But the un-Homeric version was adopted by several poets,[112] including Vergil, who in the First *Aeneid* definitely says that Achilles dragged Hector three times round Troy, and in the Second shows, by his reference to Hector's swollen feet, that he must have been alive when he was dragged. The reason for this action has been brilliantly suggested already.[113] Achilles dragged Hector in order to counteract the magic of the Trojan wall. This means that he performed something like the Roman rite of an *amburbium* but with the opposite intention, to neutralize, instead of to reinforce, the magic. For this negative magic there are parallels, in which a destructive effect is intended by circular movements in the opposite direction to the movement of the sun:[114] similar thinking is implicit in the Black Mass. The author of the *Culex*[115] confirms the suggestion. He says that Achilles contrived some magical effect on Troy by the body of Hector, using the word *lustrauit*. *lustrare* means to make movements, up and down or round about, which have some ritual effect, generally of 'purification'. The kind of purification or magical effect intended by Achilles was more like exorcism. He meant to drive the magical power out of the wall of Troy. If so, he might claim to have succeeded, because after some further steps in the process Troy fell.

Hector, therefore, must have had some special importance if he could be used in this way. A little examination of him suggests what kind of importance he may have had. His name, at least, is significant. It is one of the nouns in -τωρ which denote the agent. The root is the root of ἔχειν; and so *Hector* means 'he who holds'. What he held is obvious: he was the holder of the πόλις. In fact, his name has generally been regarded as a short form of a longer name, and it has been suggested that the longer name was Ἐχέπολις.[116] Another suggestion, based on the names of his relatives, is Ἐχέλαος;[117] but the other peculiar qualities of Hector, and the name of his son Astyanax, make Ἐχέπολις much more likely. Euripides calls Hector πολίοχον κράτος,[118] a 'city-holding might', and seems to refer to his position at Troy as a 'city-holding princedom'.[119] Apparently this adjective is applied only to Hector and to the protective divinities of cities. This helps the interpretation forward. Hector was in some supernatural sense the protector of Troy or the walls of Troy, which are frequently mentioned in close connection with him. Vergil writes of the wounds which he received, fighting round them. Homer,[120] again, says that Hector alone protected Troy. That is simply untrue in the natural sense, as we have seen; and the line has been taken as an example of the excessive tendency to individualize in early attempts at recording history, to support a theory of historical determinism.[121] If Hector had some special magical importance, no such explanation is needed. In another passage of the *Iliad*[122] Hector is asked tauntingly if he thinks that he can guard Troy 'alone'—but Homer adds then, 'with the help of his kinsmen'. This has been called a supposed pun on the meaning of *Hector*,[123] for the word ἔχειν is used. But, as in the leap of the wooden horse, the development is really in the other direction; and here an old supposed truth has survived as something like a play on words. Elsewhere in the *Iliad*[124] Hector is reproached for claiming too much care and maintenance from the other Trojans. This taunt seems quite inapplicable to Homer's Hector; but by analogy, if he was a magical personage,[125] some special sustenance is just what the Trojans would have been only too willing to provide for him, in the belief that all their lives depended on his. Achilles even threatens to eat Hector raw,[126] an unusual breach of taste for Homer. It is just possible, but more cannot be said, that this represents an original plan of superstitious significance, by which Achilles meant to make himself fully master of Hector's spirit.[127] Hector was, at any rate, precious indeed to Troy, if he thus had in him the very soul of the city's defence. He recalls other usages of ancient times by which the true names of cities and of gods were kept secret,[128] and by which the soul of some being was sometimes committed for safety to another.[129]

Whatever exactly may have been the nature of Hector's importance, the supposition that he had such an importance throws light on an old difficulty. The name of Hector, with one other doubtful instance, is known in early Greece only at Troy and at Thebes.[130] The Theban Hector has been used in argument to support the theory of *Sagenverschiebung*,[131] according to which the whole story of the Trojan War is supposed to have originated in Greece, to have been transferred to Asia, and to have been falsely localized there. Hector then would have been a Theban hero with nothing originally to do with Troy at all. This theory receives little favour in England. The Theban Hector is interesting, nevertheless. The Thebans sent to the Troad for the bones of the Trojan Hector in some uncertain time of stress.[132] Just why they chose Hector has been obscure. It has been suggested that they did so because they were at the time on the side of Persia, and Hector was a 'champion of Asia'.[133] This is unlikely, partly because it is practically certain that the event happened some time before the Persian Wars.[134] The truth is, perhaps, shown by what the Thebans did with the bones when they received them. They buried them outside their Proetidian Gate.[135] This suggests that they needed Hector, in his capacity of 'city holder', to defend them in a general way. It has often been thought[136] that they had an indigenous heroic Hector of their own. If so, either supposing him by mistake identical with the Trojan Hector, or merely wanting to reinforce their own Hector, they quite naturally sent for the bones to strengthen the heroic protection of their city. It is worth noticing that there are several parallels in the beliefs of Troy and Thebes. Above all, each city had a κρήδεμνον; and as Poseidon held it at Thebes and guarded the city, so Hector guarded Troy. The words used of both are the same. At Troy Hector seems to have been a kind of human counterpart of Poseidon. That may be why at Troy Poseidon is said to have had no priest. It has already been remarked that the idea of the magic circle and the dangerous jump over it occurs in Boeotia. Furthermore, the walls of Thebes were built to the music of Amphion and Zethus,[137] who, whatever the reason may be, are sometimes called 'colts'.[138] It seems that Apollo's part in building the walls of Troy was musical: Callimachus[139] writes as though the services of Apollo, to play when foundations were laid and walls built, were necessary and usual. Apollo is certainly associated with the walls of Troy. According to Tryphiodorus[140] he sadly departed to Lycia, in grief for his holy walls. Stesichorus says that Hector was his son; and incidentally, among other 'mythological rarities', that Medusa was the daughter of Priam.[141] Both statements are interesting comments on the strong defensive sanctities of Troy. Homer,[142] in his usual way humanizing the old stories, presents a magnificent picture of Apollo defending the walls of Troy like a human warrior; but there still remains some of the old mystery and awe in the dread of his great voice from the bastion.

At the end of the Trojan War, therefore, Hector was already dead, and in a sense Achilles had won the victory. At least, it was now to be expected that the wall was open to attack of the right kind. Besides, the pallas of the citadel had been evocated, and she would, if all went well, help the Achaeans, not the Trojans. Poseidon and his wall remained: and much skill and knowledge were needed if the right manipulation was to be tried.

In this part of the story it was recorded[143] in the *Ilias parva* that the Achaeans took Helenus prisoner and made some arrangements with him about the capture of Troy; apparently Helenus gave some secret away. There are different versions of this, and Dares[144] so far magnifies the incident that he makes treachery alone account for the fall of the city. This is clearly an exaggeration, but that there was some treachery is well attested and probable. If so, it is clear what the secret was that was given away. It was a secret of the wall. Helenus or some other Trojan told the Achaeans how the magical defence could be defeated. In fact, one writer seems to have preserved the exact truth: Conon,[145] who records that Helenus suggested the wooden horse.

It is of some interest that the siege of Troy and the siege of Veii are closely parallel. At each there was an *euocatio* of the city's goddess by means of an underground entrance. Odysseus went in by such a way, and Servius, with his description of the incident, invites comparison with the phraseology used by Livy about the plan practised by Camillus.[146] The secret of the

wall was given away at Troy by some Trojan, perhaps the seer
Helenus, and at Veii by an Etruscan seer.[147] Finally, the gods of
each city were supposed to forsake the city walls.[148] Vergil
says that all the gods left their shrines in Troy and that Neptunus was seen by Aeneas destroying his own work. In Euripides,[149] Poseidon says a sad farewell to his own holy bastions.
Why this happened, of course, is one of the questions to be
answered. At Veii, according to Livy,[150] it was prophesied
that 'the gods would not forsake the walls of the Veientines'
until the water was drained from the Alban Lake by some
unusual channel. The relevance of the Alban Lake has been
missed, but it is clear enough, and of some interest in this
context. The confine of the lake was in magical sympathy with
the walls of Veii.[151] The normal outflow would, however,
correspond with the gates, which were profane or magically
neutral. Therefore, the device of sympathetic magic required
the water to be released across the magic circle itself; and, in
fact, under it, as Camillus undermined the Veientine wall.

On the information, then, of some Trojan, the Achaean
adepts knew how to proceed. They were probably Calchas and
Odysseus, who had a large share in the affairs of supernatural
manipulation, possibly because he was not really an Achaean,
but belonged to some other, Mediterranean, stock.[152] They
planned and built the horse, and left it, bearing an inscription saying that it was dedicated to Athena. Then the Achaeans
sailed away, perhaps leaving Sinon in hiding.

The Trojans decided to take the horse into Troy. Vergil may
be right to say that they had to fix wheels or rollers under it,
though other accounts say that it had them already. The Trojans, with religious festivity, drew the horse in, dancing and
singing, and delighting to put themselves in contact with a holy
thing by touching the rope.[153] They seem to have thought that
their goddess would return to them with this new symbol of
divine protection. There may have been a ramp leading
up to the Scaean Gate, as there certainly was—and is—elsewhere, as excavation has proved. If so, Vergil's expressions
scandit fatalis machina muros, and *illa subit*, are easily explained.[154]
But when the horse reached the gate itself, it was too large to
enter. Vergil implies this by saying that the Trojans 'severed
their walls', but he does not make it at all clear whether the

horse went through a breach in the wall, through the gate, or partly through both. He seems to have left everything vague on purpose, to the advantage of the poetry. He then relates that at the very threshold the horse halted four times. To Roman thought a stoppage in a procession or any other ritual was a bad omen, a stoppage at the threshold a worse omen still,[155] and, since all even numbers, and four more than two, might have sinister connotations, four stoppages at a threshold must have been a very bad omen indeed.[156]

Apparently Vergil has produced this very powerful effect by a simple transference, according to his manner. He has made the Trojans demolish their wall before, instead of after, the horse stopped. Tryphiodorus betrays the secret. He says[157] that the gate was too narrow, but that Hera helped to free the horse in it, that Poseidon struck with his trident, and that Athena drove the horse forward on its way. This is clearly something like the original circumstances. At this point Poseidon turned against Troy; and the other divinities were already supporting the Achaeans. It is probable that Poseidon acted in the persons of his worshippers; for there is some emphasis on the necessity for the Trojans to take the horse in, and presumably to demolish part of the wall, with their own hands.[158]

It is not likely, however, that the narrowness of the gate was the important point. It mattered more that the horse was too high to go through. Plautus[159] records that there were 'three fates of Troy which would mean her ruin: first, if the statue on the citadel perished; second, if Troilus were killed; and third, if the upper threshold of Phrygia were torn'. The reference to the palladion is clear, and the efficacy of Hector seems to have been transferred to Troilus. The 'upper threshold of Phrygia' is more mysterious. Fortunately Servius[160] explains that it was above the Scaean Gate, and that Laomedon was buried there. This is likely enough. Herodotus[161] relates that the Babylonian queen Nitocris had herself buried above one of the gates of Babylon: and burials in walls are a very common part of foundation ceremonies in various parts of the world. It is clear that the burial of Laomedon was a strong supernatural agency designed to protect Troy at a dangerous point. The demolition, at any rate, broke the magic circle, probably both above and beside the gate, and Troy was no longer impregnable.

But, according to Dares,[162] there was something else also at the outside of the gate: an emblem of a horse's head. If Dares is right, and there seems no reason to doubt him, this clearly also had an apotropaic purpose, like several instances of horse emblems found among other devices at gates in North Greece.[163] The supernatural connotations of horses have a limited area: they are not found, for example, so far as can be determined, in Egyptian, Minoan, and Mycenaean thought.[164] But there is a parallel to the Trojan propylaic in Mycenae: the Lion Gate itself, which seems exceedingly likely to have been apotropaic in its purpose also. That lions, in the southern area, could be thought to have such a quality is proved by the Sardians,[165] who carried a lion round their city to strengthen the defence of their wall. Aeschylus,[166] not quite by chance, calls the wooden horse, at its jump, a lion.

A reason why Laomedon was associated with a horse's head above the Trojan gate may be suggested. Laomedon was famous for his horses in mythology: so famous that he has been thought a chthonic deity, not a man at all, on the ground that horses have so strong a connotation of sinister things.[167] This is certainly to go too far. But it is worth recalling that Heracles attacked Troy 'for the sake of the horses of Laomedon';[168] and that on the same occasion Telamon his ally, having found the secret of the defence and breached the wall of Troy, hastily constructed an altar to Heracles with the stones, and successfully allayed his furious jealousy.[169] The horse's head, therefore, and the bones of the great horse-hero, Laomedon, seem to have been expected to exercise a combined apotropaic effect, each reinforcing the other with a kind of mutual symbolism.

The tradition of the horse's head is mentioned in a different version by Servius.[170] He says that the form of the wooden horse was chosen possibly because the Trojans were defeated in a cavalry action, but possibly also because the doors of the houses of those Trojans who were friendly to the Achaeans were marked with the sign of a horse's head as an indication that they were to be spared.[171] Neither of these possibilities seems very likely: the first partly because we are credibly informed[172] that the Achaeans left their horsemen—presumably their chariot arm—behind when they returned from Tenedos for fear of the noise which the horses would make; and the second because it seems to furnish no sufficient reason for the choice of the form. But both the possibilities may contain some truth. The Trojans were, in fact, defeated, not in a cavalry action, but in a contest of horse-magic; and an element in this contest seems to have been the apotropaic emblem over the gate in the wall, connected with treachery because some Trojan divulged to the Achaeans the secrets of the wall and the gate.

The Trojans accepted the 'gift', for they were bewitched, *immemores*—as Vergil says—and possessed by *oblivio*, according to Servius,[173] 'as at an *euocatio*'. In delight at what they thought their new protection, they forgot their old, and 'released the sacral veil of their great city' with rejoicing, thinking that they would need it no more. They even seem to have done so with a special emphasis and concurrent sympathetic rites; for Tryphiodorus[174] says that a Trojan woman untied the κρήδεμνον of a jar of wine and poured the contents on the ground, and that others released their μίτραι, probably girdles of maiden-hood, and therefore something very like the third of the three known kinds of κρήδεμνον. These actions all seem to fit to-gether; and it has been shown that many different kinds of 'loosening magic' are often practised at the same time when some important free passage is required.[175] The Trojans must have felt as if they were removing a taboo on first-fruits, and that due sympathetic ceremony was needed if all was to be well for them.

But their action was a violation of their own sanctities; the god of the wall deserted them, as the goddess of the citadel had been taken from them before. When the Achaeans returned, they easily surprised the piquets, and occupied the city either by assault or by infiltration. We may allow the rationalists to say that the attackers really owed their success to military surprise and to the neglect by the Trojans of the tactical principle of security. If they say so, they may be right. But they would hardly be right to say that Calchas, Odysseus, or even Aga-memnon himself would have thought of making such a claim on the night of victory.

There is a little more to say about the magical attack on Troy. When Aeneas is waking from sleep to the horror of battle, Vergil says that the notes of trumpets rang out clear.[176] There is nothing surprising in this, because the trumpet-calls may have been attempts to direct military operations; and although it has been argued that trumpets are an anachronism in a heroic context, Homer[177] himself recognizes them once, though he seems to dislike them for some superstitious connotations, which are about to appear. However, Servius[178] goes out of his way to say in his note that it was an ancient custom to take cities to the sound of a trumpet, and he gives as an instance the capture of Alba Longa by Tullus Hostilius. It seems that Vergil has very nearly suppressed some old superstitious significance, as he nearly suppressed the causal connection between the wooden horse and the storm. The proof of this is given by Tryphiodorus,[179] who mysteriously records that a trumpet in the sky, sounded at the instance of Zeus, prophesied that 'war' was being drawn into Troy when the Trojans were pulling in the horse. This at once confirms an old suggestion,[180] made nearly a hundred years ago, that in the earliest saga the Heracleidae captured Argos by the use of trumpets. In other words, Greeks of early times seem to have had the same beliefs about the use of trumpets as the priests of Israel before Jericho. Homer himself confirms the probability, in the sole passage where he mentions a trumpet. He compares the voice of Achilles, when he shouted from the ramparts of the Achaean camp, to the sound of a trumpet used by besiegers. Again a poetic figure betrays an old superstition. Seneca[181] says that Hector feared the music of Achilles, when he stayed in his tent playing, more than other dangers. It is difficult not to connect these two passages together and ask whether Achilles after all was not sulking, but trying to work some spell on Troy. It is of some interest to remember that when the long walls of Athens were destroyed after the Peloponnesian War the work was done to the sound of flutes.[182]

Tryphiodorus probably made a mistake when he attributed the trumpet-call to Zeus. He should have attributed it to Athena, goddess of defence and sometimes of attack. Athena is closely connected with trumpets, perhaps especially in her early history. Pausanias[183] records that a dedication to Athena Salpinx—she was thus actually called 'Trumpet'—was made at Argos by the son of Tyrsenus, the inventor of the *salpinx*. The early worship of Minerva on the Capitol at Rome was accompanied by *tibicines*; and an important part of the religious ritual of the Roman army was the *tubilustria*, the purification of trumpets. How the trumpets were supposed to work at a siege has been suggested,[184] though the relevance of them at Troy has been missed in this context. They were supposed to produce, presumably by a kind of sympathetic magic, a pressure of wind which should blow the ramparts flat. They are thus all the more appropriate to Athena, if her aegis is rightly interpreted as symbolic of the storm.

The Achaeans, having occupied Troy, refrained, except in special instances, from taking prisoners among the combatants. They committed terrible atrocities, perhaps because they thought that all divine sanctions were withdrawn by the departure of the gods of Troy. Their task was easy, because the Trojans were drunk. Vergil's suppression of this is typical of him. He admits once shortly that the city was buried in sleep and wine; but that is soon forgotten in the night fighting. How he dealt with this difficulty elsewhere has already been shown. Bigger changes were necessary, too. In earlier versions Aeneas, Helenus and Antenor fell alive into the hands of the Achaeans:[185] in some, one or more of them even betrayed the city to the besiegers.[186] In one version the Achaeans allowed Aeneas to escape from the burning city,[187] and in another[188] he went before the capture, warned by the fate of Laocoon. Vergil makes all three found settlements in the west;[189] in his account only Helenus is captured, and the description of him in his new home is partly constructed with elements from the captured Aeneas of other versions.[190]

By slight changes Vergil interpreted the traditions of the entry of the horse so that the result was congenial to Roman ideas. He did the same at the death of Priam and in the Helen scene. Priam's palace is Romanized, and seems to have an *impluuium*.[191] The laurel tree by the altar belongs to old tradition;[192] it may be a sacred tree like the *ficus Ruminalis* and many that have been connected with the security of habitations in other parts of the world.[193] The Romanization of the Trojan Pallas is more interesting still. Helen is found hiding. Originally she was probably found in the house of Deiphobus; but later, sometimes with Cassandra in the temple of Athena at the foot of her large statue (not the stolen palladion, of course), and sometimes in the temple of Aphrodite. Vergil restores her

partly and vaguely to the temple of Athena, for she is found by
Aeneas hiding at Vesta's threshold. With characteristic genius
Vergil has identified the Trojan defensive Athena with the
Roman defensive Vesta, since this, according to his principles
of method, fitted his poetic plan. That Vesta had defensive
attributes is fairly clear. Her temple was round:[194] on the purity
of Vestal Virgins the safety of the city was thought to depend:[195]
impurity was corrected by burial alive, a practice which has
been hard to explain otherwise, but which is appropriate to
defensive magic;[196] and it seems[197] that the Roman Minerva,
the Trojan Athena, and probably Vesta herself might not 'be
seen by men', whose particular magic appears to have counted
against the security of a defence.

After the sack of Troy, the Achaeans did not yet apparently
feel safe. They seem to have thought that many unpleasant
acts of propitiation were required of them. Achilles demanded
the sacrifice of Polyxena, almost certainly as a bride to take
with him to the world below.[198] He influenced the winds to
prevent the Achaeans sailing home until his wish was satisfied.
This, together with the not quite parallel instance of the sacrifice of Iphigeneia at Aulis for a fair wind on the outward
journey, has led to some confusion, legitimate in poetry, but
difficult for investigators. A predecessor of Vergil seems to
have made this combination and to have used it for his Sinon.
Originally, Sinon seems merely to have been meant to show by
a fire signal that it was time for the Achaeans to return. This
fire signal Vergil has transferred partly to Helen and partly to
the flagship of the Achaean fleet.[199] The intended sacrifice of
Sinon is a great help in creating the Vergilian situation, because poetic emphasis can be laid on the imaginary cruelty of
the Achaeans to one of their own men, and the contrasting
kindness of the Trojans can be exalted.

Another confusion is more important still. It does not strictly
fall within the subject of the Second *Aeneid*, but it is closely
connected with the ideas involved in the taking of Troy.
When the Achaeans had won the last battle, they systematically
razed the walls of Troy. Euripides[200] says that no trace remained; Alexander the Great had to be shown the site; and
archaeology has already given evidence for such an intentional
destruction.[201] Apparently the Achaeans, like Plato,[202] thought

it wrong to stop a story in the middle. This is a principle of early thought: a thing once begun must be finished, or the magical loose ends may be dangerous. If so, the Achaeans must have wanted to complete their work on the Trojan wall because it was divine. The way in which they did it has been overlooked, and it is still partly obscure. They sacrificed Astyanax, the son of Hector, the 'holder' of the city wall. There are various accounts of his death, but there is a general insistence that he was thrown from the wall. Only Apollodorus[203] and Seneca[204] seem to record that it was a kind of sacrifice; though that could have been guessed easily from the nature of the variants in other writers.[205] But even the writers who admit the sacrifice seem to think that it was a sacrifice for a fair wind. They have confused Polyxena with Iphigeneia and Astyanax with both, as the contradictory motives explicit in Seneca[206] show. Even Euripides,[207] who here disregards the magical tradition which undoubtedly existed, says that Astyanax was mounting 'his father's bastions' for his death. Seneca[208] says that one sole tower of the wall remained, from which Astyanax could be thrown. Sacrifices are so often connected with the building of walls, and reversals are so usual in early rites, that the sacrifice of Astyanax is likely enough to have been intended to lay the ghosts of Hector, of Astyanax himself, and of the wall at once; especially since other instances of death by throwing from a wall[209] seem to occur in contexts of defensive sanctity.

These, then, are, if I am right, some of the thoughts of hope and fear which have gone to make up the dark mysteries of Vergil's tale. Vergil has used old things which Homer discarded. The heroes of Homer were not what Homer has represented them to be. They, too, shared the old awe common to the generations among which they were interposed. But the men of the Homeric poems are not altogether lost to history. An age of humanity derives self-identity and characteristic quality neither from an idea nor from any unity of orientation, but from a dynamic opposition of ideas forcing in contrary directions. The heroes were superstitious and of the past. But they were also intellectual, enlightened, aweless, of the far future too; and it was in he tension of this polarity that they struck off the short bright spark of the Heroic Age. So Vergil saw them, a vision worth including in his majestic picture of falling Ilion and arising Rome.

NOTES

1. For examinations, to which the view here adopted owes much, of this question of Homer and the facts of the war, *cf.* T. W. Allen, *Homer: The Origins and the Transmission* (Oxford, 1924) 73, 130 ff., esp. 161 note 1, 177 ff., 191; A. R. Burn, *Minoans, Philistines, and Greeks* (London, 1930) 210 ff.

2. Walter Leaf, *Troy* (London, 1912) 254 ff., esp. 257, 261, 264; *cf.* 292–3, 315 ff.; id. *Homer and History* (London, 1915) 65 ff., esp. 72, 74.

3. J. L. Myres and K. T. Frost, *Klio* 14 (1915) 447 ff.

4. Ibid. 462.

5. Burn (above, note 1) 202, 212 ff., 222.

6. For an imaginative reconstruction of the conditions, *cf.* Alan Sims, *Phoinix* (London, 1928) 181 ff.

7. W. R. Paton, *CR* 26 (1912) 1 ff., esp. 4.

8. Andrew Lang in *Anthropology and the Classics* (Oxford, 1908) 44 ff., esp. 47–8.

9. Procl. *epit. Ilias parva*; Eur. *Rhes.* 501 ff.; Dion. Hal. *Ant. Rom.* I, 69; *Aen.* II, 163 ff.

10. Dion. Hal. *Ant. Rom.* I, 68; for parallels to this talisman, *cf.* Sir J. G. Frazer, *Pausanias's Description of Greece* (London and New York, 1898) IV, 433 ff. on Paus. VIII, 47, 5.

11. Liv. V, 21–2.

12. Eur. *Troad.* 971 ff. (a criticism of the story of the judgment of Paris).

13. Ibid. 45 ff.

14. M. P. Nilsson, *Minoan-Mycenaean Religion and its Survival in Greek Religion* (Lund: Oxford, 1927) 419 ff.; *q.v.* for reff.; *cf.* id. *A History of Greek Religion* (Oxford, 1925) 26 ff.

15. A. Fick, *Vorgriechische Ortsnamen* (Göttingen, 1905) 95; Paus. VII, 17, 5.

16. Fick (above, note 15); *cf.* W. F. J. Knight, *JHS* 51 (1931) 174 ff., where these questions are discussed in relation to Salamis.

17. For the reff. *cf.* C. D. Buck, *CP* 21 (1926) 10, citing Wide, Kretschmer, and Wilamowitz; but *cf.* also the claim of L. Malten, *Arch. Jahrb.* 40 (1925) 121 and note 5. It is unlikely that the suggestion was never made till recent times.

18. G. H. Mahlow, *Neue Wege durch die griechische Sprache und Dichtung* (Berlin-Leipzig, 1926) 419.

19. Knight (above, note 16) 176.

20. Apollodor. III, 12, 3.

21. Ibid. I, 6, 2.

22. Ibid. II, 7, 3–4.

23. L. Malten (above, note 17) 156 and note 6 (where reff. are given); *cf.* 121 ff. *passim.*

24. Knight (above, note 16) 176–7.

25. Hdt. VIII, 36–9; Diodor. XI, 14, 3.

26. Diodor. XI, 15, 2.

27. Plut. *Them.* X; *cf.* Aristot. *Ath. pol.* XXII–XXIII.

28. Hom. *Il.* VI, 297–8.

29. Tryph. 302, 390.

30. There seems some probability (as I hope to show elsewhere) that the 'Locrian curse' was inflicted for excessive or misguided manipulation of Athena's defensive power, and that the terms of the curse were meant to restore that power. *Cf.* note 209 below. [This 'probability' was subsequently developed within the article, 'Myth and Legend at Troy', *Folk-Lore* 46 (1935) 101–2, esp. 101 note 9. J.D.C.]

31. *Cf.* C. G. Heyne, *P. Virgilius Maro* . . .[4] rev. G. E. P. Wagner (London, 1830–41) II, Exc. III, 401 ff., esp. 403: 'sed haud dubie in veteris Graeciae prisco sermone, audaces et insolentes figuras sectante, obscura huius Equi origo latet.' He refused to believe the old soldier's tale as an explanation, or the siege-engine theory (403 ff.). For the first statement of the theory here advanced, *cf.* W. F. J. Knight, *CP* 25 (1930) 358 ff.

32. Eur. *Troad.* 537–8; J. W. Mackail, *The Aeneid of Virgil* (Oxford, 1930) 62.

33. Tryph. 62 ff., 185; *cf.* Ap. Rhod. I, 363 ff.

34. Sir J. G. Frazer, *The Library of Apollodorus* (Loeb ed., London, 1921) II, 229 note 1 cont. 230–1 (on Apollodor. V, 14).

35. Allen (above, note 1) 159 ff.

36. A. Severyns, *Rev. belge de phil. et d'hist.* 5 (1926) 297 ff.

37. Dar. Phryg. XL–XLI.

38. Dict. Cret. V, 11.

39. A. B. Cook, *Zeus* II (Cambridge, 1925) 625.

40. *Cf.* Hom. *Od.* VIII, 507 ff.; Procl. *epit. Iliu persis*; *Aen.* II, 36–8; Quint. Smyrn. XII, 393; Tryph. 251 ff., with A. B. Cook, *Zeus* I (Cambridge, 1914) 180 note 5 cont. 181; Hom. *Il.* XX, 131 ff.

41. Plut. *Quaest. Rom.* XCVII.

42. A. B. Cook, *JHS* 14 (1894) 101–2, with reff.

43. *Aen.* II, 235 ff.

44. *Aen.* II, 262.

45. J. L. de la Cerda, *P. Vergilii Maronis opera omnia* . . . (Coloniae Agrippinae, 1642–7) II, 181.

46. Tryph. 352 ff.

47. *Cf.* Hom. *Il.* XVIII, 590 ff.; Plut. *Thes.* XXI; Lucian, *De Salt.* XXXIV; Pollux, IV, 101. For such temple-dancing, Minoan and Greek, *cf.* Karl Lehmann-Hartleben, *Die Antike* 7 (1931) 31 ff.; and for the probable defensive magic of maze rituals, Knight (above, note 31) 362 note 3; id. *CP* 26 (1931) 414.

48. Hom. *Od.* VIII, 493; Eur. *Troad.* 10; *Aen.* II, 15.

49. Serv. *ad Aen.* II, 16.

50. *Aen.* II, 112–13.

51. I conjectured the association myself (above, note 31, 360) before noticing that Quintus made it explicit (see note 52 below).

52. Quint. Smyrn. XII, 157 ff.

53. A. B. Cook (above, note 42) 143–4; J. E. Harrison, *Prolegomena to the Study of Greek Religion* (Cambridge, 1908) 179.

54. *Cf.* esp. Procl. *epit. Ilias parva; διελόντες μέρος τι τοῦ τείχους.

55. Dict. Cret. V, 11.

56. Tryph. 205–6.

57. Paus. I, 23, 8.

58. Hom. *Il.* VII, 452–3; Pind. *Ol.* VIII, 30 ff.; *cf. Aen.* II, 625.

59. Pind. ibid.

60. Hom. *Il.* VI, 431 ff.; Leaf (above, note 2) 156 ff.; *cf.* 88.

61. Hom. *Od.* VIII, 511–13.

62. W. R. Paton, *CR* 27 (1913) 45.

63. Eur. *Troad.* 9 ff.

64. Quint. Smyrn. XII, 440–1.

E

65. *Aen.* II, 60.

66. *Aen.* II, 234.

67. Hom. *Il.* XX, 446–7.

68. *Hom. Hymn. Dem.* 150 ff.

69. Catull. LXIV, 367.

70. Hdt. VI, 134–6.

71. Plut. *Quaest. Graec.* XXXVII.

72. W. R. Halliday, *Liv. Ann. of Arch. and Anthr.* 11 (1924) 9.

73. Apollodor. I, 8, 1. *Cf.*, for circle magic in general, and for the implications of it in Greek ritual, S. Eitrem, *Opferritus und Voropfer der Griechen und Römer* (Christiania, 1915) 6 ff., esp. 9, 14, 29, for the question whether the rites are primarily cathartic (as Eitrem thinks) or apotropaic (according to him a developed function).

74. F. Altheim, *Griechische Götter im alten Rom* (Giessen, 1930) 1 ff.; *cf.* O. Gruppe, *Griechische Mythologie und Religionsgeschichte* (München, 1906) I, 193 ff., esp. 203–4, for an estimate of the significance of mythological similarities subsisting between Arcadia and early Rome; *cf.* 360 ff.

75. Zonaras, VII, 3.

76. Aesch. *Agam.* 825 ff.

77. J. Vahlen, *Ennianae Poesis Reliquiae*[2] (Leipzig, 1903) *Alexander* fr. 10 (p. 129).

78. *Aen.* VI, 515–16. Vergil here, like Fick (above, note 15) 16, seems to have connected πέργαμα etymologically with πύργος.

79. R. S. Conway, *CJ* 26 (1930–1) 623–4, where the conclusions of Knight (above, note 31) 360–1, esp. 361 note 1, are expanded.

80. J. Conington, *P. Vergili Maronis Opera*[2] (London, 1872) II, on *Aen.* II, 237.

81. For a remarkable instance of this *cf.* G. K. Chesterton, *The Everlasting Man* (London, 1925) Pt. I, Ch. VIII, where the wooden horse of Troy is compared with the wooden Cross of Calvary.

82. Plut. *Quaest. Rom.* XXVII, with H. J. Rose, *The Roman Questions of Plutarch* (Oxford, 1924) 181 (*ad loc.*).

83. For this ceremony *cf.* Sir J. G. Frazer, *The Fasti of Ovid* (London, 1929) III, 379 ff., on *Fast.* IV, 819.

84. *Aen.* II, 185 ff.; *cf.* 15.

85. E. Bethe, *RM* 46 (1891) 516 ff.; though, according to the *Iliu persis*, Sinon entered Troy, the tradition that he remained outside to signal persisted.

86. *Aen.* II, 188. Perhaps the wooden horse, and the Roman *triumphator* and the *tensae* also, were expected to convey a magical efficacy into the centre of the defence.

87. *Aen.* II, 189; *cf.* Hom. *Od.* VIII, 509.

88. Gruppe (above, note 74) I, 689 note 2 (perhaps after Heyne, above, note 31, II, Exc. III, 403); II, 1157 ff., 1197 note 1; *cf.* for the epithet ἱππία applied to Athena, Soph. *O.C.* 1070–1, etc. *Cf.* also esp. Lamprocles, fr. 1 (Bergk).

89. Paus. VIII, 42.

90. Ovid, *Met.* IV, 798.

91. Hesiod, *Scut.* 104–5. De la Cerda (above, note 45) II, 241, on *Aen.* II, 610, noticed that Poseidon is θεμελιοῦχος.

92. Hom. *Il.* VII, 446 ff.; *cf.* 461 ff.

93. W. F. J. Knight, *CP* 26 (1931) 418 ff.; *q.v.* for further arguments in support of this theory.

94. J. A. K. Thomson, *CR* 25 (1911) 238–9.

95. Eustath. *ad Il.* X, 435; D. Serv. *ad Aen.* I, 469.

96. *Aen.* I, 469 ff.

97. Eur. *Rhes.* 600 ff.; *cf.* 613 ff.

98. Ibid. 835 ff.

99. *Aen.* I, 443 ff.

100. *Aen.* III, 537 ff.

101. *Aen.* VII, 778–9.

102. Callim. *Hymn. Del.* 275 ff.; *cf.* 23–4.

103. L. Malten, *Arch. Jahrb.* 29 (1914) 179 ff. That these associations, and not the suspicion of horses as of something new-fashioned, furnished the reason for the tabu of the *flamen dialis*, is suggested by parallels from the tabus of early Irish kings; *cf.* Sir J. G. Frazer, *The Golden Bough* (1 vol. ed., London, 1922) 173–4.

104. E. Jones, *On the Nightmare* (London, 1931) 243 ff., 273 ff.

105. Ibid. 279–80, citing the German translation of Count A. de Gubernatis, *Zoological Mythology* (London, 1872) 290; *cf.* 283 ff.

106. Herman Melville, *Moby-Dick* (World's Classics ed., London, 1930) 229–30.

107. Seneca, *Troad.*, Teubner Text, ed. R. Peiper and G. Richter (Leipzig, 1921) 128–9; *cf.* 188–9.

108. Ibid. 126.

109. Ibid. 234 ff. Seneca's sources cannot be discussed here; there are many coherent indications that he preserves a tradition neglected by other writers. [See W. F. J. Knight, 'Magical Motives in Seneca's *Troades*', *TAPA* 63 (1932) 20–33, a valuable supplement to the author's present argument. J.D.C.]

110. Hor. *Carm.* II, iv, 10 ff.

111. Hom. *Il.* XXII, 136 ff., 157, 395 ff.

112. Soph. *Ajax* 1029 ff.; Eur. *Andr.* 107–8; *Aen.* I, 483; *cf.* II, 273; Quint. Smyrn. I, 12, 112.

113. Paton (above, note 62) 45 ff.

114. W. Simpson, *The Buddhist Praying-Wheel* (London and New York, 1896) 88 ff., 103, 183 ff.; Eitrem (above, note 73) 29 ff.

115. *Culex* 324; *cf.* Pliny, *N.H.* VIII, 161.

116. A. Fick and F. Bechtel, *Griechische Personennamen*[2] (Göttingen, 1894) 389.

117. Grace H. Macurdy, *CQ* 23 (1929) 24–5.

118. Eur. *Rhes.* 821.

119. Ibid. 166: the reading πολιόχου τυραννίδος is preferred by Liddell and Scott[8], *s.v.* πολίοχος.

120. Hom. *Il.* VI, 403.

121. K. J. Beloch, *Griechische Geschichte*[2] (Strassburg, 1912) I, i, 1.

122. Hom. *Il.* V, 473 ff.

123. Macurdy (above, note 117) 24, on Fick-Bechtel (above, note 116) 389; it is not, perhaps, quite certain from their words that Fick-Bechtel were arguing from a supposed pun in Hom. *Il.* V, 473 ff.

124. Hom. *Il.* XVII, 225–6.

125. *Cf.* Sir J. G. Frazer, *The Golden Bough* (1 vol. ed., London, 1922) 168 ff. (on the tabus of the Mikado of Japan, etc.), 578 ff. (on human scapegoats in Greek cities).

126. Hom. *Il.* XXII, 346 ff.; *cf.* Gilbert Murray, *The Rise of the Greek Epic*[3] (Oxford, 1924) 120 ff., esp. 126.

127. Frazer (above, note 125) 494 ff., esp. 497 (on the practice of eating in order to assimilate qualities of the thing eaten); *cf.* 482 (on 'eating the soul of the rice'); *cf.* id. *The Golden Bough*[3] (12 vols. ed., London, 1915) III, 190 note 2; IV, 14; *cf.* VIII, 48 ff., 138–9, 167–8; *cf.* also, however, ibid. III, 174 (on the general obligation, sometimes supposed, that the slayer must eat part of the man slain).

128. Frazer (above, note 125) 244 ff., esp. 257 ff., 260 ff.

129. Ibid. 667 ff., esp. 690–1.

130. W. R. Halliday (above, note 72) 8 and note 3, citing G. Kaibel, *Epigrammata Graeca* (Berlin, 1878) 137 no. 349 (of Nicomedia).

131. *Cf.* Halliday, ibid. 3 ff. for the reff., and for arguments against *Sagenver-schiebung*, and, for reff., and recent argumentation in support of the theory, E. Bethe, *Homer: Dichtung and Sage*[2] (Leipzig, 1927) III, 76 ff., esp. 79 (citing Wilamowitz, Robert, and Dümmler), 80 (where difficulties are considered). The view here proposed may reconcile evidence hitherto apparently conflicting.

132. Halliday (above, note 72) 3 ff. (where reff. are given).

133. The suggestion is confuted by Halliday, ibid. 7–8.

134. Ibid. 4 ff.

135. Ibid. 6.

136. By Bethe and others: reff. in note 131 above. The existence of a grave of 'Hector' in Boeotia suggests that a *hector* was in some sense indigenous there.

137. The reff. are collected by Halliday (above, note 72) 14 note 3, 17 notes 5–6, 18 note 1; *cf.* 17 ff. for Asiatic affinities. The lyre is first found in Hesiod, fr. 133 (A. Rzach, *Hesiodi Carmina*, Leipzig, 1902, 367), and Eumelus (Paus. IX, 5, 7, who thinks that Amphion was taught this music from Lydia through Tantalus).

138. Altheim (above, note 74) 23.

139. Callim, *Hymn. Apoll.* 12 ff., 55 ff.

140. Tryph. 508–9.

141. W. Schmid and O. Stählin, *Griechische Literaturgeschichte* (München, 1929) I, i, 475 note 5, citing Stesichorus, *Iliu persis*, frs. 69, 22 (Bergk).

142. Hom. *Il.* XV, 318 ff.

143. Procl. *epit. Ilias parva.*

144. Dar. Phryg. XXXVII ff.

145. Conon, XXXIV.

146. Serv. *ad Aen.* II, 166; Liv. V, 15. I do not attempt here to explain the similarities: that traditions of the fall of Troy coloured traditions of the fall of Veii is an obvious, but perhaps a partly misleading, supposition.

147. Liv. V, 15.

148. *Aen.* II, 351–2; *cf.* 610 ff., 624–5; Tryph. 508–9; Liv. V, 15.

149. Eur. *Troad.* 45 ff.

150. Liv. V, 15.

151. Knight (above, note 31) 364 note 2.

152. Stanley Casson, in a lecture to the London Classical Association in 1912, as reported by Mary R. Glover, *CR* 42 (1928) 103, regarded Odysseus as symbolic of the Mediterranean race. A. Shewan, *CP* 24 (1929) 335 ff., 339 ff., esp. 341, cites Gladstone for a similar view, and further investigates the Mediterranean affinity of Odysseus.

153. Eugene S. McCartney, *CJ* 21 (1925–6) 112 ff.

154. Conway (above, note 79).

155. Eugene S. McCartney, *CJ* 19 (1923–4) 316, citing Marbury B. Ogle, *AJP* 32 (1911) 251 ff.

156. Emory B. Lease, *CJ* 19 (1923–4) 447–8.

157. Tryph. 336 ff. On the entry of the wooden horse, *cf.* W. F. J. Knight, *CJ* 28 (1932–3) 254–62.

158. *Cf.* Hom. *Od.* VIII, 504; *Aen.* II, 192 ff.; *cf.* 189.

159. Plaut. *Bacchid.* 953 ff. The source of Plautus may be Menander, who may follow Sophocles; *cf.* A. C. Pearson, *The Fragments of Sophocles* (Cambridge, 1917) II, 254 ff., citing *Myth. Vat.* I, 210, where a belief is mentioned that Troy would be safe if Troilus lived to the age of twenty. *Cf.* Apollodor. III, 12, 5, where Troilus is called the son of Apollo.

160. Serv. *ad Aen.* II, 13, 241; Quint. Smyrn. I, 802.

161. Hdt. I, 187.

162. Dar. Phryg. XL.

163. Stanley Casson, *Macedonia* (Oxford, 1926) 251–2; *cf.* 234–5; *cf.* Grant Allen, *The Evolution of the Idea of God* (Thinker's Library, London, 1931) Ch. XV, 235, for horses' heads, apparently apotropaic, pictured on churches and other buildings in later times.

164. Malten (above, note 103) 251 ff., esp. 254.

165. Hdt. I, 84.

166. Aesch. *Agam.* 827.

167. Malten (above, note 103) 192 ff., esp. 193. *Cf.*, on the other hand, for the true significance of Erichthonius, whose horses were famous, Myres and Frost (above, note 3) 461.

168. Hom. *Il.* V, 640 ff.

169. Apollodor. II, 6, 4.

170. Serv. *ad Aen.* II, 15, recognizing the Daretic variant among the others.

171. *Cf.*, for the story used by Sophocles, that a leopard's skin was hung on Antenor's door—a probable source of contamination in the notice of Servius—, Pearson (above, note 159) I, 86, citing Strabo, 608, etc.

172. Tryph. 530 ff.

173. Serv. *ad Aen.* II, 244; *cf. ad* 16.

174. Tryph. 345 ff.

175. Eugene S. McCartney, *CP* 26 (1931) 166 ff.

176. *Aen.* II, 313.

177. Hom. *Il.* XVIII, 219 ff.

178. Serv. *ad Aen.* II, 313.

179. Tryph. 326–7.

180. R. H. Klausen, *Aeneas und die Penaten* (Hamburg and Gotha, 1839–40) II, 693. *Cf.* Gruppe (above, note 74) II, 1199 note 4.

181. Seneca, *Troad.* 322 ff.

182. Xen. *Hellen.* II, ii, 23.

183. Paus. II, 21, 3.

184. Gruppe (above, note 74) II, 1199 note 4.

185. Procl. *epit. Ilias parva;* Xen. *De Venat.* I, 15; *c̦.* the reproach of Turnus at *Aen.* XII, 15, and the defence at Dion. Hal. *Ant. Rom.* I, 4.

186. Strabo, C 607–8; Paus. X, 27, 3–4; Dict. Cret. V, 10; Dar. Phryg. XXXVII ff., esp. XLII.

187. Quint. Smyrn. XIII, 333 ff.; a version probably followed by Cassius Hemina; on this whole question, *cf.* A.-M. Guillemin, *L'originalité de Virgile* (Paris, 1931) 42 ff.

188. Procl. *epit. Iliu persis.*

189. *Aen.* I, 1 ff. etc.; III, 294 ff.; I, 242 ff.

190. *Cf. Aen.* III, 294 ff. with Tzetz. *ad* Lycophr. *Alex.* 1232, 1268, citing the *Ilias parva* of Lesches (there seems insufficient reason to think that the *Ilias parva* could not have included the episode); *cf.* Dict. Cret. IV, 18; V, 9.

191. Heyne (above, note 31) II, Exc. XI, 430.

192. E. A. Gardner, *JHS* 14 (1894) 177.

193. L. D. Burdick, *Foundation Rites with Some Kindred Ceremonies* (New York, 1901) 149–50.

194. Ibid. 165–6, citing Simpson (above, note 114) 258, etc. (For other explanations *cf.* Frazer (above, note 83) IV, 184 ff. on *Fast.* VI, 257.) The defensive symbolism of circular movements and of wheels (*cf.*, for wheels built into pillars in Japan, Simpson, ibid. 116, citing Miss G. Cumming) is apparently reproduced in the round form of the temple of Vesta. 'Cyclopean walls' in Greece were probably at first merely 'circle walls', and were attributed to the Cyclopes by a later mistake. The Cyclopes are, in fact, the sons of Poseidon (Eur. *Cycl.* 262, etc.). Sophocles

(fr. 227; Pearson, I, 169) used the phrase κυκλώπιον τροχόν, 'cyclopean wheel'; and Hesychius explains that the 'wheel' is 'the walls'.

195. Liv. XXII, 57; G. Wissowa, *Arch. für Religionswiss.* 22 (1923–4) 214.

196. Wissowa, discussing the practice (ibid. 201 ff.), found mediaeval parallels, but did not connect the whole series of phenomena with foundation ceremonies. For the custom of such burials at foundation ceremonies, *cf.* Grant Allen (above, note 163) Ch. XII, 173–84; and, for a recent English survival (a builder wished to bury the shadow of an onlooker into the wall), *cf.* C. S. Burne, *The Handbook of Folklore* (London, 1914) 150.

197. Lucan, I, 598; Ov. *Fast.* VI, 234; Lucan, IX, 993–4; Claudian, *Eutr.* I, 328–9.

198. P. Stengel, *Griechischen Kultusaltertümer*[3] (München, 1920) 129.

199. *Aen.* II, 256; *cf.* Guillemin (above, note 187) 46–7.

200. Eur. *Hel.* 108.

201. Leaf (above, note 60) 102.

202. Plato, *Gorgias* 505 C-D; *cf.*, for the explanation, H. J. Rose, *CQ* 19 (1925) 147 ff.

203. Apollodor. V, 23.

204. Seneca, *Troad.* 358 ff., 634 ff.

205. Knight (above, note 93) 416–17.

206. *Cf.* Seneca, *Troad.* 365 ff., 524 ff., 546 ff., 605 ff.

207. Eur. *Troad.* 783–4; *cf.* 1173–4.

208. Seneca, *Troad.* 621–2; *cf.* 1068 ff.

209. With Apollodor. III, 14, 6, on the death of the daughters of Cecrops, thought by A. Mommsen, *Heortologie* (Leipzig, 1864) 12, to imply an original human sacrifice, *cf.* Liv. I, 11 (*cf.* 55), on Tarpeia, and Plut. *Rom.* XVII–XVIII, on her significant burial. A death by throwing befell one of the maidens (compared by Mommsen, ibid., with the daughters of Cecrops) sent according to the terms of the Locrian curse; *cf.* Lycophr. *Alex.* 1159; Apollodor. VI, 22; Tzetz. *ad* Lycophr. *Alex.* 1141, 1159. *Cf.* also here reff. at note 47 above; and E. Hommel, *OLZ* 22 (1919) 63 ff., who deduces the spiral labyrinth (which I think frequently a device of obstructive magic) from the microcosm of human anatomy, connects its symbolism with the underworld, and actually compares the wooden horse of Troy with animals (usually minotaurs or centaurs) pictured in the nuclei of labyrinths.

II. Maiden Castle from the South

Maiden Castle is a hill town in Dorsetshire. The ramparts with their labyrinthine entrances, as shown in this aerial photograph, are dated to the Iron Age, scarcely earlier than the third century B.C. They represent, however, an original component of the Initiation Pattern, which had been evolved thousands of years before. This component is the tactical labyrinth, in which a maze-like winding approach is used as a method of military defence. Its principle, the principle of exclusion with conditional entry, became important on many levels of action and of thought, especially in

PART TWO

CUMAEAN GATES

*A Reference of the Sixth Aeneid to the
Initiation Pattern*

(1936)

With Drawings by L. J. Lloyd

GENITORI

PREFACE

This book is a sketch in outline of something rather hard to define. I could call it defensive sanctity in the ancient world; or aspects of mortuary belief; or the ritual pattern of initiation, in the primary sense, especially as it is seen in Vergil's poetry. The strange thing is how these questions, which I had begun to approach in former work, have been coalescing to give a slightly changed outlook on ancient and indeed generically human ideas.

The book is a sketch only, because the investigations in this field are going fast. A simple outline is more wanted than any attempt to fix the meaning of everything that seems to be involved. Accordingly, I have postponed many obvious questions which I hope to treat eventually. I have not, for example, included a full comparison of all ancient mortuary myths; or full discussions of work on the labyrinth and defensive sanctity, done by others since my own earlier publications; or a history of the 'initiation pattern' and mystery religions in general; or any thorough attempt to evaluate theories of diffusion. Meanwhile, I hope my outline will be clear, and as fair as can be expected, as a short account of some of the old stored energies of heart and mind, that have gone to make a small part of Vergil's poetry. In fact, I prefer to regard the book as a note on some things in lines 9 to 44 of the sixth book of the *Aeneid*; a short list of some considerations which one reader has found it helpful to remember.

I cordially thank Mr Basil Blackwell for his confidence and encouragement; Mr Robert W. Cruttwell, for most kindly showing me, and letting me use, his unpublished researches in Legends of the Holy Grail; Professor T. J. Haarhoff, Signor Emanuele Cesareo, and other scholars who have printed gratifying approval or useful criticism of my former work; Mr John Layard, to whose publications, letters, and ready help in conversation I owe a great debt; Mr L. J. Lloyd, who drew the illustrations, and all to whom information used in them is due; Professor F. Muller, Junior, who has given me much help and encouragement by accepting my former results and publishing expansions of them and other researches on cognate topics; and Mr G. A. Wainwright, who has with the greatest generosity allowed me the advantage of his wide and exact learning, not only on questions of Egyptology but on others also, supplying references and reading some of this book in manuscript. These acknowledgments are in alphabetical order. Naturally, I am alone responsible for the use I make of the help which I have had, and for the opinions which I express. I also thank cordially editors and others who have helped me to publish investigations in the past, or who have invited me to read papers; and Mr J. D. Denniston, whose kindnesses are too many to describe.

W.F.J.K.

University College of the
South-West of England
Exeter
12 *July* 1936

CUMAEAN GATES

This book is in the form of a quest. It is a quest for a clear identification of certain facts in man's religious history which have hitherto been both important and obscure, especially obscure in their relation to each other.

1964   W.F.J.K.

CUMAEAN GATES

At pius Aeneas arces quibus altus Apollo
praesidet horrendaeque procul secreta Sibyllae,
antrum immane, petit, magnam cui mentem animumque
Delius inspirat uates aperitque futura.
iam subeunt Triuiae lucos atque aurea tecta.
  Daedalus, ut fama est, fugiens Minoia regna
praepetibus pennis ausus se credere caelo
insuetum per iter gelidas enauit ad Arctos,
Chalcidicaque leuis tandem super adstitit arce.
redditus his primum terris tibi, Phoebe, sacrauit
remigium alarum posuitque immania templa.
in foribus letum Androgeo; tum pendere poenas
Cecropidae iussi (miserum!) septena quotannis
corpora natorum; stat ductis sortibus urna.
contra elata mari respondet Gnosia tellus:
hic crudelis amor tauri suppostaque furto
Pasiphae mixtumque genus prolesque biformis
Minotaurus inest, Veneris monimenta nefandae;
hic labor ille domus et inextricabilis error;
magnum reginae sed enim miseratus amorem
Daedalus ipse dolos tecti ambagesque resoluit,
caeca regens filo uestigia. tu quoque magnam
partem opere in tanto, sineret dolor, Icare, haberes.
bis conatus erat casus effingere in auro,
bis patriae cecidere manus. quin protinus omnia
perlegerent oculis, ni iam praemissus Achates
adforet atque una Phoebi Triuiaeque sacerdos
Deiphobe Glauci, fatur quae talia regi:
'non hoc ista sibi tempus spectacula poscit;
nunc grege de intacto septem mactare iuuencos
praestiterit, totidem lectas de more bidentis.'
talibus adfata Aenean (nec sacra morantur
iussa uiri) Teucros uocat alta in tecta sacerdos.
  Excisum Euboicae latus ingens rupis in antrum
quo lati ducunt aditus centum, ostia centum,
unde ruunt totidem uoces, responsa Sibyllae.

Vergil, *Aeneid* VI, 9–44.

CUMAEAN GATES

Another way went Aeneas the true, to the towering fastness where Apollo reigns, and, near, that monstrous cavern, dread Sibyl's seclusion; where he of Delos, he the prophet, breathes into her spirit's visionary might, revealing things to come. Now they came near the woods of the goddess three-wayed and near that house of gold.

There is a tale of Daedalus, how, in flight from the land where Minos ruled, he took headlong wings and dared his life in the sky; by track unknown right out toward the icy north he swam, till he lightly hovered above that fastness of Chalcidic men. Here, in the first land where he found safety, he hallowed to Phoebus his slant-oar wings, in a monster temple which he founded. There, on the temple doors, Androgeos dying; there next, oh sad, command given to sons of Cecrops to pay annual retribution in seven of their fine sons, the urn visible, the lots just drawn. Opposite, balancing, the land where Knossos is, standing up from the sea. In it, that bull-love, love callous; Pasiphae, bride in secrecy; and there, record how wicked love can be, hybrid procreation, two shapes in one, Minotaur in the midst; and all the old wandering ways of the house that was there, weariness of work inextricable, except the Builder himself pitied the Queen, that her love was strong, and unwinding the craft and the coils, guided sightless footprints with his thread. And Icarus, his share in that grand sculpture would have been great indeed, had grief allowed. Hands of an artist twice had tried to mould out his fall in the gold; hands of a father twice had fallen from the trying. . . . Why, straight had they read on, every pictured word, had not Achates, sent ahead before, returned already, and with him she, priestess of Phoebus and of the goddess three-wayed, Deiphobe her name, Glaucus her father. Like this she spake to our king: 'Now is no time that commands staring at sights, as you stare. No: from a herd without spot seven heifers be your sacrifice, seven sheep too, and choose them ritually well. Better so, might it be.' So spake she to Aeneas. They were not slow to do the rite instructed. Then she called the two Trojans into the tall house where she was priestess.

Cleft out is the flank of that Euboeic rock into a cavern terrific. To it a hundred broad accesses lead, a hundred their mouthways. From it a hundred come the streams of sound, the Sibyl's answerings.

I

WALA

The strange participation of present in past or past in present has lately been winning a new notice and importance, even if long ago Vico and even Zeno raised suspicion against time and its powers of separation. On the one hand it can now be maintained that all history is contemporary history; and, on the other, psychic experiences, not all unconvincing, have been showing that events, belonging in the ordinary sense to different times, can exist together within one consciousness. Not only are the old philosophic attacks on time thus reinforced, but from another direction literary criticism is compelled to enlarge its conception of tradition in order to face the facts of literary dependence; and it would have needed to invent the theories of racial memory and a collective mind, if they had not already been provided by psychologists. Jung in particular describes a situation in which mysterious but attested participations and communications are intelligible; a situation in which Chesterton's epigram, 'The oldest things last longest', is clear. The greatness and originality of a genius may even consist in power to find contacts farther back in time, beyond the reach of others, and to evoke latent stores of feeling and of meaning in the collective mind of the present, just because his power penetrates deeply into the unconscious memory of the race. That is how symbols and patterns have permanent vitality; for thought follows the same 'archetypes' again and again. Among the archetypes of greatest universality is the ritual pattern of initiation, which seems to have begun as a burial rite, and to have developed into a scheme of religious cult, myth, and hope, carrying high spiritual meaning in the shape of the ancient mould.

It may be centuries yet before much is known about the Sixth *Aeneid*, and longer still before the message of it is understood. There is, however, a small thing to be said at the present moment, in explanation of the place of the Sixth *Aeneid* in the thought of the world, as it stretches from the Stone Age down to today. It is this small thing that I try to say here.

The Trojans on their pilgrim's progress, looking for a new city of the gods, reached the middle of their course when they came to the western land. There is rich symbolism in any western land that is a journey's end. So it is at Cumae, for it is a western land of death and new birth that there is reached. Aeneas goes to the temple of Apollo, and on the gate of it there is a picture of Attica and Crete, and the labyrinth, with the Minotaur inside, to which Attic boys were sent. The problem is to find the poetry and meaning in the pictured gate, and to see how it colours and fixes the poetic world of the *Aeneid*. The problem is not insoluble, at least in part.

The story of Vergil's Cumae is this. Aeneas with his Trojans sailed westward after the fall of Troy, and after several visits, including one to Carthage and two to Sicily, landed at Cumae in Campania. Near Cumae was the supposed access to the world of the dead, controlled by a priestess of Apollo and Diana, the sibyl, who guarded a temple of Apollo and a cave. Aeneas went to the temple; and stayed 'reading' the picture of the Cretan labyrinth on the gates. Then the sibyl appeared, and told him not to waste time, but to offer sacrifices. He obeys; she prophesies his future to him; and he asks to be shown how to visit his father Anchises in the world of the dead. The sibyl tells him that there are difficulties, especially in returning; that he must find and pick a 'golden bough' as a passport; and that he must bury a dead friend, whose death is unknown to him. He obeys; and, with the bough, he is guided through the cave by the sibyl. Seeing the bough Charon unwillingly ferries him over the river Styx. Aeneas meets the ghost of his helmsman Palinurus, who fell overboard on the voyage, taking the tiller of the ship with him; and of Dido, whom he deserted in Africa. He sees evil spirits on the way and hears about the punishments suffered by the wicked in the depths of Tartarus. Eventually he finds Anchises in Elysium, open country bounded by 'walls built by the Cyclopes'; Anchises shows him a vision of Roman history and explains the moral government of the universe; and at last Aeneas returns to his ships, coming through the ivory gate, one of the twin gates of sleep; the gate by which, as it seems, untrue dreams come. After the great experience, there is a change in Aeneas; he is firmer, with a stronger faith.

The meaning of myths current in antiquity which describe the descent of a hero to the world below has been variously estimated. Four kinds of theory have been counted; the dogmatic, the astral, the physical, and the psychological.[1] On the whole, they all belong at least partly to obsolete mythological thought. It is probably safer to prefer a new kind of explanation, which can perhaps be called the ritual.

Anthropologists have now collected many examples of these myths which are still current today in many parts of the world. It is immediately obvious that the ancient and modern myths belong to the same class, and demand the same kind of explanation. It is also clear what kind of explanation is required by the modern myths. They are found among people whose myths and methods of burial agree. There are certain principles. The myths describe the supposed origin of men at their birth and their supposed destination at death. It is found that the two are the same; for example, men are believed to come from a cave at birth and to return to it at death. Next, it is also found that methods of burial agree with the believed destination, and are designed to help the dead to reach it; interment implies a land of the dead under the earth, and cremation some kind of heaven in the sky. There are many examples of the two most important classes of myth; the ocean type, in which the dead are supposed to cross the ocean, and the cave type, in which they are supposed to enter a cave, on the way to their rest. The two types are also found fused in various composite forms. There is also a strong tendency to think that men come from stones or monoliths and return at death to them. The dead sometimes enter volcanic clefts.

There is a useful collection of the modern myths, derived principally from tribes of the Pacific islands and mainland coasts, and of North America.[2] The myths are found associated with megalithic monuments; they are thought to prove a diffusion of peoples of the so-called 'archaic' culture from some central area such as Egypt; a theory which needs very careful and qualified statement if it is to fit the complicated evidence. The collection of myths however is valuable; some examples of beliefs held, which are most relevant at present, are these.

'The peoples of the archaic civilization tend to claim descent from a race ancestress, one of the forms of the Great Mother', who 'should be found in the land of the dead'. 'Interment is the means of returning the dead to the place of origin, the underworld.'[3] A Pueblo ghost 'finds its way back into the underworld through the hole whence its ancestors emerged'.[4] 'A tribe in Upper Burma, called Bunjogee or Pankho, who inter their dead, claim that their ancestors came out of the underworld by means of a cave,' which they locate near a place called Vanhuilen in the Lhoosai country. 'They believe that the deceased go into the large hill whence man first emerged.' 'Certain tribes believe that their ancestors came out of stones, among them being some Naga tribes of Assam. They inter their dead and place a stone on the grave, or else put the body in a cave in the side of a mountain, the mouth of which is filled with stones.'[5] The Toradja were created from stone images animated by breath. Their ghosts go underground, but the 'life' of a dead man goes to the sky.[6] 'The mountain Toradja . . . place their land of the dead on the earth in the direction whence they believe themselves to have come.'[7] The Karen of Burma take their dead annually to the 'Hill of Bones'.[8] 'The Bahau of Kutei on the east coast (of Borneo) hold that men come from trees and to trees they shall return. . . . When a Bahau woman bears a child before the appointed time, it is placed in a tree; it is, as it were, returned to the place which it has lately left.'[9] 'In the Fiaralang district of Belu in Timor the people believe that they are descended from an ancestress who came out of Mt Lekaan. Their ghosts go to Mt Lekaan after death, but as to whether they go underground or not is not clear. Evidently they went underground at first; but migration has caused them to remember only their place of origin, and to forget the fact that their ghosts went underground.'[10] 'Dr Codrington has put on record the striking difference between Northern and Southern Melanesia in the beliefs concerning the abode of the soul after death. In the Banks and Torres Islands, and in the New Hebrides, it is the almost universal belief that the dead live underground, the way to the home beneath the earth being in some cases through the volcanic vents which occur in these islands. In the Solomons, on the other hand, the prevailing belief is that the dead find their way after death to islands, either in other parts of the Solomons, or more remotely situated. Here and there in the Solomons, however, as in Savo, we find, either alone or in conjunction with the more widely diffused belief, the idea that the dead go into volcanic craters or caverns, while in at least one place in Southern Melanesia, in Anaiteum, it is believed that the dead reach their future home by sea.'[11]

These beliefs illustrate the characteristics of this whole series. They are descriptions of the origin and the destiny of man in close relation to ritual acts. In some of the examples, as among the Naga, Karen, and Bahau, beliefs and actions can be seen to agree. The Malekulans of the New Hebrides, of whom there will be more to say, have elaborate initiation ceremonies which closely represent their 'journey of the dead'. That is, they use their myths for practical rites; or alternatively they describe in their myths their rites and the effect which they expect from them. It is worth while to suggest that the principle of initiation, that is, birth into a new life by ritual, either at physical birth or death, or at any other time, was evolved from a very simple myth-ritual pattern of birth and death, until the exalted spiritual conceptions of the Eleusinian mysteries, Vergil, and Dante were attained.[12] Fundamentally, the myths concern new birth by entry again into earth, the universal mother. That is why caves are so important. According to Porphyry, the Persians initiated mystics into secret rites in a place which they called a cave; and so after them other races habitually performed their mysteries in caves, either natural or artificial.[13]

Passage through a cave is a mighty poetic symbol for a change of state. But the mature use of the symbol, as in Plato and Vergil, is ultimately developed out of simple superstitions concerned with the motherhood of earth and with the return of the dead to her.

A good example of a cave myth, that must surely be one of the simplest known, has lately come from Australia.[14]

'Two churingas, slabs of stone thought by some native tribes to be a repository of men's spirits, have just arrived at the British Museum from the Ngalia and Loritja tribes of Central Australia.

'Strange legends are attached to these stones. One is of some grasshoppers that turned into men. The grasshoppers, at a place called Ngapatjimbi, flew out of the ground one day into the air. They came down again, it is alleged, as men.

'The men went to Wantangara and, having gone into a cave there, turned into churingas.

'That is the story, indicated by mysterious circles and symbols, on one side of one of the churingas in the Museum.

'The other churinga has an equally queer legend of some wild cat men and their attempts to make a cave to live in.'

This is of course much more likely to be an account of old ritual than a fairy tale. The churingas are 'spirit houses', characteristic of the people who built the megalithic monuments in Europe and Asia. The story is a myth directing the ritual life of men from the time when they come from the earth mother till their return to her to live on as ghosts in monoliths, either within the earth itself or within a tomb that represents it. An alternative to the last explanation is this. The dead man went into the cave for burial; his ghost remained in or on a monolith erected to him; and the two parts of his destiny have become confused in the myth. Without knowing the details, it is hard to be confident about the legend on the second churinga. It looks much the same; an account of funerary ritual, designed to secure survival and comfort for the dead when they were buried in a cave, or when their ghosts departed to a cave. That part of the legends is expressed by circles on the churingas is no surprise, in view of the importance of ring magic for mortuary cult.

The 'archaic myths', including the myths on the churingas, clearly picture beliefs characteristic of 'stone' cultures. These beliefs are widely encountered among people of advanced neolithic technique, and in particular among builders of megalithic monuments. There is great emphasis on monoliths, in or on which ghosts reside; on burial rites in general; stone circles; and on caves and on other underground chambers; and there is a surprising capacity for long sea voyages.

Whether it is legitimate to speak of 'megalithic people' or whether it is not, and however much or little truth there may be in theories of a 'megalithic diffusion', there seems little doubt that the classical civilizations rested on a foundation of 'stone culture' in the special sense. There are obvious parallels with the few examples of belief that I have given. There is the whole pre-Hellenic 'Tree and Pillar Cult'. Niobe, transformed to a rock, and Daphne, changed into a tree, recall an age when human beings were thought to come from trees and to return to them. So does the regular Homeric formula, used in asking a

stranger who he is: 'For I do not think you came out of a tree or
a stone.' Perhaps this began as a joke against some remnant of the
stone people, known to the earliest speakers of Greek in Greek
lands. This is the impression given by one unusual occurrence of
the formula.[15] Hector, about to fight Achilles, says that he
cannot talk to him 'as if from a tree or a stone'; that is, apparently, he cannot treat him as one of the old population of
Greece, whose day is done; for Achilles is above all a master, not
to be restrained. Many more comparisons might be made. It is
entertaining to notice the grasshoppers of the churingas, and to
remember that the Athenians wore grasshoppers of gold in their
hair, actually to show that they, unlike others, were 'indigenous', 'αὐτόχθονες', sprung from the soil on which they lived.[16]
The Myrmidons claimed to have been at first 'ants', 'μύρμηκες',
as their name distantly suggested.[17] There is plenty of evidence
that Greeks thought that men had once been 'stones'. 'Zeus
made men into stones', 'λαοί', a word which is in fact from the
same root of an old word for 'stone', λᾶας.[18] The same root
occurs in the name of Deucalion, who created men again after
the flood by throwing over his shoulder stones, 'the bones of his
mother, the earth'; and the stones became men.[19] There is also
here a reference to the belief in earth, the universal mother, as in
the 'archaic' myths. 'One is the origin of men and gods alike',[20]
as Pindar said of his 'earth broad-breasted'.[21] There are the
stories of men who sprang from the earth when 'snakes' teeth'
were sown, at Colchis, and also at Thebes,[22] a particular home
of old and often pre-Hellenic ideas. In the *Odyssey*, Heracles is
met in the world below; but Homer adds, in words that have
been thought an interpolation, 'only his ghost; for he himself
had gone to Heaven'.[23] That is just like the 'archaic' division of
the personality at death, shown in the example of the Toradja.
As for the fusion of the ocean and cave types of mortuary myth,
that is obvious at once in classical examples of journeys to the
land of the dead.[24]

Without, apparently, much consideration of the so-called
'archaic' culture in distant parts of the world, a bold but enlightening theory about 'stone men' in the Mediterranean area
has lately been published.[25] They are given the appropriate
'megalithic' attributes: caves and underground dwellings, stone
'Cyclopean' walls, round stone buildings, such as the tholos at

Tiryns, for the living and the dead, stone pillars supposed to be homes of the dead, and a particularly advanced system of mortuary belief. They are stated to have spread from Asia Minor, from which in legend the Cyclopes came, across the Mediterranean to Africa and western and northern Europe; to have left behind in Italy besides much else the name and cult of Acca Larentia and of Laverna, goddess of a cleft in the rock on the Aventine;[26] and to have been the first to use the *nuraghi* of Sardinia, apparently called Daidaleia in antiquity.[27] There is special interest in Acca Larentia and Laverna, for they are earth goddesses whose names contain the root LA-, 'stone', by which the stone men are particularly traced; and there are many other residual, pre-Indo-European words in various places which they seem to have left behind. From this root LA- not only ordinary words for 'stone' are derived, as λᾶας, 'lapis', λευσίμος, '[death] by stoning', but others, such as 'Laurentum', and, above all, 'labrys', 'λάβρυς', taken to mean 'a stone axe', and 'labyrinth' itself, 'λαβύρινθος', now shown to mean simply 'place of stone'.[28]

These people seem to be historical; they have been accepted as forerunners of the Etruscans, bringing eastern influence to Italy over a thousand years before the Etruscans came.[29] There is no doubt that a culture that can be called 'megalithic' spread, for that is clear from the remains. There has been an uncertainty whether it was communicated by migrating tribes, or merely by contact; but such contact over so extensive an area involves at least small parties of settlers, and probably a small ruling class, established here and there along the coasts.[30]

Two questions now arise. One is, whether the classical myths of the world below can be associated with such a pre-classical 'stone' culture;[31] and to answer it another must first be asked, whether there is any access to the detailed beliefs of 'stone men' anywhere in the world, especially as they ought to understand the use and meaning of caves and also 'labyrinths'. For it was to explain the cave at Cumae, and the pictured labyrinth on the temple gates there, that this argument was started; and any discovery about the relation of the picture to the cave should be enlightening.

The island of Malekula[32] is in the New Hebrides, an archipelago occupying a central position in the long series of Melanesian Islands, along which at least one wave of megalithic culture spread from south-eastern Asia into the Pacific. The inhabitants of Malekula, who use polished stone tools, believe in a future life, to be attained through a complicated series of rites during lifetime. These rites are mainly concerned with the erection of monoliths representing ancestors; and with a journey said to be undertaken after death, whereby the ghost of a dead man reaches the land of the dead. This journey presents features so impressively similar to elements in the Sixth *Aeneid* that the comparison cannot be refused. First, it sheds far more light on the connection of the maze pattern with the cave; but that is only a start. Meanwhile, the Malekulans are above all 'stone men'. They believe in 'petromorphic' supernatural beings; and stone is in great evidence in their cult, especially in their mortuary rites and their attention to rocks, caves, and stone circles.[33]

From the island of Malekula, which shows great diversity of culture within given limits, four versions of the mortuary myth have been recorded. They differ in detail, but all present the same ritual pattern, and all begin with the entrance of the ghost into a cave.

I start with the district of Seniang, where these beliefs are said to have been introduced by a white-skinned,[34] narrow-nosed race, now vanished, whose chief is said to have been buried sitting on a stone seat inside a chambered tomb covered with a mound of earth and stones, his body being incorruptible. These folk are also held to be responsible for the existing practice of attempting mummification, and for the introduction of the dog, since lost until it was reintroduced by modern Europeans.

'Ghosts of the dead of the Seniang district pass along a "road" to Wies, the land of the dead. At a certain point on their way they come to a rock called Lembwil Song lying in the sea at the boundary between the Seniang and Mewun districts, but formerly it stood upright. The land of the dead is situated vaguely in the wooded open ground behind this rock and is surrounded by a high fence. Always sitting by the rock is a female ghost Temes [i.e. "ghost"] Savsap, and on the ground in front of her is drawn the complete geometrical figure known as "Nahal", "the Path". The path which the ghost must traverse lies between the two halves of the figure. . . . As each ghost comes along the road, the guardian ghost hurriedly rubs out one half of the figure. The ghost now comes up, but loses his track and cannot find it. He wanders about searching for a way to get past the Temes [i.e. guardian ghost] of the rock, but in vain. Only a knowledge of the completed geometric figure can release him from this impasse. If he knows this figure, he at once completes the half which Temes Savsap rubbed out; and passes down the track through the middle of the figure. If, however, he does not know the figure, the Temes, seeing he will never find the road, eats him, and he never reaches the abode of the dead.'[35] The figure is one of a series, now drawn by men as an artistic game of skill in which 'Each design is regarded rather as a kind of maze, the great thing is to move smoothly and continuously through it from starting-point to starting-point.'[36]

Temes Savsap was however eventually killed by a great warrior, who revived after death to call for his weapons; and that night her rock crashed into the sea.

'The ghosts of the Lambumbu district on their way to Iambi, the land of the dead, have to pass through an analogous, but not identical geometrical design, the Nevet hor Iambi, "Stone of the land of the dead" . . .'[37] 'The home of the dead, Bwialou, of the Big Nambas of the north of Malekula is entered near a big rock in the neighbourhood of the village Ten Marou. . . . There are said to be "pictures" on this rock. The ghosts on their way to Bwialou have to pass a ghost called Lisevsep, who destroys the ghosts of evil men, but there is no mention that the ghosts have to pass through a geometrical design. Lisevsep is, however, represented by a geometrical design which precisely resembles the Nahal [i.e. the "Path"].'[38]

In the foregoing quotations the sequence of events in the journey of the dead as described in Seniang is not fully clear. The following adventures are involved, in the following order. The ghost crosses a channel called Niew, and then a lagoon. It then comes to the rock Lembwil Song and Temes Savsap, completes the maze-figure, goes through a hole in Lembwil Song, climbs a tree, leaps into the sea, and finally reaches the land of the dead, which is 'a short distance underground'.[39]

The three other versions of the journey of the dead are recorded from the three small islets lying off the north-eastern coast of Malekula.[40]

On the most northern of them, called Vao, a dead man is said

to enter a 'Cave of the Dead', but it is not his final resting
place.[41] In the cave his way is blocked by a female guardian
spirit, called on Vao Le-hev̄-hev̄. This name is a dialectal variant of the more usual Le-saw-saw. Le- being a female prefix, the
name of the ghost is Saw-saw,[42] and she is equivalent to the
Temes Savsap of the Seniang version. If the dead man has duly
offered a pig, he is rescued from Le-hev̄-hev̄ by another spirit
called Tagar-lawo, who says, pointing to the inside of the cave,
'Leave him alone. Let him join his friends over there.' He then
goes more than forty miles down the coast, until he is opposite
to an island named Ambrim. To this he is ferried, on some small
object such as a piece of banyan bark, by the ferryman of the
dead; and he is then led by him up to a volcano on the island,
where the dead are supposed to survive.[43]

The words of Tagar-lawo show that the cave was once believed to be the final resting place of the dead. This has been
proved to be the earlier version.[44] It is known elsewhere in this
area. 'In Raga (Pentecost), from which one Vao village claims
its origin,' the good spirit Tagaro, corresponding to Tagar-lawo,
is said to have sent the male evil spirit Supwe, corresponding to
the female spirit Le-saw-saw, 'to a place where there is a bottomless chasm, somewhere inland in Araga (Raga), where he
rules over the ghosts of the dead'.[45] Accordingly, for both the
Raga and the Vao versions, the tale must once have ended in
the cave.[46]

On the neighbouring islet of Atchin the dead man is buried
wearing all the insignia of the degree in the pre-mortuary hier-
archy which he has reached. With him in the grave is laid a
cane cut to the length of his body. With it he is said to strike a
canoe belonging to living men as he passes it on his way. He
visits the same Cave of the Dead, but no other dead, or spirits,
are there, and he goes on down the coast, presently meeting the
guardian ghost Le-saw-saw, to whom he offers a pig. He is next
ferried to the 'place of ghosts' on Ambrim.[47]

In the version from the third small island, Wala, the cane
buried with the dead man is called ne-row, translated 'measuring
stick'. Here also it is cut to the length of the dead man's body;
and here the use of it is understood. The dead man at his departure slings a sacrificed fowl on the cane. He then gnaws the
bark of a certain magic tree, walks straight through the Cave of

the Dead to the shore, and crosses a river by striking it with the cane, and thus parting the waters. He meets the petromorphic guardian spirit Le-saw-saw, and is ferried to Ambrim.[48] A story is told on Wala that two women made the journey of the dead in their lifetime, and thus became the source of knowledge concerning the future life.[49]

The fruit of the magic tree, the bark of which in the Wala account is gnawed by the dead man, has life-giving properties, for babies whose mothers' milk has failed are fed on it.[50] Elsewhere, in another myth a tree, apparently, but not certainly, the same tree, has 'forbidden fruit', which is eaten in disobedience.[51] There is no stated connection between the magic tree and the cane. But there can scarcely be doubt that the cane in some way represents the dead man; it has been suggested that it is his double.[52] It is not impossible that it was expected to communicate vitality to him, besides possessing the qualities of a magic wand.

This mythical system closely corresponds with the Sixth *Aeneid*. The Malekulans and Vergil have these elements in common. To reach the land of the dead a cave near the sea shore, guarded by a female guardian, is entered. Clearly the sibyl corresponds with Temes Savsap. Near the entrance is a maze or labyrinth which delays the journey. Only those who are qualified may enter, and qualification depends on ritual, wholly or partly. Even then there are serious difficulties to pass. The traveller has to be provided with a 'bough' or wand from a specially effective tree to help him on his journey and above all to enable him to cross water. There is a ferryman of the dead. There are hostile spirits on the way who punish evil doers. Some of the dead, at least, live in open country somehow below ground and out beyond the cave. There are hostile spirits consigned to an almost bottomless chasm by a spirit friendly to man. Living human beings can visit the land of the dead and return with news of it. These are the most important of many obvious similarities.

The immediate question is whether any link can be discovered to connect the ancient beliefs of Hellenized Italy with modern beliefs held on the shores of the Pacific. If so, it is worth while to ask whether the similarities are more than a coincidence. Such a link exists.

The Sumerian *Epic of Gilgamish* may be the earliest mortuary myth in the world. It has already been shown to be closely comparable to the myths of Malekula;[53] but there is something left to add.

When his friend Enkidu died, Gilgamish decided to learn the secret of immortality from his ancestor, Ut-napishtim, who had escaped the flood, and had been granted immortality. In the Sumerian version of the flood, Ut-napishtim lived on an island at the head of the Persian Gulf; but in the epic Gilgamish goes westward to Mount Mashu, a mountain behind which the sun set.

Gilgamish arrived at the mountain, and found two scorpion-men, or a man and woman, guarding its cave-like entrance. 'Their backs mount up to the rampart of heaven, And their foreparts reach down beneath Arallu (the Underworld). . . . From sunrise to sunset they guard the sun.'[54] Their very sight was death. However, recognizing the divine origin of Gilgamish, they received him kindly; but they told him that he might not continue, because only Shamash the sun-god had ever succeeded in crossing the mountain, a journey which took twelve double hours. In the end, Gilgamish persuaded them. 'There was a door on the cave, and Gilgamish was allowed to pass through it to penetrate the dark tunnel leading to the Sea of Death, which only Shamash (the Sun) could cross.'[55] But there were difficulties still in the way. For the first twelve hours the darkness increased, but then it became lighter, and at the end of twenty-four hours Gilgamish reached a place of bright daylight, the garden of the gods, where the tree of the gods grew.

Here Shamash himself met him, and tried to dissuade him, but in vain. Gilgamish came to the place of the goddess Sidurri by the sea. She also opposed Gilgamish, advising him to enjoy life while he still could, as all must die. But he persisted, and was again told that only Shamash had ever crossed the ocean, and that even if he succeeded there still remained the waters of death to pass. At last she suggested that he should cross with Ur-shanabi, the pilot of Ut-napishtim. When Gilgamish found him, he too sought to dissuade him. But in the end he told Gilgamish to go into the forest and cut down 120 poles, each sixty cubits long, to use as punt poles, throwing each one away after one stroke, so that the waters of death might not touch his hands. It appears that the poles were necessary because he had lost some essential part of the boat; but what the part was cannot be made out. Gilgamish obeyed the instructions, and together they crossed. Ut-napishtim saw them coming and noticed that the part of the boat was missing. To the account of his presence which Gilgamish offered, he replied that Mammitum, 'the fixer of destinies', had settled the fate of every man, and, in answer to a further question, that he himself had escaped the flood and had been granted immortality then. Finally, he told Gilgamish to keep awake for seven days; but he fell asleep, and only woke on the seventh day. When he woke, Ut-napishtim told him how to cross the sea, and how to find at the bottom of it a plant which restored youth. Gilgamish dived and got the plant, but on the way home he lost it, for a snake ate it while he bathed. That is why a snake's youth is renewed, but a man's is not.

The *Epic of Gilgamish* and the Sixth *Aeneid* are alike in these particulars. The heroes are in search of human princes, now enjoying a certain immortality, one of whom is an ancestor and the other a father. The heroes start by travelling westward. The entrance to the land of the dead is a cave in a rocky place near water, with supernatural guardians who discourage intruders, and strong apotropaic agencies: the Scorpion-people's dangerous glance, and the Cumaean labyrinth, which is, as will appear later, an apotropaic symbol. The guardians relent when they discover the heroes' divine origin; but they explain that only the divine have passed that way before. There are traces of solar cult. There is a pilot or ferryman of the dead, who attempts dissuasion, but agrees to co-operate on the condition that the hero is provided with poles or a 'bough'. There are boats, and a part of a boat is lost. Water is crossed twice on the journey; one crossing at least is beyond the cave entrance. The personalities who are sought tell the heroes secrets of fate, and explain the privilege of survival after death. The living contrive to return, after sleep, or by way of a symbol of sleep, having found the way, and learnt part of what they would know. There are other similarities; but these are the most obvious and important.

If these other myths are to be compared to the *Aeneid* with any suggestion, however tentative, of affinity, it is of course necessary not to forget the many intervening Greek versions.

These versions are naturally taken as Vergil's immediate sources and indeed there is little doubt that he used every one of them which was extant in his day. But, according to the most elaborate of recent commentaries on the Sixth *Aeneid*,[56] the differences between the account there given, and other known versions of the journey to the world below, are more numerous than the similarities. This cannot now be said, if the eastern myths are included for comparison. The eastern myths therefore fill a gap, which needed to be filled; unless it can be proved quite incredible that between then and the *Aeneid* any connection might subsist.

Among the unexplained details in Vergil two of the most important were the labyrinth on the temple gate, and the golden bough.

The labyrinth has been said to delay the action of the poem needlessly.[57] But it had already been shown that it is an effective poetic symbol, suggesting the difficulty and confusion involved by a journey into the earth, and expressing in advance what is to come.[58] That is in Vergil's manner; and the labyrinth does, of course, represent the complications within the earth's frame. It represents them in a far stricter sense than could be known when the suggestion was first made, but still in a sense true to Vergil's words, applied to the return journey, 'hoc opus, hic labor est'. Later another suggestion was made,[59] that this symbolism contained also the more developed and spiritual implications of secrecy, appropriate to a revelation of esoteric truth, 'sit mihi fas audita loqui', and of the moral disintegration and bewilderment which initiation in the mysteries will cure.

It is an entertaining thought that all these notions about the Cumaean labyrinth, even though they contradict each other, turn out to be partly true. The labyrinth certainly 'delays the narrative' when Aeneas looks at it; but this is right, and in conformity with its true nature, as the Malekulan maze, which delays the ghost, clearly shows. In Malekula, the maze is a test of fitness to enter the world of the dead. The ghost has to supply the other half of the pattern and find its way through it by a straight path. The original plan is forgotten; clearly at first the ghost had to find its way right through the whole winding course of the complicated figure. The Cumaean labyrinth may also be, not only a delay, but also a test; if so, that is not made

FIGURE I

The Cave of the Sibyl at Cumae—a transverse gallery (after A. Maiuri, *Associazione Internazionale Studi Mediterranei, Bollettino*, III, 3, August–September, 1932, front cover).

obvious by Vergil. How the other two guesses are right will appear better later; at present it is at least easy to see that the maze or labyrinth in some sense belongs naturally to a cave or the earth, and that it might carry spiritual ideas appropriate to initiation. The Cumaean cave and the labyrinth on the Cumaean gates do not occur together by chance. Perhaps it is not chance either that the word 'labyrinth' belongs to the language of 'stone men', of whom cave myths appear to be characteristic.

The golden bough has always been bewildering; it is 'an otherwise unknown folk-lore motive'.[60] But it has been shown that Cornutus, though elsewhere he is mistaken, is to be trusted when he says that in his day the antecedents of the golden bough were unknown.[61] There were of course rites of fertility, in which boughs were presented, corresponding to the surviving cere-monies of the maypole and 'Jack in the Green', and perhaps comparable to the beliefs and myths connected with the mistle-toe.[62] Such suggestions are present in the Sixth *Aeneid*, but it is recognized already that Vergil must have used some unknown source of knowledge concerning the 'rites of Kore', from which he got some of the folk-lore of the golden bough; and the source may or may not have been a written document.[63]

The unique thing about the golden bough was its use as a means of crossing the waters of death. It seemed to be a kind of passport; but no other boughs known had such a function.[64] The eastern parallels are quite decisive. The Sumerian myth mentions poles for punting, cut from the forest near, like the golden bough. The Malekulan ghosts use a wand to cross rivers and to tap the canoe of a living islander on their way to the ferryman of the dead. The three myths have these things in common. (1) The travellers get specially provided sticks. (2) They must have them for their journeys. (3) Their use is to cross the waters on the way to the land of the dead. (4) They are in one way or another closely connected with boats. The affinity between the three versions is absolutely clear; but the original use has been forgotten and changed.

Two ideas are involved. The traveller wants a magic wand, which may have been a charm against water, and may have had something to do with water divining, but which more pro-bably is a symbol of fertility and an influence for life and revival.

With this idea is combined another. Just as, nearly everywhere, it has been usual to bury with the dead things which will be useful to them on their journey, so, at some unknown place and time, it seems to have been thought that the dead should carry with them some nautical instrument such as an oar or punt pole. The first idea belongs to the cave type of myth, and the second to the ocean type. When the types were combined, the oar or punt pole, and the wand or bough became one, preserving what use and attributes were best understood. But in Vergil, characteristically, nothing is wasted. What has not gone into the golden bough has been used for Palinurus the helmsman whom Aeneas meets on the way to the lower world, dead, for he fell overboard, taking the tiller with him. Clearly, this is the 'missing part of the boat' in the *Epic of Gilgamish*; and indeed, though at this point the text is obscure, the actual meaning 'paddles' for the missing part has been suggested.[65] When he redistributed the pattern, Vergil, with his usual economy, found a new place for the remaining poetic content, which the golden bough had left unexpressed.

The three myths, therefore, have the same pattern. But in each the pattern has suffered alterations and combinations before it appears in the stories. There are two principal elements.

The dead cross the sea to an island. But they also enter the earth by means of a cave. In the *Epic of Gilgamish*, Ut-napishtim lives in the Sunset Mountain corresponding to the Egyptian Sunset Mountain; but in the Sumerian version of the story of the Flood he lives in an island at the north of the Persian Gulf. This simpler account has gone to make the developed myth in the *Epic*; and there an account of the sun's journey, and also a belief that the dead lived beyond the sea to the west of Asia, have also been included, besides the originally different myth that the dead went into the earth through a cave. The separate nature of this element is seen best in Malekula, where it is original, and where it is clearly shown to have been combined afterwards with a myth of a journey above ground and across water; for the adjustments are imperfect, and the cave of the dead has lost its original importance. In the *Aeneid* the journey to the west is so obvious that it is hard to notice; for Aeneas is making that journey, as he sails from Troy. After it, he too goes underground by way of a cave. In all three journeys, also, water has to be crossed beyond the cave, with the help of a cane, bough, or poles, specially provided; and there is also open country, where the dead have peace.

There is a strong solar element in the Sumerian myth. As in Egyptian mortuary belief, where there is even more emphasis on this element, the dead seem to follow the path of the sun.[66] Solar myth is far less important among the Greeks and Romans; but there are hints of it in the Sixth *Aeneid*. The sibyl is partly priestess of Apollo, who has some solar affinity which must not be exaggerated. Like Shamash, the Sumerian sun-god, Hercules, or Heracles, has crossed the waters of death before; and according to Stesichorus[67] it was Heracles who travelled over the ocean in the 'cup' of the sun, which corresponds to the boat of the sun in Egyptian myth.[68] Characteristically, when in Vergil the sibyl says that only beings of divine descent have crossed to the land of the dead before, she adds to the description of them 'and of unvanquished might'. Vergil also, following Pindar, makes special mention of the bright sunlight in Elysium.

NOTES

1. *RE*, X (1919), *s.v. Katabasis* (Ganschinietz), 2359–2449, esp. 2449; for later work *cf*. Friedrich Pfister, *Die Religion der Griechen und Römer, Darstellung und Literaturbericht*, . . . 1918–29/30 (Leipzig, 1930) 168–9.
2. W. J. Perry, *The Children of the Sun* (London, 1923) 254–70.
3. Ibid. 255.
4. Ibid. 266.
5. Ibid. 255.
6. Ibid.
7. Ibid. 259.
8. Ibid. 255.
9. Ibid.
10. Ibid. 260.
11. W. H. R. Rivers, *The History of Melanesian Society* (Cambridge, 1914) II, 261–2; Perry (above, note 2) 261–2. We still continue these alternative beliefs in ordinary talk, for we say both 'Go west' and 'Go under' to mean 'die'.
12. *Cf*. A. M. Hocart, 'The Life-Giving Myth', *The Labyrinth* . . ., edited by S. H. Hooke (London, 1935) 261–81, explaining the creation of myth from ritual.
13. Porph. *De Antr. Nymph*. VI.
14. *The (London) Observer*, April 14, 1935, 28; I avoid the question of the cultural contacts of the Australian tribes, and indeed I am concerned much more with the development and occurrences of a certain pattern of ritual and belief than with any attempt to determine how it spread through the world or part of it.
15. Hom. *Il*. XXII, 126–7.
16. Thuc. I, 6.
17. Strab. VIII, 375.

18. Hom. *Il.* XXIV, 611; Hermann Güntert, 'Labyrinth . . .', *SHAW*, Ph.–hist. Kl. (1932/3) 1 Abh., *passim*, esp. 19.

19. Pind. *Ol.* IX, 44–6; Ov. *Met.* I, 381–415.

20. Pind. *Nem.* VI, 1.

21. Ibid. VII, 33.

22. Id. *Isthm.* I, 30; Apollodor. III, 4, 1.

23. Hom. *Od.* XI, 601–4; *cf.* G. Rachel Levy, *JHS* 54 (1934) 40–53, esp. 41–2.

24. Carlo Pascal, *Le Credenze d'Oltretomba nelle opere letterarie dell'antichità classica*[2] (Turin, 1911) I, 35–6, II, 114–16.

25. Güntert (above, note 18) *passim*, esp. 10–11, 18–19, 30–6, 41–3.

26. Plut. *Sull.* VI; Güntert (above, note 18) 10–11.

27. *Cf.* Diodor. IV, 30, 1.

28. Güntert (above, note 18) *passim*, esp. 4–6.

29. E. Kornemann, *Die Antike* 8 (1932) 105.

30. No simple theory is safe for the very complicated evidence. For the difficulties *cf.* Jacquetta Hawkes, *Antiquity* 8 (1934) 26.

31. For former comparisons of the classical myths of descent with others *cf.* reff. given in *RE*, X (1919), *s.v. Katabasis*; Eduard Norden, *Publius Vergilius Maro, Aeneis Buch VI*[3] (Leipzig, 1926); Pascal (above, note 24) II, 49 note 1; Pfister (above, note 1) 168–9.

32. A. Bernard Deacon, *Malekula, A vanishing people in the New Hebrides* (London, 1934) *passim*, and other reff. cited below. For information about the Malekulans for which I cite no ref. I am deeply indebted to the kindness of Mr John Layard, to whose brilliant investigation and reconstruction much of the knowledge of the Malekulan mortuary beliefs is due. For the first publication of the comparison here suggested *cf.* W. F. J. Knight, *TAPA* 66 (1935) 256–73. [A preliminary account of Dr Layard's Malekulan researches has now been published in *Stone Men of Malekula* (London, 1942) dealing mainly with the culture of the small island of Vao. Publication of his more detailed field work on the neighbouring small islands of Atchin and Wala is still to come. J.D.C.]

33. Deacon (above, note 32) Index *s.v.* 'stone', 'sacred stones'; John Layard, 'The Journey of the Dead', *Essays presented to C. G. Seligman* (London, 1934) *passim*, e.g. 135–6.

34. [Dr Layard writes: 'In this context "white-skinned" means "shining-skinned" or "refulgent", the whiteness referring to the "ghostly" or "pure" whiteness of the moon, or of moonlight, this symbolizing in the Malekulan mind "spirituality" or "psychic force".' J.D.C.]

35. A. Bernard Deacon, *JRAI* 64 (1934) 130 (edited by Camilla H. Wedgwood, with notes by A. C. Haddon).

36. Ibid. 129–30.

37. Ibid. 131.

38. Ibid.

39. Deacon (above, note 32) 554–6.

40. Layard (above, note 33) *passim*.

41. Ibid. 131–3.

42. Ibid. 131–2.

43. Ibid. 118–20.

44. Ibid. 131–3.

45. Ibid. 132 (quoting R. H. Codrington, *The Melanesians*, Oxford, 1891, 169).

46. Ibid.

47. Ibid. 120–2.

48. Ibid. 122–6.

49. Ibid. 126–7.

F

50. Ibid. 123 and note 1.

51. Ibid.; *cf.* 139.

52. By Mr Layard, in conversation.

53. S. H. Hooke, *Folk-Lore* 45 (1934) 195–211, citing *The Epic of Gilgamish*, translated by R. Campbell Thompson (London, 1928). I am much indebted to Professor Hooke's comparison of the Sumerian and Malekulan myths, which I only read after I had done my comparison of the Sixth *Aeneid*. I give the results of Professor Hooke's investigation here, addding further detail, and continuing his analysis. He includes Biblical material which I must leave aside. For former comparisons *cf.* P. Jensen, *Das Gilgamesch-Epos in der Weltliteratur*, I (Strassburg, 1906), II (Marburg a.L., 1929), and *RE*, X (1919) *s.v. Katabasis*.

54. Donald A. Mackenzie, *Myths of Crete and Pre-Hellenic Europe* (London, 1917) 303–4.

55. Ibid. 304.

56. Norden (above, note 31) 163–76.

57. Ibid. 120, on Verg. *Aen.* VI, 14 ff.

58. [Mrs] Margaret de G. Verrall, *CR* 24 (1910) 43–6, esp. 44.

59. W. F. J. Knight, *CR* 43 (1929) 212–13.

60. Norden (above, note 31) 163, on Verg. *Aen.* VI, 136 ff.

61. Ibid. 169–70.

62. Sir James Frazer's comparison of it with the mistletoe, whatever view is taken of his system, is on the one hand enlightening and on the other not fully satisfactory. *Cf.* Norden (above, note 31) *ad loc.*

63. Norden (above, note 31) 163–75, on Verg. *Aen.* VI, 136 ff.

64. Ibid. 173, citing Servius.

65. Thompson (above, note 53) 46 note 3.

66. A comparison of the Egyptian myths would be too long here. I refer to details when it seems necessary. For the myths *cf.* esp. Sir E. A. Wallis Budge, *From Fetish to God in Ancient Egypt* (London, 1934) 351–81.

67. Stes. fr. 8 (Bergk).

68. *Cf.* Budge (above, note 66).

II

OGYGIA

It is not easy to get on without some more help from Homer; and he can now be approached. In Homer, the pattern exists in fragments; its disintegration has gone much farther than in Vergil.

In the Eleventh *Odyssey*, Odysseus, having reached the land of the Cimmerians, 'covered with mist and cloud', beyond the streams of Oceanus, pours sacrificial blood into a trench, and talks to the ghosts who come to drink it. Half way through the book something has happened; Odysseus as he tells the tale, instead of saying 'Then up came the ghost of . . .,' as each ghost comes to the trench, begins to say 'Next I saw the ghost of . . .'; and it is clear that he is wandering about in the world below, not waiting above ground for the ghosts.[1] Here again, obviously enough, is a combination of the two types, the ocean type and the cave type. The ocean type is thought to be more Homeric, and the cave type is regarded almost as a long interpolation, of Orphic origin. Orphic belief sometimes emphasized the journey to the world below, with details to which the best parallels have been found on 'Orphic' vases in South Italy.[2]

But the Homeric myth as it is given in the Eleventh *Odyssey* would not have helped Vergil much with the structure of his lower world. Nor is it necessary to suppose that the cave type used by Homer waited for Orphism to develop. More probably descents to the lower world, which came to be considered Orphic, developed long before Orphism from simple cave myths. Orphism only adopted them, anyhow; they were not originally part of an early Orphic system.[3]

The cave element in the Eleventh *Odyssey* seems to have already reached a developed form before Homer or a predecessor blended it with an ocean myth to make the extant combined version. Therefore Vergil probably had myths of the cave type in Greek, which are now no longer extant in documents. Many 'necyiae' existed; there were several in the old Greek epic, not Homeric, which is now lost; and cave-type myths were almost inevitable for cave cults, better illustrated, as they now are, by the Malekulan evidence.

Vergil could have got the two types, which are fused in Homer, from Greek poems, and fused them again himself. The Greek types may have been near to original forms. Geography is right. There is no difficulty about underground rivers, known, of course, from Aristophanes, or about a western land of the dead. This western land of the dead, reached by Odysseus, has lately been identified as Britain, which is famous as the land of the dead to Celts,[4] unless it is more exact to say that that was the Scillies. This might show that the myth was originally European; or at least a myth affected by knowledge of north-west Europe; but even if the land of the dead was Britain to Homer, it need not have been Britain to Homer's predecessors, though even to them 'the ocean' must surely have meant the Atlantic. At least the western land as a home of the gods is old in Greece.[5] But there is still no sign of the maze or the golden bough, or of several other elements common to Vergil's and the eastern myths; and Homer's fused version is so simple that it gives no one a right to say that Vergil could find all he needed in Greek sources. Elsewhere in Greek literature the pattern is scarcely more intact.

Fragments of mortuary myths appear in other parts of the *Odyssey*. There is the 'cave of Eileithyia',[6] the goddess of birth and also of death, clearly recalling a cult of the primeval goddess from whom all come and to whom all return. There is also another not less important cave, the cave of Calypso the 'nymph', who keeps Odysseus there for seven years. Calypso is very much like a sibyl.

It is on the fringe of the Greek world that sibyls occur.[7] They are un-Greek both in nature and in name;[8] but Manto at Delphi is once called a sibyl,[9] and there is even a record that a sibyl actually prophesied against Apollo there,[10] a memory of the time when the possession of the oracle was not finally settled.

Sibyls are very ancient; and they are all partly divine instruments of necromantic prophecy, not purely upper world, Apolline prophecy.[11] This may mean that other sibylline oracles never became so strongly Hellenized as the Delphic. However, sibyls were generally connected with Apollo.[12] His cult in Asia Minor, where the earliest sibyls were, goes back to 'Homeric' times;[13] but the sibyls must have been older still, and Pausanias is probably right to say that there was a sibyl at Erythrae before the Trojan War.[14]

It has been said that the sibyl at Cumae is, strictly, Apollo's priestess only, and that Vergil himself made her Hecate's priestess also, in order that she might lead Aeneas through Hades.[15] If so, that is because Apollo's conquest was by then in appearance complete, and Vergil, by the extraordinary poetic imagination which enabled him to reconstruct ideal realities, restored a connection which was there before Apollo came.

Sibyls belong to the earth and caves. There was a cave, where the Erythraean sibyl was born, on Mount Corycus.[16] She was the daughter of a man and one of the nymphs of Ida. Not far from her home, by Marpessos, there was the river Aidoneus, which disappeared into the ground and reappeared several times.[17] The name suggests the truth, that this sibyl, like others, was in an important sense chthonic.[18] The Libyan sibyl has a valuable genealogy. She was the daughter of Lamia, who was a daughter of Poseidon:[19] Poseidon is an earth god, especially in early times, and Lamia actually means a cave.[20] There was a play by Euripides called after her, now lost.[21] In it the myth of her transformation was probably described; for this is the ghost Lamia who ate human flesh, and who was, according to Stesichorus, the mother of the cave monster Scylla.[22]

The name 'Scylla' itself is explained to be cognate with 'Skerrig', 'Skerry', and 'Scilly', all meaning 'a rock in the sea'.[23] Scylla in the *Odyssey* swallows sailors. So Lamia, a cave on land, swallows children; that is a pessimistic description of the fact that all return at death to earth, the universal mother. To be daughter of Lamia is, in a special sense, to belong to the earth and its caves.

That sibyls were not purely Apolline, but belonged to the earth in their own right, is shown by what are supposed mistaken identifications. Albunea,[24] the spirit of the prophetic cleft and spring in Latium, and another spirit, in a cave, with springs in it, under the Palatine,[25] are called sibyls. If they were prophetic personalities attached to caves and in communication with powers of earth, the name fitted them. Sibyls are not wholly human, and perhaps need not be more human than any other heroic being supposed to survive after death as a ghost. In fact, it is sometimes rather as a ghost than as a living person that

a sibyl is regarded. In historical times graves of sibyls were
known, at Gergis in the temple of Apollo,[26] and at Cumae,
where the grave was a small stone urn with bones.[27] There the
sibyl was heard, not seen;[28] Apollo married her, but she grew
old and prayed for death; and he let her voice live on after her,
echoing from the many orifices in the stone.

It is easy to miss Calypso's prophetic function in the *Odyssey*;
but it is quite clear. She prophesies to Odysseus;[29] and even her
particular epithet means something like 'eloquent', αὐδήεσσα.
This is not her only connection with sibyls. She belongs to the
earth. Her name means 'she who covers' or 'hides',[30] and it has
been supposed that Homer invented her and her name simply to
use her to delay the return of Odysseus. She has been considered
as merely the double of Circe, and the name of her island
Ogygia has been thought to be the double of Circe's land,
Aeaea, and indeed to be derived from the same northern root,
a root meaning no more than 'land'.[31] Aeaea has however also
been derived from a Semitic word meaning 'hawk';[32] the very
meaning of Circe's name in Greek, except that, on this theory,
the Greek common noun, the same for both masculine and
feminine, has been equated with the Semitic word by being
given a special feminine termination in '-e'. This is of great interest, if it could be more certain. But even if it is not true, it is
probable that Vergil thought it was true. He mentions 'the
island of Aeaean Circe', 'Aeaeaeque insula Circae'.[33] It is suggested that in so repeating what is said to be the same idea in
adjective and noun he displays ignorance of this possible meaning.[34] More probably, he displays knowledge of it; for it is his
way to use words 'etymologically', and especially to reproduce
the meaning of a noun in an adjective chosen for it, a true and
legitimate exploration of poetic resource.[35] But, whatever is the
truth about Aeaea, Ogygia has lately received a clearer account.[36] The name is from an adjective meaning 'of the earth';
and Calypso has been proved to be an old death goddess, whose
name means 'she who hides' the dead in the earth, and is
ultimately cognate with our word 'Hell'.[37]

Clearly, a 'journey of the dead' is an important constituent of
the *Odyssey*. Odysseus sails over western waters, and enters a
cave of the goddess who hides the dead in the earth; and that is
like the Malekulan pattern. This is not all. Gilgamish, coming

to the Waters and the Tree of Life, meets Sidurri Sabîtu, whose first name has been translated 'ale wife', and who has in her gift some kind of strong drink. Her Greek equivalent was originally thought to be Calypso, but lately she has been regarded as nearer to Circe, who also dispensed a strong drink, which effected magical transformations. According to the usual complications, Sidurri is nearly certain to be partly both. Her second name helps.[38] It is convincingly equated with the Semitic Sa(m)bethe, the name of the 'Jewish Sibyl', and a form of the word 'sibyl' itself. Other names in Greek mortuary myth have been traced to Semitic words; they are 'Erebos'[39] and 'Acheron',[40] both originally meaning 'west', and Oceanus itself;[41] not to mention the word 'labyrinth', which on one theory comes from a Semitic word for various internal organs of the human anatomy.[42] Of this there will be more to say. What matters now is that Sabîtu really seems to have the same name as the sibyls, and also some of the nature of Calypso. How nearly Calypso actually is Vergil's sibyl is disclosed by Dio Cassius.[43] He seems to say that there was a goddess of water and of the earth in western Italy, actually called Calypso; that she was worshipped at Lake Avernus which was sacred to her; and that here Odysseus came. The whole story could hardly be more precisely told. The Cumaean sibyl is then Vergil's, and indeed in all probability Homer's, Calypso, the guardian of the cave; she is part of Sidurri; but Vergil does not forget the other part of her, for he places Circe on the coast of Italy, to be passed by Aeneas on his right as he sails, not long before he comes to Cumae and the cave.

That sibyls belong to what may be called a stone daemonology is shown by the account of the Idaean sibyl given by Pausanias.[44] She was born in a cave, in which were statues of the nymphs; they belong to a very old layer of belief, and like sibyls, or indeed Temes Savsap, are only in part divine, for they are liable to death. The Idaean sibyl prophesied standing on stone. With her in her cave was a stone Hermes. Now Hermes is one of the Greek divinities nearest to the stone culture. His name seems to denote some kind of fixed standing stone; that is what he was at first, a reason he has so many different meanings, which bewildered antiquity.[45] Among other things he is a grave-stone; obviously a monolith 'spirit house', half remembered in the 'herms' of classical times, stone blocks sculptured to a head only at the top, as monoliths are sculptured in the Pacific still. Hermes is a male partner of the guardian of the cave, the sibyl.[46] It is not surprising that in classical myth he guided ghosts to Hades, or evoked them from there.

There is a descendant of the female petromorphic spirit still farther to the west in one or more of the personalities called 'Cailleach',[47] which means 'old woman', by the Celts, who of course, like other people, believed in a world of the dead below.

Like the madly prophetic sibyls, there is a Cailleach with a 'roaring mouth', associated with water. She (or another) had seven periods of youth; and she appears before a hero as a repulsive hag and suddenly transforms herself into a beautiful girl. Sibyls too had an ambiguous longevity in myth; and there was doubt whether they should be pictured as young and beautiful, or old. Like the nymphs with whom the Idaean sibyl is associated, sibyls are not quite immortal.

Nor is the Malekulan guardian Temes Savsap; or in one form the Celtic Cailleach, who is said to have been transformed into a standing stone, looking out over the sea. This happened after she had thrown away her magic wand, with which she struck standing stones, and turned them into fully armed warriors. Again she is like Temes Savsap, who was fought and defeated by one of the dead, with the result that the rock which represented her fell into the sea. Her power of transforming stones into men recalls the legends of 'stone men' in Greece, and the earth-born men there, sprung from the dragon's teeth.

The persistence of the faith in monoliths is shown by the tradition of the alchemists.[48] The monolith ancestor god became the 'philosopher's stone'. In Salomon Trismosin's *Aureum Vellus* (1598) there is a symbolic picture of the Hermetic Spring which is 'surmounted by a royal crown . . . in conformity with the tradition of the alchemists, most of whom call the stone "our great King" '. In Limojon de Saint-Didier's *Le Triomphe Hermétique* (1710) there are depicted two caverns, with a Latin legend: 'He who is the stone whom we must worship is hidden in the caverns of the metals' (or 'of the mines').[49] It is doubtful whether the same tradition helped to form the conception of St Peter, the Rock, guardian of the gate of Heaven, against whom the gates of Hell shall not prevail.[50] The words about St Peter in the New Testament are a quotation from the Old; there they refer to the foundation stone of the temple at Jerusalem, which separated the temple from the waters of the abyss below the earth. This seems to be a different kind of stone, effective and in a sense divine though it may have been considered to be.[51]

But it is hard to deny altogether that the old stone daemonology has coalesced with other thoughts into the poetic symbol of the rock—now almost fixed as 'The Rock' by the culmination of the symbol's history in Eliot's work. Rocks are very frequent in Eliot, changing in colour and form with the poetic mood, until the red rocks of *The Waste Land* and the blue, cool rocks of *Ash Wednesday* become, in his church 'pageant-play' *The Rock* (1934), the Rock which is St Peter; and St Peter was portrayed in the first production with the formality of a petromorphic spirit or herm. Again, in Auden's *The Witnesses* the rocks are there, guardian rocks each side of the path to the wilderness. It is not even really fanciful to wonder, not whether, but by what history and in what sense, Leonardo's Madonna of the Rocks, remembered by Eliot, is herself a sibyl.[52]

There is another cave in Homer, the cave of the Cyclops. For Greeks, caves and walls belong to Cyclopes, which would have been surprising, if it had not been for the identification of them with the stone men, already noted for both walls and caves.[53] A Cyclops is a man, who by the action of legendary wonder has grown to be more than a man, and who builds Cyclopean walls, and makes or uses caves under the earth. The name Cyclops comes from the adjective 'Cyclopean', which means little more than 'circular', and is applied to 'ring walls'.[54] Now the name seems to have been applied to men of an ousted population here and there in Greece, of a lower civilization than the true Greeks, and of a different physical type, perhaps rather like Socrates. Homer describes their lawless ways. That is, the old people who built the walls were known both in the legendary form of monsters with one eye, and also as a surviving class of ordinary, if inferior, human beings.[55] It is as ordinary but violent human beings that the Cyclopes drive Nausithous from his old home, wherever that was, to Scheria.[56] Such survivals are argued for Britain, where it is thought that a stone-age folk lingered in small groups, helping to create the folk-lore of dangerous fairies.[57] Strangely, such a group is said to have existed at Cumae, where they were still more strangely called Cimmerians.[58] As human beings, the Cyclopes were believed to have come from Lycia, and to have built the ring wall for Proetus at Tiryns.[59]

The Cyclopes in the *Odyssey* may therefore represent the old stone folk who built the walls, but they are a blend of their surviving, disparaged selves, and their monstrously idealized ancestors. There are, however, further blends.

The next thing is the eye of the Cyclops. Babies are of course occasionally born with one central eye. The old men may have had large, round eyes. The meaning of the act of Odysseus in piercing the eye of a Cyclops has been guessed to be this. The real act of Odysseus was to pierce the Cyclopean wall of Troy at the capture of the city; it is noticed that he manipulated the wooden horse, and that he was persecuted by the gods who were the gods of the Trojan wall, Poseidon and Apollo. The wall of Troy could perfectly well be called a 'Cyclopean circle'; and that could equally mean, also perfectly well, the eye of a Cyclops. This created the legend, with an easy adoption of the widely known folk-tale of 'No man' which elsewhere, so far as I know, except for the *Arabian Nights*, which may have been influenced by the *Odyssey*, does not say that the villain's eye was put out.[60]

But a new discovery has just been reported.[61] On a Babylonian relief, centuries older than Homer, an armed god is shown killing a creature that has one eye and is identified as a fire god: two attributes of the Cyclopes, on the more mythical side of their nature. They are partly human and distantly historical; and partly also they are eastern gods, passed on like others to Greek tradition.

This is not all that can have helped to make the story. At the same time, the eye of a Cyclops, living in the west, and throwing rocks and endangering travellers, means the crater of a volcano. This is usually, and rightly, said. It immediately suggests the volcanic entrances to the underworld which are known to the 'archaic' myths.

The Cyclopes, well known at first as hard workers above ground and in a human fashion below ground, became famous afterwards for their imaginary supernatural work at the bottom

of volcanoes. Besides other things, a Cyclops is a volcano and his
eye a crater. Now on Ambrim the dead live on or in a volcano.
There may be an echo of such a myth in Vergil. For round
Elysium, corresponding to the 'high fence' surrounding the land
of the dead of Seniang, are walls either 'built high' or 'forged
out' by the Cyclopes.[62] The word is 'educta'; probably it is a
fine Vergilian ambiguity, meaning both things at once. However, the Cyclopean walls are new. What they mean cannot be
asserted; but there are several things that they might mean, and
probably they mean them all. The walls correspond to the 'high
fence' of a very early myth. They also correspond to the 'orbes
aenei', kept in the temple of Jupiter as god of oaths;[63] effective
symbols of binding and constraint, fixing an oath on earth, and
fixing the state of the blessed below. Seven such bands are also
on the shield of Aeneas, made by Cyclopes.[64] Next, the work of
the Cyclopes in the world below may well mean that Vergil is
giving what is partly their myth; that he is setting forth truth as
old as the old men of stone, perhaps of the very same lineage as
the surviving 'Cimmerians' of Cumae, from whom he may even
have gained some secrets, which others did not know. This,
however, is only a possibility.

On his last journey, according to Homer,[65] Odysseus will
carry an oar, travelling inland, until he is told by a man he
meets that he is carrying a winnowing fan on his strong shoulder.
Of course the oar is to cross the river or ocean of death; and it
has been confused with the 'mystic winnowing fan of Iacchus',
which was important in rites of fertility. Obviously, too, it is to
cross the waters of death that Aeneas plants on the grave of
Misenus the oar that he used.[66] Here is one of the surprises; the
oar of Misenus is part of the golden bough.

In Greek myth there are now signs of many of the common
elements, but not of all, and not of the golden bough as a passport, except in so far as the oars of Odysseus and Misenus go
some of the way to meet the 'maypole' folk-lore which helped to
form the conception. The oars are also represented by the helm
carried by Palinurus with him as he fell overboard, the counterpart of the missing gear of the boat of Gilgamish. That it really
is this will, I think, be admitted immediately by those who have
chanced to develop their intuition for Vergil's sources. The gap
is where the ideas of the magic wand and the dead man's double

should come. Vergil practically calls the bough a magic wand, 'fatalis uirga'; and it is surely as his double that Aeneas carries it to Proserpina as his gift to her and fixes it to the lintel. For these two ideas, especially, no link seems known; apparently Vergil had knowledge of them from secret traditions left behind in Italy or Greece.[67] Or he may have acquired his knowledge from eastern doctrines, such as the death myth lately identified in Elijah's story, and in the folk-lore of Aaron's rod.[68] But no known material would fully supply the pattern as it appears in the *Aeneid* and in Malekula.

In the three 'journeys of the dead', the Vergilian, the Malekulan, and the Sumerian, the combination of elements is complete at the start; they have approximately the same conflation of 'cave' and 'ocean' myths, even down to similar incoherences. Apparently there was a single original for all three, an original which was already composite; though in a long and complicated history countless adjustments, many of them adjustments to local geography, must have been made. There is interest in the crossing of water; and in this question it is hard to resist the temptation to ask how the combined myth first arose.

NOTES

1. Vittorio D. Macchioro, *CP* 23 (1928) 239–49.
2. Ibid.
3. *Cf.* W. K. C. Guthrie, *Orphism and Greek Religion* (London, 1935) 52–3; *cf.* also, on the history of eschatology from Homer to Orphism, Carlo Pascal, *Le Credenze d'Oltretomba* . . .[2] (Turin, 1911) I, 163–93.
4. R. Hennig, *Die Geographie des homerischen Epos* (Leipzig, 1934) 50.
5. Sam Wide, in A. Gercke and E. Norden, *Einleitung in die Altertumswissenschaft*, II[2] (Leipzig, 1912) 185; M. P. Nilsson, *A History of Greek Religion* (Oxford, 1925) 23, says that the isles of the blest are pre-Hellenic.
6. Hom. *Od.* XIX, 188.
7. R. H. Klausen, *Aeneas und die Penaten* (Hamburg and Gotha, 1839–40) I, 203–318; L. Malten, *ARW* 29 (1931) 37.
8. *RE*, II.A (1923) 2075 (A. Rzach).
9. Klausen (above, note 7) I, 215.
10. Clem. *Strom.* I, 323c.
11. Klausen (above, note 7) I, 224.
12. Malten (above, note 7) 37.
13. Ibid. with reff.
14. Paus. X, 12, 2; *cf.* Schol. Plat. *Phaedr.* 244B.
15. Eduard Norden, *P. Vergilius Maro, Aeneis Buch VI*[3] (Leipzig, 1926) 118, on Verg. *Aen.* VI, 35.
16. Paus. X, 12, 7.

17. Ibid. 12, 3–4.
18. Klausen (above, note 7) I, 207.
19. Plut. *De Pyth. Orac.* IX; Paus. X, 12, 1.
20. *Et. mag. s.v.*: σημαίνει τὰ χάσματα.
21. Schol. Plat. *Phaedr.* 244B; Lact. I, 6, 8.
22. Philostr. *Vit. Apoll.* IV, 25; Klausen (above, note 7) I, 207.
23. J. Rendel Harris, *Scylla and Charybdis* (Manchester, 1925) *passim*, esp. 1–8.
24. Varro *ap.* Lact. I, 6, 12.
25. Schol. Plat. *Phaedr.* 244B.
26. Steph. Byz. *s.v.* Γέργις, citing Phlegon.
27. Paus. X, 12, 8; Schol. Lycophr. 1278.
28. Ov. *Met.* XIV, 152–3; Serv. Verg. *Aen.* VI, 321.
29. Hom. *Od.* V, 206–7.
30. Hermann Güntert, *Kalypso* (Halle, 1919) 28–36.
31. J. Rendel Harris, *Apollo's Birds* (Manchester, 1925) 39–42.
32. Victor Bérard, *Calypso et la Mer de l'Atlantide* (Paris, 1929) 293; id. *Nausicaa et le Retour d'Ulysse* (Paris, 1929) 287–8, 486–8.
33. Verg. *Aen.* III, 386.
34. Aurelio Espinosa Pólit, S. J., *Virgilio, el poeta y su misión providencial* (Quito, 1932) 69 note 2 cont. 70.
35. Bernhard Rehm, *Philologus*, Suppl. 24 (1932) 27–40, 103–6; W. F. J. Knight, *CR* 48 (1934) 124–5.
36. Güntert (above, note 30) 167–70.
37. Ibid. 36–44.
38. Ibid. 24–5, with reff.; Güntert, 25 note 2, admits with Zimmern the probability that the names Sa[m]bethe, Sibylla, and Sabîtu are akin, but does not admit the connection of these personalities with Calypso.
39. Harris (above, note 23) 24–5, citing Bérard.
40. Pascal (above, note 3) I, 37 after Lewy.
41. O. Gruppe, *Griechische Mythologie und Religionsgeschichte* (Munich, 1906) II, 1113; Charon is Egyptian according to Diodorus, I, 92, 2; 96, 8.
42. E. Hommel, *OLZ* 22 (1919) 64. See below, Ch. VII, esp. pp. 231–3.
43. Dio Cassius, XLVIII, 50: ἐργαζομένων δ'αὐτῶν εἰκών τις ὑπὲρ τῆς 'Αουερνίδος, εἴτ' οὖν τῆς Καλυψοῦς, ἢ τὸ χωρίον ἀνατιθέασιν, ἐς ὃ καὶ τὸν 'Οδυσσέα ἐσπλεῦσαι λέγουσιν, εἴτε καὶ ἑτέρας τινὸς ἡρωίνης οὖσα, ἱδρῶτος ὥσπερ τι σῶμα ἀνθρώπινον ἀνεπλήσθη. On this *cf.* Güntert (above, note 30) 13: 'Ob das Standbild das Kalypsos war, ist ganz gleichgültig; beweisend ist, dass an einer Stelle, die seit alters als Eingang zur Unterwelt galt, dort wo die Sibylle hauste und der finstere Hain der Hekate lag, auch ein Kult Kalypsos bezeugt ist.'
44. Paus. X, 12.
45. *Cf. RE*, VIII (1912) *s.v.* (S. Eitrem).
46. The Cumaean sibyl had once the apotropaic name of Taraxandra, 'she who alarms men' (Schol. Plat. *Phaedr.* 244B), which suggests the severity of a guardian at a gate.
47. D. A. Mackenzie, *Myths of Crete and Pre-Hellenic Europe* (London, 1917) 67–9, 183.
48. Grillot de Givry, *Witchcraft, Magic and Alchemy*, translated from the French by J. Courtenay Locke (London, 1931) 360–1.
49. Ibid. with figs. 337 and 338.
50. *Cf.* F. Muller, Jun., *Mnemosyne* Ser. III, 2 (1935) 207 note 2.
51. Eric Burrows, S. J., 'Some cosmological Patterns in Babylonian Religion', *The Labyrinth* . . . , edited by S. H. Hooke (London, 1935) 57–9, comparing Isaiah xxviii, 16, with Matth. xvi, 18.

52. [See also Grover Smith, 'T. S. Eliot's Lady of the Rocks', *Notes and Queries* 194 (1949) 123–5, with its reff. to *Cumaean Gates*. J.D.C.]

53. H. Güntert, *SHAW*, Ph.-hist. Kl. (1932/3) 1 Abh.

54. See above, pp. 133–4, note 194.

55. J. L. Myres, *Who Were the Greeks?* (Berkeley, California, 1930) 18, 306.

56. Hom. *Od.* VI, 1–10.

57. M. A. Murray, *The God of the Witches* (London, 1931) 39–60.

58. Strab. V, 244; Pliny, *N.H.* III, 5, 9; Klausen (above, note 7) I, 209.

59. Paus. II, 16, 6; 25, 8.

60. W. F. J. Knight, *Folk-Lore* 46 (1935) 118–19, with reff.

61. Henri Frankfort, *The Times*, 1 August, 1936, 13–14.

62. Verg. *Aen.* VI, 630–1.

63. Franz Altheim, *Römische Religionsgeschichte*, I (Leipzig, 1931) 103.

64. Verg. *Aen.* VIII, 447–9.

65. Hom. *Od.* XI, 128; XXIII, 275.

66. Verg. *Aen.* VI, 232–5.

67. G. Funaioli, *L'Oltretomba nell'Eneide di Virgilio* (Palermo, 1924) 23–4, supposes that Avernus had a folk-lore of its own: 'La mossa di principio avvia al regno del fantastico, sulla solida base di secolari narrazioni e credenze: quello che il poeta vede e canta ha, di nuovo, tutta l'apparenza del vero. Accreditata dai sussulti vulcanici del suolo, dalle mefitiche esalazioni lacustri, dalle solitudini selvose, da caverne sotterranee, invalse diffusamente l'opinione fra gli Italici che presso il lago Averno in Campania fosse l'ingresso dell'Ade . . .: spelonche, burroni, cisterne, profondità della terra insomma, immettono di frequente laggiù, nelle concezioni e nei racconti popolari . . .; e presso l'Averno, fin dai tempi più antichi, esisteva un oracolo dei morti, e ancora all'età di Varrone e di Lucrezio si favoleggiava di volatili ivi precipitanti senza vita nelle acque, e vi si facevano scongiuri di anime.'

68. S. H. Hooke, *Folk-Lore* 45 (1934) 201–4.

III

ELEUSIS

That the underground rivers of the classical underworld are not original, but have taken the place of ocean in the myths, has been recognized.[1]

They look like an adjustment, to keep the cave and the crossing of water too. The Malekulans have real rivers, not underground, but sometimes beyond the cave. There seems little point in the rivers, as they are; especially as the dead cross the sea as well, and it is for crossing the sea that their 'ferrymen of the dead' is imagined. Elsewhere in the Pacific area the ferryman transports the dead over a river. Apparently the Malekulan myth once had rivers underground, but they were afterwards conceived to be above ground, so that they could be fitted into real geography. The cave at least is original, since anyhow the dead go into the earth. It is less clear why water should be crossed. Tribes which have migrated are known to believe that their dead return to the old home by crossing the sea. This may possibly be the origin of the idea everywhere. The next step is to suppose that the dead enter the earth in their new home, where of course they are buried. This means that either they cross rivers before they enter the earth, or, if they still cross the sea, they must cross it, irrationally, afterwards. These two possibilities, combined in a natural attempt at adjustment, result in a theory of underground rivers beyond the cave.

But another manner of development cannot be left out of account. Myths in general, and perhaps myths of creation and death in particular, arose in at least some places in a remarkable way.[2] They describe ritual, which itself describes the world, and action designed to 'create' the world for certain special purposes. For example, the sun in a myth is not so much the real sun as a human officiant, representing the sun in ritual; and so also a sacral king and queen, in their sacral marriage, may in myth be described as the heaven and the earth, which in some sense they represent. It is noticed that in some languages of the Pacific the word for 'create' means to effect or affect by sacrifice, to the complete exclusion of the idea of creating out of nothing. The most important thing now is the 'creation' of the universe by the construction of an altar or tomb. This is specifically asserted in India. 'As to why he [the builder of an altar] encloses the household altar with enclosing stones, that household altar is this world, the enclosing stones are the waters; he extends the waters round the world. It is the ocean he thus extends round it; on all sides, therefore the ocean flows round the world on all sides; clockwise, therefore the ocean goes round the world clockwise.'[3] The altar may belong to a barrow tomb; and together the tomb and altar represent, and are even thought to cause, the world, surrounded by the ocean. In the same way, the old German cosmology of the earth surrounded by the sides, therefore the ocean flows round the world on all sides; tomb. The world tree, Ygdrasil, is really the tree planted on a barrow. The German myth, like others, 'is a very bad description of the world, so bad that one wonders how anybody could have imagined it, but it is an excellent description of our circular mound enclosed by a ditch representing the Ocean, and by a railing to keep out the lurking demons, surmounted by the sacred tree which overshadows the enclosure of the gods on the top and with its roots penetrates down to the earth and what is beneath'.[4]

The picture of the world presented by a myth may, therefore, be mediated by the ritual of the tomb. A myth that seems to describe something else may be conditioned by the form in which the tomb is built, and by the ritual with which the tomb is tended; the ritual being meant for the preservation of the efficacy of the king buried in the tomb, which is a centre of the life and prosperity of the community,[5] or for the 'initiation', in some sense, of individuals. How near such 'initiation' is to classical Italy is shown by the probability that the very word in English comes from a special use of the Latin word 'inire', 'enter', to signify 'ritual entry into the earth'.[6] Two hundred years ago it was acutely seen that there is a strong element of 'initiation' in the Sixth *Aeneid*,[7] but the discovery was exaggerated and has been mistrusted. The 'archaic' myths support the truth of it: and it must not be forgotten that Porphyry says that according to Eubulus, Zoroaster, when he was the first to consecrate a natural cave 'in the Persian mountains' to sacred purposes, made it to represent the whole universe.[8] That is, a cave

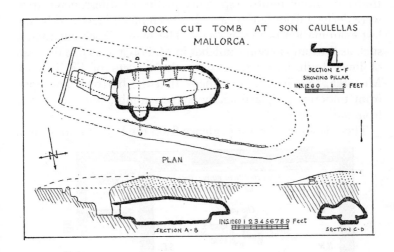

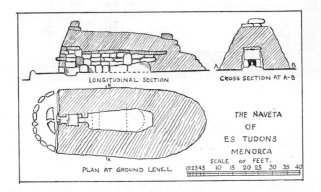

FIGURE 2

The Rock-cut Tomb at Son Caulellas, Mallorca, and the Naveta of
Es Tudons, Menorca, showing the probability that burial barrows
developed from the subterranean tombs and ultimately from caves
(after W. J. Hemp, *Proceedings of the Prehistoric Society*, I, 1935, Plate
IX, Fig. 1, facing p. 110, and Fig. 2, p. 111).

can carry the cosmic symbolism of a built tomb. The probability
that megalithic tombs, especially in the Mediterranean area,
were derived from burial caves has been much increased by the
last examination of the problem. The plan of rock-cut tombs,
such as the tomb at Son Caulellas in Mallorca, is so like the plan
of long, built barrows, such as the Naveta of Es Tudons,
Menorca, that it is hard to deny that the barrows developed
from underground, artificially shaped tombs, and ultimately
from natural caves.[9]

There is some relevant evidence from the hall of initiation in

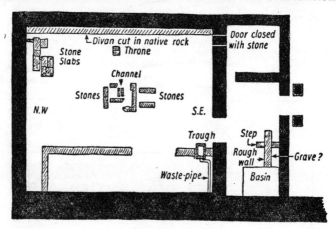

FIGURE 3

Plan of the Hall of Initiation in the Sanctuary of Men, excavated in
1912 and 1913 (from W. M. Ramsay, *BSA* 18(1911–12)41, Fig. 1;
with acknowledgment to the British School of Archaeology at
Athens).

the Phrygian mysteries at Antioch.[10] Firstly, it was called a
'cave', ἄντρον. The first two letters of the word depend on a
restoration of an inscription, which may be considered certain.[11]
Interestingly, the comment given on the use of the name 'cave'
is the suggestion that the word could be used for any building,
above or below ground. The point is rather that 'cave' is an
appropriate name for a hall of initiation, beyond all other
buildings. The hall here has in fact been compared with the
'cave' of Mithras and the Christian Bethlehem. As Porphyry
says, caves are the right places for initiations. The building

represented what had originally been a cave. Inside, on the left as the hall is entered, was a high shallow trough for preliminary purification. Farther inside must have been the usual 'lake', λίμνη, like a Roman 'impluvium'; there is at least a trace of it in a water channel.

An Orphic fragment[12] gives these directions to the dead initiate entering Hades. 'You will find a spring on the left as you go in, and a white cypress by it. Go not near the spring. You will find another, cool water flowing from the Lake of Memory. There are guardians in front of it. You must say "I am the child of earth and starry heaven; but of the heaven is my lineage. . . . I am withered by thirst. . . . Give me cool water quick from the Lake of Memory." ' This is ritual turning into myth. Pausanias discloses similar circumstances at the prophetic cave of Trophonius. The water near the entrance in the Orphic fragment is Lethe, water of oblivion, not however in its late identification with a river. Pausanias[13] says that those who entered the cave of Trophonius for prophecy first drank Lethe, to forget their former thoughts, and then the water of memory, to remember the prophecy, which was communicated in a dream during sleep.

The Phrygian mysteries have more help to give.[14] In a different inscription final initiation is indicated by the word ἐνεβάτευσε, 'he stepped on', a word appropriate to stepping on to a ship or on to a road. 'The entrance on a new life, the settlement in a new home—that is ἐμβατεῦσαι' (an infinitive of the same verb).[15] 'To be identified with the god and goddess was the goal of human life. The goal was attained, as many epitaphs in Phrygia show, at blissful death, when the dead returns to the mother who bore him; and it was attained also as the result of initiation and *Embateuein*' (another infinitive, transliterated).[16] One of the epitaphs says 'ἐκ γῆς εἰς γῆν τἀγαθά', 'from the earth come good things and to the earth they go'. This word for 'entry on' or 'stepping onto' like the Latin 'inire', 'to enter', was originally an expression of the primeval thought of 'entry' into the earth, or any new life, which is consequently the truest meaning of our word 'initiation' also. That is not all. The same idea is expressed exactly on coins of Asia Minor, to mean the act of colonization;[17] that is, setting foot on a new life in a new home, again just one of the sorts of initiation which Aeneas undergoes, when he sails to his Western Land.

The Phrygian mysteries indicate that the simple entry into the cave is not lost in developed Greek belief. Next, the Orphic myth corresponds with the built hall of initiation, developed from the cave. The waters of forgetfulness and memory are in the same places in both. At death, an initiate need not, apparently, drink the first; it is to be supposed that this is excused by his initiation. The evidence suggests that in Greek religion as elsewhere mortuary and initiation ritual created myth; and that myths of descent to the world below are indirect descriptions, mediated by ritual versions of the hall of initiation, and ultimately the built tomb and the cave. The cave of Trophonius, compared with the other facts, is evidence that originally earth-prophecy shared with initiations and myths of descent a common derivation from the primary cult of caves and tombs. When the Orphic calls himself child of earth and heaven, he refers to the marriage of heaven and earth. They are the 'great gods' of the Samothracian mysteries, who seem to be a necessary part of the primary beliefs.[18] The earth, as mother of all, has the sky for her husband.

Of the ritual actions belonging to caves in antiquity not much is known.[19] Caves were entrances to the earth conceived as universal mother. To assist the process of fertilization from the sky magically, double axes, which are the almost universal symbol of the imaginary 'thunderbolt' and therefore of the real lightning stroke, were thrown into caves. They are found inside the Cretan caves in great numbers. Axes of course 'split', like lightning and meteorites. So general and explicit was this conception of the earth in early times that it gave the name Delphi to the most famous chasm of all; for Delphi means the female generative organ, and is the same word from which the Greek for 'brother', ἀδελφός, is derived.[20] Plato himself writes that women, in conception, imitate the earth, and that it is not true to say it the other way round, that the earth copies the women.[21]

Now the motherhood of earth is relevant not only to marriage and birth but to death also. There is strong reason to think that some barrows in Britain were designed to represent the anatomy of a mother, in whom the dead might rest, in a pre-natal condition.[22]

To many peoples at an early stage of development all the

phases of life are passed with ceremonies of initiation or 'threshold rites', and they are all rituals of rebirth. At each stage a
man is reborn; and this applies to death. At death men are
consigned to the earth, the universal mother from whom all
came. They return to the earth, to be reborn. That this was the
outlook of the Greeks, at least of some of them at an early time, if
not of all at all times, is known, and does not need new proof.[23]
The belief is most clearly expressed in the famous mystic formula
ὑπὸ κόλπον ἔδυν χθονίας βασιλείας,[24] 'I have entered beneath
the lap of the queen of the earth below.' It means that the
initiate is qualified for spiritual rebirth. Whether physical birth
was enacted for this may be doubted. The enactment of it was,
however, emphasized in Egyptian mysteries,[25] and known in
Greek civil law; for when a man was wrongly supposed dead, he
had to go through the movements of physical birth before he
could be officially readmitted to life.[26] At Eleusis there was a
sacred marriage, and the announcement was made that Brimo
had borne a son Brimos. The Eleusinian Mysteries closely correspond in details and intention with savage initiations;[27] and
there is sufficient evidence to justify the theory that developed
Greek initiation contained the idea of rebirth by entry into the
earth, originally by a cave.

The principle of initiation by a form of rebirth into a new
phase of life is far more general, even in civilized modern countries, than is easily suspected. One of the best instances is coronation,[28] partly because in many places ordinary initiates were
crowned as kings to entitle them to enter the next stage of their
life. Both coronation and death meant rebirth, sometimes specifically imagined as rebirth in the form of a baby. One of the
most impressive survivals of this is the fact that the coronation
robes in England can be shown to represent symbolically the
condition of a baby at birth.[29] The nature and affiliation of such
threshold rites has been traced among modern peoples of the
Pacific and elsewhere. 'The conception of death as a rebirth is
one of the most widespread, and the Fijians were no strangers to
it, for in Nakelo when a chief dies "they conduct the body to the
river-side where the ghostly ferryman comes to ferry Nakelo
ghosts across the stream. As they attend the chief on his last
journey, they hold their great fans close to the ground to
shelter him, because 'His soul is only a little child'. " '[30] Initia-

tion is normally derived from installation.[31] Adolescent initiation involves rebirth. For example, among the Kipsiki of Kenya Colony 'the ceremonies seem to indicate a return to pre-natal condition by the mother's skirt being worn over the body'.[32]

Initiation by rebirth is not less Christian.[33] In early centuries, 'catechumens underwent their baptismal rebirth in the waters of regeneration, whence they emerged as new creatures, as from a spotless womb, ready to receive their unction to complete their initiation as citizens of the heavenly kingdom'.[34] Men 'could become raised to the supernatural order by a process of initiation, and so attain immortal life. This was the theme of the Pauline doctrine of rebirth, according to which the catechumen by being baptized into the death of Christ passed through a mystic grave to a newness of life. . . . As in other initiation ceremonies, the catechumen died and was reborn a "new creature".'[35]

The earth cults and mortuary myths of ancient Mediterranean lands and elsewhere persistently suggest a certain anatomical symbolism. Positive knowledge is incomplete. There is, however, some.

Greeks in classical times knew the conception of the earth as a mother, whose travail was copied by human women, and to whom the dead returned, a conception practically used for initiation. Ovid writes of the entrails of the earth[36] and the entrails of the god Hades are mentioned in the Greek Anthology.[37] That the whole universe had human shape was certainly an Asiatic belief in times before the Trojan War. An interesting example of the effect of this belief on Greeks and Romans is the use in Babylonian, Greek, and Latin of the same word for the palate of the mouth and the universe or sky.[38] In Latin the word is mundus, which seems to be at least cognate with the French for 'world', 'monde', and the German for 'mouth', 'mund'. That the dead enter the body of a living being is almost a commonplace of eastern myth; the entry of Jonah into the whale is only one example of many, and the conception is emphasized in several forms by Egyptian belief.[39] Osiris himself surrounds the lower world; and the earth is considered to be a god, Geb, married to a goddess, Nut, who is the sky.[40] The Egyptians are unusual here, because elsewhere the earth is predominantly the goddess. Perhaps they affected the Greeks, who regarded the earth as a mother, but could say that to be within the earth was to be in the entrails of the god Hades.[41]

This physical human nature, certainly to some extent attributed to earth, explains classical references. Deucalion had to throw the 'bones of his mother', that is, stones, over his shoulder, to repeople the earth. This is well understood; and indeed Deucalion's name is thought to contain the root of a word meaning 'stone', as in λευσίμος, an adjective meaning 'by stoning', applied to death, the λ, *l*, having become δ, *d*.[42] Of the others, two are worth noticing, because they have not so far as I know been so explained before. One belongs to the Corycian and Olbian caves in Cilicia. 'In the battle of the gods and giants, which was fought out in Egypt, Typhon hugged Zeus in his snaky coils, wrested from him his crooked sword, and with the blade cut the sinews of the god's hands and feet. Then, taking him on his back, he conveyed the mutilated deity across the sea to Cilicia, and deposited him in the Corycian cave. Here, too, he hid the severed sinews, wrapt in a bear's skin. But Hermes and Aegipan contrived to steal the missing thews and restore them to their divine owner.'[43] Now the conjecture that such stories arise from large fossilized bones of prehistoric animals found in caves is unproved; and a likelier account is that the caves were in fact entrances to the body of the earth mother or of a male divinity such as Hades.[44]

Secondly: at three places where sibyls were there was red earth. The places are near Cumae, near Marpessos, and in Epirus.[45] Sibyls are intimately connected with this same religion of caves; and it is not a rash guess to see in the red earth a material interpreted as the very blood of the earth mother.

From 'initiation', cave prophecy can be derived; for if a cave was an entrance to the land of the dead, it was access also to truth which great men of the past, now ghosts in the world below, could tell. There may have been added a belief that the sound of running water in caves was able to communicate prophecy. The muses were at first water spirits. At any rate, earth is generally prophetic, as in the *Niebelungenlied* and other northern folk-lore. There still survives in poetry the notion of 'the prophetic soul of the wide world dreaming on things to come'. Prophetic caves became famous, without remaining subject to chthonic powers alone. At Delphi Apollo was supreme in fully Hellenic times. But Aeschylus, at the beginning of the *Eumenides*, clearly remembers that the oracle belonged first to Earth, whom he calls 'primal prophetess', πρωτόμαντις, then to Themis, who is near to identity with Earth, and lastly to Phoebe, who gave the shrine to Phoebus as a 'birth gift'. Phoebe may be already the moon, and if so is comparable to the crescent in a labyrinth on a Cretan coin; she is at any rate earth-born, a Titanis, for Aeschylus says so. Why the female personality should have been projected into the moon, as well as the earth, is not yet certain; the explanation by means of a dual world egg is probably a late attempt at reconciliation. It is more certain that all these forms of the earth goddess at Delphi are the female partners in the cosmic sacral marriage. Another of them, killed by Apollo according to the Homeric Hymn to him, was Telphousa; and her name, cognate with Delphi itself, connotes with Delphi the female generative organ.

It is a central part of the design of Aeschylus to reconcile the powers of the dark below with the powers of the light above. By facing this fierce antinomy he found his solution to the riddle of the universe. Accordingly, he is very careful to present the changes in occupation of the Delphic shrine as a peaceful inheritance by consent. In this he is in sharp opposition to the less philosophical but more historical older theory, preserved in the Homeric Hymn. There Apollo, and probably a very Hellenic Apollo, violently dispossesses an older earth goddess and her natural attribute, the snake. Much earlier cults are at the base of the Hellenic worships, as they were in classical centuries; and this is true of both the ordinary forms of the cults of caves.

The Greek mysteries, Eleusinian, Orphic, and Samothracian, all seem to be survivals from pre-Hellenic times.[46] At Eleusis in particular there was a Mycenaean cult of Eleutho in 'the laughless rock', ἀγέλαστος πετρά; though the telesterion itself is later.[47] Now the object which lay in the holy chest has been shown to have been a model of the female generative organ.[48] This was represented by the name of Baubo, which was considered the name of a divine personality. The remarkable thing about the name is that it has a credible etymology in Ancient Egyptian, an etymology accepted by at least some Greeks.[49] If it is right, Baubo and Telphousa appear to mean the same thing, a point of interest, apart from the possibilities concerning early

Egyptian influence on Greece which are suggested. Further, although mysteries were secret and investigation is accordingly difficult, it is now clear that at Eleusis two results were both sought by ritual enactment: the fertilization and renewal of the earth each year, and personal rebirth, in at least one of the many senses, for the individual initiate.[50]

NOTES

1. *Cf.* G. Funaioli, *L'Oltretomba nell'Eneide di Virgilio* (Palermo, 1924) 36–7, who clearly states this: 'Dal vestibolo dell'Averno all'Acheronte è breve il tratto. Le acque sono il primo ostacolo sulla via dei morti: mare, fiumi, laghi, variamente nei miti. Ma fiumi e laghi non sono originari; da principio è l'oceano che separa i vivi dai morti, la terra dall'isola funerea: laghi e fiumi sono un'immagine dell'oceano. Nei testi letterari è rimasta sempre una grande incertezza topografica delle correnti, attraverso le quali si penetra nell'Ade, in Virgilio del pari che in Omero o in Platone e in Aristofane. Una salda tradizione non si è mai stabilita.' He observes, 37, 38, that Charon is of 'popular origin', showing signs that he belongs to the sea rather than to rivers: 'Della provenienza manifestamente volgare serba più d'un tratto rude: l'irsuta canizie; il lurido mantello, il *palliolum* degli uomini di mare, e annodato, non affibbiato, sulle spalle; la pertica, tipica nella tradizione, anzichè il remo.'

2. A. M. Hocart, *Kingship* (London, 1927) 189–203.

3. Ibid. 176, quoting *Satapatha Brahmana* VII.

4. Ibid. 188.

5. Ibid.

6. Eugen Täubler, 'Terremare und Rom', *SHAW*, Ph.-hist. Kl. (1931–2) 2 Abh., 60–1.

7. William Warburton, *The Divine Legation of Moses* (London, 1738) I, 182.

8. Porph. *De Antr. Nymph.* VI; *cf.* VII, where it is said that a cave is a symbol of the universe, that Kronos made himself a cave 'in Ocean', where he hid his children, and that Demeter brought up Kore in a cave with the nymphs; and VIII, where Porphyry says that Plato and the Pythagoreans declared the universe to be a cave. Cato said that a 'mundus' in Italy was like the sky, in some sense. *Cf.* also Sidney Smith in Sir E. A. Wallis Budge, *From Fetish to God in Ancient Egypt* (London, 1934) 516: 'Osiris was buried in an island tomb, perhaps in deference to a Nubian custom, for many of the Kings of Ethiopia were buried in islands in Lake Sânâ (or Tânâ as it is called in some dialects).'

9. W. J. Hemp, *Proceedings of the Prehistorical Society* I (1935) 108–14.

10. Sir William M. Ramsay, *JHS* 32 (1912) 151–70; id. *BSA* 18 (1911–12) 37–61.

11. Ramsay, *JHS* 32 (1912) 162–3.

Ξένοι Τεκμορεῖοι
ἐπεσκεύασαν τὸ [ἄν-]
τρον καὶ τὸν δάον εἰσ-
ανέστησαν.

Porph. *De Antr. Nymph.* VI implies that the Persians conducted initiation in a building that was only called a cave.

12. *IGSI* no. 638 (Kaibel).

> εὑρήσσεις δ᾽ ᾽Αἴδαο δόμων ἐπ᾽ ἀριστερὰ κρήνην,
> πὰρ δ᾽ αὐτῇ λευκὴν ἑστηκυῖαν κυπάρισσον·
> ταύτης τῆς κρήνης μηδὲ σχεδὸν ἐμπελάσειας.
> εὑρήσεις δ᾽ ἑτέραν, τῆς Μνημοσύνης ἀπὸ λίμνης
> ψυχρὸν ὕδωρ προρέον· φύλακες δ᾽ ἐπίπροσθεν ἔασιν.
> εἰπεῖν· γῆς παῖς εἰμι καὶ οὐρανοῦ ἀστερόεντος,
> αὐτὰρ ἐμοὶ γένος οὐράνιον· τόδε δ᾽ἴστε καὶ αὐτοί.
> δίψῃ δ᾽ εἰμὶ αὔη καὶ ἀπόλλυμαι· ἀλλὰ δότ᾽ αἶψα
> ψυχρὸν ὕδωρ προρέον τῆς Μνημοσύνης ἀπὸ λίμνης . . .

[On this inscr. see D. Comparetti and C. Smith, *JHS* 3 (1882) 111–18. J.D.C.]
13. Paus. IX, 39, 7–8.
14. Sir William M. Ramsay, *BSA* 18 (1911–12) 44–50; where he shows the general similarity of the Phrygian and other 'mysteries'.
15. Ibid. 48.
16. Ibid. 50.
17. Ibid. 47–8.
18. F. Muller, Jun., *Mnemosyne* Ser. III, 2 (1935) 46–7, on Varro, *De Ling. Lat.* V, 58–61.
19. M. P. Nilsson, *A History of Greek Religion* (Oxford, 1925) 12–13, explains how slight is the evidence for Cretan cave cults. There are, however, the axes which were thrown into caves.
20. F. Muller, Jun., 'De "Komst" van den Hemelgod' *MKAW*, Afd. Lett. 74, B, 7 (1932) 32–6. [See also: C. Autran, 'ΠΑΤΗΡ et ΑΔΕΛΦΟΣ', *Revue des Etudes Indo-européennes* 1 (1938) 330–43. J.D.C.]
21. Plat. *Menex.* 238A: οὐ γὰρ γῆ γύναικα μεμίμηται κυήσει καὶ γεννήσει ἀλλὰ γυνὴ γῆν. *Cf.* Macrob. *Saturn.* V, 19, 15–18, where a strange story about the Palici is told. They were swallowed by the earth, and returned from it. Macrobius gives a derivation of their name from 'returning'; 'ἀπὸ τοῦ πάλιν ἱκέσθαι, quoniam prius in terram mersi denuo inde reuersi sunt.' I owe this interesting ref. to the kindness of Mlle A.-M. Guillemin.
22. [Miss] Tony Cyriax, *Archaeological Journal* 78 (1921) 205–15: 'To enter the next world therefore the spirit would have to be *reborn* . . . The object of the tomb-builder would have been to make the tomb as much like the body of a mother as he was able.'
23. A. Dieterich, *Mutter Erde* (Leipzig, 1905) 56 and *passim*.
24. Otto Kern, *Orphicorum fragmenta* (Berlin, 1922) 107, fr. 32c.
25. A. Moret, *Mystères Egyptiens* (Paris, 1913) 85–9.
26. Sir J. G. Frazer, *The Golden Bough* (abridged ed., London, 1922) 14–15.
27. Felix Speiser, *Zeitschrift für Ethnologie* 60 (1928) 362–72.
28. Hocart (above, note 2) 70–98; esp. in Egypt, 83–4.
29. Ibid.
30. Ibid. 75, quoting the Rev. L. Fison after Sir J. G. Frazer, *The Golden Bough*[2] I (London, 1900) 250.
31. Hocart (above, note 2) 134–61.
32. Ibid. 149, with ref.
33. E. O. James, 'The sources of Christian Ritual and its Relation to the Culture Pattern of the Ancient East', *The Labyrinth* . . ., edited by S. H. Hooke (London, 1935) 237–60.
34. Ibid. 241.
35. Ibid. 241–2.
36. Ov. *Met.* I, 138.

37. *Anthol. Palat.* XV, 40, 42.
38. E. Hommel, *Orientalistische Studien Fritz Hommel* I (Leipzig, 1917) 233–52, esp. 234.
39. E. Hommel. *OLZ* 22 (1919) 65–6, citing Robert Eisler, *Weltenmantel und Himmelszelt* (Munich, 1910) II, 387, 431: 'Nun ist ferner die Idee weitverbreitet, dass der Mutterleib einem Tiere gleicht oder selbst ein Tier ist, in welchem eben die werdende Seele gefangen liegt, bis sie aus diesem engen Gefängnis zum Leben hinaustritt und frei wird.'
40. Budge (above, note 8) 436–7.
41. Muller (above, note 18) 49, 175, regards the labyrinth as a symbol of the body of the earth mother or rather a deity of scarcely determined sex, citing, 48, Margaret C. Waites, *AJA* 27 (1923) 29.
42. Muller (above, note 18) 203.
43. Sir J. G. Frazer, *Adonis, Attis, and Osiris, The Golden Bough* IV (London, 1914) I, 156–7.
44. *Cf.* the Orphic fragment *ap.* Aristot. περὶ Κόσμου 401A (*Orph. fr.* Kern, 21a).
45. R. H. Klausen, *Aeneas und die Penaten* (Hamburg and Gotha, 1839–40) I, 222.
46. Otto Kern, *Die Religion der Griechen* I (Berlin, 1926) 135–47, etc.
47. Friedrich Pfister, *Die Religion der Griechen und Römer, Darstellung und Literaturbericht . . . 1918–29/30* (Leipzig, 1930) 273, with reff.
48. A. Körte, *ARW* 18 (1915) 116–26, and other reff. given by Pfister (above, note 47) 274.
49. Margaret A. Murray, *JRAI* 64 (1934) 95–6.
50. Fritz Wehrli, *ARW* 31 (1934) 77–104, esp. 104.

IV

ABYDOS

The opinion that the labyrinth on the Cumaean gate and the rest of the pictures there are irrelevant and needlessly delay the action of the narrative, could not have been held, if the task of considering the labyrinth, and its history in thought, had not been neglected. To understand the meaning of the parts of the *Aeneid*, a symbolic language must be known, so that the emotions that had gathered round each poetic conception in a long history can be apprehended. If the effect is not now immediate, and the symbolic language has been forgotten, there is one thing to do: to trace the history of the image or conception which is obscure. This time it is very well worth doing, because a labyrinth is a most central thing to ultimate thought through thousands of years. It has had many forms[1] and variations of meaning, and has been adjectival in many ways to many facts and beliefs; but at the start its principle and meaning are transparently obvious and clear.

The pattern of a labyrinth is the pattern of a maze. Frequently, a labyrinth is a maze pattern, rendered in brick or stone; but the words, labyrinth and maze, can without much danger be used interchangeably to indicate the pattern. The simple and obvious meaning of the pattern comes directly from its plain description; and there is good reason to think that early man understood the pattern as we have to understand it now. There is an area, with the outside and inside sharply distinguished. There is a long path from outside to the inside, which is usually called the nucleus. Sometimes the path has turnings, so that a wrong turning, not leading to the nucleus, might be taken, by one who does not know the way. Sometimes there are no turnings which lead wrong, but only a very long path from the outside to the inside, a path which can bend in many different shapes, but cannot possibly be straight. With alternatives, the pattern is 'multicursal'; without them, 'unicursal'. The description shows the meaning and purpose implicit in the shape. There are two opposite objects: exclusion from the nucleus, and admission to it. Mazes and labyrinths provide correlatively obstruction to those who would enter the middle point of a certain area, and at the same time a conditional penetration to that point. They serve in fact the purpose of gates, giving entrance on certain terms. The terms may be knowledge of the way, or merely ability to traverse a long course. From these two kinds of terms many sorts of elaboration come.

This plan was worked quite certainly in a simple and sensible

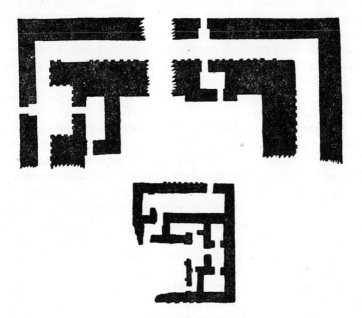

FIGURE 4

Entrances at corners, and central keep, of the Second Dynasty fort at Shuneh (from E. R. Ayrton and others, *Abydos*, Part III, London, 1904, Plate VI, with acknowledgment to the Egypt Exploration Society).

way, a very long time ago, when what might be called the 'tactical' labyrinth was first used. In military tactics the defenders of a position have an advantage if they can compel attackers to approach by a long route, wasting energy, perhaps losing their way, and if possible under fire from the defence for a long time, in enfilade. This is as strong a principle in modern defence as it has ever been. Defended localities are disposed so that when one is attacked, the attackers are under fire in enfilade from the others. When there is time to erect barbed wire obstacles, they are planned to make attackers bunch together at points enfiladed by the defence. A fire trench is dug with traverses, things which are too well known to need description, so that the whole trench cannot be enfiladed, and some chance is given of enfilading a party of the enemy, attacking one bay, from either flank. From the air or on a map these trenches look like a weak maeander pattern, a derivative from the tactical maze. Modern methods represent something like a return to Roman practice. The Roman 'quincuncial' disposition, with units in lines, and gaps covered by units in rear, is in essence the same as our 'diamond' formations. All are akin to the tactical labyrinth.

The earliest tactical labyrinths are in some Egyptian forts of the First and Second Dynasties, about 3100–2700 B.C.[2] They have a system of walls with openings not opposite to each other but staggered, so that attackers have to take a long crooked path, moving laterally between the opening in one wall and the opening in the next. The plan enforces a labyrinthine path, and therefore achieves the correlative principles of conditional exclusion and conditional penetration. Friendly troops can freely use the path of entry; but an enemy, under enfilading fire for a long distance, is severely obstructed.

So simple and necessary a device does not need much illustration. The example of Maiden Castle[3] in Dorsetshire is sufficient. It is a hill town, oval in plan, with the shorter sides towards the east and west. The rampart now visible belongs to the early Iron Age, about 300 B.C.; and in it, at each shorter side of the hill town, is an entrance of an elaborately labyrinthine design. Like the Egyptian entrances, they are severely practical, not stylized and ornamental. In time, however, the Egyptian and British examples are separated by about 3,000 years. The principle used at Maiden Castle is evident elsewhere in Western Britain at about the same date, but not in earlier hill towns, except perhaps in the spiral rampart of the neolithic Trundle.

But probably the labyrinthine principle might be found in far the greater number of defended places of many times in some form or other. It tended to be applied more simply, as engineers acquired the power to build very strong defensive walls of stone. To use an elaborately labyrinthine plan would then have been much more laborious, and scarcely necessary, since the large stone walls themselves afforded a nearly impregnable protection. But the labyrinthine principle was not usually abandoned. A characteristic of the strong fortresses of Mycenaean times in Greek lands, and also of Hissarlik, Homer's Troy, is the customary approach to the gates. The road reaches the foot of the wall, and then turns, and following the wall, close under it, leads up a ramp, until the gate itself, at right-angles to the wall, is reached.

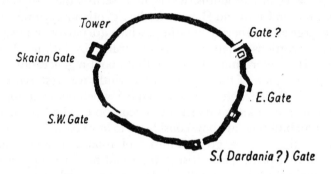

FIGURE 5

The wall at Hissarlik, which protected Homer's Troy, showing the enfiladed gates (from Walter Leaf, *Troy*, London, 1912, 154, Fig. 8).

Attackers are therefore enfiladed from the gate and under fire from the wall all the way. Troy itself is thus in a broad sense a labyrinthine place; a fact which will turn out to be of some significance.

The tactical labyrinth is used in principle at almost all times and places at which it can give common sense a chance to improve any military defence. The simple plan is obstruction and entry on right terms. Everyone may not enter; and everyone is not necessarily excluded. The tactical labyrinth is equally acceptable and intelligible to modern and ancient thought, in any part of the world.

The principle need not work in one direction only. It can be used to make escape difficult, from the inside to the outside of any place. This is asserted of the most famous and perhaps the

most mysterious labyrinth of all, the legendary labyrinth in
Crete. Of this the Cretans themselves are said to have affirmed
that there was nothing awful about it; it was merely a prison,
difficult to enter and still more difficult to leave.[4] This definition
fits the story of Theseus, Ariadne and the Minotaur quite well;
and it agrees with the simplest, tactical part of the early history
of the labyrinthine plan. But we should not get far in the investigation if we stopped here.

However, at the start the certain facts of the tactical labyrinth
must be firmly emphasized. Among other things they illuminate
the passages in Herodotus, where he describes the 'labyrinths'
of Knossos in Crete and Hawara in the Egyptian Fayyum.[5] Both
were large and elaborate buildings, which are partly understood
from excavations. There is no sign of a truly labyrinthine plan in
either. It is entertaining to notice that about a generation ago,
the ground plan of the 'Egyptian labyrinth' was restored with
an imaginary maeander maze round it,[6] which does not appear
in a more recent and authoritative restoration.[7] The Cretan and
Egyptian buildings are now considered to have been 'labyrinths'
because they had a great number of rooms, arranged in a
complicated plan. This satisfies the usual modern supposition
that a labyrinth is essentially a place inside which it is easy to
lose your way. That is true of both the Cretan and Egyptian
buildings. In fact, there has been for about a generation a pre-
ponderant belief that the Minoan palace at Knossos was in a
sense the original labyrinth, and that the very name 'labyrinth'
was derived from the 'hall of the double axes' there; 'labrys'
being a name for 'double axe', and 'inth' a suffix in one of the
pre-Hellenic languages, widely known and credibly supposed to
mean 'place'.[8] This is hopelessly insufficient; and not far from
the root of the matter is the fact that a labyrinth has only as a
secondary implication the danger of getting lost inside it; the
primary and essential quality is the power to obstruct entry, but
also to allow it on proper terms.

Part of the truth seems to be that, certainly in Egypt and
possibly in Crete, the labyrinthine principle applied to defended
buildings in early times somehow left a name (though the actual
word 'labyrinth' is not Egyptian) to other buildings which might
have been built on a strictly labyrinthine plan, but which in
practice were not. Pliny says, in an important passage which will

help again later, that a labyrinth is suitable for a king's palace, or a tomb, and that Daedalus, who was supposed to have built the labyrinth at Knossos, was anticipated by the Egyptians long before.[9] This agrees well with the facts; but Pliny does not explain the difference between the true labyrinth, with a tortuous exclusive path of entry, and the two buildings described as labyrinths by Herodotus, one the palace at Knossos, and the other the burial place at Hawara. To understand this, the more abstract kinds of exclusion must be noticed, and labyrinthine entrances to tombs.

There is a certain commentary on this development which is worth offering for the sake of its interest and of the possibility that future discoveries may increase its importance; but at present much doubt is involved. It looks as if Egyptians and Greeks, and possibly Minoans also, considered the labyrinthine pattern an appropriate symbol for any house. The Egyptian hieroglyph ⌷, a form of *h*, represents the ground plan of a courtyard. On Greek vases the maeander pattern is thought to show, when it surrounds a scene of action, that the action is taking place indoors; and the maeander pattern, which appears in Egypt by the Eleventh Dynasty, about 2000 B.C., is mainly a repetition of the Egyptian hieroglyph.[10] However, it is scarcely derived from the hieroglyph alone; and indeed such designs appear first at a time of strong North Syrian influence, and partly depend on it. Lately two attractive objects from the Greek geometric age have been found; earthenware models of small houses, on each of which a firm maeander pattern is painted, perhaps to assert that the objects are meant for houses, and perhaps by some method to bring good luck.[11] This is where the next problem begins.

To exclude the unfriendly, and yet when necessary to admit the friendly, the labyrinthine pattern was sensibly used as a tactical device of military engineering in widely separated places many centuries ago. The practice and in particular its devolution set at work a process of ideas. One result is that something like a labyrinthine quality tends to become the attribute of any house, expressed by drawings or words. But now something has occurred which makes explanations by practical common sense look insufficient. The maze-like maeanders on the models of Greek houses insistently invite, even in the historical context

G

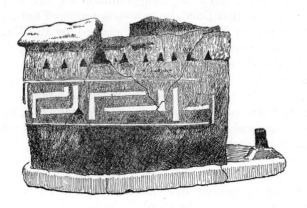

FIGURE 6

Clay models of Greek buildings of the Geometric Age found in 1933 in the Heraeum at Perachora near Corinth, which show for the first time how close was the ideal connection among Greeks between the maze or maeander and the walls of houses (after H. G. G. Payne, *JHS* 54, 1934, 191, Figs. 3, 4).

which we have already identified, the explanation that they
are some kind of charm. These patterns evoke at once comparison with the well-known 'tangled threid' designs which are
still drawn on doorsteps and elsewhere in Northern England and
Scotland. They, also, are charms of a kind. The intended effect
is clear. Tangled drawings are meant to entangle intruders, as
the tangled reality of a labyrinthine construction at the approach to a fort actually helps very much to entangle attackers.
There have been entanglements of brickwork, stonework, and
earthwork; and there have been barbed wire entanglements on
just the same principle. Now in the war of 1914–18, British
soldiers had a joke which could be made when something was
wanted, but was not to be had. They said that they would
'chalk one out', as if the wish would be father not only to the
thought, but to the fact also, for chalking out a drawing is
nearer to willing a thing than to making it. Here there is a
survival of early thinking in modern talk. Like the soldiers,
Greeks of the geometric age, and cottagers of North Britain,
planned to chalk out an entanglement, in lack of the reality; but
the Greeks and the cottagers thought, unlike the soldiers, that
the chalked-out drawing might have something like the practical effect of the real thing copied by the drawing. That is, they
sought to apply 'sympathetic magic', a practice which, whatever the uncertainties about its origin and exact nature, is
proved to have existed in almost every part of the world.

Authorities are less inclined now than they were, to think
that magical beliefs are original or strictly primitive in mankind.
It is more usual to hold that early people start like others with
concrete fact, and then seek explanations of what they see
occurring. The explanations are often very far from the truth;
but even then they have to provide the theory on which action
must be based, frequently enough. Much of the theory and
practice may remain sound; but much also, of the sort which
we should now consider less sound, belongs to the class called
magical. A sub-division of magic is sympathetic magic, in
which it is assumed that the effect is like the cause, and that an
event in one place can be made to produce by its very nature a
similar event far away. Another subdivision, most often at the
same time sympathetic, and almost safely to be called a sub-
division of sympathetic magic, is the apotropaic class, in which

attempts are made to avert evil influences by magical means. The maeanders on the models of Greek houses and the 'tangled threid' drawings are alike devices of sympathetic apotropaic magic.

They however belong to an abstract kind of magic, not in any very obvious contact with concrete reality. The supposed value of the patterns is quite formal, as if what mattered was what they were, not anything that they could do. An earlier stage seems to have concerned ghosts. The evil influence was not supposed to be an abstract force, but a dangerous ghost, who would behave like a living human being, and could be resisted

FIGURE 7

Second Dynasty mortuary chapel (from Sir W. M. Flinders Petrie, *Medum*, London, 1892, Plate IV; with acknowledgment to the Egypt Exploration Society).

in a similar way. Now living beings can be excluded by labyrinthine approaches which make access to a centre of resistance difficult or impossible, as in the Egyptian forts and Maiden Castle. The Chinese still resist ghosts in just this way. At the entrances to their cities they have their well-known 'spirit walls', set transversely, like the baffle-plates in a petrol engine's silencer, to enforce upon the undesired spirit or ghost a tortuous and therefore difficult path. The same plan is followed at the entrances of houses. 'If there are fine houses, they are concealed behind walls, and you cannot see into their courtyards through the gateways, because the gates are masked, on the inside, by another short section of wall, designed to prevent the ingress of evil spirits which (as everybody knows) can only fly in a straight line.'[12] Early funeral processions often take a zigzag path to deceive ghosts.

This partly explains the development of the labyrinthine idea

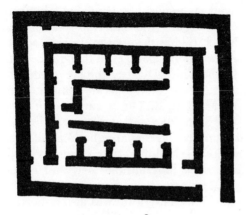

FIGURE 8

Tomb of King Perabsen, Second Dynasty (from Sir W. M. Flinders Petrie, *Royal Tombs of the Earliest Dynasties*, London, 1901, Part II, p. 11, Plate LXI; with acknowledgment to the Egypt Exploration Society).

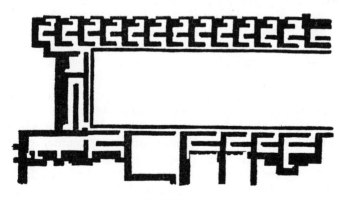

FIGURE 9

Northern end of the court of the Sed Festival, in the area of the Step Pyramid at Saqqarah (from J.-Ph. Lauer, *Ann Serv. ant. de l'Égypte*, 28, 1928, Plate I).

from natural to supernatural uses. There are clear signs of the
development in Egypt. Buildings with labyrinthine entrances
are of two sorts. Some are forts; but others are tombs and mortuary chapels.[13] The tomb of King Perabsen, of the Second
Dynasty, about 3000 B.C., is specially labyrinthine.[14] After
devolution has begun, the innermost small chamber of a
mortuary chapel still has the door to the side, so that all who go
to it must take a bending path, even though the path now bends
very little. In the Third Dynasty the labyrinthine construction
is very apparent in the small funerary temple of Sneferu, about
2600 B.C., at Medum, and it is carried out on a wholesale
scheme in the Step Pyramid at Saqqarah.[15] Here there are
many small rooms round the large building of Zoser, Sneferu's
predecessor. Zoser's building thus seems to be intermediate
between the earliest labyrinthine forts and chapels, and the
'labyrinth' at Hawara, belonging to the Twelfth Dynasty,
about 1800 B.C. This 'labyrinth' was also a mortuary building.
So far, there is confirmation of Pliny's remark, that a labyrinth
is suitable for a king's palace or a tomb, for the forts and burial
places fit his statement. There is, however, a distinction. The
forts are practically defensible; but in the burial places there is
no question of defence by force. The labyrinthine pattern may
well be meant to resist hostile ghosts, like the 'spirit walls' of
China. In the Egyptian *Book of Gates*, a 'journey of the dead',
compiled perhaps about 1300 B.C., behind gates passed on the
way are mysterious 'double walls'.[16] They clearly have the
function of the Chinese 'walls'; and it is hard not to think that
they represented the labyrinthine principle.

In some of these sacred buildings the labyrinthine approach
of early examples can be seen successively straightening out.
There may be an entrance in a wall, after which there is just one
further entrance to be passed, not opposite, but to the side, and
round a corner of a small inner building. Another stage is
reached when there are several openings in walls, but all
exactly opposite to each other, so that only a less essential part
of the labyrinthine shape survives. Meanwhile, there has been
a more elaborate, composite development, of which the exact
purpose is obscure, though it must have been concerned with
ritual. The plan noticed at Saqqarah has been evolved; a large
hall is built, having round it many small rooms each with a

simple but unmistakably labyrinthine entrance. This construction, which is early, since it belongs to the Third Dynasty, is intermediate between the early labyrinthine fort plans, with which it shares the labyrinthine entrances, and the shapes of the 'labyrinths' of Hawara and Knossos, which are also large buildings with a great number of interior rooms. The 'labyrinth' at Hawara is more regular, and nearer to the Third Dynasty plan, than the palace at Knossos. There is thus a complete and satisfactory archaeological series, which explains why a name, that strictly belonged to a true labyrinthine building, could have been used, after a gradual process of changes, for the two large edifices, compared together, and both called 'labyrinths', by Herodotus. But by what peoples the actual word 'labyrinth' was applied to buildings is a different question.

The further development of this supernatural exclusion can be inferred with some confidence. There are found in many places dances which follow the track of a labyrinth or maze. They are, for example, still danced in Crete.[17] Maze dances can safely be said to belong to the larger class of protective rituals,[18] performed to exclude evil influences,[19] though that is not the whole truth about them. The dances elsewhere, and the Egyptian entrances, agree; and it is possible that the pattern was first represented architecturally in stone and brick, and that the dances were planned to copy the architectural application. This agreement between two uses of the pattern, in both of which the principle of exclusion is apparent, is part of the solution of a familiar problem, why dances, a certain pictorial design, large buildings, and finally caves are all alike called 'labyrinths'.[20] The rest of the solution must wait; at present it is enough to show the connection between dances and tombs.

Besides the entrances, there is evidence for the labyrinthine pattern in Egypt on seals and plaques decorated with a 'square fret', like a maeander. The square fret is confined to the Eighth Dynasty, 2200 B.C. or earlier, a time of strong influence from North Syria.[21] Accordingly, these designs need not prove anything for indigenous Egyptian cult; they may represent Asiatic influence on Egypt. One plaque of steatite is of great interest.[22] In the lower half is a square fret, a rectangular labyrinthine pattern; and in the upper part surrounded by the outer walls of the same pattern and pictured in a 'labyrinthine' or 'square fret' style, are two seated figures, facing each other. Both may be male; but possibly one is female; it is hard to be sure.

Among other representations is a schist seal, showing a single male figure, apparently enclosed in labyrinthine walls within a building.[23] A suggestion has been made[24] that the male figure is a divine king, that the labyrinthine pattern represents his sacred tomb, and that the second figure on the plaque is the divine king's consort, associated with him in a sacral marriage.

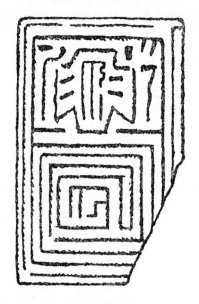

FIGURE 10

Steatite plaque of the Eighth Dynasty, showing two seated figures confined within a 'square fret' labyrinthine pattern (after Sir W. M. Flinders Petrie, *Buttons and Design Scarabs*, London, 1925, Plate IV, No. 238; with acknowledgment to the Egypt Exploration Society).

Labyrinths appear on Minoan seals, and on later Cretan coins of historical times. Inside the labyrinth on coins occur a human head, a bull's head, and a crescent moon. It is argued that the first two represent a divine king, symbolized by a bull in Egypt and Crete; and that the moon represents the king's consort. On the gate at Vergil's Cumae, in the picture of the Cretan labyrinth, Pasiphae, who was united to the bull, is shown. Her name means 'she who gives light to all;' and she is in some sense the moon.[25] In the theory of the divine king there are uncertainties, especially about details and subordinate evidence. But there is no need to doubt the importance of the Egyptian king; and the labyrinthine pattern is likely to have represented his sacred defence in the tomb.

NOTES

1. W. H. Matthews, *Mazes and Labyrinths* (London, 1922), gives a history of the maze or labyrinth, classifications, and illustrations, but avoids questions about the meaning of the designs and their purposes.
2. J. E. Quibell and F. W. Green, *Hierakonpolis* II (London, 1902) Plate LXXIV; E. R. Ayrton and others, *Abydos* (London, 1902, and later dates) III, Plate VI.
3. R. E. Mortimer Wheeler, *The Antiquaries Journal* 15 (1935) 265-75, esp. 266-70 and Plate XXIX; see Plate II, facing p. 135 above.
4. Philochor. *ap.* Plut. *Thes.* XVI.
5. Hdt. II, 148.
6. Matthews (above, note 1) 15, Fig. 3, a restoration by Canina.
7. Ibid. 16, Fig. 4, a restoration by Flinders Petrie.
8. The explanation as 'house of the double axe' was offered by Max Mayer, *JDAI* 7 (1892) 191.
9. Pliny, *N.H.* XXXVI, 84-5.
10. I owe the information on the first appearance of the maeander pattern, like much else here, to the kindness of Mr G. A. Wainwright.
11. H. G. G. Payne, *JHS* 54 (1934) 190 and 191, Figs. 3, 4.
12. Peter Fleming, *One's Company* (London, 1934) 96.
13. E.g. Sir W. M. Flinders Petrie, *Medum* (London, 1892) Plate IV.
14. Sir W. M. Flinders Petrie, *The Royal Tombs of the Earliest Dynasties* (London, 1901) II, Plate LXI and p. 11.
15. J.-Ph. Lauer, *Ann. Serv. ant. de l'Égypte*, Cairo, 28 (1928) 96 ff. and Plate 1; 29 (1929) 103-4 and Plates II, III, V.
16. Sir E. A. Wallis Budge, *From Fetish to God in Ancient Egypt* (London, 1934) 368-79.
17. Sir A. J. Evans, *The Palace of Minos* III (London, 1930) 75.
18. W. F. J. Knight, *Antiquity* 6 (1932) 445-58.
19. S. Eitrem, *Opferritus und Voropfer der Griechen und Römer* (Christiania, 1915) 6-75.
20. Richard Eilmann, *Labyrinthos* (Athens, 1931) 90-5.
21. Sir W. M. Flinders Petrie, *Buttons and Design Scarabs* (London, 1925) 7 and Plate IV.
22. Ibid. Plate IV, 238.
23. Ibid. Plate IV, 237.
24. Mrs C. N. Deedes, 'The Labyrinth', *The Labyrinth . . .*, edited by S. H. Hooke (London, 1935) 3-42, esp. 5-11.
25. Verg. *Aen.* VI, 25; for the place of the moon in the religions of initiation, *cf.* M. Esther Harding, *Woman's Mysteries, Ancient and Modern* (London, 1935) *passim.*

V

TRUIA

The primary idea of the labyrinthine form, which still demands great insistence, is the exclusion of hostile beings or influences. First this form is used in building, practically. Then it becomes more symbolic, but is supposed to be effective, even when it appears as a mere drawing on the ground, according to the theory of sympathetic magic. Even the lines of the drawing may be invisible. The very enactment by moving of a labyrinthine path may be expected to exercise a labyrinthine, exclusive effect. That is the meaning of a maze dance or other maze ritual. The movements of the performers are intended to weave a magical entanglement and spread a field of magical force to exclude all that is not wanted to enter the guarded place. The central evidence for this is an Etruscan vase and a passage of Vergil.

On the Etruscan vase,[1] the famous Tragliatella oenochoe dated about 600 B.C., armed riders are shown. A large incongruous pattern, unmistakably a maze pattern, is drawn on the vase; the riders seem to trail it behind them, as if it expresses the path they have taken. The pattern is distinctly marked by an inscription, TRUIA. The drawing is naturally and usually understood to be a picture of what is known as the Troia, Truia, or Trojan game.

The Trojan game was a mounted ceremonial, which was revived and favoured by Augustus, and maintained by later emperors. It was performed by young members of the Roman nobility, but its practice seems to have spread outside Italy. During the Principate it was mainly a social affair and an amusement; one of its advantages was that it was a bloodless sport, unlike the gladiatorial games, and for that reason commended itself to the reformed Augustus,[2] however able to endure bloodshed he may have been in his earlier years. I suppose the musical rides of today, such as are performed by British cavalry at tournaments and tattoos, are descended from the same ancestry as the Roman performance; a strange thought, in view of the nature of that ancestry, as it is now to be disclosed.

FIGURE II

The Tragliatella oenochoe, showing the protective armed ride called the Truia, and also, apparently, a protective march on foot (after W. H. Matthews, *Mazes and Labyrinths*, London, 1922, 157–158, Figs. 133–135, and F. Muller, Jun., *Mnemosyne*, Series III, Vol. II, 1935, Plate IV, 3, 4; with acknowledgments to Messrs Longmans, Green and Co. Ltd. and Messrs E. J. Brill, Leiden).

According to Vergil,[3] the performers of the Troia did just
what can be seen in modern musical rides. The movements have
been worked out and are not hard to understand. Their details
are not relevant here, except the undoubted fact that they
followed the pattern of a maze or labyrinth. This has long been
recognized. Apart from guessing, Vergil himself hints this when
he actually compares the Truia, as I propose to call the performance here, to the labyrinth at Knossos.[4] He says that the
movements were labyrinthine. The Truia must have been intended to create a magical field of exclusive force, an abstract
defensive entanglement.[5] Vergil significantly uses the word
'impediunt' to describe the movements.[6]

The Truia in Vergil was part of funeral ceremonies performed by the Trojans for Anchises,[7] a year after his death,[8] in
Sicily. After the revival, the rite continued to be performed at
funerals; it was enacted at the funeral of Gaius and Drusilla.[9]
The maze dance is in fact appropriate to funerals, just as the
labyrinthine plan is described as appropriate to burial places.
That it was a rite, and not merely an ornamental military drill,
is shown by notices in which it is described as a sacred ride, ἱερὰ
ἱπποδρομία,[10] and a mystery, μυστήριον.[11] It has been supposed
that the first description is inexplicable;[12] and the second has
not been explained. To explain them it must be shown how the
Truia can be a sacred rite; and this is clear enough if the
Truia was a ceremony designed to enforce magical exclusion.[13]
The actual word used for 'sacred' is 'ἱερός', which means
rather 'magically or divinely potent' than 'holy' or 'pure' in a
milder sense, which would be ἅγιος. The application of the
word 'mystery' is more obscure, and for the present must remain obscure. Two things are to be noticed now. 'Mystery'
comes from a word which means 'shut', 'μύω'; in the ancient
sense it means a series of rites belonging to a secret and esoteric
religion closed to all but the initiated. How appropriate the
notion of shutting is to the present interpretation of the Truia
is at once obvious; it is also clear why the true meaning of the
rite seems to have been little understood in full historical times,
since it is the very nature of a 'mystery' to be beyond the knowledge of all but those who manipulate it, and, believing in it,
keep the secret.

The probability that the maze movements of the Truia were

meant to enact magically the exclusion of undesired beings or influences from a grave, and at the same time to admit those who were authorized to visit it,[14] is confirmed, without any

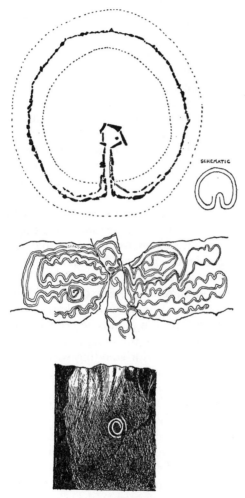

SCHEMATIC

FIGURE 12

The three occurrences, two spiraliform, of the principle of the maze in the Chambered Cairn of Bryn Celli Ddu in Anglesey; in the plan of the monument; on a stone found lying flat, embedded in the soil; and on an upright stone (after W. J. Hemp, *Archaeologia*, 80, 1930, 179–214, Fig. 1, facing 184, Pl. XLIX, Figs. 1 and 3, XLV, Fig. 1).

reference to Egypt, by a very remarkable megalithic monument in Britain, the chambered cairn of Bryn Celli Ddu in Anglesey.[15] This is the first megalithic burial cairn of its time to be so well and carefully excavated that a chance is given to discover the burial rites practised by the megalithic folk.[16] The remarkable thing about this monument is for the present enquiry the occurrence in it no less than three times of a pattern which has or suggests the exclusive characteristics of a labyrinth or maze. On a standing stone there is a small broken spiral.[17] On another stone, found carefully buried on the site in a floor of purple clay, is a large leaf-like spiraliform pattern,[18] obviously rendering the memory of a maze. Lastly, the whole structure is based on the plan of a spiraliform maze; for the entrance does not lead directly to the central chamber, but only reaches it after making two complete circuits of the monument, confined by stone circles.[19]

The excavator's comment on the buried stone with the zigzag pattern is this: 'The recumbent position of the stone . . . and the disposition of the pattern inevitably suggest that it was intended to be set upright in the ground at some stage in the funeral rites in such a way as to display the pattern.'[20] The meaning of the pattern was unknown to the excavators; but it was suggested that some form of magic was perhaps the most obvious explanation. The spiraliform plan is described by the excavator as follows. 'Further study of the design brought to light a very surprising fact. To a spectator standing without the outer passage the monument appears to have a perfectly symmetrical arrangement of four converging walls, all terminated at the portal by upright stones. . . . Analysis of the plan, however, reveals a very different position. . . .

'This end of the inner circle therefore is continuous with the north wall of the passage. This wall runs on without a break, curving round to form the chamber, and returning as the south wall of the passage, to complete the circuit of the monument . . . the line of walling therefore runs without a break twice round the monument. . . . In fact the two "circles" may be considered as together forming a gigantic spiral, in which is a loop comprising the passage and chamber.

'If, then, the whole inner area of the monument enclosed by the ditch is a "holy place", the burial chamber is in it but not of it, being completely shut out by the "loop" in the spiral.'[21]

The chambered cairn seems to belong to the range of full 'megalithic' influence. Its date is in the Bronze Age, apparently. But it immediately recalls the 'stone men', with their emphasis on stone circles and burial rites, and their word 'labyrinth'.

The spirals in this monument invite the explanation that they were all intended, with more or less clearness of purpose, to shut or seal the burial, or at least to suggest or assist that requirement. The spiral plan can hardly mean anything else, with its long and bewildering path. The stone with the leaf-shaped, zigzag, maze-like pattern may have been set up during burial rites, either as a chart to direct dancing, or as a symbol of exclusion from the land of the dead, and correlative admission to it; no doubt it was carefully buried inside the monument in order to maintain a similar effect by its sympathetic presence.[22]

The exclusive complications of this chambered cairn illuminate the Truia. It also was exclusive, connected with burials and the need to shut or seal them. The involved movements were thought to create a field of magical force, active by apotropaic magic. It was therefore rightly called a 'mystery' or act of secrecy, for the exclusion of the uninitiated; and 'sacred' in the magical sense was a fair description of it. It is clear also why Seneca called the Truia an annual or at least regular rite, performed on a fixed day of 'lustration';[23] for initial ceremonies have to be periodically performed again to renew their effect, and 'lustration' or purification, the ejection and exclusion of impure and dangerous influences, agrees well with the purpose of the Truia as it has now been defined.

Graves therefore were sealed to protect the dead inside; there was sometimes a secondary motive, to preserve the living from a return of the dead. The ghost of Patroclus returned, before his funeral. Here I cannot refrain from a modern parallel. 'From the United States I hear a pleasant story now going the rounds. A tourist visited the tomb of Huey Long, erstwhile "Dictator" of Louisiana, a huge concrete block in front of his £1,000,000 Capitol. Massively built, "tough"-looking, and rather aggressive guards were patrolling the site. The Northern visitor murmured to a Louisianian friend, "To keep away souvenir hunters I suppose?" "Well," said the local man thoughtfully, "that was the general idea. But most of the folks around here think that they aim not so much to keep people out as to keep Huey in." '[24]

This account of the funerary purpose of maze movements and patterns is reached without reference to Egypt. The Egyptian evidence confirms it independently; and the convergent probabilities can be said to unite into a certainty.

This mysterious matter does not, however, finish here. So far the tactical maze and partly the funerary maze have found an explanation. The next question is their effect on each other; or at any rate the approach of the one to the other within the realm of magical thought. There are signs of a magical application of the idea of the labyrinth or maze to a tactical purpose. This happens in the magical defence of cities and their walls—a subject little considered until quite lately.

The Truia was performed by Ascanius (or Iulus), according to Vergil, not only at the funeral games of Anchises, but also 'when he was surrounding Alba Longa with walls', afterwards, in Italy.[25] Vergil uses a verb for the act of Ascanius which does not very clearly admit that the Truia had been already performed in Sicily, and Servius explains that what Vergil meant was that Ascanius revived or renewed the Truia, since it had been instituted before.[26] The difficulty which Servius seems to have felt arose because Vergil offers two origins for the Truia, one in funeral rites and the other in the foundation ceremonies of a city. These points have been missed; but I think they are not easy to question when once they are stated; and there is evidence to show why they are to be accepted, and how this double origin could be sensibly supposed. The truth is that exclusion from a city was regarded in much the same way as exclusion from a burial.

That the Truia was a kind of foundation ceremony becomes clearer from a comparison of it with the dance of the Salii, which has actually been called by a modern scholar 'a Truia on foot'.[27] There can scarcely be doubt that the Salian dance was intended to help the defence of the city. Like the Truia,[28] it was a 'Pyrrhic' or war dance. Two origins are given for the Salii. It is said that a certain Salius, an Arcadian, came with Aeneas and taught the Trojan settlers an 'armed dance'.[29] It is also said that the Salii came from Samothrace, where they were called Sai, and were in charge of household gods, 'penatium antistites'.[30]

Though a Thracian tribe on the mainland near Samothrace carried the name Sai, the use of the same name for the Salii looks like a statement that they were 'men of safety' or 'saviours', since such is the meaning of the name, especially as they are supposed to have had a leader called Saon,[31] a form from the same root which must literally mean something like 'preserver'. The names agree well with the charge over the household gods. The Sai were they who 'stood in front' of them, and accordingly protected them and the habitation which they were thought to preserve. It is also said that a Salius danced in honour of Alesus, son of Poseidon.[32] That too seems to confirm the argument; Alesus can be connected with Alea, a name of Athena apparently meaning 'defensive' or something like it, and this Poseidon may be identified as the well-known Poseidon who was god of city walls. The Salii take part in an elaborate 'amburbium' to preserve the city at a time of danger by circular movement round it; and Lucan[33] describing the scene attributes to the procession a zigzag course, which would be appropriate to maze movements, if it were certain that the changes of direction were not merely due to the configuration of the ground. The Salii wore military dress and armour, and carried large shields, which they beat not with spears but with long drumsticks.[34] The noise therefore was an important part of the ritual; and it is usually thought that, like the Curetes who were akin to them, they sought to frighten away evil spirits. The movements might do this in some sense alone, but the noise, and the magical suggestion of the arms and armour, would be expected to help also. The Salian rite, therefore, was defensive or apotropaic, though other functions may have been combined with this. It has been thought that they were primarily cathartic, expected to purify and so strengthen the place or object round which they danced.[35] This intention is clearly emphasized elsewhere, especially in the circumambulations of sacred persons or objects in eastern religions, such as the circumambulation of the sacred stone in the Kaaba at Mecca. Here there is no sign of defensive requirement. It has been shown however that there is little real distinction between the two purposes; since an act of expulsion of evil from a place, person, or object is involved in the idea of purification and strengthening, from which are descended circular movements which are little

more than marks of respect. Again, it is likely enough that the
Salii danced to make the crops prosper. The higher they
jumped, the higher, probably, the crops were expected to grow.
There are modern parallels for this, and the Curetes, who,
according to the Palaikastro hymn, jumped 'to a fine harvest',
may have been expected also to operate in this way. It is clear,
however, that such an expectation may have been added at any
time, without interfering with the apotropaic function, which is
sufficiently established. It has been remarked already that this
new purpose, to make the crops grow high by jumping high, was
imposed on protective dances in Egypt. The Salii, and the Mars
who is partly a projection from them, at first guarded crops;
afterwards, when city states developed, they came to be concerned principally in the city's defence.[36]

The Truia, then, and the Salian dance were both apotropaic
in a similar way. Their movements were designed to create a
field of defensive magical force. The differences are that the
Truia was a mounted performance, and the Salian dance was
not; and that the Salian dance is not known to have followed a
labyrinthine course, with allowance for authorized admission
correlative to the magical exclusion. Details concerning the
Salian dance can hardly be recovered, though some, including
the places which they visited, are known; but it is just worth
while to mention a modern example of a similar dance, recorded from western Australia, in which dancers carry round
with them gates, clearly intending to admit good influences
while they exclude the bad. The other is capable of more investigation, for the significance of horses in early thinking is
known. Roman cavalry commanders had to be present when
the Salii danced.[37] Horsemen and horses were not irrelevant to
such rites.

The horse in early European thinking means on the one hand
fertility[38] and on the other hand death.[39] The first meaning has
been understood longer than the second; but the second is now
well realized. Horses are messengers of death among northern
races, and among the Greeks; the Erinyes were at first horses.[40]
The first Roman circus started with rites to Neptunus equester,
who was Consus.

The immediately important significance is the second, of
death. In this sense horse magic is strongly negative. Therefore,

the Truia, performed by mounted men, could be thought to exert an apotropaic effect strengthened by the participation of horses. The horses, by their mere presence acting in sympathetic magic, were expected to repel hostile influences. This is confirmed by the Tragliatella oenochoe, which shows performers mounted on horses, with a possible extension of apotropaic magic in the boars represented on the shields of the walking figures.[41]

With the Truia are to be grouped other ancient practices. British barrows in general, like other burials, were sealed by their circles[42] and horses may well have been used; as, with or without horses, Bryn Celli Ddu was clearly sealed.[43] This, too, is what Achilles did to the body of Patroclus, when he drove his chariot three times round it,[44] to prevent interference with the rest of his friend and perhaps also to prevent his ghost returning as indeed, before his burial, it did return:[45] a comparable custom is reported from Arabia, practised however not at deaths but at the ceremony of circumcision when 'mounted horsemen ride three times round the tent where it takes place'.[46] In a similar practice the chariot races of the Roman circus had their origin.[47] They at first averted evil from the mysterious Roman god Consus, who is equated by Livy with an equestrian Neptunus.[48] Consus, whose name is from 'condere', which means 'to hide' and therefore either to store provisions or to lay foundations in the earth, was one of the many gods of safety and stability worshipped in Italy. His sacred place was a 'mundus', a hole in the earth giving communication to the world below, kept shut, except at the Consualia, the festival of Consus. He had a consort called Ops, 'wealth'.[49] The horse ritual therefore secured the dependence of the city on the earth, in which it was founded, and its store of food, given at harvest; and at the same time it prevented evil influence from outside evoking excessive activity from the chthonic powers, symbolized by Consus in his equine shape. His own instrument or symbol, the horse, was used for this ritual. On a like principle, the Romans regularly sacrificed 'the October horse', enacting in this way something like a death of death. There is a very remarkable instance of the same process used with something like an opposite intention. Achilles, in the version of the story which Homer altered, dragged Hector three times round Troy, behind his chariot and horses. The writer of the *Culex*, in a passage which has lacked explanation, says that he 'purified', 'lustrauit', Troy with Hector's body.[50] The purification was more like exorcism; the movement must be supposed to have gone 'widdershins', against the sun, in order to unwind, not to make secure, the magic of the city's defence.[51] Perhaps this is the meaning of Lucian, when he says that Pyrrhus, the son of Achilles, invented the 'Pyrrhic' war dance, and by means of it captured Troy, invincible before.[52]

NOTES

1. G. Q. Giglioli, *Studi Etruschi* 3 (1929) 111–59, and Plate XXVI, with reff.
2. The late Professor R. S. Conway kindly explained to me this motive for the action of Augustus in encouraging the Truia.
3. Verg. *Aen.* V, 545–603.
4. Ibid. 588–93.
5. W. F. J. Knight, *Antiquity* 6 (1932) 445–58.
6. Verg. *Aen.* V, 593.
7. Ibid. 42–71.
8. Ibid. 46–8; F. Muller, Jun., *Mnemosyne* Ser. III, 2 (1935) 167–71, esp. 170 note 2.
9. Dio Cass. LIX, 11.
10. Plut. *Cat. Min.* III.
11. Galen. *Ad Pis.* 930–1; cf. A. von Premerstein, *Festschrift für O. Benndorf* (Vienna, 1898) 261–6.
12. F. Rasch, *De Ludo Troiae* (Progr. Gymn. Jena, 1882) 7.
13. Knight (above, note 5) 449–55.
14. Ibid. 457.
15. W. J. Hemp, *Archaeologia* 80 (1930) 179–214.
16. Stanley Casson, *The Progress of Archaeology* (London, 1934) 19: 'For the first time we know something about the ceremonial which accompanied a Bronze Age burial, for no similar mound has hitherto been so carefully examined.'
17. Hemp (above, note 15) 184, and Plate XLV, fig. 1.
18. Ibid. 197–8, and Plate XLIX.
19. Ibid. 200–1, Fig. 1, and Plate LVI.
20. Ibid. 197–8.
21. Ibid. 200–1.
22. Knight (above, note 5) 456–8.
23. Sen. *Troad.*, Teubner Text, ed. R. Peiper and G. Richter (Leipzig, 1921) 775–82:

> non arma tenera patria tractabis manu
> sparsasque passim saltibus latis feras
> audax sequeris nec stato lustri die
> sollemne referens Troici lusus sacrum
> puer citatas nobilis turmas ages.
> non inter aras mobili uelox pede,

reboante flexo concitos cornu modos,
barbarica prisco templa saltatu coles.

24. *The Daily Telegraph*, January 3, 1936, 12 col. 6.
25. Verg. *Aen.* V, 596–602:

> hunc morem cursus atque haec certamina primus
> Ascanius, Longam muris cum cingeret Albam,
> rettulit et priscos docuit celebrare Latinos,
> quo puer ipse modo, secum quo Troia pubes;
> Albani docuere suos; hinc maxima porro
> accepit Roma et patrium seruauit honorem;
> Troiaque nunc pueri, Troianum dicitur agmen.

26. Serv. *ad loc.*: rettulit: innouauit quod ante iam fecerat.
27. von Premerstein (above, note 11) 265.
28. Suet. *ap.* Serv. Verg. *Aen.* V, 602.
29. Festus, p. 439 (Lindsay).
30. D. Serv. Verg. *Aen.* II, 325.
31. O. Gruppe, *Griechische Mythologie und Religionsgeschichte* (Munich, 1906) I, 199, note 11.
32. Ibid. note 12.
33. Lucan, *Phars.* I, 592–606.
34. J. E. Harrison, *Themis*[2] (Cambridge, 1927) 194–5.
35. S. Eitrem, *Opferritus und Voropfer der Griechen und Römer* (Christiania, 1915) 27–8.
36. Inez Scott Ryberg, *TAPA* 63 (1932) lxiii–lxiv.
37. Eduard Meyer, *Kleine Schriften* (Halle, 1924) II, 278 ff., accepting after von Premerstein (above, note 11) 265, this interpretation of the *Fasti Praenestini*, *CIL* I, part 1[2], 234, which had been criticized by J. Toutain in Daremberg et Saglio, *Dictionnaire des Antiquités* V, 493–7, *s.v. Troia*.
38. *Cf.* Julius von Negelein, *Das Pferd in arischen Altertum* (Königsberg, 1905) 3–4, etc.; W. Mannhardt, *Mythologische Forschungen* (Strassburg, 1884) 156–201; E. Jones, *On the Nightmare* (London, 1931) 269, giving psychological reasons for the connotation of fertility.
39. L. Malten, *JDAI* 29 (1914) 179–256; *cf.* F. Altheim, *ARW* 29 (1931) 22–32.
40. A. H. Krappe, *RM* 81 (1932) 305–20.
41. *Cf.* Tac. *Germ.* XLV, 2.
42. *Cf.* A. Hadrian Allcroft, *Archaeological Journal* 78 (1921) 331–3; Eitrem (above, note 35) 23, 27.
43. Knight (above, note 5) 456–8.
44. Hom. *Il.* XXIII, 13.
45. Ibid. 65.
46. L. D. Burdick, *Foundation Rites with Some Kindred Ceremonies* (New York, 1901) 161–2.
47. *Cf.* Allcroft (above, note 42) 331–3 with reff.; he is, however, inclined to treat the races as fortuitous additions.
48. Liv. I, 9: [The new city seemed already doomed to perish because the Romans had no women, before the rape of the Sabines] ... Romulus ... ludos ex industria parat Neptuno equestri sollemnis; Consualia vocat; *cf.* Muller (above, note 8) 185 note 4, who adds to my account of Consus the point that he was propitiated because the city was threatened with death, of which horses are symbols. *Cf.* Allcroft (above, note 42) 321–40, on Consus.
49. G. Wissowa, *Religion und Cultus der Römer*[2] (Munich, 1912) 201; F. Altheim, *Römische Religionsgeschichte* I (Leipzig, 1931) 61, 65: II (Leipzig, 1932) 26.

50. *Culex*, 322–4:

> hos erat Aeacides uoltu laetatus honores
> Dardaniaeque alter fuso quod sanguine campis
> Hectoreo uictor lustrauit corpore Troiam.

51. Knight (above, note 5) 454–7.
52. Lucian, *De Salt*. IX.

VI

TROIE-ILIOS

'After all,' said the retired colonel in Tchehov, 'a pig's a pig; and it is not for nothing that it is called a pig.' Nor is it for nothing that Homer's city, the Italian military ride, and indeed mazes and maze dances in distant parts of Europe, all carry the same name of Troy.

To discover why, two principles have to be remembered. One is the general principle of the maze, exclusion, with conditioned admission. The other is the rule that in the development of legends facts attract to themselves as mythological accretions those myths which are in form similar to themselves.

In trying to find out what happened at any time in the legendary past, it is not enough to say that some element in a tradition is myth, and the rest probably fact. It is necessary to see fact and myth in a special relation. There must be a reason for the mythical accretion which comes to overlay a net of facts. Facts are of a certain class or shape. Mythical stories are attached to them and alter the tradition of them; but the particular mythical stories will usually be those which have already a form similar to the facts. That is, *any* facts cannot be presented in *any* mythical form. There is a limit to the change which mythology will effect. Myth first arises from some single event of human and personal relations and acts, then becomes in a sense general, as a statement of truth rather than an account of what once happened, and lastly is used as a mental container to hold the facts of some new event. The container can be called an archetypal pattern.

The principle has a firm psychological foundation;[1] and its point is this. The mind cannot think just anything. There are certain shapes in which it must think, varying at different times, of course. In Homer's mind the events of the *Iliad* fell into a flexible symmetry according to the habits of geometric art; and that is therefore the organization of the poem. Herodotus is influenced by pedimental sculpture and Attic tragedy; his account of Peisistratus, for example, is organized by central and supporting groups, as in a pediment, and he tells the story of

Cleomenes as if it were a myth of the shape of 'Hercules furens'. Even Thucydides is affected by 'myth'; quite without his knowledge, probably, his history is controlled by a current moral philosophy, in which punishment follows sin, and without conscious distortion or suppression his natural interest alone, by omissions and emphasis, channels history into an ethical shape.[2] This need not spoil the work; they say that a historian should be biased, and the truest things are often exaggerations. Such 'patterns' are found in most poetry. For example in *Paradise Lost*[3] Milton's mind worked according to two patterns of filial relationship, the pattern of love and respect for a father, in which Milton's God is formulated, and a contrary pattern of revolt, equally sincere, which allows Satan to be often the real hero of the poem. The New Testament itself is an example; for although the effect of pre-existing form on new content has been estimated without sufficient restraint, and there is still much disagreement about it, there is little doubt that the Gospel story, however accurate historically, is told in extant accounts, and reproduced in the ritual of worship, in a form that agrees with the ancient pattern of the king-god's death and resurrection. The same pattern dominates tragedy; and, following it, the tragedy of Shakespeare himself is strongly ritual.[4]

The story of the fall of Troy is not less preserved in an 'archetypal pattern'. I think it is clear that the pattern is in some sense the 'labyrinthine', and that Troy was very much a 'labyrinthine' city. Accordingly, 'labyrinthine' myth would be expected to provide the accretion, with the result which we find, a 'labyrinthine' account of the events.

Wherever the line between fact and mythic distortion ought to be drawn, there is at least one fact which I believe no one would deny. Troy was labyrinthine in being hard to enter, just like the prison which the Cretans, according to Plutarch, explained the real labyrinth to have been. Even the stone walls with the defended ramped gates were enough to evoke the metaphor of the labyrinth; as a recent writer has lately described the difficult country in Abyssinia as a labyrinth impassable to the uninitiated. If labyrinths or mazes were common objects of thinking at or soon after Trojan times, they offered a very ready description of the almost impenetrable Trojan defence. This might even have been enough; this is where fact might end and mythical metaphor begin; if there were not the reasons already given for believing the Troy of history to have been even more 'labyrinthine' than that.

But as soon as Troy is seen to be labyrinthine in any sense at all, another thing in the traditions becomes clearer. That is the part played by Helen. Helen has usually seemed to be either human or divine. The Trojan War is a historical event, intelligible against the background of the known world situation of that time; the walls of Hissarlik are tangible enough, and the Achaean League operates as the analogies of other heroic ages would suggest. There is not even any improbability that Helen, an heiress on whom the Achaean right to the Spartan throne depended, was one of the causes of the war.[5] Her abduction, whether its main motive was political or not, is by no means unlikely to be fact. Against this, Helen also looks divine, and this is inconvenient; Homer's line, 'terribly is she like the immortal goddesses to look into her face',[6] claims assent from investigators, as much as any it might claim from the Trojans. Helen was worshipped as a vegetation deity. At Sparta her cult was in the 'Menelaeion', which makes Menelaus look like a god also.[7]

Alexandros, who in Homer is synonymous with Paris, is known as a typical robber of folklore.[8] And Helen is carried away not only by Paris but also by Theseus, like Ariadne and Persephone, both goddesses of fertility. Theseus is strongly mythical, in the sense that the historical solidity of him and of his relations with others is slight, though there is little reason to doubt that a historical Theseus performed some of the acts attributed to him.

Now Paris has another name, but Helen has not, at least now. This is a hint. 'Paris' is not Greek; 'Paris', 'Priam', 'Anchises', and 'Aeneas' are probably the only true Trojan names which have survived in legend. But in telling the tale of Paris someone substituted the Greek name Alexandros, belonging to a typical robber. Both Alexandros the robber and Paris the Trojan steal Helen: I think because Helen and Alexandros were both mythical names in relation to the Trojan war, and a composite story of the abduction by a robber (from one context) of a goddess (from another) has become overlaid on another story, of the abduction by the Trojan prince Paris of a Mycenaean princess, whose name is lost for ever. If so, the masculine name Helenus, which is anyhow a little suspicious, may well be a divine name, more or less adapted to human use in northern Greece, and used for a Trojan who was a prophet and of some importance in the stories, though like his nameless counterpart, the Etruscan seer in the siege of Veii, he was not well equipped with any convincing name.[9]

Though a real princess was carried away to Troy, the presence of a goddess in the middle of a place with a labyrinthine name and attributes is not inappropriate. A labyrinth is at first a kind of tomb, and tombs are regularly in the earth. Therefore the entry to a tomb is the same, at least often, as entry into the earth. Helen the fertility goddess, worshipped in Rhodes as a tree spirit, is in 'Troy' as if she were below the earth, to be rescued by Theseus or another hero, in order that the fields may flower again.

The point is that facts have attracted as an accretion myths which are morphologically similar to them, for the very reason of their similarity. It was impossible in narrating the story of Troy to avoid confusion with the myths, and the story of Troy became clothed in them because they fitted. In this instance, furthermore, there is more than Helen, because there are also Athena, her palladion, and Cassandra, all female personalities in Troy, having some supernatural sympathy with the city itself. According to the ideal contemporary facts, Troy was in a sense a labyrinth and the defensive maiden powers were the object of attack.[10] The adjustment to myth was very easy; especially since Troy was a magical city relying on supernatural defence.

The broad question whether ancient cities were thought to depend on supernatural defence needs certain distinctions. Individual tribes, nomadic or settled, have had their own gods whom they supposed to fight the gods of other tribes on behalf of their worshippers. There may even be a divine conflict, which decides the issue of the fight on earth. The battles of the gods in Homer, which have not much result, are derived from earlier versions in which they were more effective. In earlier saga the gods must have gone far towards deciding the Trojan war. When a population was settled in a city, its gods became the gods of the city, and were expected to save the city from the enemy and to resist the enemy's gods. There were many sequences of development, tending towards more truly religious and more moral conceptions of divine protection.

Connected more or less closely with belief in the defensive efficiency of personal gods is a different principle of protection, by means of talismans.[11] They may have been sometimes little more than lucky objects, expected to bring good fortune by undefined means. At other times their supernatural attributes are clearer. Some were of meteoric origin, preserved for the invincible potency associated with metal from heaven. Others came to present a personal divinity with defensive powers, such as the palladion at Troy, representing Athena. Again, artificial objects were sometimes credited with an ability to fulfil their natural purposes by magical or at least supernatural means, as the sacred shield of Diomedes at Argos,[12] and the 'ancilia', the sacred shields at Rome. The fire at the public hearth, dimly personified as the Greek Hestia and the Latin Vesta, can perhaps be included among talismans; but that is too elusive a question for any single answer.

Lastly, there is the magic circle of the city wall. The signs of this in Greece are few and they are already dim in Homer. But Homer himself frequently mentions the 'sacred veil', 'ἱερὸν κρήδεμνον', of a city, which it is necessary to 'break' or 'undo' before the city can fall. The name is applied at Troy and Thebes to the sacred walls said to have been built by gods. A memory of early thought on such matters appears in the Homeric Hymn to Demeter, where kings are said to maintain the 'sacred veils' of cities by right judgments. Here the moralizing process has begun. Other signs of circle magic are to be discerned in the actions of Poemander, Toxeus, and in historical times Miltiades, all of whom jumped over a magic wall and suffered death in consequence, like Remus, whose story seems to be based on a Greek original. It is my suggestion that all these acts represent attempts to vitiate magic circles by crossing them, a suggestion supported by Plutarch's strong distinction between the profanity of a gate and the sanctity of a wall, and by the Roman rule of inflicting the death penalty on any soldier who crossed the wall of a camp at any place except the gates.[13] That an encircling wall was in early Greece connected with strong religious feeling is shown by the care with which at Mycenae the wall was constructed in relation to the graves.

A peculiarly interesting example of different kinds of supernatural defence is furnished by Egypt.[14] To the north-east of
Egyptian Thebes there is a fortress of Ptolemaic date, Medamud, and within it was a temple of the war god Montu. The
temple stands on a site which goes back to the nineteenth
century, but the plan of it, as it is disclosed by excavation, was
developed by the Lagids. This plan was for some time a mystery. All the Middle Kingdom texts mention Montu as lord of
the site; but excavation revealed a sanctuary of Amon, god of
Karnak, in the middle of the temple of Montu.[15] In the temple
were four statues of the armed Montu, designed to constitute the
'spiritual stronghold' of Thebes.[16] The explanation of the
sanctuary of Amon is now given by this conception, with new
help from an inscription of the time of Tiberius.[17] Part of the inscription is translated as follows. 'All that Thebes is Medamud
is: the Eye, complete [in all its elements], because His Majesty
[Amon Re] is one of the five gods who make Thebes exist like a
complete right Eye. The four Montus are his guard. They are
united in this town to repel the enemy from Thebes.' Now the
'Eye' mentioned is the sacred eye of Horus, which is found on
amulets. It has an eyebrow, and an appendage below and to the
side which is called 'menti'.[18] The buildings of Thebes are
actually planned to follow the lines of this eye, and there the
temple of Montu corresponds with the 'menti'. The 'menti' was
thought to be of great religious importance. At Medamud there
is the same design; and Amon has his own place in the temple of
Montu to represent Thebes itself there, so that by sympathetic
magic Thebes might be safe from all attacks, which Montu
repelled from his own temple and from Amon, protected within
it. This implies faith in two kinds of supernatural defence, firstly
direct protection by a god, and secondly magical efficacy inherent in a kind of palladion constituted by the association together of Amon and Montu.[19] That exactly these ideas were
held in Egypt at early dates is not yet proved. However, there
are strong reasons to think that magical protection of cities was
known long before the time of the evidence from Medamud.
The protective symbolism of the 'Eye' is proved for the reign of
Pepi II, in the twenty-fourth century, and it may be prehistoric.[20]

That there were sacred cities in other eastern lands is clear apart from the example of the fall of Jericho. The Babylonians, and neighbouring peoples also, firmly believed in sacred cities.[21] There is a sense in which the Babylonian ziggurats were focal points of sacred cities, holding them together.[22] The ziggurats affected Greek thought, for from them comes the belief in the soul's ascent to Heaven by way of seven circles, a belief which reached Dante by way of Spain from the Arabs, who adopted it for their beliefs about Heaven. The doctrine reached the Greeks in the fifth century B.C.[23] It is well worth while to suggest that the Greek sacred city, Thebes, the city of the seven gates, which are more ideal than real, itself contains a memory of the ziggurats.

The example from Egyptian Thebes shows one of the requisite distinctions very clearly, the distinction between the divine defence of a god and the magical defence of a palladion or talisman. Perhaps the distinction would have been shown more clearly still, if the god Amon Re himself, or at least his sanctuary, had not constituted the palladion. It is possible that two theories, one religious and one magical, have become fused; though it is not very safe, especially in the present state of knowledge, to say what is magical and what is religious, with any attempt at exact definition. On the other hand, there is some probability that talismans, valid for their material or their shape, were trusted before anthropomorphic protective deities, who in many instances were partly developed by personification of objects that were conceived to have power. Whether the objects were at first regarded as potent because they contained *mana*, or were the home of the ghost of a dead man, or the home of a spirit that had never been human, is a question that is important enough, but scarcely to be fitly discussed here. Perhaps it is sufficient to notice roughly the distinction between the potent object and the god; and to remember that the most important talisman of all, the Trojan palladion, which, like the ancilia, fell from Heaven, and, like or unlike the ancilia, was at first a meteorite, was treated by ancient writers as if it was a statue of the goddess Athena, who was herself closely associated with the defence of cities.

In classical Greece the magical defence of cities is not much emphasized; but, though there has been a tendency to deny that there was any belief in it, there are sufficient indications to prove that the belief existed.[24] Very different are the conditions in Italy. There magic circles round settlements are normal, and maintained by careful ritual throughout the historical period of ancient history. The Iguvine tablets declare very clearly how explicit was the care for the safety of a citadel and its people, manifested in conducting circular rituals of defence.[25] The ceremonies with which cities were founded unmistakably prove that there was reliance on the validity of a magic circle round them, first traced by the furrow ploughed. This faith may well be Etruscan; but it is important to recognize that its counterpart was at least as strong among the settlers of terramara villages, and before that of pile dwellings in the north. Indeed it has been shown that the Roman religion of supernatural exclusion from the city's area is partly descended from the inhabitants of terre-mare and pile settlements.[26] The Roman pontifices themselves were at first adepts who contrived the pile bridges across the magical confines, which led into early villages, and performed the delicate task of maintaining the magical safety of the in-habitants, in spite of the risk, which the construction of a bridge entailed, by cutting the circle. This is a strange origin for the pontifices, and for the name of the Pope himself, still called Pontifex Maximus.

Those who choose may consider that the name now legiti-mately means, 'builder of the bridge between God and man', the very meaning once thought to have been authentic among the Romans.[27] Stranger survivals than this might be found; and it is of their nature, and of the nature of the human progress which they sustain, that content should change and meet new truth, the old form remaining yet.

Now the pontifices, and the rest of the exclusive religion derived from terremare and pile dwellings, raise another ques-tion. Magical defence, by means of some kind of magic circle, survived strongly in Italy. It did not survive strongly in Greece; though even there the name of a clan at Athens, Gephyraioi, which means 'bridge men', may be a faint echo of some history parallel to the history of the pontifices in Italy, and it is even possible that sacred furrows at Athens, as in Italy, once had a defensive meaning.[28] It is more than likely that Italy and Greece both had a common layer of population, installed in those countries at a very early time, and that the survival of defence by magic circles in Italy, but not in Greece, can be partly explained because in Italy that layer of population remained at or near the top, but in Greece it was submerged, and lost its effect.[29] The explanation is not, of course, complete without the recognition of a further influence in Italy, the influence from the north, which brought the ritual of terremare to be blended with other methods of defence by magical means. Italian circle magic must therefore be composite, owing elements certainly to the Etruscans and to the incoming tribes from the north, and possibly to a layer of population which had been in Italy before either came.

Such ritual of defence is not necessarily to be thought strange or in any sense solitary. Full information is not yet available; but there are signs that the Greeks are much more remarkable for their failure to retain it than the Italians are for having it in several forms. In fact, a parallel to the Italian terramara settlements has actually been found in China;[30] and indigenous peoples in America, Africa, and Japan show signs of comparable defensive rites.[31]

The argument so far is sufficient to show that cities in the ancient world were, at many places and times, but not at all, supposed to depend on a scheme of magical defence, which might fitly be instituted by rites involving circular movements, and restored or maintained by repetitions of those rites. The circumstances in Italy, with the Italian foundation ceremonies and amburbia, are the best known; but signs of a similar system of beliefs, with local variations, are to be found elsewhere, even in Greece, where the traces in historical times are faint. The Italian ceremony of the Truia is therefore appropriate to the foundation of a city, and above all to the moment when the founder 'girds' the city 'with walls', as Vergil says of Ascanius and Alba. The Truia creates a magical entanglement to obstruct attackers on the old principle of the tactical labyrinth, translated into magic. This purpose is just as appropriate as the other purposes, of securing magical obstruction to protect a grave. On the temple gates at Cumae there was a picture of the labyrinth at Knossos, because they were near the entrance to the land of the dead, and to the City of God beyond.

Notes

1. Maud Bodkin, *Archetypal Patterns in Poetry* (London, 1934) 1–8, and *passim*, citing, p. 1, C. G. Jung for the description 'psychic residua of numberless experiences of the same type', some of them inherited in the structure of the brain from remote ancestors. Jung also called these residua 'archetypes'.

2. For patterned composition *cf.* J. T. Sheppard, *The Pattern of the Iliad* (London, 1922) *passim*; J. L. Myres, *Who Were the Greeks?* (Berkeley, California, 1930) 511–25, and 604–5 note 112, with reff.; id. *The Mythical Element in History*, a paper read to the Society for the Promotion of Hellenic Studies in London, February 5, 1935, in which the conclusions of F. M. Cornford, *Thucydides Mythistoricus* (London, 1907) *passim*, are developed. [Summary in *JHS* 55 (1935) xiii–xiv. J.D.C.]

3. Bodkin (above, note 1) 217–70 esp. 230–48.

4. G. Wilson Knight, *The Principles of Shakespearian Production* (London, 1936); now *Shakespearian Production* (London, 1964) Chapter V.

5. See above, pp. 103–4, with reff.

6. Hom. *Il.* III, 158: αἰνῶς ἀθανάτῃσι θεῇς εἰς ὦπα ἔοικεν.

7. For the reff. and the latest discussion of Menelaus, Helen, and Paris, *cf.* M. P. Nilsson, *Homer and Mycenae* (London, 1933) 251–3.

8. Ibid. 252–3.

9. See above, pp. 119–20.

10. Cassandra is called a sibyl (Suid. *s.v.*). Another sibyl is called Athenais (Strab. XIV, 645). Cassandra, also, and sibyls have similar relations with Apollo in myth. Apparently Cassandra is partly a human girl in Troy and partly a supernatural being in or at the entrance of a cave or labyrinth. There was a myth of Cassandra, and of the burial of herself and her twin sons, at Mycenae, in a context of wall sanctity (Paus. II, 16, 6–7); the twins are of course appropriate.

11. Sir J. G. Frazer, *Commentary on Pausanias* (London, 1898) IV, 433–7, on Paus. VIII, 47, 5, has an indispensable collection of instances.

12. R. H. Klausen, *Aeneas und die Penaten* (Hamburg and Gotha, 1839–40) II, 1192–3, 1203. See below, note 24.

13. See above, pp. 103–28, esp. 110–13 and notes, for this account of sacred walls. F. Muller, Jun., *Mnemosyne* Ser. III, 2 (1935) 182–7, restates much of the evidence and the conclusions, sometimes with expansions.

14. Étienne Drioton, 'La protection magique de Thèbes à l'époque des Ptolémées', *L'Ethnographie* N.S.23 (1931) 57–66, citing, 57, Lefébure, *Rites égyptiens. Construction et protection des édifices* (Paris, 1890) 15.

15. Drioton (above, note 14) 57–8.

16. Ibid. 58–9, citing, 58 note 2, for the theory of a 'spiritual stronghold' ('forteresse morale'), Bisson de La Roque, *Fouilles de l'Institut français d'Archéologie orientale du Caire* (1926), *Rapports préliminaires* IV, Part I, Medamud, 110–16.

17. Drioton (above, note 14) 59 note 1, citing Étienne Drioton, 'Les quatre Montou de Médamoud, *palladium* de Thèbes', *Chronique d'Égypte* 12 (Brussels, 1931) 259–70.

18. Drioton (above, note 14) 60; whether the general apotropaic significance of the eye is concerned here is uncertain. A gate to the Egyptian underworld hinged on an eye.

19. Ibid. 61.

20. Ibid. 62–6. Doors were sacred to Egyptians as to Greeks: Porph. *De Antr. Nymph.* XXVII: οὔκουν οὐδ' ἐπὶ τῶν ἄλλων θυρῶν ἐφ' ὁποίας οὖν ὥρας ἐξῆν λαλεῖν ὡς ἱερᾶς οὔσης θύρας, καὶ διὰ τοῦθ' οἱ Πυθαγόρειοι καὶ οἱ παρ' Αἰγυπτίοις σοφοὶ μὴ λαλεῖν ἀπηγόρευον διερχομένους ἢ πύλας ἢ θύρας, σεβόμενοι ὑπὸ σιωπῆς θεὸν ἀρχὴν τῶν ὅλων ἔχοντα.

21. E. Kornemann, *Die Antike* 8 (1932) 105–12, distinguishes sharply between cities in Italy and Asia, which were primarily homes of the gods, and cities of Greece, which were above all homes of human societies. They were far less 'hierocentric'.

22. Eric Burrows, S.J., in *The Labyrinth*, ed. by S. H. Hooke (London, 1935) 45–70, esp. 60, on 'the idealization . . . of the sacred cities and temples'.

23. Ibid. 67; F. Cumont, *Religions Orientales* (Paris, 1906) Ch. V note 88, and Ch. VI note 69. See below, p. 231, on the êkal tîrâni tablet, which has seven 'walls'.

24. Besides the signs of the sanctity of walls, gates, and cities in Greece already found, there are some others. The *Septem contra Thebas* of Aeschylus is partly a conflict between supernatural means of attack and defence, especially the magic of emblems on shields, and other more rational methods. The practice of demolishing city walls to admit an Olympic victor looks like a means to facilitate the entrance of good magic with the victor, who had proved his possession of it. The Roman triumph is similar in intention. Then there is the Pelargikon at Athens (Thuc. II, 17). The root ΠΕΛ means circular movement; and the oracle which said that the Pelargikon was 'better idle' seems to have been protecting a magic circle from profanation. The defensive rite of Diomedes at Argos is instructive. Diomedes was a hero specially attached to Athena. His shield, with the statue of Athena, was carried round the city of Argos, and on account of him both Argos and Arpi were supposed impregnable (Klausen, above, note 12, II, 1203). At Arpi were statues made of stones which Diomedes had brought from the walls of Troy. Daunus threw them into the sea, but they returned to their pedestals (Timaeus and Lycus *ap.* Tzetzes, Lycophr. 615). This is clearly magical defensive efficacy. (*Cf.* Klausen, above, note 12, II, 1192–3.)

25. *Tab. Iguv.* VIA–VIB, 47: an *amburbium* with sacrifices went round the city and at each gate prayers were said for the citadel and for the state, and for their names.

26. E. Täubler, *SHAW*, Ph.-hist. Kl. (1931/2) 2 Abh., *passim*.

27. Klausen (above, note 12) I, xxv.

28. Sam Wide, in A. Gercke and E. Norden, *Einleitung in die Altertumswissenschaft* II² (Leipzig, 1912) 197, notes that the sacred furrows, ἄροτοι ἱεροί, transferred from Eleusis to the Acropolis at Athens, took the place there of what was really a *sulcus primigenius* as in Italy: '. . . ursprünglich hatten doch die heiligen Pflügungen unterhalb der Akropolis von Athen einen anderen Sinn. Sie sind gewiss mit dem um die palatinische Burg von Rom gezogenen *primigenius sulcus*, und mit den noch bestehenden slavischen Umpflügungsriten zu vergleichen, bei denen es sich um die Abwehr jeden Übels handelt, sei es in Gestalt von Pest und Verderben bringenden Dämonen, sei es von menschlichen Feinden.'

29. E. Kornemann (above, note 21) 110.

30. Täubler (above, note 26) 80–1 with reff.

31. *Cf.* W. Simpson, *The Buddhist Praying-Wheel* (London and New York, 1896) *passim*, and L. D. Burdick, *Foundation Rites with Some Kindred Ceremonies* (New York, 1901) 149–66.

H

VII

TĪRĀNI

Troy was a sacred city, with a magic circle of walls. Much manipulation seemed necessary to the Achaeans, if the magic was to be neutralized. One of the most important instances of this is the act of Achilles who encircled Troy with horses, as he encircled the body of Patroclus; but he wanted to bind up the magic of the grave, and to unwind and loosen the magic of the city walls.

The labyrinthine epithet has found its way on to the Trojan tradition. The scene of festivity, when the Trojans were pulling in the wooden horse, is compared to a labyrinthine rite, the crane dance. Now it is also compared to a rope-dance, partly with reference to the rope by which the wooden horse was towed.[1] The connection between these two dances is nearly, if not quite, clear. The rope of a rope-dance represented either the navel string, or, on a later theory, the intestines. Both are appropriate to the anatomical meaning of a labyrinth, and incidental to a ceremony enacting birth or death, and assisting in that way the strength of life. Indeed, it is now argued that the Greek for 'dance', χορός, is cognate with χόρδη, 'gut', and therefore that a dance fundamentally is a movement representing the convolutions of the internal organs.[2] The full relevance of this must wait. Meanwhile, to accept the scene at the entry of the wooden horse as 'labyrinthine', the following point can be made. Troy is in the story entered with movements fit for a labyrinth, and therefore is treated as in some sense a labyrinth itself. Strangely, this might have been expected.

In Italy, the 'Truia' or Trojan game is known to have been 'labyrinthine' in its movements. It is therefore conceivable that its name means something like 'labyrinthine'. Accordingly, the Latin evidence from the name and its cognates may be useful. The correspondence of many such words with words known east of the Aegean was long ago noted and explained as a surprising coincidence.[3] But now another reason has become more probable than chance.

There are several ancient comments on these words. Festus[4] says that cavalry were called 'trossuli' because they took the Etruscan town of Trossulum without the help of infantry. Pliny[5] adds that they were also called 'flexumines' and quotes Junius Gracchanus for the belief that the name 'trossuli' was no longer understood, and that the cavalry were sometimes ashamed to be called that name. Junius was a friend of the Gracchi; so that the name 'trossuli' was old in the second century B.C., whether or not Sulla in any sense introduced the Truia from the east, as Plutarch[6] has been wrongly supposed to suggest. It is hard to dissent from an old view,[7] which connects the words 'Troia' ('Truia') and 'trossuli' together, and with other words 'troare', 'redantruare', meaning some kind of active movement, probably to and fro and possibly round about as well.[8] The name 'flexumines', which must mean something like 'benders', is instructive too. This is not the only word of the kind used of cavalry, for according to Servius,[9] who cites Varro, they were called 'flexutes'. All this goes to show that in early times vigorous movements, returning on themselves, zigzag, or backwards and forwards, were a sufficiently appropriate duty of cavalry to furnish names for them. As for the derivation from the town Trossulum, that is clearly the wrong way round, and no objection to the argument; though the mistaken etymology gives some help. At present it is enough to suggest that Trossulum may equally be called so because it was a town strengthened by magical movements indicated by such words as 'troare'. Two more remarks are wanted. 'Redantruare' is a technical word for part of the Salian dance,[10] and it is recorded that 'torosuli' was a form of 'trossuli',[11] a matter of some interest.

'Troy' means a maze or labyrinth in several places far outside Asia Minor. In England there are at least four examples of mazes called 'Troy', or still more impressively 'The Walls of Troy'. The name 'Troy' designates mazes in many parts of Europe, even as far away as Russia.[12] There are two questions. One is, whether the names all came from the same place and if so where; the other, whether the 'Troy' words are derived from a proper name or a descriptive word originally, and if they are from a descriptive word, what that word principally means. The questions cannot easily be kept apart.

The most elaborate system of thought about all this material is concerned mainly with the northern labyrinths.[13] One in

Germany is said to be dated by finds to the later part of the Bronze Age.[14] Of course, Bryn Celli now proves that the labyrinthine idea occurred, in its true application to a tomb, still earlier in northern Europe. But that has been discovered since. The inference drawn from the northern evidence was that the name of Troy, the labyrinthine pattern, and rites and myths belonging to it, came down from the north to Mediterranean lands;[15] that the intention of the structures and rites was solar, concerned to maintain the beneficent activity of the sun and stars;[16] and that the Greek stories of Troy and Knossos were simply northern myths, adopted by Greeks, with no reference to the places where they are localized.[17] The original meaning of the Troy words, found in northern Europe to mean 'castle' or 'fort', 'breast', and 'dance', is referred to a central idea of 'surrounding'.[18]

Against the theory of the northern origin of the Troy names, myths and rites, are opposite theories that they came from the south, introduced from Italy by the Roman occupation, or ultimately from Egypt much earlier, by a diffusion of megalithic people. The Roman theory cannot possibly fit the evidence. Roman influence could never have imposed elements of culture so permanently and so far away, even if that influence had been active early enough, as it was not.[19] The Egyptian theory assumes that the cult of the king-god and his tomb spread from Egypt, and became firmly established in Troy; and that for that reason the name of Troy, originally the proper name of Homer's city, came everywhere to be applied to mazes.[20] Against this is the lack of evidence that there were any king-gods at Troy, or even in a great majority of the places where mazes occur; and also it is strange that the Troy names should have spread so far and remained so tenaciously if they were all copied from a single city's proper name. Further, it was Crete not Troyland that was remembered by tradition as the home of labyrinths.

The Egyptian theory at least recognizes where the earliest maze patterns were made and used. They are about a thousand years earlier in Egypt than anywhere else. There they are used for exclusion, first at forts and then at graves and temples. Northern influence is unnecessary. But the mazes and maze names appear early in the north, and are associated with nothing that looks Egyptian. The maze idea may have originated independently in many places. On the other hand, northern mazes are far most often near the sea, associated with signs of the sea-borne megalithic culture. With that the maze idea may have spread from the eastern Mediterranean; possibly the megalithic culture may have had some loose contact with Egypt, but Asia is more likely to have been its origin. Relevant discoveries are to be expected when Cilicia is better explored. Cilicia is now proved to be the home of the Keftiuans, well known from Egyptian monuments; and it is likely to have been the centre of a strong culture, hitherto scarcely known.[21] It is from Cilicia that the 'Cyclopes', identified with the 'stone men', are said to have come. And meanwhile it must not be forgotten that even in Egypt the explicit 'square fret' mazes on seals and plaques, associated with human figures, occur suddenly after a period of strong eastern influence.

There are of course 'Troys' and 'Troy' names in Italy. The names long ago received an approximately right explanation, by reference to a root meaning primarily 'turn', or, 'move actively'.[22] That is, the 'Troy' names were not all either due to settlements of Trojans, or invented to confirm a developing belief that Trojans had settled in Italy. They had nothing therefore to do with Homer's Troy; and the occurrence of the same name for the city and the maze-places and maze-rite had to remain a coincidence. But the theory was nevertheless a great advance.

The 'Troys' in Italy needed an explanation. It is hard to think that they only started after the literary legend of Trojan foundations took shape. 'Troys' in Italy were noted as confirmation of those legends; and not many have been ready to accept the legends of Trojan settlements at all literally. A 'Troy' therefore was a place for moving quickly to and fro; and that is, apparently, an important part of the truth. Meanwhile, a similar suggestion was made for a maze in Wales called Caer Droia.[23] 'Caer' is 'camp'; 'Droia' was referred to a Celtic root TRO, meaning 'turn' in many slightly varying senses. This applied well to the turns of the maze, like the Latin word 'tro-are'. The occurrence of words from similar roots in Latin and Celtic is of course likely; and there is always a possibility that the root may belong to an earlier linguistic layer.

There are other views concerning the meaning of the root from which Troy names, supposed originally descriptive words, may come. It has been referred to geographical features, such as a valley.[24] A root can usually be found to fit a theory. But on this occasion the root chosen should at least fit mazes generally; and this the geographical roots scarcely can, for a maze need not be in any particular geographical situation. A word meaning some kind of movement is therefore best. Now comes the question of the 'labyrinthine' city, Homer's Troy.

The safest thing to do is to suppose that Homer's Troy and all the other Troys were called after the word used for mazes and labyrinths. Troy was called Troy because it had some quality of a maze. The obvious definition of this quality is as follows. A maze is a material or magical instrument of shutting, and Troy was very much a shut city. This is preferable to another proposal that has been made, attractive as it is:[25] that Troy was called Troy because it shut the trade-routes, between north and south and between east and west, which crossed commanded by the city's walls. This is to be doubted because it seems to involve a strange use of the still religious word for shutting, especially at such an early time, and again it is most uncertain that control of trade was explicitly considered as a motive of national policy in Trojan times. Troy, like other places that had the name, was rather shut than shutting; and it was in all probability so called because it was at some time thought to be shut by magical power.

This belief has had some support and agreement, with a further definition of the meaning of 'Troy' as 'sacred or magically encircled city', the proper name of the place being Ilios or Ilion:[26] this is all right except that the Ilian words themselves actually and impressively seem to be nearly synonyms for 'Troy'. Their easiest derivation is from a root 'wal', or 'wel', 'ϝαλ' or 'ϝελ'; there is the digamma in the root and in 'Ilios' also. Cognate with 'Ilios' is an important verb, ϝείλω, which has a rich variety of meanings, some quite close to the meanings of the Celtic 'tro'. Among the meanings is 'roll up tight, pen into a narrow space'. Nothing could be much nearer to the meaning of maze movements, as they have been quite independently inferred.[27]

This opens the question of the Ilian Athena and the Ilian

Aias. It is too soon to be sure. But it looks possible that the defensive Athena and the hero connected with her may have been called 'Ilian' as a description of defensive powers. The name may mean the same thing in Greece, among the Locrians; and even in Italy; for there Athena and Minerva are often 'Ilian', Ilia is the name of the vestal who was mother of Romulus and Remus, and Iulus himself, who significantly conducts the Truia, was said to have been originally 'Ilus'. This, however, must wait for new evidence, or new ingenuity in interpreting the old. The suggestion may turn out to be helpful, but it must not be pressed now.[28]

'Troy' and 'Ilios' applied to Homer's city, and ultimately personal names also such as 'Tros' and 'Ilus', appear to express the particular defensive quality thought to reside in Troy. 'Trojans' and 'Ilians' are then the 'men of the magically defended city'. What is otherwise known of these names does not apparently contradict this. They have been identified in contemporary Egyptian records, where 'Taroisa' are possibly Trojans and 'Wilusha' quite probably Ilians.

Of the Ilian name so much only can be said, but about the Trojan there is something to add. Some years ago some Babylonian tablets were discovered, marked with maze patterns. The date is about 1000 B.C.[29] The patterns mean the intestines of animals used for entrail divination; this is proved by inscriptions on them, especially on one, inscribed 'êkal tîrâni', which is translated 'palace of the intestines'. The name of Homer's city has lately been compared to the word 'tîrâni', 'intestines', so that 'Troy' is cognate with 'tîrâni'.[30] This conjecture can be strengthened by the further comparison of the word 'Taroisa', and the root of 'troare' in Italy. The appearances of the root in Italy are bewildering in their variety, from 'porca troia', 'a pregnant sow' to 'redantruare' in its sense of 'repay a kindness', and 'trulla', 'a cooking pot'.[31] Whether the human mind has a right to unity or not, it demands it; and I risk saying that the unity binding these words is the notion of 'to and fro', applicable to the movements of a maze, to the returning anatomy of the intestines, and to reciprocations of goodwill. If so, the sow is called 'troia' because it has young within it; and the 'trulla' is called a 'trulla' because it cooks one sort of cheap meat. Further if a 'Troy' is a defended place of certain magical

FIGURE 13

Babylonian Tablets, connected with entrail divination, with patterns
in the form of a spiraliform maze (after F. Muller, Jun., *Mnemosyne*,
S. III, vol. II, 1935, Plates VI and VII; with acknowledgments to
Messrs E. J. Brill, Leiden).

power, 'Trossulum' in Etruria is explained; and 'trossuli', also vocalized 'torosuli' resembling 'tîrâni' and 'Taroisa', are seen to be cavalry, who, by performing a Truia, a function expressed also by the names 'flexutes' and 'flexumines', magically strengthen the defence. It is also now clear why Roman cavalry objected to their old name.

If this is the root-meaning of 'troia', 'truia', it fits the occurrence of the word 'truia' inside the maze pattern of the Tragliatella oenochoe very well. [See p. 203 above.]

There is more to say of the pictures there. In the latest discussion it is suggested that the riders are coming out of a labyrinth; if so, the maze drawing does not express a track they have followed in the open.[32] The objection to this is that horses ridden inside a labyrinth are hard to parallel, even if the interpretation otherwise fitted. The proposal that the inscription MI FEΛENA ('mi welena') elsewhere on the vase means that Helen is pictured is only made to be rejected, since that is not the Etruscan form of Helen's name. Therefore, it cannot be shown that the group of figures in front of the men marching on foot represents Paris and Helen, although the object held by the large female figure has generally been considered an apple. If the scene had been the judgment of Paris, three female figures, not two, would have been expected, for the three goddesses. The scene, therefore, is better regarded as ritual than as mythological; and in fact in this same interpretation the two pairs of figures to the right of the maze engaged in physical union are said to mean a sacral marriage. This may be accepted, especially as it is supported by very similar scenes on Babylonian seals.[33] If so, no account can yet be given of the three or four figures outside the scenes of marching, riding and marriage. However, the supposition that the marching and riding men are engaged in ritual can stand. Therefore we have a performance of a Truia, and something like an amburbium on foot, both apotropaic. Meanwhile, the marriage scenes, also ritual, are going on. All that is shown intelligibly to us is two sorts of ritual observance; the sacral marriage on which fertility depends, which is a rite of freedom and communion, and the converse rites of exclusion and constriction, designed to preserve the other enactment from external harm.

This then is a picture of a foreign, eastern observance, united to an eventually Italian rite, called by a name, 'truia', that is found over a wide area. It is safest to say that the name spread over that area from an unknown source, whence it reached both Italy and Homer's Troy.[34]

If all this is fair, it is also fair to ask whether the Trojan 'game' was ever 'played' at Homeric Troy. Besides the memories of the act of Achilles, who dragged Hector round Troy, the only direct assertion of anything of the kind is in Seneca. He is of course late, but he certainly used old material now lost in which the magical tradition about Troy had left more traces than it has in extant works. This old material he handled by recombination of its elements, comparable to the method of Vergil, but different from it, since the transferences of Seneca are less violent. It is sometimes possible to detect that Seneca and Vergil are using the same source, Seneca more conservatively.[35] This is so when they mention the Trojan Game. In Vergil, Iulus leads the Truia in Sicily and Italy, and it is used as part of the ceremonies connected with the burial of a prince and afterwards with the foundation of a city.[36] In Seneca, Astyanax leads the Truia in Troyland; it is called a rite of purification, and connected with temple dancing.

It would be characteristic of the two poets if they proved to be using a single source, in which Astyanax led the Truia in Troyland. That Seneca is not merely thinking of the Imperial, social Truia of his own day, is shown by the religious quality he gives to the observance, a quality little remembered, even if understood at all, at that time. And Euripides has a passage which, if it is cleared of emendations, hints that he knew of such a ritual also.[37]

There is archaeological evidence for contemporary belief at Homer's Troy in supernatural defence. Two small standing stones at a gate of Hissarlik have been compared to the Biblical Jachin and Boaz, with the convincing suggestion that they guarded the gate.[38] So also it is hard to think that the newly investigated large stone pillars at the south gate, already accepted as religious in purpose,[39] are not apotropaic.[40] Near to them is still the projecting tower, on which Penthesilea was said to have been cremated 'near the bones of Laomedon'. This looks like a memory of a defensive sacrifice, in the context.[41]

Labyrinthine dances still survive in Crete and elsewhere, and

they survived in classical Greece. Homer's reference to a dancing-floor like Ariadne's (see below, p. 239) proves the existence of labyrinth dances; it is likely that they happened at many
temples,[42] and possibly in the theatre at Athens, where a
labyrinth of Roman pattern is to be seen on the floor of the
later orchestra.[43] Protective dances were danced in Egypt, and
probably everywhere else. It is more likely than not that protective and labyrinthine dances were performed at Troy, to
protect some temple or tomb, or perhaps the city itself.

If so, the description of the scene at the entry of the wooden
horse can be explained as follows. When the Trojans pulled the
wooden horse in, they behaved as in a labyrinthine dance.
Whatever the horse itself may mean, it looks as if a dance of this
kind might fitly be danced outside the walls of Troy, whether
the account of it belongs to this place in the tradition or has been
transferred to the entry of the horse from some other occasion.
The dance then may have been a protective dance, performed
outside the city of Troy to strengthen the divine defence. If so,
the origin of such dances, of which there will be more to say, in a
representation of anatomical forms may have been remembered
dimly in the derivation of the supposed cordax rope-dance from
the rope that pulled the wooden horse.

The connection of the Trojan horse with mortuary myth,
readily suggested by the well-known folk-lore of the horse as a
symbol or agency of death, is confirmed by close Egyptian
parallels.

In the Egyptian *Book of Gates* the sun-god comes to the funerary mountain Amenti, which counted as the first gate on the
journey.[44] By the use of magic it is split open, and the gods of the
desert and mountain lands assist Afu, the sun, to pass through
the gap. Presently the third gate is reached. 'This is a very strong
gate. Behind the door is a sort of double wall which is guarded
by two gods in mummy form'.[45] When the eleventh gate is
reached 'the gods of this gate welcome the arrival of the Boat of
Afu, and when it closes after his entrance the gods on the battlements wail'.[46]

The sun-god is towed in by eight gods, who draw the boat
through the body of the 'Boat of the Earth', which is a sort of
tunnel, each end of which terminates as the head of a bull. 'The
text states that the soul of Ra has been absorbed by the Earth-

God, and he who is in the Boat of the Earth is holy.'[47] Apep, the snake that is the enemy of the sun-god, is held down by a rope, pulled by gods.[48] Rope spells, also, are used.[49] There is, as in the Sixth *Aeneid*, a place at the entrance of the world of the dead for those who have been drowned.[50] Spells were built into the walls of Egyptian tombs,[51] comparable to the apotropaic agencies built into the wall of Troy.[52]

Some writers, ancient and modern, have treated the wooden horse as a ship. The horse has been explained as a ship, on the theory that the story merely means that the Achaeans sailed to Troy. Again, the Trojan and the Egyptian gates are opened in magical circumstances. The double wall behind an Egyptian gate is obstructive, like entrances in Egyptian architecture and at Troy, like Chinese spirit walls, and indeed the whole labyrinthine idea. The Trojan south gate was guarded by two pillars, like the two Egyptian gods in mummy form. The horse, like the Egyptian boat, is helped through by gods, and as it passes, gods on the wall and citadel cry aloud. In both accounts there is emphasis on ropes. The anatomical symbolism suspected in the Trojan story is explicit in the Egyptian.

Much might be argued from this comparison, but only a little is safe. Probably enough there was contact between the myth of Egypt and of Aegean or Asiatic lands at or soon after Trojan times. It is of some interest that the conception of men inside the Trojan horse has already found a comparison, in an Egyptian version of the story of *Ali Baba and the Forty Thieves*;[53] which is not of course to be supposed a peculiarly Egyptian motive. However, what can be said is this. The story of the Trojan horse has been affected by contact with mortuary myth. The entry into Troy is conceived as entry, at death or initiation, into the earth.[54] The horse may be many things. In part it is the death horse of folk-lore,[55] and also possibly a symbol of fertility and sexual strength.[56] There may be in it a memory of some boat that crossed the waters of death; and possibly too of some beast, centaur or minotaur, from the middle of a maze or 'Troy'.[57] Many elements of mortuary myth are unmistakably present in the legends of the city's capture.

It is hard to see, however, how such conceptions could have turned into the story. Not less attractive is the possibility that the Trojan horse has the same place in folk-lore as the horses of

Siegfried and other northern heroes, on which they ride over walls.[58] The parallel is exact; and it is said that the same act is known in actual ritual.[59] But no unilateral solution is sufficient singly, if only because so many of them are well supported. The composite mortuary motive has been imposed on the facts of a magical attack on the historical city's sacred walls. Rather than to leave out the factual part, it is preferable to find in the facts something to attract a particular kind of myth. The facts at Troy are the magic circle of the wall and attempts by the attackers to break it. These facts attracted mortuary myth, mainly from the south, including Egyptian myth; and also the folk-lore motive of the mounted hero, mainly from the north. The important conclusion now is, that the labyrinthine quality of Troy attracted mortuary myth because the labyrinth is appropriate to mortuary belief concerned with tombs and caves.

There is one more question at this point. The earth was pictured by Egyptians, Asiatics and classical Greeks in human form, according to the system of microcosm and macrocosm.[60] The myth makers treated Troy as the earth.[61] In Italy, Vesta is clearly, on the one hand, the earth, and, on the other hand, the city of Rome.[62] The Sumerians believed in heavenly counterparts of earthly cities; and their ziggurats were meant to bind together both the land of men, and the upper and lower worlds also.[63] Certainly, the sky, at least in later Gnosticism and astrology, was mapped out to correspond with the human body; that is how the influence of the stars on destiny and character was plotted.[64] It remains to ask whether a city could be pictured as a human being.

This has been suspected, by inference from the maidenhood of city goddesses, which seems to have been in some magical sympathy with the unbroken defence of a city.[65] This explanation fits the myths of the capture of Troy; especially the act of a Trojan woman, releasing her girdle of maidenhood, κρήδεμνον, when the sacred wall of Troy, also called by the same name, κρήδεμνον, was 'released' or broken to admit the wooden horse.[66] It also fits the evidence concerning the terms of the Locrian curse, which look as if they were meant to restore the maiden purity of Athena;[67] and the practice of burying Vestals, as if their default weakened the city's defence.[68] The assault of Hephaestus on Athena at Athens[69] seems to be at once a myth of a sacral marriage of heaven and earth, and also a myth of an attack on the city. Tarpeia is clearly a defensive sanctity at Rome, and her maidenhood is in sympathy with the city's preservation.[70]

The possibility has now been brilliantly stated,[71] but on different evidence, chiefly poetic metaphors in Latin comedy which need not, of course, be reliable indications of far earlier belief. The statement is that ancient cities in prehistorical thinking were in certain places regarded in the human image of maidens; the violation of the maiden being a description of the breach of the city wall, and the capture of the city.[72] The further comparison of the êkal tîrâni tablets adds some credibility; the name 'palace of the intestines', with other details, suggests that the mazes on the tablets mean both intestines and architectural structures, cities, temples, forts or tombs.[73] This is argued, but might be doubted; and anyhow the intestines belong to animals, and may have no reference to human anatomy. For Troy there is a further argument that Priam himself represents the city in a special way, as if he personally symbolized it, and in fact was his city.[74]

Not only has the evidence of the êkal tîrâni tablets been accepted as showing that anatomical images were applied to sacred cities,[75] but a similar opinion has been reached on quite different evidence, the argument starting from the Malekulan geometrical drawings.[76]

They are all based on two types: 'Class A composed of a continuous line having a definite beginning and end, meandering on a linear framework, and Class B composed of a continuous never-ending line enclosing a space.' The extract of the paper on the subject, from which these words come—the whole paper is not yet published goes on: '. . . The mortuary mythology connected with the Malekulan geometric drawings is then discussed, and the conclusion is drawn that the basic origin of Class A is the delineation of the path (the continuous line having beginning and end) traced when threading the mazes of the labyrinthine tomb (the linear framework), and that the basic origin of Class B is the human form representing the body of the dead king, Lord of the Underworld.'[77]

That might mean that though, possibly, the tactical labyrinth came first, and determined the shape of tombs, anatomical symbolism was applied early in the development, and controlled the scheme of maze dances and continuous line drawings within a wide area. It does not seem necessary to deny the tactical origin of the labyrinthine pattern, which is hard to doubt. The application of anatomical forms might have been the easier for the conception of earth as universal mother; but it is to be noticed that the labyrinthine tomb is conceived to represent the anatomy not of a mother but of a king. Both principles seem to become fused; and it is to be observed that in Egypt the earth is male and the sky female, as pictures show, though this reverses the usual belief of other parts of the world. The Egyptian sky-goddess was Nut, and the earth-god Geb; there is however also Osiris, type of dead king-gods, who is pictured as coiling round the underworld, like Oceanus in Greek imagination. Possibly Homer himself has blended both the images, in the Shield of Achilles, where Oceanus is represented encircling the shield, and near the middle is a dancing-floor like the 'dancing-floor of Ariadne', which is of course a maze.[78] If so, this is another residual piece of the old initiation pattern disintegrated by Homer. On the whole, if the anatomical theory is accepted, it is not yet very safe to differentiate too sharply the male and female principles. They seem to meet in lands within Greek influence; the cave mouth certainly belongs to the earth mother, but there are signs of the male principle.[79] It is, however, mainly apparent in an intelligible and secondary way. Caves were places of burial, and of birth; and principally of the birth and burial of kings and gods. Zeus was born in a cave, and part of the old beliefs survives in the accounts of this. One account worth quoting is as follows:

'It is said that in Crete is a sacred cave of the bees, in which according to the myths Rhea gave birth to Zeus. No one, either god or mortal, may pass into it. But each year at a fixed time there is seen a great blaze of fire shining from the cave. The myths say that this occurs when the blood of Zeus, shed as a result of his birth, boils over. The cave is occupied by the sacred bees, who fed Zeus. [Certain men wearing bronze armour against the bees] ventured to go in; there they saw the infant clothes of Zeus, and immediately the bronze they wore burst open. Zeus thundered, and lifted his thunderbolt; but the Fates and Themis stayed his hand, for no one might die in that hallowed place. [So the men were turned into birds.]'[80]

How the anatomical symbolism may have helped to develop maze dances in Egypt has been suggested. The dead Egyptian king was eviscerated, and his intestines were put in Canopic jars. The suggestion is that 'the bearers of the Canopic jars on their way to, and within, the Pyramids, performed evolutions symbolical of the bowels which they were carrying'.[81]

There are then probabilities that the maze belongs to the anatomy of the buried king-god and of the earth mother, and that cities were conceived in human imagery and in imagery of the earth and of the tomb. That the earth, sky and universe were at different times and places equated as macrocosm with human beings is known; and something is known also of the magical defence of cities. Therefore, there is not much risk in saying that defensive cult at Troy, Rome and elsewhere, and myth derived from it, were strongly affected by habits of thinking applicable primarily to a human maiden, in whose form, with greater or less clarity, the city goddess, and then the city, were seen. Athena, Cybele who came near to identity with her, and Vesta all wore the towered crown in later centuries; the personification must have been still more easy and obvious in earlier times.

The mortuary pattern is clearly applied to a city in mediaeval myths preserved in Russia. In one,[82] a foundling king rebuilt Babylon, after a plague, on seven hills and seven terraces, like a ziggurat, or ideal Thebes or Rome. The city wall had only one gate, for stronger defence; and it was in the form of a coiled serpent, devised to emit flames upon attackers. The serpent naturally represents the maze or waters of death or the body of an earth god or goddess in mortuary myth; which here as elsewhere has blended with conceptions of the city and its defence.

The conclusion at this point is that Homer's Troy was a 'labyrinthine' city, and that it was called 'Troy' or 'Ilios' because those names expressed what it was; and that names cognate with 'Troy' spread at some early time with the religion and pattern of the 'labyrinth' and remained in some ancient layer of language in many parts of Europe. I take it that a 'labyrinthine' city fulfils some or all of the following conditions. It must be supposed to depend on supernatural defence, inaugurated and sustained by magical or religious ceremonies, which are meant, either always or at least often, to create or strengthen the ring magic of the wall, in particular by means of 'labyrinthine' movements. The labyrinthine city is imagined, either originally or later, in human shape; and the defences are directly or indirectly pictured according to human anatomy, under influence of the symbolism of earth the universal mother, and the later development of the labyrinthine tomb. To this complex, at Troy, has been applied both the northern folk-lore motive of the mounted hero, and elements of mortuary myth.

NOTES

1. A. B. Cook, *JHS* 14 (1894) 101–2; W. F. J. Knight, *Folk-Lore* 46 (1935) 104–6.
2. F. Muller, Jun., *Mnemosyne* Ser. III, 2 (1935), 201–2, quoting on the word χόριον Hippocr. I, 461; Aristot. *Hist. An.* VI, 158; etc.; and esp. Varro, *De Re Rust.* II, 1, 19: 'dicuntur agni cordi qui post tempus nascuntur ac remanserunt in volvis intimis...; vocant chorion (=χόριον) a quo cordi appellati.'
3. R. H. Klausen, *Aeneas und die Penaten* (Hamburg and Gotha, 1839–40) I, xvii.
4. Festus, p. 505 (Lindsay): Trossuli equites dicti, quod oppidum Tuscorum Trossulum sine opera peditum ceperint.
5. Pliny, *N.H.* XXXIII, 2, 9.
6. Plut. *Cat. Min.* III.
7. Klausen (above, note 3) II, 823.
8. Festus, p. 9 (Lindsay): *Antroare* gratias referre. Truant moventur. Truam quoque vocant, quo permovent coquentes exta. *Andruare* id est recurrere a Graeco verbo ἀναδραμεῖν venit; hinc et drua vocata est. *Cf.* ibid. p. 334: *Redantruare* dicitur in Saliorum exultationibus: 'cum praesul amptruavit', quod est, motus edidit, ei referuntur invicem idem motus. Lucilius: 'praesul ut amptruet inde, ⟨ut⟩ vulgus redamptruet †at†.' Pacuius: 'Promerenda gratia simul cum videam Graios nihil mediocriter redamptruare, opibusque summis persequi.' *Cf.* also Nonius, p. 165: redantruare, redire.
9. Serv. Verg. *Aen.* IX, 606 (flectere ludus equos): flectere autem verbo antiquo usus est, nam equites apud veteres flexutes vocabantur, sicut ait Varro rerum humanarum.
10. Festus, p. 334; see above, note 8.
11. Nonius, p. 49: Trossuli dicti sunt torosuli.
12. W. H. Matthews, *Mazes and Labyrinths* (London, 1922) 4, 23, 52, 71, 81, 88, 89, 91, 93, 94, 98, 129, 151, 156, 162, 181, 197, 202, 211, 216, 225, 233.
13. Ernst Krause, *Die Trojaburgen Nordeuropas* (Glogau, 1893) *passim*.
14. Ibid. 33–6.
15. Ernst Krause, *Die nordische Herkunft der Trojasage* (Glogau, 1893) 41–8.
16. Krause (above, note 13) 156–94, etc.
17. Ibid. 277–300, esp. 279–81.
18. Ibid. 11.
19. An argument for the Roman origin of 'Troy' names is the occurrence of other names, almost certainly derived from the *Aeneid*, in similar contexts; for example, 'Juliberry', recalling Iulus who led the 'Truia' (Matthews, above, note 12, pp. 71,

78, 90, 173, 230). But what will not account for all the facts may account for some; these names might easily have been imposed on much earlier 'Troys'.

20. Mrs C. N. Deedes in *The Labyrinth*, ed. by S. H. Hooke (London, 1935) 36–41.
21. G. A. Wainwright, *JHS* 51 (1931) 1–38 (and several other important articles there cited), has proved the Cilician origin of the Keftiuans against the formerly accepted opinion that they are Cretans.
22. Klausen (above, note 3) II, 810–34.
23. Matthews (above, note 12) 92, attributes the suggestion to W. H. Mounsey who made it in 1858. I owe the following information to the kindness of Professor J. E. Lloyd. In old Welsh literature the city of Troy is sometimes styled 'Caer Droia'; and the same name is also applied, for reasons difficult to apprehend, to a maze or labyrinth. On the second point Professor Lloyd refers to a notice, with plan, furnished by Peter Roberts, *Cambrian Popular Antiquities* (London, 1815) 212–13, who also suggested that the real connection of the name is not with Homeric Troy but with the word 'tro', 'turning'. Mr W. J. Hemp kindly informs me that the ordinary Welsh word for 'to turn' is 'troi'. The best dictionary (Anwyl) gives: TROI: to turn; to revolve; . . . to stir; . . . to convert; . . . to become; to plough. TRO -ION -IAU: turn; . . .curve; screw; twist; time; . . . occasion; . . . walk; tour; conversion. TROAD: bend, turning, twist, flexion.
24. J. Carcopino, *Virgile et les origines d'Ostie* (Paris, 1919) III, 404–8, gives recent opinions.
25. G. D. Hornblower, *Antiquity* 7 (1933) 94–5.
26. F. Muller, Jun., 'De beteekenis van het Labyrinth', *MKAW*, Afd. Lett. 78, B, 1 (1934) 15, thinks 'Ilios' the city's proper name: '*Troia* zou dan ± 'kringstad, heilige stad' als appellativum kunnen hebben beteekend, waarnaast dan Ἴλιος nomen proprium kan zijn geweest.' I doubt if 'Ilios' is really much less descriptive even than 'Troia'.
27. Liddell and Scott[8] *s.v.* εἴλω give: '*to roll up* or *pack into a close compass* . . ., κατὰ τείχεα λαὸν ἐέλσαι, *to roll up* the host *and force* it *back* to the walls, *Il.* 21, 295 . . ., *to go to and fro*, . . . *to wind, turn round* . . .' Most of the important meanings are here too, therefore; and since the root of εἴλω, Fαλ or Fελ, is identified also in ἴλιγξ, ἴλιγγος, ἰλιγγιάω, the etymological connection with 'Ilios' is satisfactory (W. F. J. Knight, *Antiquity* 7, 1933, 132).
28. 'Ilu' in Babylonian meaning 'god' appears on a tablet for entrail divination (Ernst F. Weidner, *Orientalistische Studien Fritz Hommel* I, Leipzig, 1917, 192–3). If Vergil meant to recognize such an etymological meaning for Ilium in 'o diuom domus Ilium et incluta bello/moenia Dardanidum' (*Aen.* II, 241–2), this would be only characteristic of him; for a similar use of word play, *cf.* 'Aeaeaeque insula Circae' (*Aen.* III, 386) (see p. 166 above). Babylon, 'Bâb-ili', actually means 'door of the gods': E. Kornemann, *Die Antike* 8 (1932), 109.
29. Weidner (above, note 28) 191–8; E. Hommel, *OLZ* 22 (1919) 63–8.
30. The suggestion was made by Dr Böhl, in a paper read to the Societas Classica at Leiden in March, 1931. I know it only from the reference to it made by Muller (above, note 26): 'Ons medelid Böhl heeft in een voordracht, gehouden voor de Societas Classica te Leiden in Maart 1931, op hoogst verrassende parallellen gewezen. Zoo staan bij een in Babylon gevonden Labyrinth de woorden '*êkal tîrâni*', 'paleis der ingewanden'; de lobos pyramidalis geldt als tempeltoren 'Zik-kurat'; lever en ingewanden samen worden als burcht en als wereld opgevat met bij voorkeur *zeven* muren. Het bewuste woord *tîru*, ouder *tajaraj* zou, aldus coll. Böhl, met *troia*, etr. *truia* verwant of identisch kunnen zijn: Hethieten en Etrusci zouden tusschenschakel zijn geweest. Dankbaar deze bloemen uit vreemden tuin plukkend, geloof ik echter, dat de naam van de stad *Troia* aan den Hellespont niet later en volksetymologisch met deze taalgegevens uit Mesopotamië verbonden is,

maar dat hier historische samenhang mag worden ondersteld, zonder dat men voorloopig zich uitspreekt over de richting der ontleening.' That is, Troy got its name from historical circumstances, but whether the name came to Troy from the East or to eastern languages from Troy, Muller does not decide. He interprets it, ibid., to mean 'city in a circle' or 'holy city'. I should think, if the etymologies are sound, Troy was at first a common name in an eastern language, communicated to the city and to many objects in Italy.

31. Klausen (above, note 3) II, 829–33, collects the notices, but thinks the words in Latin connected with 'Troia' indigenous and referred to Homer's Troy by mistake. I say they came to Italy from Asia. Klausen takes the principle of the Italian words to be the meaning 'surround'.

32. Muller (above, note 26) 12.

33. Id. (above, note 2) 229, and Plate IV, 1, 2, citing H. Frankfort, *Iraq* I (1934) Plate I (2).

34. Klausen (above, note 3) I, xvii, was impressed by the coincidence of names including 'Troy' names, and other matters also, in Italy and in Greece and Asia Minor. On his theory he had to accept the coincidence; but he honestly recognizes that it is surprising.

35. W. F. J. Knight, *TAPA* 63 (1932) 32–3, on Sen. *Tro.* 775–82.

36. It is to be noticed that, at the beginning of the Troia, Iulus is specially called 'impubes' (*Aen.* V, 546); so, in the parallels cited by Sir J. G. Frazer, *The Fasti of Ovid* (London, 1929) III, 383–4, circular furrows to protect cities in east Europe must be ploughed by unmarried boys and girls.

37. Eur. *Troad.* 151–2, where the text of the MSS.,
παιδὸς ἀρχεχόρου πληγαῖς Φρυγίαις
εὐκόμποις ἐξῆρχον θεούς
means that a boy led a Phrygian, that is, Trojan, dance. But for 'παιδός', 'ποδός' and for 'Φρυγίαις', 'Φρυγίους' are now read. *Cf.* above, p. 212, on Lucian, *De Salt.* IX, where dancing is said to have captured Troy, and also on *Culex* 322–4, a similar magical attack on Troy. *Cf.* W. F. J. Knight, *CP* 26 (1931) 414.

38. Walter Leaf, *Troy* (London, 1912) 90–1.

39. C. W. Blegen, *JHS* 53 (1933) 298.

40. W. F. J. Knight, *JHS* 54 (1934) 210.

41. Ibid., with reff.

42. Karl Lehmann-Hartleben, *Die Antike* 7 (1931) 31.

43. Deedes (above, note 20) 32, observes this, and supposes that it means a spread of the labyrinthine ritual of the king-god to Greece.

44. Sir E. A. Wallis Budge, *From Fetish to God in Ancient Egypt* (London, 1934) 369; *cf.* above, pp. 103–28 with reff. and esp. Quint. Smyrn. XII, 421–43, Tryph. 305–57.

45. Budge (above, note 44).

46. Ibid. 377.

47. Ibid. 369.

48. Ibid. 377.

49. Ibid. 374.

50. Ibid. 373.

51. Ibid. 33–4.

52. See above, pp. 121–3.

53. T. W. Allen, *Homer: The Origins and the Transmission* (Oxford, 1924) 159; M. P. Nilsson, *Homer and Mycenae* (London, 1933) 256; *cf.* A. Erman, *Die Literatur der Aegypter* (Leipzig, 1923) 215–16.

54. Knight (above, note 1) 98–121.

55. L. Malten, *JDAI* 29 (1914) 179–256; Muller (above, note 2) 182–7, who

adopts the unilateral explanation that the horse is simply the 'death horse' sent
to warn the city of its approaching end; with the suggestion that the heroes entering
the horse were really entering the earth at death.

56. E. Jones, *On the Nightmare* (London, 1931) 273–319.
57. Hommel (above, note 29) 68.
58. Krause (above, note 13) 126, 280.
59. Ibid. 46.
60. E. Hommel, *Orientalistische Studien Fritz Hommel* I (Leipzig, 1917) 233–52; id.
(above, note 29) 63–8; R. Reitzenstein, *Die Hellenistischen Mysterienreligionen*
(Leipzig, 1927) 15–17 note 1, citing the Zend-Avesta (a clear statement of the
microcosm); *cf.* James Morgan Pryse, *A New Presentation of the Prometheus Bound of
Aeschylus* . . . (Los Angeles and London, 1925) 103, etc.
61. Knight (above, note 1) 98–121, esp. 100–1, 120–1.
62. Ibid. 102 and note 11; for reff. and earlier discussions of Vesta *cf.* Frazer
(above, note 36) IV, 176–87, on Ov. *Fast.* VI, 257; Klausen (above, note 3) II,
620–36.
63. Eric Burrows, S.J., in *The Labyrinth* . . ., ed. by S. H. Hooke (London, 1935)
45–53.
64. Grillot de Givry, *Witchcraft, Magic and Alchemy*, transl. Locke (London, 1931)
240–8.
65. W. F. J. Knight, *JHS* 51 (1931) 176 note 6 (which I think is the first suggestion
of the matter).
66. See above, pp. 114, 123, etc.; Knight (above, note 1) 104–5.
67. Ibid. 101–2, esp. 101 note 9.
68. Ibid. 102 note 11.
69. Apollodor. III, 14, 6.
70. Knight (above, note 35) 30–2, with reff., esp. A. H. Krappe, *RM* 78 (1929)
249–67, on stories of the same class as the stories of Tarpeia and Nisus at Megara;
the main point is that (*a*) sacrifice of maidenhood, (*b*) the capture of a city, and
(*c*) death by throwing from a wall or rock, occur in the same context several times;
cf. also esp. Plut. *Rom.* XVII–XVIII and the lines of Simylus on Tarpeia there
quoted.
71. Muller (above, note 2) 180–94.
72. Ibid. 186–7: 'Proinde ut virgo nuptiarum die "cingulo" ligabatur, quod vir
solvere solebat sequenti nocte, ita urbs condendi die "cingulo" (>bat. "singel" =
fossa extra secundumque muros urbem ambiens) ligabatur, cuius rei ritus condendi etruscus, quem Romani denuo asciverunt, praeclarum testimonium est.
Quae ei respondet conclusio, scilicet urbis talis rite conditae et "ligatae" expug-
nationem antiquis idem fuisse atque *violationem virginis*, id quod haud scio an hodie
quoque superstes vivat in nostra appellatione "stedemaagd, stadsmaagd"—ea,
opinor, revera locis ex antiquis scriptoribus, Vergilio imprimis, sumptis stabiliatur.'
73. Id. (above, note 26) 15.
74. J. D. Meerwaldt, *Mnemosyne* 59 (1932) 184–215; *cf.* the suggestion concerning
Hector made by W. F. J. Knight, *CP* 25 (1930) 364.
75. Muller (above, note 2) 174–80; id. (above, note 26), 15 and *passim*.
76. John Layard, 'The Labyrinth in the megalithic areas of Malekula . . .';
summary in *Man* 35 (1935) 13. [See below, Layard p. 284; also *Folk-Lore* 48 (1937)
115–82. J.D.C.]
77. Ibid.
78. Hom. *Il.* XVIII, 607–8; 590–2; Muller (above, note 2) 163.
79. *Cf.* above; p. 182, on ἐν ἔγκασιν Ἅιδου; p. 165, on the Corycian cave. It
might be asked whether names from the stem Tark- found near in great numbers by
Sir J. G. Frazer, *Adonis, Attis, Osiris, The Golden Bough* IV (London, 1914) 144–8,

and probably belonging to priest-kings, are connected with a root of 'Troy' and 'tîrâni'.

80. Boios *ap*. Anton. Lib. XIX: [ἱστορεῖ Βοῖος ὀρνιθογονίας β'.] ἐν Κρήτῃ λέγεται εἶναι ἱερὸν ἄντρον μελισσῶν, ἐν ᾧ μυθολογοῦσι τεκεῖν Ῥέαν τὸν Δία καὶ ⟨οὐκ⟩ ἔστιν ὅσιον οὐδένα παρελθεῖν οὔτε θεὸν οὔτε θνητόν. ἐν δὲ χρόνῳ ἀφωρισμένῳ ὁρᾶται καθ' ἕκαστον ἔτος πλεῖστον ἐκλάμπον ἐκ τοῦ σπηλαίου πῦρ. τοῦτο δὲ γίνεσθαι μυθολογοῦσιν, ὅταν ἐκζέῃ τὸ τοῦ Διὸς ἐκ τῆς γενέσεως αἷμα. κατέχουσι δὲ τὸ ἄντρον ἱεραὶ μέλισσαι τροφοὶ τοῦ Διός. εἰς τοῦτο παρελθεῖν ἐθάρρησαν . . . καὶ τὰ τοῦ Διὸς εἶδον σπάργανα καὶ αὐτῶν ὁ χάλκος ἐρράγη περὶ τὸ σῶμα. Ζεὺς δὲ βροντήσας ἀνέτεινε τὸν κεραυνόν, Μοῖραι δὲ καὶ Θέμις ἐκώλυσαν. οὐ γὰρ ἦν ὅσιον αὐτόθι θανεῖν οὐδένα. . . . I owe this ref. to the kindness of Professor H. J. Rose, who lets me use his translation.

81. This suggestion was very kindly made to me by Mr R. W. Cruttwell, in a letter dated May 30, 1936. He traces survivals of the practice in the myths of the Holy Grail. I print below, pp. 253 ff., further information from him, showing the general presence in Grail myths of the initiation pattern.

82. Krause (above, note 13) 103–5, etc.; *cf.*, for a magic wall built by Sargon II, Robert Eisler, *Weltenmantel und Himmelszelt* (Munich, 1910) II, 741.

VIII

KNOSSOS

Troy is an ideal equivalent to the earth because it is ideally a labyrinth. And there is all the more reason for it to contain female personalities of ritual importance because labyrinths contain them also.[1]

The folk-lore of labyrinthine dances furnishes instances in which a maiden stays in the middle or nucleus of the labyrinth during the performance. It is thought that Ariadne was at first not a princess outside, helping Theseus to get away, but a figure corresponding to these maidens of ritual, having her place in the middle. The ritual is an approach to the maiden in some sense, and is best connected with sacral marriages.

In the next place, a labyrinth was not only a tomb, built of brick or stone. The arguments concerning the 'original' Cretan labyrinth have now reached a conclusion that the palace at Knossos cannot be that, because there is too much evidence in favour of identifying the original 'Cretan labyrinth' with some cave. This has taken time, since, when the 'hall of the double axes' was excavated, it seemed to fit so exactly the name 'labyrinth', convincingly explained to mean 'place of the labrys or double axe'. Etymological doubts were soon felt and expressed.[2] For example, the transposition of the y in 'labrys' was a difficulty; and besides the marks in the hall of the double axes were said to be more like mason's marks than religious symbols. But these objections were not at first much noticed; and confirmation came in the end from a new examination of the literary notices.

Now most of the earlier literary records of the Cretan labyrinth indicate a place built by Daedalus in which was the Minotaur, and into which Theseus was made to go. This strongly suggests some part of the palace at Knossos, perhaps the 'theatral area'; as if the palace or part of it was the labyrinth, and the Minotaur was either a bull inside, employed for 'bull jumping', or a symbol of the king-god Minos, represented as in Egypt by a bull. The notion that the Minotaur was partly human might easily have been assisted by the actual presence in the palace

of priests wearing the masks or heads of animals, and in particular of bulls. They were worn both in Egyptian and also in
Minoan-Mycenaean observances; and European parallels help
to explain the meaning of them. The bull may be a king-god in
his tomb; or he may be the monster who devours the ghosts of
evil men.[3] There seem to be two main classes of myth here; but
the question how far each extends must wait for a special
investigation.

After classical antiquity, and till the end of the nineteenth
century, the 'Cretan labyrinth' was regularly described as a
cave, and travellers who refer to it usually identify it confidently
with the system of rock chambers at Gortyn. Some ancient references imply the same identification; but the most explicit of
them are late.[4] It is now safe to say that in Crete caves were just
as much entitled to the name 'labyrinth' as the palace; and
probably more. This emerges from the criticism of the authorities.[5] The Minotaur is in one reference actually said to have
lived in a cave in the mountains.[6] In another, Theseus pursued
it 'into the land of labyrinths', and killed it in a cave where it
hid.[7] In another version of this, the Minotaur fled not from
Knossos, but from Gortyn.[8] In a third, the Minotaur has become 'Tauros', a young man, sent by Minos into the mountains, where, later pursued by Minos on account of a quarrel,
he shut himself in a deep hole dug in the earth.[9] Apollonius of
Tyana, with his followers, went to Crete. He allowed them to
see the 'labyrinth' at Knossos; but he himself, saying that 'he
refused to look at the lawlessness of Minos', went to Gortyn to
see Mount Ida.[10] Many guesses might be made about his real
thoughts and their connection with fact. Near Nauplia there
were caves, 'with labyrinths built inside them', called 'Kyklo-
peia', that is, 'Cyclopean work'.[11] There was a built underground
labyrinth under the tholos at Epidaurus. The truth is betrayed
very clearly by one reference: the labyrinth in Crete was a cave,
hard to enter and just as hard to leave, with the added remark
that the word is used for inescapable dilemmas in argument.[12]

The theory that the real 'Cretan labyrinth' was a cave and
not a palace can be confidently accepted, without further discussion, as far as it goes. Now soon afterwards it was followed
by another theory,[13] apparently independent of it, and very
remarkable. This theory has been met already. In it a return

was made to the etymological approach, and the word 'labyrinth' was shown to mean 'place of stone', from the root of 'lapis' and 'λᾶας', 'labrys' being now explained as 'a stone axe'.[14] This too can be accepted, so far; it helps to make clear the application of the name 'labyrinth' to caves, which is already established.

But the older opinions have left behind a difficulty which demands reconciliation. The labyrinthine shape is now known to belong to a protectively constructed tomb or fort, but the labyrinthine name belongs to a cave or system of caves in the earth. The shape is clearest in Egypt, and the name is clearest in Crete. With the new etymology of the word from the root meaning 'stone' the explanation was given that when the palace of Knossos fell into decay it was called a labyrinth because the ruins looked like caves in the earth to any who wandered about them.[15] This is insufficient, because the Egyptian evidence, and the notices in Herodotus, Pliny and other writers, are quite enough to prove that edifices, underground or above ground, did not have to fall into ruin before they could accurately be called labyrinthine. It is not safe to limit the enquiry to Crete or any other single place, or to leave out of account labyrinthine rites, especially dances. Now with the restoration of the name labyrinth to caves rather than buildings a clear distinction was made between labyrinths of three kinds; rock labyrinths, natural caves sometimes improved by hewing the rock; the labyrinthine or maze pattern, including the maeander; and thread or rope dances, following a labyrinthine track.[16] This brings in the rites, but leaves out Egyptian and other distant evidence including much available mythology; the distinctions, honest and useful as they were, left it to seem that labyrinth dances were called that name, because sometimes, apparently by chance, they were performed at the entrances of caves;[17] and chance again must be invoked to explain the use of the word labyrinth for caves and palaces also. The first act of chance would have seemed still more strange, if it had been remembered that Japanese drama arose from dances danced in front of caves, to honour the earth mother, the universal ancestress, who is said to have hidden in a cave.[18] There is even a Greek notice of labyrinthine dances, performed at caves;[19] but no connection with any earth goddess is stated.

Two things are wanted; a principle of unity in matters that seem so different, and an insight into an ancient way of thinking, now obsolete. Happily, the principle that has served before will serve again: the principle of exclusion, and conditional penetration. This fits all three 'labyrinths', the palace or tomb, the rock cave, and the labyrinthine dance. That such a notion was not strange to antiquity is proved by Simplicius,[20] who, in a comment on the Aristotelian conception of infinity, chances to group together, as things which have or almost have no exit, a kind of ring, a labyrinth, and a hole in the earth in Messenia called a 'Keadas', famous as the escape by which Aristomenes, the Messenian hero, was led to safety by a fox, when he was surrounded by the Spartans. The ring meant must have been a tight spiral, like our key rings; and if so here are all three kinds of labyrinth grouped together as things with a difficult passage, the pattern, the architectural labyrinth, and the cleft in the earth.

The 'Keadas' has an interest of its own. The word comes from κεάζω, 'split', a verb used by Homer of the 'splitting' of a ship by a meteorite. In funerary rites the Egyptians used meteoric stone or metal to 'open the mouth' of the dead man, because the material had naturally the power of splitting well.[21] Since Aristomenes is a hero with strong chthonic affinity, it is not rash to think that as usual similar facts have attracted similar myth, and that the 'Keadas' was a cleft supposed to have been made by lightning or a meteorite, at a place where heaven and earth became married in a lightning flash.

Maze dances,[22] with special reference to the maze dance said to have been instituted by Theseus at Delos to commemorate his rescue by Ariadne, are already thought to form part of marriage rites. There are the modern Cretan maze dances, still danced 'widdershins' before a wedding.[23] Now there is an answer, which the Japanese parallel might suggest, to connect the dances with the caves. Both are relevant to marriage; primarily the divine marriage of the sky with the earth, but secondarily the marriages, or cognate 'threshold rites', of human individuals, and correlatively also the converse of marriage rites, at funerals, when the dead return to the body of earth, the universal mother.

There are two representations, one on a bowl from Corneto[24]

and one on a vase in the Louvre,[25] of Theseus killing the Minotaur. On both Ariadne is seen with a coiling thread; on the vase
it seems to start from the top of her chest, and coil in front; on
the bowl she holds it in her hands, and the coiled part is under
the left foot of Theseus. It has been thought that the coil really
belongs to the anatomy of Ariadne,[26] and this is possible, but
hardly to be proved on the evidence which there is at present.

All this involves a responsibility to offer at least a possible
development for the story of Theseus and the Minotaur. The
main elements seem to be two, one legendary and one mythical.
This is, of course, a simplification. For one thing, Oriental myth,
here as so often elsewhere, lent its forms to Greek imagination.[27]

During the time of Minoan sea power, Cretan fleets operated
in the Saronic gulf, and imposed a temporary Cretan sovereignty
in the Megarid and in Attica. Some form of tribute was exacted,
and either as part of the tribute, or simply to convey it to Crete,
young people of Attica visited the imperial island. There they
had adventures. They may have got into serious trouble; and it
is possible that they were made to take part in the bull-jumping
games, or were actually sacrificed in this or some other way.
Anyhow, stories of excitements reached Attica; how hard it was
to find your way about the palace; how absolute and stern, and
yet how just was the king (two views of him existed, not always
both stated at once); and how elaborate was the culture and
material civilization. With these accounts of facts came descriptions of religious beliefs and practices. Bull-masked priests were
reported, and confused with participants in bull-jumping. The
theology of the bull, possibly representing the divine king Minos,
was recounted too; and a ritual like the ritual of royal tombs in
Egypt may have been described, either as it was seen to happen,
or more probably in the form of a ready-made explanatory
Cretan myth. Then there were the dances, either part of the
ritual of the royal tomb, or detached from it, or both; they were
maze dances and thread dances, possibly both at once, and almost certainly some were performed at the entrances to caves.
If so, that may well have been a survival of an older cult of the
earth mother, existing before the cult of the royal tomb came
from Egypt. A maiden taking a central part in the dance could
easily be identified with a Cretan lady who befriended an Attic
prince. Such were the main elements, one legendary and one,

FIGURE 14

Ariadne's coil of thread, shown on a bowl from Corneto and a vase in the Louvre; recalling the intestinal spiraliform labyrinth of the Babylonian Tablets in Fig. 13 (after Th. Leslie Shear, *AJA* 27, 1923, 136, Fig. 2, and 141, Fig. 7, and F. Muller, Jun., *Mnemosyne*, Ser. III, 2, 1935, Plates VIII, 1, and VII, 2).

at least, mythical. The composite tale was now told in Attica, and approached existing forms of Attic myth.[28] The bull of Marathon, and Ariadne, were reflected in the stories. To the other adventures of the great Attic hero Theseus were added adventures in Crete, where he was rescued by Ariadne from bull-masked priests, from the bull King Minos, or from the Minotaur of the pictures; and then in turn rescued her. He and she thus become the partners of a sacred marriage in a labyrinthine dance. The identification of the rock labyrinth of cult with the palace of Minos was confirmed later, when in the earliest historical age Greeks could still see the fresco labyrinth, above ground, when all else was ruin, at the palace gate at Knossos.

The religion of the cave keeps a certain identity at many places and times. How old it is cannot be safely said; it may even be palaeolithic, for many of its elements seem present in palaeolithic caves of France and Spain.[29] There the dead are buried in a prenatal posture, as if expected to be born again; the rites performed within the caves seem to have been esoteric, purposely remote from the daylight; there are even maze-like lines at the entrances as if to assert the principle of exclusion and conditional entry; and there is evidence for dances, which have been compared to the dances of the Curetes, and therefore, if this is right, are likely to have been concerned with the same principle. Describing these caves, the highest authority[30] cannot escape using the word 'labyrinth'; and, if a cave in Crete containing drawings of buffaloes like the pictures in the cave of Altamira had been known, there would have been little hesitation in seeing in it the original of the Minotaur itself, in a rock labyrinth. However, though the Cretans have actually been thought akin to Cro-Magnon palaeolithic men,[31] it is best not to extend this argument so far back in time as that.

The start in the sanctity of caves is the belief that men come from the earth, and return to the earth, as to a mother. Access to her is by caves, used for burial, and then for initiations of other kinds. This meant cave rites. From the cave rites come firstly initiation ceremonies of many degrees, secondly prophecy, since access to the dead might be access to ancestral wisdom, and thirdly the myths of descents to the lower world.

Complications soon begin. The burial cave turns into a

building, perhaps a pyramid or burial barrow. Migrations occur; and the dead are supposed to travel to their old home before re-entering the earth, with the result of an endless confusion between the real geography of the world, with rivers, seas and mountains, and the imaginary, symbolic geography of the cosmic tomb, with its lustral waters and sometimes mountain form, the tomb itself having been imagined from the real world at first. Then there is the religion of the sky, the husband of earth, identified sometimes with a divine king. Meanwhile, monoliths of ancestors become gods, and monoliths representing the earth or female guardian spirits become goddesses. The labyrinth is the boundary between without and within; it is the entrance to the tomb, it is the cave which is the entrance to the earth, and possibly it is the body of the earth mother, and of the divine king also.

From the sanctity of caves and tombs comes the 'initiation pattern', in Mediterranean lands, and elsewhere also, especially in many parts of Europe, where Troy myths connected with mazes and 'Troy' castles have already been compared with the myths of Knossos and Homer's Troy.

The northern myths would take long to examine afresh; but the appearance of the 'initiation pattern' in one group, the myths of the Holy Grail, must not be missed.[32]

'Miss Jessie Weston, in her *Quest of the Holy Grail*, London, 1913, writes thus: "The Grail Quest should be viewed primarily as an Initiation Story. . . . The quest, properly speaking, begins only when the hero, having failed at his first unpremeditated visit to the Grail Castle to fulfil the tests to which he has been subjected, sets out with the deliberate intention of finding the vanished Temple of the Grail, and of fulfilling the conditions which shall qualify him to obtain a full knowledge of the marvels which he has beheld. . . . Professor Heinzel had already seen that the peculiarities of the Grail story, the nature of the test employed, the mysterious question, all partook of the character of an initiation, and that one of its elements was the record of a failure to pass an initiation test."

'Miss Weston in 1920 elaborated her theory in *From Ritual to Romance*, Cambridge, 1920, in which she dealt fully with the Initiation and Mystery elements in the Grail Legends. Dr Nitze has equated the Grail Mysteries with the Eleusinian Mysteries,

whereas Miss Weston connects them with the mysteries of
Adonis, Tammuz and the Divine King.

'So much is sufficient to prove that the initiatory character
of the Grail Legends is no new or unsupported theory. Indeed
it had been worked out at great length many years earlier by
A. E. Waite in his *Hidden Church of the Holy Graal*, London, 1909,
which equates the Grail with the Philosopher's Stone, and cor-
relates the Grail Legends not only with Alchemy, but also with
Freemasonry, Rosicrucianism and Occultism. It is, however,
necessary to emphasize that neither Malory nor Tennyson gave
us the genuine Grail Legend, but only popularized and senti-
mentalized echoes at a far distance of far earlier stories which
they failed to understand. The real canon of the Grail Legend
covers roughly the years 1150–1200, during which it appeared
in many and varied forms in many languages. But the root ideas
(completely lost in Malory and Tennyson, but restored by
Wagner in his *Parsifal* opera) are invariable and persistent.
They centre in a mysterious Castle or Temple, situated always
by water, often on a mountain, wherein dwells an equally
mysterious King Priest, who is *both Dead and Alive* and who
guards certain talismans or symbols—Lance, Cup, Sword and
Dish (or Stone). The object of the innumerable hero-questers is
to find this Castle, to witness the manifestation of its symbols and
to restore the Priest King to life and health. The country round
the Castle is the Waste Land: it was wasted by the King's illness
and "death"; and it will be restored to fertility by his recovery
or "resurrection". The difficulties in the way of finding the
Grail Temple are both numerous and fearsome. There are
many guides to it, not all of them reliable; but the chief guide
is a woman called the Grail Messenger (Kundry in Wagner)
who is sometimes a hideous old hag and sometimes a lovely
young girl. She is found usually by water, and near the Castle
entrance, both before and after the visits of the questers. She is
also, often, the bearer of the Grail, whether a cup or stone (it
may be either); and she alternately urges the hero to the quest
or warns him from it. When he fails, she upbraids him for not
passing the necessary tests. When he succeeds, she often becomes
his bride, and changes from ugliness to beauty. The quester not
only finds it almost impossible to *find* the Temple. When at last
he has found it, it becomes almost impossible to *enter*. There are

innumerable obstacles against entry. Sometimes there is a portcullis or a drawbridge; when the hero ventures on to the bridge, either the portcullis falls with a crash and nearly beheads him, or else the bridge itself suddenly rears in the air, so that he nearly falls off it into the waters beneath, which are a wide moat, or a lake, or the sea, or a river, which is itself perilous both from its raging waves and from the water beasts which wait to devour him. In several versions, however, the quester is met by a boatman who is fishing on the castle lake, and who (if satisfied of his credentials) rows him across to the Island Temple. When at last the hero succeeds in entering the Hall of the Grail Castle (or Temple), his troubles are far from over. In many versions he is attacked from all sides, now by ghosts, now by armed knights, now by fierce beasts, who appear from the many chambers and corridors which surround the central Hall. Then often there is a sudden storm—thunder, lightning, hail, wind, so that all the windows suddenly clap to, and shrill birds are heard screeching in the hurricane.

'When at last all these obstacles are overcome (they do not, of course, *all* appear in any *one* version), the hero may be welcomed to the presence of the Priest King of the Grail, who turns out to be none other than the Boatman of the Lake who rowed him across, or else one of his other previous guides in various forms. Now comes the initiation test. The King is sorely wounded unto death and of extreme old age—in fact he is really dead—the Dead King in his Ritual Tomb. The function of the hero is twofold (a) to pass an initiatory test, to prove his own fitness, and (b) to restore the Dead King to health and life. A procession appears from the various side chambers of the Hall of Initiation, and slowly *passes to and fro and round and round* the table at which King and guest are seated. The procession consists of young girls and young men, bearing the 4 (or 5) Grail symbols. The hero is expected to ask their meaning. If he fails to ask, the test has failed; if he asks, the King begins a long story of explanation, during which the hero falls asleep. In either case of failure, he is summarily ejected from the Temple (as Parsifal in Act I of Wagner's opera) either by main force, all the inhabitants of the building rushing at him and mishandling him as an intruder, or by simply falling asleep and waking up in a meadow by the water-side, the Castle having completely vanished.

It is here that the Grail Messenger lady invariably appears, and reproaches the quester for his failure to pass the initiatory tests. Now, she says, he will have to wander long years (as in Wagner) before he can find the Castle again, and overcome many fresh obstacles both human and superhuman during his quest. As a rule, the quester does at long last succeed in reaching the Castle once again, and often he is successful this second time in passing the tests, and in healing the King and restoring the Waste Land. His reward is succession to the Grail Kingdom, and the Grail King's daughter (really the Grail Messenger) as his bride. There are also innumerable visits to *Magic* Castles, with *Magic* Kings, *Magic* Symbols, *Magic* Ladies; and in these versions the hero usually kills the Magic King or Giant, and marries his queen or his daughter. Or he beheads the giant, who thereupon is released from a spell and becomes a handsome youth.

'The above summary is perhaps sufficient. Now for comments. To begin with, the root ideas of the Grail Legend are these:

(1) *A Dead King* in a Castle or Temple, who is really both alive and dead at the same time, and who needs to be rescued from this condition *from outside*.

(2) *A Water Lady* who carries the chief talisman of this Castle, and who is found sometimes inside the Castle, sometimes outside. The hero usually weds her, or in some way receives her favours.

(3) *A Castle*, or *Temple*, or *Palace*, always situated by water, often on an island in a lake, or by the seaside; often on a mountain; always mysterious, hard to find, liable to be lost; only found after much difficulty.

(4) *Obstacles to entry into the Castle*. These are of every conceivable kind, and extend over the entire story, increasing however as the Castle draws nearer, and reaching their maximum at the actual moment of entry and reception.

(5) *A Quester* or *Hero*, who under innumerable names and guises is alternately urged to, and warned from, the Quest; who seeks now a *Dying King*, now a *Dead Father*, now a *Hidden Bride*, and now a *Lost Mother* (corresponding to Herzeleide of *Parsifal*, Act II).

(6) *A Grail Procession*, round and round and to and fro, in and out of Hall, Chambers and Corridors.

(7) *The Quester's Mother*, who is either lost or dead and who is sought and found by him.

'I think it will be clear by this time that I equate the Dead King of the Grail with the Divine King in his tomb; the Water Lady Messenger of the Grail with (a) the Earth Mother, (b) the Hidden Bride; the Grail Castle with the Cave or Hall of Initiation, which is both the Tomb of the hero's father and the Womb of his mother, as well as the Vagina of his bride; the obstacles with the Maze or Labyrinth, both within and without the Fort, i.e. Castle; the Quester with the candidate for initiation, whose object is both personal and cosmic; the Procession with the Initiation Dance; and the Quester's Mother with the Earth Mother.'

In the Grail myths an exceptional number of the elements which belong to the initiation pattern appear obviously. Some have special interest. The sibyl at the entrance and the ferryman of the dead are seen to have a lasting place in the complex. The sleep of Gilgamish reappears; as it does in Vergil, and, dislocated, in Homer, who has his 'gates of sleep', and who says that Odysseus slept on the last stage of his journey to Ithaca, on a Phaeacian ship, that travelled 'like sleep'. The sleep of visitants to the cave of Trophonius is also to be compared, and the pattern confirms the affinity of the prophetic cave with the cave of initiation. The maze and Oceanus or water of death have, as often, coalesced; even the nine coils of Styx are a form of the maze idea; and in the Grail itself there is a recurrence of the waters of life within the tomb, or initiation hall. The perpetual obstructions and warnings again, as in the *Epic of Gilgamish* and indeed all the myths, have their cardinal place; and the variety of the personalities sought, mothers, fathers, or brides, suggests that all three principles involved belong authentically to the early pattern. Except at the start, it must be hard to find times and places where the object of the quest was in no sense a return to the prenatal condition, the revival of the divine king, and the satisfaction of love, all together. Another thing must be noticed. The rushing sounds, from many openings and passages in the Grail castle, belong clearly to Sibylline caves,[33] perhaps to rock labyrinths as at Gortyn, and certainly to the 'Egyptian Labyrinth', if Pliny's explicit description of the terrifying sounds, which some Egyptian 'temples' in the 'Labyrinth' were planned to make, comes near the truth.[34]

I

NOTES

1. Ernst Krause, *Die Trojaburgen Nordeuropas* (Glogau, 1893) 262–300, has already classed together the myths of Troy and Knossos, supposing both to be forms of the northern 'Troy' myths which have penetrated into the Aegean area.
2. W. H. D. Rouse, *JHS* 21 (1901) 268–74.
3. Mr T. H. Harrisson kindly tells me that in dances observed by himself in Melanesia, beings corresponding to the Minotaur are always hostile monsters rather than king-gods. A mask, of course, indicates generally that a ghost is represented; more than that cannot be said.
4. E.g. Claudian, *De VI Cons. Honor.* 633–6.
5. Richard Eilmann, *Labyrinthos* (Athens, 1931) 74–80.
6. Rouse (above, note 2) 274, citing Eudocia, 253.
7. Suidas, *s.v.* Αἰγαῖον πέλαγος.
8. Malalas, IV, 108.
9. Palaephatus, *Mythogr. Graec.* II, 7.
10. Philostrat. *Apoll. Tyan.* IV, 34.
11. Strab. VIII, 369.
12. *Et. mag.* 554, 26.
13. Hermann Güntert, *SHAW* Ph.-hist. Kl. (1932/3) I Abh., 4–6, esp. 6.
14. Ibid. 4–6.
15. Ibid. 5.
16. Eilmann (above, note 5) 90; *cf.* 77, 80.
17. Ibid. 80.
18. *Japanese Drama*, Tourist Library: 6 (Tokyo, 1935), (National Committee of Intellectual Co-operation of the International Assoc. of Japan; revised edition, Yoshio Yoshikawa): 'The origin of the Japanese drama is said to have been the sacred dance which was performed before the heavenly cave, in which the great Ancestral Goddess had hid Herself, long ago, in the mythological age of the Gods.'
19. Eustath. 1166, 17 *ad Il.* XVIII, 590: the words for 'cave' are emendations, but practically certain. [See below, p. 280, note 64. J.D.C.]
20. Simplic. *Aristot. Phys. Comm.* 204a, 2 (Diels, p. 470, 24–9).
21. G. A. Wainwright, *JEA* 18 (1932) 6–8.
22. *Cf.* R. Winter, *Neue Jahrbücher für Wissenschaft und Jugendbildung* 5 (1929) 707–20.
23. Sir A. J. Evans, *The Palace of Minos* III (London, 1930) 74–8, esp. 76.
24. Th. Leslie Shear, *AJA* 27 (1923) 136.
25. Ibid. 141.
26. F. Muller, Jun., *Mnemosyne* Ser. III, 2 (1935) 176, 226.
27. Shear (above, note 24) *passim.*
28. *Cf.* M. P. Nilsson, *The Mycenaean Origin of Greek Mythology* (Cambridge, 1932) 163–80; E. Bethe, *RM* 65 (1910) 200–32, puts almost all the story in Attica.
29. Th. Mainage, *Les Religions de la Préhistoire* (Paris, 1921) 206, 214, 217–20; H. Breuil, etc., *La Pasiega* (Monaco, 1913) 54; D. S. Merezhkovsky, *The Secret of the West*, transl. J. Cournos (London, 1933) 174–5, 177.
30. Breuil (above, note 29).
31. D. A. Mackenzie, *Myths of Crete and Pre-Hellenic Europe* (London, 1917) 163.
32. [The author's original text reads: 'Mr R. W. Cruttwell has sent me the following account of the Grail myths and initiation which he generously allows me to use. It is so good that I print it almost in full, as he wrote it.' We now print the material as subsequently published in *Folk-Lore* 49 (1938) 244ff. J.D.C.]

33. *Cf.* Ov. *Met.* XIV, 152–3 and Serv. Verg. *Aen.* VI, 321, on the survival, after her death, of the sibyl's voice; *cf.* also Verg. *Aen.* VI, 42–4, a passage which, with a little exaggeration, agrees with the existing cave at Cumae: A. Maiuri, *Associazione internazionale studi mediterranei, Bollettino*, III, 3 (1932) 21–9.

34. Pliny, *N.H.* XXXVI, 13.

IX

CUMAE

There is much difficulty in getting the right mental picture of ancient Italy in its prehistoric relations. The Romans believed that an important element among them came from Asia Minor —Trojans who escaped at the sack of Troy and followed Aeneas. In modern times this belief has been sharply criticized and contradicted.[1] The legends of Trojan foundations are certainly incoherent; and in fact it is not hard to watch them developing, and to suggest that transplantation of Greek stories, and political expediency, can quite well account for their origin, without any need to suppose that they are true.[2] In the last few years, however, there has been a strong tendency to reverse this decision, and to think that the legends contain a memory of something that really happened; but for lack of evidence it is difficult to prove what their relation to facts exactly is. It is not, however, quite impossible to discover within certain limits what those facts, and the relation of the legends to them, may provisionally be thought to have been.

The important principle is not to expect too much from legend, but to understand its method of preserving fact. This method is forcible. Fact is coerced to fit one of the available archetypal moulds of thought and narrative.[3] Just as tyrannical man almost has to have a tyrannical, appropriate end, even if he is quite a historical person, such as Alcibiades, so it is found that arrivals in Italy from the east are compelled to take certain forms. This makes them look artificial and unconvincing; but in reality their formal aspect ought to recommend them to the right sort of trust. In fact it may be said that, if allowance is made for the archetypal forms, though individual legends do not agree very well with individual sets of facts, yet on the whole the totality of the legends represents the totality of the available facts quite well; and this is, of course, a distinct help in controlling the mental picture of early Italian relations.

Before or soon after 1000 B.C. settlers were said in antiquity to have come from Crete and from Troy to Sicily, from Greece to south-west Italy, from Greece to Apulia, from Asia Minor and Greece to Etruria, from Asia Minor to the Po valley, from Crete and Greece to Campania, and from Troy and Greece to Latium.[4] This makes seven groups of legends. Of the seven, five have some archaeological support, if simple adjustments are allowed: for example, the finds near Arpi in Apulia suggest arrivals from Illyria where Diomedes was worshipped rather than a settlement founded, as the legends say, by the Homeric Diomedes himself.[5] But such coherence is more than good enough for legendary tradition; scientifically it is more satisfying than a suspiciously exact correspondence. It happens that the only two legends which have no archaeological support are those that are most relevant now, the legends of a Cretan foundation of Cumae and of a Trojan settlement in Latium.

There is, however, evidence of a kind. For Latium, there is language. Latin is a Q dialect surrounded by P dialects, in a geographical situation which has been thought to show that the Latins arrived on the west coast of Italy by sea, as the legends of Aeneas say.[6] Roman soldiers at the time of the Punic Wars were armed as were the land raiders of Palestine in the thirteenth century B.C. in some particulars.[7] A shield of almost Mycenaean shape survives in the equipment of the Salii.[8] There are at Rome clear signs of an old layer of religion of the general Mediterranean kind to which the Mycenaean religion mainly belongs.[9] The Roman Vulcanus has a Cretan name, for he must be Welchanos (Ϝελχανός); he was worshipped near the mouth of the Tiber, apparently because a small group of Aegean settlers landed there.[10] Place names in Latium suggest intrusions, apparently from Illyria.[11] The Roman alphabet is even thought to show in the forms of some letters contact with a very early alphabet of the Levant, not far in development from the Minoan linear script.[12] It has been argued that the Roman practice of 'euocatio', by means of which the gods of enemies were thought to be persuaded to change sides, was used by the Hittites.[13] Whether either the Phrygian or Hittite languages show contact with Latin seems to be still uncertain; but it can at least be said that an investigation of Hittite pronouns has elucidated Latin grammar.[14]

Twenty-five years ago it was possible to say that a great drift of population came from the east towards the west of the Mediterranean at about 1000 B.C.[15] More recently it has been said that the Iron Age in Italy began and developed under strong Aegean influence.[16] There is a theory, supported by finds of Italian 'spectacle' fibulae in Greece, that the Mycenaean civilization was overthrown by Italian tribes, who are the same as the Sekelesa and others mentioned in the Egyptian lists of sea raiders.[17] In this interesting theory it is supposed that Achaeans visited Sicily at the time of the migrations, but strangely nothing is said about the legends concerning arrivals in Latium. That the sea raiders overran Greece before they attacked Egypt is an attractive suggestion, but uncertain; it is much more certain that afterwards they settled in the west of the Mediterranean.[18] One of the tribes, the Mashwasha, settled according to Herodotus in Libya. He mentions their strange method of hair dressing, with vermilion dye; and he is confirmed by a recent observation that this particular dye came only from Asia Minor.[19] Accordingly, the historical context is not against settlements in Latium, though they are not proved.

Apparently the legends represent more or less obscurely one or more of several probabilities. Aeneas is brought in the legends to Latium by three main routes or stages; by Sicily, by Arcadia, and by Chaonia in Epirus. There are facts of some sort for each version. Elymoi and Dardanians seem almost certainly to have come from Troy and near Troy to Sicily in the twelfth century, and they may have had a leader with the characteristic Dardanian name of Aeneas.[20] Their language survives in legends, on Sicilian coins, and in Sicilian place names. In Arcadia are found Dardanian names, apparently a sign that a branch of Dardanians split off from those of them who settled in the Troad, and penetrated into the Peloponnese; and since Roman stories agree impressively with Arcadian in their mythical form, it is possible that the legendary Arcadian settlement on the Palatine may represent a reality which has been confused with other foundation legends.[21] The supposed arrival of Aeneas from Epirus may be a way of recording the arrivals of Illyrians, who certainly came; an interesting commentary on this is the name Ulixes, which shows by its form that it was adopted not from Homer, but from the western coast of Greece or Illyria.[22] Another point is this. Chronology is likely to be telescoped, and 'Trojan War' settlements may really belong to an age centuries before the fall of Troy, which was after all a typical point of time, often meaning not much more than 'a long time ago'.[23] In fact, there seem to have been Greeks in Sicily before the Trojan War.[24] Early Helladic pottery is found in Apulia;[25] and the persistence of Greek in Southern Italy has been thought to show that it was spoken generally there even before the first Achaean colonies, assumed to have been founded about the fourteenth century.[26] Legends of Trojan settlements may therefore mean some very early event, perhaps even the stream of influence called sometimes 'megalithic', the influence of the stone men, who are said to have carried Oriental culture to Italy, like the Etruscans, but many centuries before them.[27]

Whatever the facts were, they have, of course, been forced into available morphologies. The Greeks heard the stories, and retold them in a shape habitual to them, making the readiest identifications, if possible Homeric, and unconsciously and tacitly omitting whatever was intractable. No 'Trojan War' settlement has to be discovered in Latium or Campania before the evidence of the traditions can be accepted. We do not know what we are looking for at first. It is therefore difficult to say that we have found it, and still more difficult to say that it was never there to be found. The local inhabitants may not even have known whence some party of new arrivals came, or the arrival may have been remembered, without the origin—an ignorance which would not be unparalleled.

Vergil treats Cumae as a place where Daedalus, flying from Crete, built a temple of Apollo, and dedicated his wings in it.[28] Vergil mentions no city, and does not say, with others, either that Daedalus had already visited Sicily, or that he went on to Sardinia, where the structures called *nuraghi* are in some sense attributed to him. The one hint that there was already a city, Greek or other, at Cumae, is sought in Vergil's words 'Chalcidic stronghold', 'Chalcidica arce';[29] but even if 'stronghold' must mean more than a hill of natural strength, which is doubtful, the words may well be not assertion but association, directed on the dramatic future.

Vergil does, however, certainly guide readers to think that Daedalus, whatever he may mean, instituted something at Cumae in the Bronze Age. This suggests that Cretan influence reached Cumae then. It certainly reached Sicily, where Minoan pottery renders easily credible the legend of the Minoan voyage

to Sicily in which the Minoan débâcle culminated; and Daedalus was said to have gone on that voyage. Vergil may have
transferred this influence from Sicily to Central Italy by imagination. He seems to lay some stress on Cretan influence, and to
mean something by it. The gold foil of the golden bough has
been compared to Minoan-Mycenaean work,[30] the cave at
Cumae to the palace at Knossos,[31] the bright air of Heaven
beyond to a scene on the Mycenaean 'ring of Nestor',[32] and the
newly found entrance of the Cumaean cave to the dromos of a
Mycenaean tomb.[33] Possibly Vergil wants to assert that Cretans
were the founders of civilization,[34] as elsewhere[35] he asserts the
religious dependence of Troy on Crete, and the Cretan origin
of the Trojan Teucer. These guesses do not go very far, but they
may well go in the right direction.

There is no sign of any Bronze Age settlement of people from
the Aegean at Cumae. It is possible that wanderers like Odysseus
landed there, but no trace of them has been found. The earlier
foundation-date for Greek Cumae in the eleventh century had
some support recently, but has now been abandoned.[36] It is
clear that the Greek city started suddenly about 800 B.C., rather
earlier than the later traditional date. Before that there was only
the native city. The negative evidence is so far convincing;
though of course negative evidence is seldom safe, a principle
proved once again actually at Cumae, where the Sibyl's cave
was found a short time ago, after it had been for years supposed
to be known in quite a different part of the area where Cumae
was. Here again there is no evidence of occupation before the
fourth century B.C., though no doubt there is a distant possibility
that early evidence may have been obliterated by the engineers
of Augustus, or other agencies. It is conceivable that the Etruscan
or Mycenaean style of the entrance may indicate contact with
some old tradition. There is now again a slight tendency to date
Greek influence in Central Italy early, for Greek vases were
there in some quantity before the first Greek cities.[37] Again, the
Etruscans seem to have had a strong Greek element among their
mixed racial constitution when they arrived from Asia.[38] But
there is no sign of foundations or arrivals as early as Trojan
times.

Yet there is much still unexplained concerning eastern influence on Italy. There are hints that the Italy of the Romans was

partly the result of this influence, centuries old, and now atrophied and stylized. Roman religion looks like something that has suffered an artificial fixation followed by decay, not merely something which has been naturally arrested in development. Evidence has been found for the practice in Italy at an early time of the bull-sacrifice of the eastern Mediterranean.[39] Even the Sumerian king-god and his sacral marriage have been supposed to have reached Italy and helped to create Janus;[40] a surprising suggestion, after all the controversy which there has been about divine relationships in Italy, and which seemed to show that there divine beings were never conceived to be married. Another indication is the persistence with which ideas of defensive sanctity, as they are now disclosed, occur in the east and in Italy. It has been said that a layer of population which was submerged in Greece was at the top in Italy and the near east.[41] That is why Greek cities are not 'hierocentric', like the cities to the east and west. Of course, some 'hierocentricity' clings to the Greek city-goddess Athena; and it is remarkable to notice how important forms of her are in Italy,[42] and how closely she is connected with Vesta there.[43] For Vesta is 'hierocentric'.[44] She cannot be proved an indigenous Italian goddess; and strangely she is found only in Latium. She shares with the shadowy Greek Hestia some 'hierocentric' qualities, and with her and with Athena the quality of maidenhood, which seems to have been associated with defence. She appears indeed to be part of the old world, of which Vergil made a world that is for ever new.

The past which Vergil handled in the *Aeneid* is complicated and uncertain. Vergil's poetic meaning is concerned with old values and symbols which are eloquent below the threshold of full consciousness; he assimilates them, and renders them in his poem, in the full characteristically poetic manner, mysteriously conscious of the common racial past alive to his own individual apprehension. The collective mind had inherited something of evocative power from old facts of history that joined Italy to the very ancient east, and to its values, and religious thought. Some old streams of culture had come to Italy from the east, and perhaps many at many times. Antiquity had dimmed the outlines, but pent up symbolic power, which Vergil could release. Such is the truth of the *Aeneid*, spoken by a single man, to single but connected minds in the present and far future, but spoken through the living past, and out of it. That is why it is worth while to enquire into many things which Vergil himself could not consciously know, for they have helped him to make what he and we through him can feel and see. These things have their richness from the years and the countless spirits of men that have enlivened them. Among them are the kinship with God and earth and king, the sacred city, and the labyrinthine cave that means them all, reaching from the simplest form to emotions that are still deep, and reverences that still are real.[45]

That the 'mysteries', perhaps mainly the Eleusinian, were in some sense recalled in the Sixth *Aeneid* has for some time been admitted by some scholars, and by others disbelieved. About two hundred years ago the opinion was very firmly stated.[46] 'We hope to make it very evident that the masterpiece of the *Aeneis*, the famous Sixth Book, is nothing else but a description, and so designedly, by the author, of his hero's initiation into the mysteries of one part of the Eleusinian spectacles.' Of course, it is never safe to say that Vergil's meaning is exclusively one thing or another. But that some of the ritual pattern and the doctrines of the mysteries are expressed and used in the Sixth *Aeneid* is much easier now to believe. Vergil's knowledge and intuition were so comprehensive that it is scarcely necessary to prove that he was himself initiated. His method is better understood; especially his fusion of different originals in a new whole,[47] and his habit of letting historical fact 'shimmer through' his narrative, instead of reporting it.[48] Further, the community of principle in cave rites is clearer, so that the cave at Cumae can now be expected to recall the pattern belonging to other cave rites, from which the mysteries themselves, besides much else, were derived. Once more, the very word 'initiation' comes from a use of 'inire', 'enter', in the ritual sense of 'enter the earth'.[49]

The mysteries, the Sixth *Aeneid*, and much else besides are, or can become, expressions of a 'universal myth' of the soul's journey to perfection. This has been proved.[50] Now there is a trace of maze movements used as an introduction to the moment of revelation in the ceremonies reflected in the myth. In Shakespeare's *Tempest* the court party comes through 'forth-rights and maeanders', which mean a maze. At Eleusis there was a 'blind march', preliminary to full initiation.[51]

On the other hand, the ritual origin of these motives had still to be guessed. That the 'blind march' at Eleusis was a maze movement seemed almost certain, but was still an inference. Excavation has discovered no architectural maze in the telesterion there. But now the gap is filled by the Malekulan evidence, which for the first time gives a parallel to the location of a maze design at the entrance to a cave entered at death, indicating of course a change of state, from one kind of life to another. The evidence even goes further still, for the Malekulans search blindfolded for the anklets which they wear when they perform maze dances at funeral rites, doubly emphasizing the principle of the 'blind march', and showing that for them it belongs to the maze, at the point where the ideas of exclusion and secrecy meet.[52] The Cumaean maze, therefore, represents in something like an original form a part of the pattern, which survives indistinctly in the 'universal myth' elsewhere, just as it might have been conjectured from the survivals; and the astonishing thing is that the obscure element is kept explicitly and exactly in its place by Vergil and Pacific islanders alone.

The place of the maze or labyrinth in Greek mysteries is not very clear in literature, nor is it proved by pictures, but it has been inferred, and, I think, quite certainly. In 'the universal myth',[53] 'this passage through the Labyrinth or purgatorial Wilderness is . . . the main ordeal of the Lesser Initiation';[54] for example, the Temptation in the Wilderness of the Gospels, and the 'forthrights and maeanders' through which the Court Party comes in Shakespeare's *Tempest*. That this goes back to Greek cult has been guessed, without reference to the new evidence, partly from Plato, who, judging from Greek sacrifices and religious ceremonies, believed that the road travelled after death was not plain and straight, but had several turnings and cross-ways.[55] This implies a maze movement in cult,[56] perhaps the same as the blind march in darkness mentioned by Lucian.[57] 'Without doubt, in some of the ancient ritual initiations the neophyte was required to pick his way, actually or by representation, through a labyrinth or maze.'[58] Allegory already begins with *Ecclesiasticus*, which declares 'that the aspirant walks in "crooked ways", wherein he is tormented by the laws and discipline of Wisdom, before he finally wins her by the "straight way".'[59] But the meaning of *Ecclesiasticus* may have been too closely defined; and it is hard to find early evidence for an elaborately moralized meaning of mysteries. It has been held that 'while the Lesser Initiation was concerned with life and purgation from sin, the Greater Initiation was concerned with death and rebirth. For, as in the former, the aspirant trod the winding paths of an intricate maze that signified our mortal life, and came at last through repentance to that clarity of intellect which is self-finding and self-mastery, so in the latter he was deemed to go through the grave itself, that thereby he might come face to face with the gods and learn the ultimate mysteries of existence.'[60] The same writer goes on, 'True, I have argued that the Lesser Initiation comprised a passage through Purgatory, generally known as a "Descent into Hell"; but it does not follow that a ritual death was implicit in this Degree. Indeed, an essential feature of the traditional "Descent into Hell" is that it is made by one who is still alive. . . .'[61] Later, he suggests that the wanderings on the shore at Eleusis, recalling the search of Demeter for Persephone, were, like the search of Isis for Osiris, and of the Court Party for Ferdinand, really an expression of the search for truth. 'Every seeker must pass through this Labyrinth or Wilderness (MIST), and mount thence into the clear AIR of reason.'[62]

Purification does, of course, come before full initiation. Whether Greek belief reached the conception of clarity of intellect and self-mastery, won by ritual, before contact with Hebrew thought, may seem more doubtful. Such conceptions are, however, characteristically those which the mysteries were naturally able to attain; and something like them had been attained before Vergil's time, and may legitimately be apprehended from the Sixth *Aeneid*.

The search for Persephone was not, perhaps, at any early time a search for truth. But it was a kind of maze movement. That it happened on the shore is significant. Mazes are often found near the sea. It has been thought that they were located there because a maze ritual was performed by sailors, who, putting to sea, were going from the realm of life to the realm of death, and therefore guarded themselves by entering it ceremoniously through the doors of the 'house of death', the labyrinth.[63] I suggest that the original reason is that the cave type of myth has not quite lost contact with the ocean type; and mazes on the shore, or maze movements there, recall that the dead had once started across the sea on their journey.[64] The mazes at Lembwil Song in Malekula and at Cumae in Vergil agree with this proposal.

The connection of the labyrinthine idea with 'initiation' in the widest sense is shown by mediaeval church mazes.[65] It is now possible to say that the beliefs of contemporaries and the conjectures of modern scholars concerning them are much more certain than might have been supposed.

The earliest church maze is dated long before the Middle Ages. It is at Orléansville in Algeria, and it belongs to the fourth century A.D. 'At the centre is a "jeu de lettres" on the words SANCTA ECLESIA (Holy Church) which may be read in any direction except diagonally, commencing at the centre.' But most church mazes belong to the twelfth century. Two, at Lucca and Pavia, have words which refer to the story of Theseus, without Christian allusions. But at Piacenza there is a maze, said to date from A.D. 903, which has a Latin legend of four hexameters declaring the Christian symbolism. According to this the maze is the world, easy to enter but hard to leave, so that one who is caught in it, weighed down by his sins, can scarcely succeed in returning to the true doctrine of life. The labyrinth in the church of Santa Maria in Trastevere in Rome has three concentric circles inside, which have been thought to refer to degrees of beatitude, like Dante's circles. Dante's circles go back, through the Arab myth of Heaven, to the Sumerian ziggurat; so that here there seems to be one of the neatest fusions of the religion of earth and of the sky. There are church mazes known as 'Chemin de Jérusalem'; and at Lyons there is an inscription, clearly referring to a maze though it is not associated with any actual maze design, which again treats the maze as the world. 'Learn by looking at this that you will die. Pray to Christ. He rescued me from this labyrinth.'

The inscriptions show that the exclusive quality of a maze, and its appropriate place between life and death or between two sorts of life, were well understood. It is easy to believe theories that have been published, that the mazes were used for symbolic pilgrimages; the penitent either finding his way through the maze on his knees, or simply tracing it with his finger, instead of making a real pilgrimage or crusade. There is one difficulty. Heaven, or some equivalent to it, may be inside or it may be outside. Originally it was inside, that is, in the place of peace within the universal mother, earth. Therefore the earliest example at Orléansville is strictly right. So are the mazes with 'Jérusalem' in the middle. The old earth cult was not quite forgotten. But sometimes the prevailing conception of a Heaven in the sky reversed the meaning. This is an old difficulty. Vergil, and even the Malekulans of Seniang, have to imagine open country under the earth. It was, however, easy to think of the upper air as home, a conception fully perfected in Cicero's *Dream of Scipio*. According to Elias Ashmole's *Theatrum Chemicum Britannicum*, even the alchemists, seeking the philosopher's stone in the earth, thought that they needed 'an influx from the sky for obtaining the secret fire which allows the Stone to be achieved'.[66]

The same general pattern is clear in Chinese mysticism. Circular symbols are used to draw 'a *sulcus primigenius*, a magical furrow around the centre, the *templum* or *temenos* (sacred precincts) of the innermost personality'.[67] 'Magical practices are nothing but the projections of psychic events'; and the circle reacts on its maker, with fixation and concentration. Then Tao, the supreme life principle, takes leadership, and opposites are resolved in harmony. 'The interest is brought back to an inner, sacred domain.' The Chinese have names for this which suggest the pattern: 'the golden castle', 'the Heavenly Heart', 'the terrace of life', and 'the land without boundaries'.[68] They also remember the symbol of the cave.[69] There is a 'quieting of the spirit in the space of the ancestors'. 'It is safe within the cave of power, where all that is miraculous returns to its roots.' 'One fans the "fire in the middle of the water", which is in the middle of the cave.' That is the bright light seen beyond the waters of death by Gilgamish, the mystae in Aristophanes, and Aeneas too. A modern western mystic's vision also fits the pattern, but rather on the side of the ziggurat, the microcosm, and Dante's circles. The mystic had the impression that he traversed successive spheres or belts, and mounted a ladder leading to the centre of the system, which was equally his own system, the solar system, and the universal system, 'the three systems being at once diverse and identical'.[70] Then he saw the great light, and in it God, 'proving through His duality that God is Substance

FIGURE 15

A 'Mandāla' drawn by a European patient (after Richard Wilhelm
& C. G. Jung, *The Secret of the Golden Flower*, London, 1931, Plate
10; with acknowledgments to Messrs. Kegan Paul, Trench, Trubner,
& Co. Ltd.). '*Mandāla* means a circle, more especially a magic
circle, and this form of symbol is not only to be found all through the
East, but also among us; *mandālas* are amply represented in the
Middle Ages' (Jung, ibid. 96–7). 'Among my patients I have come
across cases of women who did not draw *mandāla* symbols but who
danced them instead' (ibid. 97). The picture here given is described
as: 'A *mandāla* as a fortified city with walls and moats. Within, a
broad moat surrounded by a wall, fortified with sixteen towers and
another moat following this wall. The last moat surrounds a central
castle with golden roofs whose centre is a golden temple' (ibid. 138).
If to this description is added the statement that the *mandāla* includes a surrounding maze as one of its most obvious characteristics, it becomes clear that this *mandāla* is a perfect illustration of the
'Initiation Pattern', as it is still apparently remembered in the unconscious; in particular the *mandāla* closely agrees with the Legends
of the Holy Grail. The *mandāla* has been slightly simplified for clearness in the drawing here given.

as well as Force, Love as well as Will, Feminine as well as Masculine, Mother as well as Father'. That is the synthesis which Vergil sought; to it the universal collective mind, in which he shared so sensitively, has tended since the idea of initiation began with the motherhood of earth and the cave.

Aeneas descends into the earth in submission to Apollo and Diana; and in submission to them Augustus instituted his 'secular' games, as the sibylline books commanded.[71] Apollo and Diana are not only of the world above; in fact they represent Dis and Proserpina, to whom the secular games really belonged.[72] The transference was made easier because the old chthonic god Veiovis of Bovillae, a particular god of the Julii, was much identified with Apollo; and Augustus himself thought of appearing as Veiovis.[73] Vergil[74] regards this chthonic policy with some deprecation; and in the Sixth *Aeneid* he applies his intuition to chthonic theology, in quest of a true marriage of heaven and earth. But it is not only Augustus that started, nor even only the Sixth *Aeneid* that declares, his quest.

The cave at Cumae is not the first which Aeneas enters. He also entered a cave for his union with Dido.[75] Both caves mean a change of state, enforced by the very ancient symbolism of caves. Dido's cave recalls the sacral marriage of heaven and earth, which is localized at caves. The marriage of Peleus and Thetis happened in a cave, and so, in effect, did the marriage of Jason and Medea. Important marriages of heroes and heroines are put in the mould of the old earth marriage; at some point like facts attracted like myth. Not much of this sort loses its force in Vergil. Dido's cave is an initiation into a new phase of life, and the marriage ought to mean the start of a great creative process, like the first marriage of heaven and earth. At Dido's marriage, the nymphs, old deities of nature, cry aloud on the mountain crest. Lightning flashes, as when the earth is fructified by the sky.[76] But there is no blessing; Dido has no son. It is by Juno's favour that Aeneas came, thought Dido, and Juno orders the wedding. It was Hera-Juno who persecuted Heracles; and myths of Heracles gave much help to the myth of Aeneas. There is a difficulty in seeing what the personality of Juno means, and why a goddess, honoured at Rome, should be so hostile. The answer is that Juno is fiercely feminine. She was not among the principal early deities of

Rome, and was never one of the greatest. Rome worshipped male gods first; Rome began, because Juno acknowledged defeat.

Vergil knew the cost of empire; the cost in suffering, and the cost to conscience and to so many graceful things. That he knew the cost his poem shows so clearly that it has lately been thought to be a savage attack on Augustus and autocracy.[77] This is half the truth. The Trojans cannot prevail, and start the Roman race, without many horrors, and without some guilt. Vergil saw the world whole, and faced everything. But in many moods he accepted autocracy, partly because he stepped into the tradition, which had already gathered strength, in which the highest law is not abstract but personal, incarnate in the lawgiver or king.[78]

In so far as he accepted the resignation of so much that he loved, before this destiny of a greatness sometimes hard, he accepted it seeing, and feeling.[79] The male principle, which is seen in Fascism now, is always fighting a form of the female principle, which has found its way into Communism, and lost much of itself as it went.[80] Vergil found some consolation in courage and national honour and in the generosity which a conqueror can reach. To such things poets will return. T. S. Eliot has returned to them, in 'stone, bronze, stone, steel, oak-leaves, horses' heels'. He trusts 'in the hands, quiet over the horse's neck'. But, still like Vergil, he has to cry 'O hidden under the dove's wing, hidden in the turtle's breast . . . , At the still point of the turning world. O hidden.'

Juno is what the female principle may become, as cruel as the male principle itself, and less rational. When Juno and Venus pull one way, great havoc is done. It is no wonder that even within the *Aeneid* there is not one single Venus only. At the last, Vergil trusted the male force more, with a hard hold on his hate. 'Bridesmaid', 'pronuba', to Dido was Juno;[81] but bridesmaid to Lavinia, with the same word used, the only other time in the *Aeneid*, was Bellona.[82]

The wedding with Dido failed, because such love alone was not enough. This is an initiation. A soft love had sent Aeneas safe out of burning Troy. But something different is demanded as the time goes on, something less free. Yet Vergil never forgot how much Rome was built on love, 'mother of Aeneas' sons', filling all the world with life, bringing into light all happy and lovely things, as Lucretius said and saw.[83] There was love in Julius and Augustus, though there was wickedness along the way. Other despotic men have burnt with a fiery love, and started so. However, not only the adherents of autocracy were wicked. The extreme republicans, as Vergil with a miracle of subtlety says, were not better; Brutus had tyranny in the soul.[84]

In the myths of the Grail the initiation pattern, which Vergil also used, is exceptionally complete; and there are present in it survivals of the earth mother, the princess won from the castle or the earth, and the divine king. Vergil, sensitive to world tradition, has all three, symmetrically spaced however, with dramatic dissociation, in the second, fourth, and sixth books of the *Aeneid*. Aeneas leaves Troy, in an almost passive trust in his mother who is the universal mother also. She is fitly inside 'Troy'; the maze can even be called the earth mother's symbol.[85] And Troy is the east, the softer, less forceful part of the elements that went to make Rome. Then in Africa, typically, the love is fierce and selfish;[86] Dido is partner in the old sacred marriage, and she is the erotic end of initiation; but to Vergil that alone will not do. Africa has not full partnership with Rome. Last comes Italy, the home of manhood and discipline and the public will. In Italy the king-god has become the leader, the providence, the protector of the nation's life; but because the king-god's folk-lore had existed and had not been lost, the Stoic Roman, who guides and foresees and in his own fashion loves, has all the more to impart to poetry. For now, Vergil stands for the father; even though Aeneas comes out of the ivory gate.

At Cumae the greater initiation comes. Whether Aeneas fully lives through the experience, or dies, half or more, is a question to be asked, but not with any attempt to answer it. There is a taint of death on Odysseus, from the old death-myth of Calypso's cave. Several modern stories, such as Bruno Traven's *The Death Ship*, and Graham Sutton's *The Damnation of Mr Zinkler*, show a soft and bewildering passage between life and death. And Aeneas comes out of the cave by the gate of false dreams. Strangely, that old bewilderment was not used in the attempt to show that Vergil hates Augustus and his rule, though it might have been interpreted to mean that all the glory of Rome prophesied by Anchises was a lie.[87] Vergil has left it, carrying that meaning as much as it may; but to Vergil truth is not truth while only one side of it is seen.[88] Perhaps Aeneas, coming through the gate of false dreams, is a false dream too, and never came through the gate, a living man, at all. He had seen Dido within the Cumaean cave.

But however much of these meanings, which are all there, each reader should at each time accept, only each reader can decide. There are clearer lines on the Cumaean entrance gate, a pictured warning against wrongful love.[89] The love of the bull is 'callous', 'crudelis', a strong oxymoron, and Pasiphae, 'she who gives light to all', met him in secrecy of sin. So far, it is the old myth from Egypt and Crete. The minotaur is the king-god, and perhaps a devil too, and Pasiphae, the moon, who is shown in labyrinths, is somehow his queen-goddess, perhaps because she is also the earth. Vergil has quite transformed the myth in the labyrinth for his symbolic end. In contrast is the love of Daedalus. He pities the love of the queen; and, for love of Icarus his son, he cannot make any picture of him. And all the time the labyrinth commands awe and secrecy, and presages the cave myth coming. For, in his way, Vergil takes the labyrinth which is the king-god's temple tomb and sacral marriage room, the labyrinth which is the cave, access to the earth mother, and that other dim labyrinth, in part the same, which is Anchises, to whose 'very ashes and bones' Aeneas is journeying;[90] and, blending all of them into one simplicity of words, says much in little.

Homer took the folk-tale of the unknown hero, who met a princess by chance, and, declared by success in games no common man, won her. Nausicaa he wanted, and the games; but not the ending, for there was Penelope.[91] Vergil took the beginning from Homer, in passage after passage, for the tale of Dido; but his plan was tragic. He reconstructed Homer's broken story, making it as it had once been, and bringing it to its natural end. For his Cumae Vergil reconstructed another old tale. In the *Odyssey*, Odysseus goes among the ghosts to meet his mother, and Teiresias. In most Greek myths the hero descends to recover a goddess of life, Persephone, Helen, or Ariadne. But in the *Epic of Gilgamish* it is an ancestor whom Gilgamish seeks, to gain immortal secrets from him. Vergil has made this the quest of Aeneas, a new creation, by means of one of his delicate changes, because the race memory strong in him guided him along the ancient pattern; or he may have known that pattern by more conscious means. The first possibility would be strange; but the second would be more wonderful still. Like Gilgamish, through terrible frustrations, Aeneas meets a father in a land of immortality, and brings back some of the secrets of life, but some is lost; and yet, like the king in the Egyptian myth, Anchises is installed 'as the centre of the life and well-being of the community', 'his vigour . . . prolonged and renewed', under the rays of the Elysian sun, like the sun-god to whom the Egyptian king was united after death.[92]

The frustrations and obstructions of the Sumerian myth and the myths of the Grail are reflected again and again in the Sixth *Aeneid*.[93] This agrees with a new theory of ancient belief: that a thing was supposed to remain itself on account of strong binding forces alone, so that if the binding force was relaxed, the thing would dissolve into its opposite.[94] Life unbound becomes death; death unbound, life. That is different from the usual theory, that the binding is to strengthen the known world, of the city, perhaps, or the grave, against the unknown and probably unfriendly powers of an outer world. I am not sure whether the theories are exclusive; possibly they are equally good attempts to represent irrecoverable thoughts of early man, thoughts which were perhaps themselves logically exclusive of one another. Either way, the religion of binding is strong in Vergil; he never lets the mighty constrictions separating death and life be forgotten; till all at once a change in the imagery is sudden and dynamic. As soon as the golden bough is hung up to Proserpine, the images are free; no triple walls of bronze, but bees, flying where they like, and symbolizing immortality, like the bees in the cave where Zeus was born;[95] and a new, strong thought, coming from Musaeus, that the souls in bliss have no fixed home, but wander in the woods.[96] That is, if old thought is clear, life out of the midst of death.

The motive for writing poetry, and for reading poetry, is the desire for Heaven before the time. It is Roman to wait patiently for Heaven, as Scipio was told in his dream. But this patience in waiting pent up a poetry deeper than poetry of Greeks.[97] And depth is of the earth. Psychologically, there is still a residual longing in the mind for a return to prenatal peace;[98] and the ancient association of that peace with caves of the earth miraculously survives. 'O Earth, O Earth, return!' said Blake; and Sophocles, writing the one single ending that answered all the poised questions left by his former plays, presents even an Oedipus saved when he worships earth and the sky in one.[99] So it is not too strange that great poets, in search of Heaven before the time, write again and again a song of triumph out of a funeral service, 'while jewelled unicorns draw by the gilded hearse'.[100] They are a long way from the Australian churingas;[101] but their lineage started near them. Vergil, in his unique economy, does not leave out very much. He has to let the most ancient pattern shimmer through; and he has to preserve notions adjectival to it which lesser poets lost. That is why he retains the forgotten image of the full sacred personal city, the society which is divine because it is one; perhaps passing the image on to Saint Augustine, who also remembers the old philosophy of the microcosm.[102] Vergil needed the old beliefs, in order to glean his brain; they had gone to make humanity of the present and the future, whose high prophet he was, bound to know and say what others could only be.

NOTES

1. For the legends and criticisms of them *cf.* F. Cauer, *De fabulis Graecis ad Romam conditam pertinentibus* (Berlin, 1884) *passim*, esp. 1–5 (a history of the controversy); id. *Jahrbücher für classische Philologie, Suppl.* 15 (1887) 95–182; Gordon J. Laing, *CJ* 6 (1910) 51–64 (where more recent theories are criticized); L. Malten, *ARW* 29 (1931) 33–59; W. F. J. Knight, *G&R* [6 (1937) 70–7. J.D.C.]
2. *Cf.* esp. Th. Mommsen, *History of Rome*, transl. by W. P. Dickson (Everyman Edition, London, 1920) I, 459–63, esp. 460.
3. *Cf.* above, p. 215.
4. R. H. Klausen, *Aeneas und die Penaten* (Hamburg and Gotha, 1839–40) *passim*; A. Blakeway, *JRS* 25 (1935) 129–49, esp. 134 note 21 cont. 135.
5. *Cf.* T. E. Peet, *The Stone and Bronze Ages in Italy* (Oxford, 1909) 396 (Este), 421 (near Taranto), 511 (Apulia).
6. P. Giles, *CAH* II (Cambridge, 1924) 36–7.
7. A. R. Burn, *Minoans, Philistines, and Greeks* (London, 1930) 243–4.
8. H. J. Rose, *Primitive Culture in Italy* (London, 1926) 95.
9. Sir A. J. Evans, *JHS* 21 (1901) 126–9.
10. H. J. Rose, *JRS* 23 (1933) 46–63, esp. 50–1, 62–3; *cf.* Paul Kretschmer, *Glotta* 20 (1932) 201–3.
11. H. Krahe, *Glotta* 20 (1932) 188–96.
12. F. Melian Stawell, *A Clue to the Cretan Scripts* (London, 1931) 12, 24, 25, 45, 91; these observations are not dependent on the validity of the general thesis of the

book. [But see now J. Chadwick, *The Decipherment of Linear B* (Cambridge, 1960). J.D.C.]

13. F. Schachermeyr, *Etruskische Frühgeschichte* (Leipzig, 1929) 298.

14. E. Adelaide Hahn, *TAPA* 64 (1933) 28–40.

15. *Encyclopaedia Britannica*[11] (1911) *s.v.* Etruscans.

16. Nils Åberg, *Bronzezeitliche und Früheisenzeitliche Chronologie*, I, *Italien* (Stockholm, 1930) *passim*, esp. 200–11 (conclusions); *cf.* the review of the book, by D. Randall McIver, *Antiquity* 5 (1931) 126: 'It is trade with the Mediterranean, beginning long before Greek colonization, which brings Italy into touch with Greece and the Orient at the very beginning of the Dipylon stage.'

17. Schachermeyr (above, note 13) 50–7.

18. B. Farrington, *Revue des études homériques* 2 (1932) 74–80, esp. 75–6, argues from Hellanicus, fr. 127 (Müller), Schol. Ap. Rhod. IV, 992, Thuc. VI, 2 and I, 25, Strab. I, 2, 15 that Greeks were in Sicily at a very early date.

19. S. Casson, *CR* 27 (1913) 153–6.

20. Malten (above, note 1) 33–59.

21. O. Gruppe, *Griechische Mythologie und Religionsgeschichte* (Munich, 1906) I, 193–205; *cf.* 360–5.

22. F. Altheim, *Römische Religionsgeschichte* II (Leipzig, 1931) 87.

23. Casson (above, note 19).

24. See above, p. 262.

25. H. Frankfort, *Studies in the Early Pottery of the Near East* II (London, 1927) 126–35.

26. Gertrude Robinson, *JHS* 50 (1930) 186–7.

27. H. Güntert, *SHAW*, Ph.-hist. Kl. (1932/3) 1 Abh. *passim*, esp. 12, 36, who suggests that the spread of the 'stone men' constitutes the element of fact in the legend of Aeneas; *cf.* E. Kornemann, *Die Antike* 8 (1932) 105, who independently makes the same people forerunners of the Etruscans, tracing them to Sumer.

28. Catharine Saunders, *Vergil's Primitive Italy* (New York, 1930) 13–29.

29. Verg. *Aen.* VI, 17.

30. J. W. Mackail, *The Aeneid of Virgil* (Oxford, 1930) 520.

31. Ibid. 210, 519–25, esp. 519–21.

32. Sir. A. J. Evans, *JHS* 45 (1925) 71.

33. A. Mauri, *Ass. internaz. studi mediterranei, Bollettino* III, 3 (1932) 27.

34. R. S. Conway, *New Studies of a Great Inheritance* (London, 1921) 123–4.

35. Verg. *Aen.* III, 104–13.

36. Saunders (above, note 28) 13–29.

37. Blakeway (above, note 4) 129–49.

38. Ibid. 132 note 14.

39. Franz Altheim, *SMSR* 10 (1934) 125–55, esp. 148–55.

40. [Mrs] C. N. Deedes, *Folk-Lore* 46 (1935) 194–243, esp. 229–32.

41. Kornemann (above, note 27) 110.

42. Klausen (above, note 4) *passim*, esp. II, 691–704, 1169–95; Saunders (above, note 28) 8, 59, etc.

43. Klausen (above, note 4) II, 623–4.

44. For the reff. *cf.* Klausen (above, note 4) II, 620–36, etc.; and for a selection of them relevant to this point, W. F. J. Knight, *Folk-Lore* 46 (1935) 102 note 11. The burial of Vestals who had not preserved their purity was a device to preserve Rome from enemies (*cf.* G. Wissowa, *ARW* 22, 1924, 201–14). It seems that the Vestals' purity was supposed to be in magical sympathy with the city's preservation from attack. The burials are, at the same time, like foundation-burials under walls (Grant Allen, *The Evolution of the Idea of God*, Thinker's Library, London, 1931, Ch. XII, 173–84). In Italy burials were apparently sited to protect the

living (H. J. Rose, *CQ* 24, 1930, 132, citing von Duhn). The only ancient parallel to the burial of Vestals is the burial of Antigone (Wissowa, *ARW* 22, 1924, 213). I suggest that Antigone too is defensive, sacrificed to repel the plague from Thebes, or possibly the threat of war; the incident appears displaced, but its original context in the myth is undecided. *Cf.* the prayers offered to Athena, the defensive goddess, Soph. *OT*, 19–21. Like the Sumerian ziggurats, Vesta bound the land and people together (Klausen, above, note 4, II, 625). In the story of Tarpeia maidenhood seems to be in magical sympathy with the defence of Rome (W. F. J. Knight, *TAPA* 63, 1932, 30–2; see above, p. 238 note); and there are signs of this defensive maidenhood in the terms and aetiology of the 'Locrian curse' (W. F. J. Knight, *Folk-Lore* 46, 1935, 101–2, esp. 101 note 9). All this is only one side of the question; but defensive sanctity in Italy, as noted here, and also by Muller (below, note 63) and Kornemann (above, note 27) is not without some confirmation of the legends of early influence on Italy from the east. That Athena was a maiden goddess in early, not only in late, times is well maintained against Fehrle by L. R. Farnell, *Cults of the Greek States* I (Oxford, 1896) 303.

45. *Cf.* L. R. Farnell, *The Evolution of Religion* (London, 1905) 34–5: 'A passage in the Panarium of Epiphanios is of singular interest for those who wish to study the period of transition between old things and new. This writer tells us that on the night of the 5th or 6th of January, in Alexandria, the worshippers met in the sacred enclosure or temple of 'Kore', and having sung hymns to the music of the flute till dawn, they descended by the light of torches into an underground shrine and brought up thence a wooden idol on a bier representing Kore seated and naked, with the sign of the cross on her brow, her hands and her knees.' *Cf.* ibid. 36: 'An old ritual of Kore at Alexandria, the goddess of the underworld whose statue was kept in a subterraneous cavern, may have included a kind of passion play in which a holy child was born…'

46. William Warburton, *The Divine Legation of Moses* (London, 1738) I, 182; *cf.* Maud Bodkin, *Archetypal Patterns in Poetry* (London, 1934) 122–36, where the presence of initiation in the Sixth *Aeneid* is noticed, and the symbol of the cave also, but not in close association.

47. Charles Knapp, *The [American] School Review* 13 (1905) 492–508, an excellent, but inaccessible, account.

48. E. K. Rand, *The Magical Art of Virgil* (Cambridge, Massachusetts, 1931) 3–10, 64, etc.

49. Eugen Täubler, *SHAW* Ph.-hist. Kl. (1931/2) 2 Abh. 63.

50. Colin Still, *Shakespeare's Mystery Play, A Study of 'The Tempest'* (London, 1921) *passim*; id. *The Timeless Theme* (London, 1936) *passim*, where the same theory is advanced without significant change. I cite the earlier book.

51. Lucian *Catapl.* XXII, 644; *cf.* Porph. *De Antr. Nymph.* XXXIV.

52. I owe this fact to the kindness of Mr John Layard.

53. Still (above, note 50) *passim*.

54. Ibid. 132–3.

55. Plat. *Phaedo* 108A.

56. Still (above, note 50) 133 note *.

57. Lucian (above, note 51).

58. Still (above, note 50) 133.

59. *Ecclus.* iv, 17–19.

60. Still (above, note 50) 58.

61. Ibid. 58 note *.

62. Ibid. 129–32; *cf.* 132–5.

63. F. Muller, Jun., *Mnemosyne* Ser. III, 2 (1935) 164: 'in hac re iste usus ac mos *saltatio circularis* ("Rundtanz, Kringdans") est, quem olim perficiebant homines,

quotiens mortis periculum adibant, imprimis quotiens navigationem trans mare aut incipiebant aut feliciter perfecerant.'

64. The seaside maze-dance retains its connection with caves, according to Eustathius, 1166, 17 *ad Il.* XVIII, 590: καὶ νῦν ἔτι πολλοὶ καὶ μάλιστα ναυτικοί, ὅσοι πρὸς τὸ ἀντρῶδες* παρεκνεύουσι, χορόν τινα ἐλίττουσι ποικιλόστροφον καὶ πολυκαμπῆ τὰς τοῦ Λαβυρίνθου μιμεῖσθαι θέλοντες ἕλικας. *(MS.: τὸ παλαιὸν ἀνδρῶδες; v.l. σπήλαιον ἀντρῶδες.)

65. W. H. Matthews, *Mazes and Labyrinths* (London, 1922) 54–70, from which I quote.

66. Grillot de Givry, *Witchcraft, Magic and Alchemy,* transl. Locke, (London, 1931) 359–60 with fig. 336 (359); the philosopher's stone may be represented in the Holy Grail (see above, pp. 253–7).

67. Richard Wilhelm and C. G. Jung, *The Secret of the Golden Flower, A Chinese Book of Life* ... (London, 1931) 100–2.

68. Ibid. 98.

69. Ibid. 53, 61–2, 68.

70. Ibid. 102–3, quoting Edward Maitland.

71. H. Mattingly, *CR* 48 (1934) 161–5, esp. 161–2.

72. Ibid. 161.

73. Ibid. 162, on Verg. *Georg.* I, 36–7.

74. Verg. ibid.

75. Verg. *Aen.* IV, 165–6.

76. Ibid. 166–8.

77. Francesco Sforza, *CR* 49 (1935) 97–108.

78. Eugene Tavenner, *TAPA* 64 (1933) 128–37.

79. C. M. Bowra, *G&R* 3 (1933) 8–21.

80. *Cf.* 'Gens', *The New English Weekly* 5 (1934) 322–3.

81. Verg. *Aen.* IV, 166.

82. Ibid. VII, 319.

83. Lucr. I, 1–27; that an Epicurean could write like this of Venus is not in the least the difficulty that has been supposed, provided that the symbolic apprehension of poets in general is recognized, and the religion of life, which poets must have to be poets at all, is at least partly understood.

84. W. F. J. Knight, *CR* 46 (1932) 55–7; ibid. 47 (1933) 169–71.

85. Muller (above, note 63) 49; Mr Layard tells me that in Malekula a stylized design derived from a maze is the symbol of Temes Savsap.

86. *Cf.* Liv. XXX, 12, 18.

87. Vergil does not exactly say that false dreams are sent through the ivory gate. He says that the second gate is of ivory, finished gleaming 'but false dreams the good spirits send to the sky' (Verg. *Aen.* VI, 896), with no indication that the dreams come through the gate, though that seems an obvious supposition. This is enough for Vergil's subtlety, and it enables him to mean two things equally.

88. T. J. Haarhoff, *Vergil in the Experience of South Africa* (Oxford, 1931) 111–14, explains Vergil's 'holistic' outlook.

89. Verg. *Aen.* VI, 14–33.

90. Ibid. V, 55–7:
nunc ultro ad cineres ipsius et ossa parentis
(haud equidem sine mente reor, sine numine divum)
adsumus ...
Cf. Muller (above, note 63) 177.

91. W. J. Woodhouse, *The Composition of Homer's Odyssey* (Oxford, 1930) 63–5.

92. S. H. Hooke, *Folk-Lore* 45 (1934) 208.

93. Verg. *Aen.* VI, 51–3, 81–2, 109, 126–32, 138–9, 146–8, 238, 258–9, 264–7, 316, 319–20, 327–8, 389–91, 425, 515–22, 548–56, 563, 573–5, 630–1, 640, 673.

94. Muller (above, note 63) 38–45.

95. Boios *ap.* Anton. Lib. XIX; see above, p. 239, note, and *cf.* the officiants called 'bees' at Eleusis; and for the interpretation of the bees in Vergil, *cf.* [Mrs] M. de G. Verrall, *CR* 24 (1910) 43–6.

96. Verg. *Aen.* VI, 673.

97. Aurelio Espinosa Pólit, S. J., *Virgilio, el poeta y su misión providencial* (Quito, 1932) 134–68.

98. Bodkin (above, note 46) 113–14.

99. Soph. *OC*, 1654–5; on this I acknowledge kind help from Mr G. K. Jenkins.

100. G. Wilson Knight, *The Christian Renaissance* (Toronto, 1933) 370–4, who explains the optimism of Eliot's later phase. [Not included in the 1962 re-issue, London, but likely to reappear in a volume of collected essays. J.D.C.]

101. [For 'churingas' see p. 146 above, J.D.C.]

102. E. Hommel, *Orientalistische Studien Fritz Hommel* I (Leipzig, 1917) 234–5, quoting Augustin. *De Ciuit. Dei* VII, 8.

For the golden bough cf. also F. J. M. de Waele, *The Magic Staff or Rod in Graeco-Italian Antiquity* (privately printed, 1927) *passim*. He distinguishes the shapes and uses of ceremonial and magic staffs, with short discussions of Vergil (65–9; 82–4). He thinks (82–4) that the golden bough belongs to popular belief, that it passed into the mysteries, and that Vergil derived it either directly from the mysteries, or from Hellenistic treatises. He cites a 'golden bough' found in a tomb in the neighbourhood of Colonus, and writes (82–3): 'Literary evidences, as well as some remnants of the customs and monuments, fully prove that throughout the whole of classical antiquity the dead protected themselves by carrying this golden bough.' Even if this is not an overstatement, the similarities between other golden boughs and the Malekulan wand *ne-row* still do not extend to the use of the bough as a passport or magic wand to cross water. Vergil has filled in this missing content in his golden bough, as the Malekulan parallel shows. The antecedents of Vergil's golden bough, and the fusion of ideas in it, are the same, apparently, as for the Malekulan wand. This is all the more remarkable since it cannot be shown that in any historical mysteries of classical times the golden bough had such composite attributes.

A full discussion of 'Journeys of the Dead' would have to include more eastern evidence, besides much else. The divided soul of Heracles has a close Babylonian parallel; and the partial 'initiations' of the heroes Etana and Adapa, who nearly won Heaven, need to be considered besides the journey of Gilgamish. In Babylonia the 'tree of life' was a worshipper's palm branch in a jar of water. Possibly the myths were copied from the offering; or possibly the offering was copied from the myths. In Egypt the 'sky Heaven' was imagined very early, and the conceptions of it strongly affected ideas of the underworld. Probably few variations elsewhere known have not some counterpart in Egypt and Babylonia. The cave is Egyptian: 'This is thy cavern in the broad hall of Osiris, O King Pepi' (Pyramid Texts, §§ 1551–4). The Egyptian King drew sustenance from a 'tree of life in the mysterious isle in the midst of the Field of Offerings, in search of which he sets out in company with the Morning Star' (J. H. Breasted, *Development of Religion and Thought in Ancient Egypt*, London, 1912, 133; cf. ibid. *passim*, especially 49–69 and 118–41 for the condition of the dead in the after life of the tomb and later in a celestial heaven). The king is the sun, because he starts with the

Morning Star; but he goes to an island of the blest, with a tree of life there, according to the 'pattern'. It might be asked whether in Egypt this myth has been caused by the ritual of a tomb with a sacred tree growing on it; a possibility unlikely for Egypt itself, but not for lands to the east and north from which Egypt was influenced.

For further comments on 'stone men' in connection with trees, with reference to Hom. *Il.* XXII, 126, etc., and on the stone that was Cybele, cf. F. Muller, Jun., *Mnemosyne*, S. III, 2 (1935) 203–6, with reff. Muller's suggestions are often confirmed by anthropological material not treated by him.

I suggest that problems concerning the 'Pillars of Heracles' can be enlightened by regarding them partly as real geography, but partly also as an element in a ritual 'journey of the dead'.

[An interesting application of the author's 'initiation-pattern' is made in an article described as 'A Footnote to *Cumaean Gates*': Miss Theo Brown, 'St Joseph of Arimathea at Glastonbury', *Folk-Lore* 57 (1946) 75–9. J.D.C.]

II. INITIATION

On the origin of the idea of initiation I have kept here to a very simple outline, because the subject is precarious. I think it useful to emphasize the cave, rebirth, and the maze; and if possible to make those structural lines of the pattern firm. This has meant that I have almost confined myself to the religion of earth. There is, however, the religion of the sky also; and the two cannot permanently be separated. In discussing classical antiquity it is usual and desirable to avoid exaggeration of solar elements. There is, however, a sense in which a reaction from this reaction is to be expected. Mr Robert W. Cruttwell, in a paper which he has kindly allowed me to see, and which may as I hope soon appear in print, gives a very acute and fundamental explanation of the initiation pattern by reference to early man's immediate consciousness of the alternations of day and night, and sun and moon, and to his passionate desire to prevent the extinction of himself and his world. It is not a question of worship. And the sky, not the sun, may be the primary fact; but then the sky is a clock face, and the sun and moon are the hands of the clock, necessarily mediating any behaviour towards the changing sky. Early man, then, associates sun and moon, and day and night with the personalities of his family; and the birth and death of sun and moon are identified with his own personal fears and hopes. All this must wait for the publication of Mr Cruttwell's paper.* But it is

* [This paper was published as: 'The Initiation Pattern and the Grail', *Folk-Lore* 49 (1938) 244 ff. J.D.C.]

necessary to say that some such theory seems to be ultimately required, in order to bring within our view known descriptions of the outlook of early man on alternations of day and night, such as the account given by C. G. Jung, *Contributions to Analytical Psychology*, translated by H. G. and Cary F. Baynes (London, 1928) 74, 112–18, 125–6, 374 (referring to Lévy-Bruhl's doctrine of *participation mystique*, a strong confirmation of Mr Cruttwell's view). Further, a theory of the kind is required to satisfy the evidence for cults of the moon, which I have left aside, and above all the strange identification of the moon with the earth for certain purposes; cf. M. Esther Harding, *Woman's Mysteries* (London, 1935) *passim*.

Miss Dorothea Chaplin, *Matter, Myth, and Spirit, or Keltic and Hindu Links* (London, 1935) 67–72, discusses the Abbot's Bromley Dancers, comparing Morris Dances and Hindu religious dancing. John Layard, 'Maze-Dances and the Ritual of the Labyrinth in Malekula', *Folk-Lore*, 47 (1936) 123–70, describes and analyses Malekulan maze-dances, and, comparing Morris dances and the Abbot's Bromley horned dancers, says that the horned dancers are not far removed from the bull-headed Minotaur. For further work on this whole question, this evidence from contemporary Malekulan maze-dances, which may represent an approach to a ritual tomb and sacral marriage, needs close examination.

III. MYTH AND FACT

Lord Raglan, *The Hero* (London, 1936), offers a 'direct challenge to those who uphold the historical value of tradition'; the traditional narrative 'is derived in all its forms from dramatic ritual, and never from historic fact'. This to me is half the truth. The patterns persist, and the 'heroes' have their place in them and act according to them. This does not mean that that is all that a hero of tradition can do; for if like fact attracts like myth, the facts may still be there, and partly ascertainable, when they are separated from their accretions.

IV. THE PATTERN IN LITERATURE

Much might be said about the permanence and even universality of the initiation pattern. What is remarkable is not so much the regularity of the general form as the persistence of elements in their right place, and the apparent necessity with which the spiritual quest is presented in the shape of an initiation. Besides the poems of Dante and Shakespeare, Browning's *Childe Roland* ought especially to be mentioned. On this cf. William Lyon Phelps, *Robert Browning*

(London, 1915) 232–3. 'What happened when he [Roland] blew his horn? Did the awful mountains in the blood-red sunset dissolve as the walls of Jericho fell to a similar sound? Did the round, squat Tower vanish like a dream-phantom? Or was the sound of the horn the last breath of the hero?' There is interest in this. Browning may have intended an initiation that failed, as often in the Grail legends. Further, the tower beyond the waste land assailed by a blast of a horn recalls the ideal fusion of the qualities of a city with a sacred wall, and of the earth entered at initiation. The other idea, fusion of the city with an individual maiden, is remembered by Shakespeare in *The Rape of Lucrece*, 463–76, 1527–68, where Tarquin's outrage against her is elaborately compared to an assault on a city, and in particular Troy. I owe it to Mr G. K. Jenkins that I did not overlook this valuable reference. T. S. Eliot's *The Waste Land* is of course the most impressive modern initiation myth. Cf. Edmund Wilson, *Axel's Castle* (New York and London, 1936), the chapter on Eliot's poetry, where the dependence on Grail legends is shown. I have mentioned above Eliot's symbolic use of rock and stone here and elsewhere. Among other modern examples of the pattern is Dennis Wheatley's novel, *They Found Atlantis* (London, 1936). A diving-party reaches a Utopia among Atlanteans, surviving below the sea. First sea is crossed by a westward voyage, and by the descent in a diving-sphere. The party then traverses labyrinthine caves, in which sub-human wild creatures assail them; eventually they cross a moat and enter the island home of the Atlanteans, a kind of garden of the gods, with bright light, and trees and flowers, where the motive of marriage is emphasized. As usual, the 'initiation' partly fails, and the journey ends in sleep.

V. THE COLLECTIVE UNCONSCIOUS IN LITERARY CRITICISM

The theory of a racial memory and a collective unconscious here accepted is principally Dr C. G. Jung's. Jung's theory is of course contested; for an alternative theory, nearer to 'common sense', cf. the works of Professor Bronislaw Malinowski, e.g. *Sex and Repression in Savage Society* (London, 1927) *passim*. It should not be forgotten, however, that Jung has a unique command of the psycho-analytic evidence on which his theories are based, and that, unless positive impossibility is found in the theory, equal command of the evidence would be necessary in order to disprove it. That the theory is not more, but less vague and mystical than alternatives to it, is well shown in the context of artistic and literary creation by Dr Harold Rosenberg, *The Symposium* 2 (New York, 1931) 179–91, who criticizes the theories of Freud and Jung, and shows that the more comprehensive view of the matter, which takes into account not only a 'personal myth' but a 'collective myth' also, is necessary to the facts. This article is not very accessible, but I hope soon to print a discussion of it and other theories concerned with literary tradition and dependence (probably an expanded form of a paper called *Poetic Sources* which I read to the Sheffield Branch of the Classical Association at Sheffield on March 4, 1936).* For some references, and a short statement of the meaning of literary tradition and dependence, cf. my remarks in *CW* 29 (1936), 121–2, esp. note 9.

Dr Rosenberg writes as follows. 'Jung's "collective unconscious" is a sort of four-dimensional organization of the mentality of society' (Rosenberg, 184); it is 'connectible with the plane of contemporaneous consciousness', and it 'stretches also backwards in time to the primitive beginnings of thought' (ibid.). It borders on mysticism, 'but it is saved for psychology and the scientific method by the location of its origin not in the transcendental present but in the prehistorical past' (ibid.). 'The relation of the Collective Unconscious to the poet consists in the fact that "he is the *collective* man, the carrier and former of the unconsciously active soul of mankind" ' (ibid.). That is, a *human or racial myth* is substituted for the *personal myth*. The myth is objective. 'Objective here means a fundamental unconscious mythology waiting to be related to the contemporaneous consciousness' (ibid. 185). ' "The psychic structure, exactly like the anatomical one, must bear the characteristics of the primogenital phases through which it passes" ' (ibid., quoting Jung).

This view solves difficulties of literary criticism. The expositions of Professor J. Livingston Lowes, Mlle A.-M. Guillemin, Professor E. K. Rand, Mr T. S. Eliot, Dr J. van Gelder, and others, seem to require for their reconciliation and completion the psychological theory of Jung. Artistic creation relies on recognitions and contacts that reach beyond the experience of the individual in both time and space. Cf. on the subjects of the present book, C. G. Jung, *Contributions to Analytical Psychology*, translated by H. G. and Cary F. Baynes (London, 1928) 119–20 (on prehistorical reminiscences), 123 (on the reality of mother earth as a symbol), 124 (on the mother as the hearth, 'the protecting cave', and the provident field), 396 (on the imprint of initiations on our consciousness, old and enduring). Cf. also Gustav Richard Heyer, *The Organism of the Mind*, translated by Eden and Cedar Paul (London, 1933) 107, 127–51, 237–8, etc. The only possible alternative to something like the doctrines of Jung seems to be a theory of reincarnation. Remarkably strong arguments

---

* [This paper was published in *Vergilius* 5 (1940) 7–16; a continuation was published in *Vergilius* 8 (1962) 2–7. J.D.C.]

in favour of it have lately been put forward by the Hon. Ralph Shirley, *The Problem of Rebirth* (London, 1936), *passim*. If he is right, Vergil states in the Sixth *Aeneid* what may almost be the literal truth, agreeing, too, with a surprisingly large number of poets and philosophers even in Europe.

That the earth is still able to carry a symbolism of gentleness, love and redemption is shown by a remarkable passage recently printed in a newspaper (James Douglas, *The Sunday Express*, September 22, 1935):

'How lightly we regard this wonder above all wonders, this splendour above all splendours, this grace above all grace!

'How good and pleasant this life of ours would be if we made love the victor over every evil and every ill!

'What a heavenly world we could create if we were loyal to the light of love as individuals, as nations, as races!

'The rule of love—is it an impossible dream, an unattainable Utopia, a Promised Land that mankind can never enter?

'The answer comes from the bowels of the earth to a despairing age, ravaged by hate. If love can conquer death, surely it can conquer life.'

PART THREE

THE HOLY CITY
OF THE EAST

THE HOLY CITY OF THE EAST

Reprinted from *Vergilius* 2, January 1939, incorporating a few later corrections.

The bewildering force and depth of Vergil's poetry for ever challenge new explanations. One possible explanation, accounting for something if not for everything, is this. Vergil, beyond other poets, had a strange sense of the past in the present, and sometimes of a very distant past indeed. Pent up in his poetry is the experience not of his day alone, and not even of a few generations before him besides. Nor does he read the further past by superficial records merely. He has a sensitivity to know what mattered to men in far distant days, and he retains within him some of their sight, and some of their hope and fear.

For Vergil, the old faith of Italy, in his day to become new once more, was a faith that went far back and away, beyond all known Italian places and times. He preserves what others forgot, since it mattered more to him. His Aeneas coming to Italy from Troy gave Italy her place in the long series of the cultures of the world.

In particular, Aeneas brings the sacred city, focalized in the cult of a protecting deity, who very nearly is the city itself;[1] the city that is one because it is personal, and because it is divine. It has been clearly seen that the human Greek city came to life in a central area, intruded between areas to the east and to the west, where another kind of city, the sacred or 'hierocentric' city, left a stronger imprint behind.[2] In the west was Italy; in the east were Babylonia and Sumer, and, on their western confine, Troy. Vergil bridged Greece, and traced his Italy to an eastern world.

The Troy of Vergil has far more sanctity than the brighter, more modern Troy of Homer. Vergil cannot forget the magic of the ring wall, the folk-lore of the wooden horse, the divine protection of the Trojan deities, Minerva, Apollo, and Neptunus, the palladion, Minerva's talisman, and Cassandra, maiden representative of the goddess whose maidenhood was the inviolability of her city.[3] In Troy he could see, far back, the very faith of Italy, the faith of Vesta and the Vestals, and the faith and fear clearest of all to us at Iguvium from the still-preserved ritual about its gates and walls.

But the old faith is clear too at Rome itself, in the story of the foundation and in rites, especially the Salian Dance and Trojan Game. It is clear too at Veii, the city captured according to the very pattern of the capture of Troy.[4] Juno was 'evoked' from Veii, as the power and help of Minerva were lured from Troy with the palladion. The walls of both cities were pierced; at Troy the magic of them was defeated by the wooden horse, and at Veii by violating with an outflow of water the confine of the Alban Lake, clearly thought to be in magical sympathy with the city's walls.

The city-sanctity and its elements, and their unity, have been very obscure; but lately the lines of their pattern have begun to emerge more clearly. What has remained less clear is the origin of this ideal complex in place and time. But I think it can be now shown that here is a legacy from the very ancient east, where the elements can be detected a thousand years or more before the time at which in the Troy of Vergil they first force themselves upon our observation. If so, there is interest here for those who care for Vergil's way of blending and uniting things divorced, as here he blended in one history the severed east and west.

The ideal complex of city-sanctity can be described like this. There were beliefs and practices concerning a sacred city, defended by a magical ring wall, and identified in early thought both with a maiden goddess of the city's defence, and also with the earth as well, especially the earth personified as a mother goddess. This complex can be detected especially at Troy and Rome, and, in Greece, at Thebes, where old thought lingered, in the myth and the cult.[5]

The eastern influence which left this city-sanctity strongest outside Greece yet left behind in Greece itself other effects which came much less near to obliteration.

The debt of historic Greece to prehistoric and proto-historic Asia is appearing more and more in its true proportions. Greek science is at first a restatement of Oriental myth, two or three thousand years older than itself,[6] and, in spite of exaggerations, it is clearer and clearer that Homer reflects more than a mirage of the Orient. Homer's Cyclops has now joined Hesiod's Chimaera as an eastern creature, made at home for ever in Greek story;[7] and even Athena herself, with her owl, has lately

been betrayed, if I am not mistaken, as, after all, an imper-
sonation of an old owl-attended Ishtar of the Larsa dynasty.[8]

Among myths, the tale of Prometheus becomes more and
more clearly Akkadian, and indeed cannot be fully understood
in its Greek occurrence without reference to its eastern ancestry.[9]
Even Greek Tragedy has now a similar antecedent, and very
probably an origin, in a text of the fourteenth century B.C.
found at Ras Shamra,[10] a clearing house of culture which for
centuries was in close touch with the Aegean world. The Ras
Shamra text is a passion play of the type enacted at New Year
festivals to renew the life of the King, in Mesopotamia from
Akkadian times onwards.[11]

The obscure subject of ancient Mediterranean defensive
sanctity can be further enlightened by reference to eastern
traditions. I made some attempt to consider it in *Cumaean Gates*[12]
but I did not go far enough in my conclusions.

In that investigation there appeared reason to think that the
sacred cities of Troy, Thebes, and Rome retained in tradition
memories of the Sumerian temple-towers, and of the cosmology
associated with them. That is not surprising, since so much else
that is Oriental and old has imposed itself on Greek and Roman
thought and life from the earliest times. Greece was not always
closed to foreign influence, even if at certain times that influence
was limited and obstructed by unsettled conditions; Homer
remembers not the Egypt of his own day, but the Egypt of the
fifteenth century B.C.[13]

The conclusions of my own former work on the subject of
defensive sanctity may be expressed for the present purpose as
follows:

1. Cities in early Greece and Italy were holy, and defended
by holy or magical walls.

2. They were sometimes closely identified with an important
temple.

3. They were sometimes closely identified, in personification,
with goddesses of the cities' defence, or representatives of them.

4. Such goddesses, or representatives, may be considered to
be raped when cities are captured.

5. They may be carefully removed as part of military
operations against cities.

6. They may wear a *polos*, or towered crown, indicating that

these personalities are themselves peculiarly defended by the city walls.

7. Attacks on cities may be conceived to be manipulated by divine or at least supernatural agencies.

8. The walls of cities and buildings are sacred, and their strength is increased by buried personalities, real or symbolical, particularly female.

9. This strength may be increased also by the symbolism of the nail or peg.

10. It may be increased also by circular shape.

This is the complex which can be detected in Greece and Italy. I now show that all the elements existed earlier in the cultures of the nearer east; most of them are far more evident and emphatic there.[14] I take this as some confirmation of my views; and I am inclined to suggest that there is here ground for provisional belief that the complex of myth and ritual originated in nearer Asia and was communicated to Europe from there.

The first reference proves a very early existence of a very simple form of the 'pattern'.

'At the annual dinner of the American Institute for Persian Art and Archaeology . . . Dr Elihu Grant announced the excavation at Tepe Gawra, in North-Eastern Iraq, of a site which brought to light the earliest evidence of civilization ever discovered.

'The excavation, carried out by a party from the University of Pennsylvania under Dr E. A. Speiser, shows a mound that had already been abandoned by 1500 B.C., and twenty occupational levels below it. At the eleventh level a circular citadel in excellent condition was found which combined the purposes of fortress and temple. Two levels lower an elaborate acropolis which must be at least 6,000 years old was disclosed. The buildings themselves and the objects found in them show a high degree of civilization which had not been believed to exist in so early a period. . . .'[15]

This 'circular citadel . . . which combined the purposes of fortress and temple', found so near in time and place to the earliest developed human civilization, is clearly a most important point of departure for myths and practices connected with the divinely defended city, and all that is associated with it.

Several other examples have now been published from Khafaje and elsewhere, some earlier still.

'Ur-Nina (c. 3100) is the first city-king of any Sumerian city who has left important inscriptions concerning his reign. . . . Our principal information concerning him is taken from stone tablets supported on the hands of little copper figurines of women. The body and limbs of these figurines end in a long peg planted in the unbaked bricks of the foundations of the various buildings of this King. These copper figures of women with hands folded in the orthodox pose of prayer appear to have possessed "magical" power, and their use can be traced to the foundation of the prehistoric building at Girsu. In the foundations of this building, far below the level of Ur-Nina, De Sarzec found in two recesses of the walls groups of these figures stuck in the unbaked bricks in a circle. With Ur-Nina began the custom of placing a little stone tablet on the head of each of these buried guardians of his buildings, and these tablets carry inscriptions concerning the pious architectural works of the King.'[16]

Here there is a precise application to magical defence of female personalities, buried like Vestals.[17] The figures are shaped like pegs, recalling the Roman practice of driving a nail into the temple of Juppiter Stator, and the African folk-lore of 'pegging the village to the ground'.[18] The figures are once, even, found arranged in a circle; and circles in defensive magic without doubt carry a force of their own.[19]

In the time of Eannatum, 'the canal which separated Umma and Lagash was named "Lion of the Plain". . . . According to a broken passage in one inscription Eannatum was a benefactor of the sacred city Nippur. He speaks with affection of having built the city Nina to the goddess Nina, and the wall of Uruazagga (or better Urukugga), "the holy city".'[20]

Whether the metaphor of the lion implies a faith in the apotropaic force of lions, as later, within the Greek sphere,[21] or not, this reference asserts the sanctity of cities and a close identification of city and goddess, hinting, also, at the sanctity of a city's wall.

Furthermore, the great goddess Innini of Erech was a virgin goddess.[22] At Erech, too, was worshipped a mother goddess Nin-Sun, mother of Gilgamish.[23]

In Homer the walls of a city are called its 'sacred veil', and the idea is represented in later Greek sculpture, and is conjectured to have been represented in earlier Greek work, by a towered mural crown, a *polos*, like the mural crown of the Romans. In both these ways the city is identified with the goddess of its defence; the city walls are seen encircling her head. The idea comes from the east; for the *polos* belongs to Atargatis or Nana, it occurs at Boghaz-Keui and Eyuk, and it travelled to Cyprus and to Greece.[24]

The close identification of the city goddess and the city, especially at a city's destruction, is even more plainly asserted at the sack of Lagash by Lugal-zaggisi,[25] priest-King of Umma, than at the fall of Troy. The conquerors have committed wickedness against Ningirsu, says a historical tablet—as the Achaeans sinned against Athena.[26] A hymn, popular afterwards, is a lamentation for Bau, the goddess of Lagash:

> In holy Girsu the children are in distress.
> Into the interior of the splendid shrine he pressed.
>
> The august queen from her temple he brought forth.
> O lady of my city, desolated, when wilt thou return?[27]

The conquest of the city is symbolized in the capture and removal of the city goddess.

The Babylonian chronicle attributes the disasters which befell Sargon at the end of his reign to the preceding violation of the holy city at Babylon. 'An Omen Text preserves the same tradition: "Sargon whose troops bound him in a trench and suppressed their master in a coalition." The misfortune which overtook him at the end of his career is again referred to a birth omen, "if a ewe give birth to a lion with head of a lamb, lamentation of Sargon whose universal dominion [passed away]".'[28] It is hard to doubt that a stream of influence from Asia left in Greece thoughts of divine vengeance that recur in myths of Troy, and brought to Italy the faith in prodigies which is clearest of all in many passages of Livy. When Vergil associates prodigies with the fall of Troy, perhaps he is once more reverting to an older form of tradition, preserved among classical writers by him alone.

In the twenty-fourth or twenty-third century, when the Elamites devastated Akkad, the statue of the goddess Nana of

Erech was carried off.[29] The fall of Ur in 2357 B.C. was foretold by a monstrous birth, as the omens were explained by liver-divination.[30] 'The chants redoubled in sorrow for the rape of Ishtar, torn from her shrine in Erech; they were couched as though she herself were the mournful singer, and there can be little doubt that they were shrilled by her temple-women.

Me the foe hath ravished, yea, with hands unwashen,
Me his hands have ravished, me in exile driven . . .
(Now) I tread his courts—my very person sought he
In the shrines—(alas) the day, when to go forth feared I.

He pursued me in my temple, (Oh) he made me quake with
    terror,
There within my walls; (and) like a dove that fluttereth perch I
On a rafter, like a flitting owlet in a cavern hidden,
Birdlike from my shrine he chased me—me, a queen!—yet he did
    chase me
From my city like a bird—(and) sighing 'Far behind, behind me,
Is my temple—I, a queen—(and yet) my dwelling is far distant,
Isin's walls are far behind me, (yea) too, is my temple Gal-makh.'[31]

There is a similar lamentation over the looted temple of Innini, Queen of E-anna:

'How long or ever the ruined fane unto its place be restored? . . .

Unto a foreign land the fair wife was ravished—(so also)
Unto the foreign land the fair child was ravished—(the temple),
Uncelebrated its festivals splendid, its rituals solemn
Cease from the shrine.'[32]

Such ideas can be seen turning into mythical legend. In the legend of Girra, the plague-god, a mythological text, there is clear allusion to a real attack on Babylon about 2357 B.C. Girra himself takes part; and in the same text Ishtar is angry with Erech and assembles the enemy against it.[33]

It almost seems that myth makers concerned with Troy found a very large part of their material presented to them by eastern records, which were already one, or even two, thousand years old.[34]

In 2094 Hammurabi carried off the goddesses of Emutbalum. He wrote to a minister: 'The goddesses of Emutbal, which are assigned unto thee, the troops under the command of Inukhsamar will deliver unto thee . . . detail some men to settle the goddesses into their dwellings.'[35]

The chthonic aspect of this myth-ritual system is more complicated, though it is, of course, just as emphatic in the very ancient east as the other aspects. There are virgin goddesses, earth mothers, and temples that represent the earth. That they are not irrelevant is suggested by what has long been known of similarities between the eastern and the Greek Hades.

The afterworld of the near east is dreary, like the Greek.[36] In the midst is the fortress-palace of Nin-sun or Allat, the goddess of death. Hades has seven gates, and seven warders, who stripped the spirit of the dead of all that he possessed. The entrance to Hades was in the marshes beyond the mouth of the Euphrates. The waters of life come up at the foot of the golden throne of the spirits of earth; whoever could drink might return to the upper world. There are blissful fields beyond the river of death, Datilla, and to them were translated Xisuthros and his wife. There is also a sky heaven, reached by the spirit of the friend of Gilgamish, Ea-bani, who rose like a cloud of dust out of the ground on account of the prayers of his friends.[37]

That is enough to recall the almost exact correspondence between the Greek and eastern conceptions of the world beyond the grave, which in my view are ideally connected with conceptions of the sacred city. This connection is clear in the poetry of Vergil and in myths of Thebes. As I have shown, Vergil retains ancient thought lost by others; and he emphasizes the protective fortifications of the land of Hades, and of its central stronghold, closely recalling the eastern myth.[38] So, too, Thebes in Greece is an ideal city in myth, on the pattern of ancient eastern sanctities. Its seven gates cannot be located in the wall of city or citadel; but they, and their seven warders as they appear in Aeschylus, clearly reflect first the protections of the eastern Hades, and ultimately the ziggurat, with its seven stages.[39] There is, however, more to be noticed.

'All the old cities which lay in central Sumer and in the north . . . were consistently attached to the worship of earth-deities.'[40]

'The great virgin-goddess Innini and her mystically begotten son, Abu or Tammuz, are the most impressive figures in Sumerian theology and ritual. As a counterpart of heaven she became associated from unknown antiquity in an abstract way with Anu as his female principle and acquired the title Innini, "queen of heaven". Hence her cult was associated with that of Anu, who never was much more than an abstract figure in the pantheon. The name of the principle temple at Erech was E-anna, "house of heaven"—it was apparently the earlier name of the city itself; but the cult of Innini or Ishtar, because of its more human appeal, usurped the position of the old god and dominated the religious interests. She was widely known as "the Erechian goddess". Her cult is of course found established everywhere like that of her companion (Nintud) the goddess of birth, but Erech was her home. A grammatical text records eleven epithets of this holy city, among them *Illag* or *Illab*, the enclosure; *Antiranna*, the forest of heaven (an ordinary name of the Milky Way); *Ubimin*, the seven regions; *Daimin*, the seven sides; *Geparimin*, the seven dark chambers. The three last names refer to the tower Egeparimin, whose seven stages in accordance with the usual belief symbolized the seven regions. Erech was also called "the sleeping place of Anu".'[41]

'The temple of Nergal at Cuthah was named E-meslam or House of Meslam. Meslam is an epithet for the lower world and the god Nergal has also the title Meslamtaea, "He who rises from Meslam", referring to his solar character as god of the scorching summer sun. As a god of the waning summer sun he was connected with the waning moon and the new moon, and the stage tower of Cuthah bore the name E-Nannar, "House of the New Moon". The name Nergal is derived from Ne-unugal, "Power of the vast abode", lord of the lower world where he was the judge of those that died.'[42]

'The history of every ancient Sumerian city involves its relations with Nippur, the sacred city situated on the Euphrates, in the very centre of Sumerian lands. Here was established the national cult of the earth-god Enlil whose name means "lord of the winds"; an epithet derived from the myth of a cave of the winds in the earth. His proper title Enki, "lord of the earth", was later transferred to the third member of the trinity, the water-god of Eridu, whose cult was appropriately located at the mouth of the "Great River" (the Euphrates).'[43]

'Nippur is written by an ideograph meaning "the city of Enlil"; its chief temple, E-Kur, means "house of the earth mountain"; its ziggurat has several names, Eduranki ("house of the under-world mountain"), etc., all of which connect the city, its temple and tower with cosmological ideas of the earth as a mountain in whose vast interior repose the dead. The three great deities about whom all the great Nippurian cult revolves are Enlil the earth-god, Ninlil his consort (a degraded form of Nintud, Aruru, Ninkharsag, the earth-mother as patroness of birth) and their son Ninurasha, god of the spring sun and war.'[44]

The mother-goddess at Erech, Bau or Gula, is called 'Queen who gives life to the dead'.[45]

An inscription at Abu Shahrein 'ends, "he built for Enki his beloved lord the Apsu". Enki, the god of fresh water, was worshipped chiefly here and his temple was known as *E-abzu* or "House of the nether sea". The *apsu*, or sea of fresh water, on which the earth was supposed to rest and from which fountains and rivers sprang, was often represented by a great bowl or *apsu* in the temple courts of other cults.'[46]

'Esh-girsu and E-Ningirsu are the most common names of the temple of the local god at the old site Girsu, and when this god was identified with Ninurta, son of Enlil, the name was changed to E-ninnu, temple of the "fifty", for "fifty" was the sacred number of the earth-god Enlil.'[47]

The first detail to be noticed in this material is the well known alternating virginity and motherhood of the earth goddess, comparable of course to the renewed virginity of Hera. She is earth as consort of heaven, a relationship important in Greek myth. Secondly (to omit less urgent matters), the holy city has names which belong to cosmology, or to a temple within the city, or to both. The choice of emphasis in the names meaning 'enclosure' proves nothing but is interesting; the assertions of the number seven significantly illuminate the transition from the seven-staged eastern temple to the seven-gated ideal Thebes in Greece. Of the temple of Nergal it is only necessary to remark that it represents the earth, the solar and lunar reference must wait. At Nippur, an earth god, not goddess, contributes to the comprehension of the Greek Hades, always partly anomalous in Greece. The 'cave of the winds' is yet another eastern antecedent for a conception of Greek myth. Like Poseidon, Enki is now a god of water, and now an earth god. The names of the temple E-Kur, and its ziggurat, at Nippur emphasize the connection of city, temple-tower, and earth mountain, where the dead live.

There is an earth god, and an earth goddess of birth. At Erech the earth goddess 'gives life to the dead'. Everything here has relevance to the myth-ritual complex which I have predicated for Greece.[48] Additionally there is the *apsu*, to be compared with the 'lake' of Poseidon at Athens;[49] and the temple of the fifty at Girsu, a very possible origin for the fifty rooms in Priam's palace.

When speakers of Indo-European dialects began to come south before 2000 B.C., a result was pressure exerted by culture in Asia on culture in Greece. There was certainly movement in south-eastern Asia Minor; and the famous layer of place names in *-nthos*, *-ssos* was certainly overlaid on Greek lands from Asia Minor at about this time.[50] A connected movement also affected eastern Crete. What happened may have been migration, voyages of small parties of adventurers, or in some places merely 'culture creep'. Certainly something happened; possibly even movements of Sumerians from Asia to Italy, predecessors of the Etruscans by 1,500 years, carrying across the east Mediterranean ideas of city-sanctity which were afterwards there submerged, but remained evident in their eastern home.[51]

At Delos Greek temple builders took care not to disturb an old 'megalithic' burial. There too, at Delos, is the mysterious cave temple, a cleft in the rock of Cynthus arched by the gable formed by two great 'megalithic' stone slabs. And the cleft, at the place where Apollo was born, is the shape of the cleft at Delphi, where he prophesied—the shape of a mother's organ of generation. Apollo is the son of an eastern mother, who guards the living dead within her, to speak through him.

The mental pattern of the east overlaid Troy and Trojan story, for the east was near; and overlaid Thebes too, for there it was carried by seamen settlers from the Levant; and movements made before history becomes clear taught Italians to worship Rome and Vesta, to tell the tale of Veii, and to make the *Aeneid*, guided by the same lines of eastern awe.

NOTES

1. See above, pp. 103–28, 215–41; F. Muller, Jun., *Mnemosyne* Ser. III, 2 (1935) 1–54, 179–250.
2. E. Kornemann, *Die Antike* 8 (1932) 105–12.
3. Reff. in note 1, above.
4. See above, pp. 105, 119–20.
5. See above, pp. 118–19, 221.
6. E. A. Havelock, *TAPA* 67 (1936) xxxix; a view strongly held by A. H. Sayce, *The Ancient Empires of the East* (London, 1884) 154–9.
7. H. Frankfort, *The Times*, August 1, 1936, 13–14; *cf.* above, p. 170.
8. *The Illustrated London News*, Vol. 188, June 13, 1936, 1047; Ishtar is depicted standing on lions, with an owl on each side; of course, the warlike, defensive quality of Ishtar is sufficiently clear from the beginning of Hammurabi's code.
9. Sayce (above, note 6) 157–8; W. F. J. Knight, *JHS* 58 (1938) 51–4.
10. T. H. Gaster, *SMSR* 10 (1934) 156–64, esp. 164.
11. *Cf.* Claude Schaeffer, *Ras Shamra and the Minoan and Mycenaean World*, a paper delivered to the Oxford Branch of the Classical Association on November 21, 1937; H. Frankfort, *Iraq* 1 (1934) 2–29.
12. See above, pp. 100, 264–5; I cordially acknowledge the important help of Kornemann (above, note 2).
13. M. P. Nilsson, *Homer and Mycenae* (London, 1933) 157, with ref.
14. For my purpose I have found it possible to depend mainly on the articles of the late Professor S. H. Langdon in *CAH* I. I quote them freely and gratefully, feeling sure that he would forgive the freedom.
15. *The Times*, April 2, 1937, 11.
16. Langdon, *CAH* I (1922) 378–9; for a new reference, giving evidence of a foundation burial at Maiden Castle to be added to my own statement on p. 190 above, *cf.* R. E. Mortimer Wheeler, *The Times*, February 26, 1937, 18: at the junction between the old and new ramparts was found 'a human burial, inserted in the outer slope of the old work and covered immediately by the material of the new. It is tempting to recall the Bethelite who built Jericho and "laid the foundation thereof in Abiram his first-born".' (At Jericho occur as at Troy firstly the magical defence by foundation burial and secondly, as I have explained before, a magical attack by means of trumpets and circumambulation.)
17. *Cf.* the list of foundation burials in E. B. Tylor, *Primitive Culture* (London, 1929) I, 104–8, where the female motive occurs in eight instances of the eleven in which sex is determined by the information published.
18. W. F. J. Knight, *CR* 46 (1932) 168, citing W. L. Gomme.
19. L. D. Burdick, *Foundation Rites with Some Kindred Ceremonies* (New York, 1921) 165–6; the interest of Babylonians in architectural plans is attested by Langdon, *CAH* I, 428: 'On the knees [of a statue of Gudea in the central court of Eninnu] lies a rectangular stone tablet on which is traced the ground-plan of the temple, its gates, crenellated towers and false pillars.'
20. Langdon, *CAH* I, 380.
21. See above, p. 122 with reff.
22. Langdon, *CAH* I, 387.
23. Ibid. 366–7; *cf.* 443, 457.
24. Sayce (above, note 6) 225–6.
25. Langdon, *CAH* I, 388.
26. See above, pp. 125–7; W. F. J. Knight, *Folk-Lore* 46 (1935) 98–121, esp. 101–2.
27. Langdon, *CAH* I, 388.

28. Ibid. 408.
29. Ibid. 471; cf. 423–4.
30. Ibid. 471–2.
31. Ibid. 472.
32. Ibid.
33. Ibid. 473.
34. The obvious comparisons are with the actions of Apollo in Hom. *Il.* I, and Athena in Verg. *Aen.* II; cf. above pp. 215–19.
35. Langdon, *CAH* I, 488; cf. the theft of the palladion, and the 'evocation' of Juno from Veii. 'Evocation' has already been seen to be an eastern rite; F. Schachermeyr, *Etruskische Frühgeschichte* (Leipzig, 1929) 298. Cf. above, pp. 105, 119–20, for the apparently typical, imposed morphology of the legend of the siege of Veii.
36. Sayce (above, note 6) 155.
37. Ibid.
38. See above, pp. 265–6, 275–6.
39. See above, p. 221.
40. Langdon, *CAH* I, 396.
41. Ibid. 396–7.
42. Ibid. 394–5.
43. Ibid. 391.
44. Ibid. 392.
45. Ibid. 393.
46. Ibid. 399.
47. Ibid. 375.
48. See *Cumaean Gates, passim.*
49. Cf. also above, pp. 175–6, 282, for the relation between temples and small ritual objects and the cosmological realities which they symbolize.
50. J. B. Haley and C. W. Blegen, *AJA* 32 (1928) 141–54.
51. Kornemann (above, note 2) 105–12; in so far as such mild 'diffusionism' can be accepted at all, it is preferable to the theory of wide diffusion from Egypt for various reasons, among them these: history and archaeology at least know something of movements from Asia, but not from Egypt; and the stone-working technique of 'megalithic' builders is much more likely to come from a brick architecture than from Egyptian stone-working, with its perfect technique.

INDEXES

I INDEX OF AUTHORS AND AUTHORITIES

II GENERAL INDEX